PROJECTIONS OF WAR

FILM AND CULTURE
John Belton, General Editor

FILM AND CULTURE
A Series of Columbia University Press
Edited by John Belton

What Made Pistachio Nuts?
Henry Jenkins

Showstoppers: Busby Berkeley and the Tradition of Spectacle
Martin Rubin

Laughing Screaming: Modern Hollywood Horror and Comedy
William Paul

PROJECTIONS OF WAR

Hollywood,

American Culture,

and

World War II

**THOMAS
DOHERTY**

COLUMBIA UNIVERSITY PRESS   NEW YORK

Columbia University Press
New York   Chicester, West Sussex

Copyright © 1993   Columbia University Press
Revised Chapter 11, "Legacies," copyright © 1999 Thomas Doherty

Library of Congress Cataloging-in-Publication Data
Doherty, Thomas.
    Projections of war: Hollywood, American culture, and World War II /
    Thomas Doherty.
        p.   cm—(Film and culture)
    Includes bibliographical references and indexes.
    ISBN 0-231-08244-4   —   0-231-11635-7 (pbk.)
    1. World War, 1939–1945—Motion pictures and the war.   2. Motion
pictures—United States—History—20th century.   I. Title.
II.—Series.
D743.23.D63   1993
791.43′658—dc20   93-20420
                                                                          CIP

Designer: Teresa Bonner
Text: ITC Cheltenham Light
Compositor: Impressions, A Division of Edwards Brothers
Printer: Edwards Brothers
Binder: Edwards Brothers

Printed in the United States of America
c   10   9   8   7   6   5   4   3   2   1
p   10   9   8   7   6   5   4   3

FOR MY FATHER

CONTENTS

ACKNOWLEDGMENTS

A word on form, sources, and support. As legend reminds us, Hollywood is a state of mind, not a place. It is also a rhetorical device. In the following pages, I speak of "Hollywood" not as an active agent or monolithic hegemony but as a shorthand way of conjuring a broad sense of the American motion picture industry during the Second World War. Research notes and parenthetical remarks can be found in the back of the book. In mining the usual archival sources for cultural historical scholarship, I leaned mainly on the motion picture trade press—*Box Office*, the *Film Daily*, the *Hollywood Reporter, Motion Picture Herald*, and *Variety*—as the most revealing gauge of industry dynamics and self-identity. Naturally, the movies themselves remain the best screen for historical inquiry, aesthetic enjoyment, and imaginative projection.

At the risk of evoking the spirit of Greer Garson who, upon winning her Best Actress Oscar for *Mrs. Miniver*, set an Academy record with a speech of gratitude that seemed to last as long as the film, I must express thanks to a number of kind souls. Unbeknownst to them, Richard Dyer MacCann and John Raeburn inspired this study during their "American Film and Culture of the 1940s" course at the University of Iowa. Michael Anderegg, Jeanine Basinger, David Desser, Lawrence Fuchs, Rich Horwitz, Charles Maland, Thomas Schatz, and Saul Touster were generous in criticism and gentle in correction. For advice on military matters and archival access, my siblings in uniform, John Doherty (Captain, USAF) and Sally Lengyel (Captain, USAF), were dutifully familial. Jennifer Crewe, John Belton, Anne McCoy, Roy Thomas, and Teresa Bonner at Columbia University Press handled their editorial tasks, and me, with grace and professionalism. Lending direction and expertise were Patrick Sheehan and Madeleine Klein at the Motion Picture Division of the Library of Congress; Caroline Stein at the Motion Picture Association of America office in New York; Samuel Gill at the Margaret Herrick Library of the Academy of Motion Picture Arts and Sciences; George Barringer at Georgetown University Special Collections; Mary Corliss and Terry Geesken at the Museum of Modern Art Film Stills Archive, and archivists at the Doheny Library at the University of Southern California, the New York Center for the Performing Arts, the *Stars and Stripes* office in Darmstadt, Germany; the Historical Research Center at Maxwell Air Force Base, Montgomery, Alabama; and the National Archives in both Washington, D.C., and Suitland, Maryland.

Friends at Brandeis University—Joyce Antler, Jerry Cohen, Angie Simeone, and Stephen Whitfield—and at the University of Groningen in the Netherlands—Rob Wagenaar, Tity de Vries, Annie van den Oevere, Docke Bosscher, and J. W. Drukker—were unfailingly supportive. Janaki Bahkle, Bill Brevda, Greg Burk, Chic Callenbach, Jim Deutsch, Bob Eberwein, Jim Gilbert, Mimi Hanson, Mark Hirsch, Andrew Hudgins, Bob Kapsis, Mary Kennedy, Cindy Larson, David Marc, Bob Moses, Steve Mayer, Dane Morrison, Nancy Palmer, William Paul, Gerry Peary, Sharon Rivo, Laura Shea, and Jan Simons offered suggestions, encouragement, and videos. Above all, to my wife Sandra—more than thanks, honey.

PROJECTIONS OF WAR

Hollywood's War

A montage of archival footage flashing by to an Andrews Sisters soundtrack unspools the familiar images. William Bendix shaves before a pinup of Betty Grable and sighs over the Brooklyn Dodgers. At the Hollywood Canteen, wide-eyed GIs dance with Marlene Dietrich, Lana Turner, and Deanna Durbin. Donald Duck throws tomatoes in "der Führer's face," and Bugs Bunny croons "Any Bonds Today?" The Three Stooges, whose Moe Howard had a made-to-disorder resemblance to Adolf Hitler, torment the "nutzy" Nazis. Screen celebrities hawk war bonds, donate blood, and bring shtick to remote Pacific atolls. The sacrifices of the stars can make for a press agent's dream (Veronica Lake shears her trademark peek-a-boo bob after the War Production Board warns that women workers in war plants face an occupational hazard from "eye strain and possible scalping, if dangling hair is caught in machinery") or a front-page nightmare (Carole Lombard dies in a plane crash while returning to Hollywood from a bond rally in January 1942).

The documentary footage and Hollywood films of the war years—compiled, reedited, remade, replayed endlessly—are a vivid cultural heritage and a vital historical link. The motion picture images lend contour and depth, visual presence and resonant impact, to a past that no longer recedes before the eye. A way of seeing America during the Second World War, the newsreel clips, Victory shorts, and feature-length movies invite a second sight into the most dramatic and decisive moments of the century. Flashed on screen, in the mind's eye, Hollywood's projections of war are the graphic legacy of a graphic age.

From the nickelodeon forward to the 70mm screen, the pleasures of spectacular imagery, the vicarious thrill of combat, the titillating horror of death and destruction—all enjoyed from the security of a theater seat—have lent war and cinema a tight kinship. For all its persistence and pervasiveness, however, Hollywood's vision of the Second World War has had limited currency as worthwhile art or reliable history. From the vantage of half a century, the film record of 1941–45 is condescended to as quaint or condemned as duplicitous. The technique seems hopelessly antiquated, the sensibility laughably naive. Exceptions are allowed—perhaps John Ford's elegiac *They Were Expendable* (1945) or John Huston's grim combat report, *The Battle of San Pietro* (1945)—and the newsreel record is conceded its documentary value. More often, though, Hollywood's wartime work is portrayed as a stiffly staged show of parading toy soldiers and tightly wound dolls. Writing in the film magazine *Premiere,* critic David Denby vented a common current-day sentiment: "World War II pictures (especially the ones made during the conflict) look childish and banal—morally hapless in the dehumanization of the enemy, naive in their glib underestimation of the spiritual devastations of combat, their unshadowed faith in the democratic and egalitarian American future." Against the ruthless honesty of today's R-rated, FX-laden spectacles and the searing vision of the cutting-edge auteur, classical Hollywood cinema sanitizes the horror and flinches before the ghastly realities.

Of course, one couldn't blame the moviemakers themselves. If, as Walt Whitman remarked of an earlier conflagration, "the real war will never get in the books," still less could it enter the more public, more constrained medium of the motion picture. Straitjacketed by government censorship and Production Code prudery, directors averted their eyes, and screenwriters bit their tongues. The War Department, the Office of War Information (OWI), and Hollywood's studio heads colluded in keeping the awful devastations of combat from the home-front screen—sometimes by outright fabrication, usually by expedient omission.

Disposable as art, dubious as history, wartime cinema has fared no better at the mercies of academic film theory. To dive into the swirling waters of cinematic metaphysics risks an immersion that may never lead back to the surface, but the "dominant discourse" in university-bred film studies delights in the conflation or denies the differences between the spectacle of war and the spectacle of cinema. Where the image, the gaze, the rapid eye movements of a visually oriented culture have blurred the borders of art and reality, the search for meaning is ultimately quixotic anyway. Modes of interpretation ("readings") can make any film mean just about what any critic wants it to mean. By this light, Hollywood cinema is less a window on the past than a screen reflecting the preoccupations of the beholder, a canvas for interpretative dexterity and polemical praxis. The well-traveled Paris-to-London lines of postmodernist criticism run to mind games, conceptual implosion, italicized neologisms, "scare quotes," and parenthetical puns. A web of *simulacra* and *pastiche,* signs and meanings, cinema becomes a system of codes to be broken, not a vision to be interpreted or an art to be experienced. Under this critical mass, the commonsense distinctions between art and experience, film and culture, collapse into a black hole of linguistic opacity. Thus Guy DeBord, the prophet of the voguish Situationist school, apprehends *la société du spectacle* in which "lived reality is materially invaded by the contemplation of the spectacle while simultaneously absorbing the spectacular order." For DeBord and the likeminded, "Objective reality is present on both sides" and "reality rises up within the spectacle and the spectacle is real." At some point, the au courant film theorist splits the difference with a favored, inevitable pun: in war or peace, the "real" bleeds into the "reel." *Vive la similarité.*

Back on American shores, another kind of bleeding has come to obscure the focus. Always the cultural legacy of the Vietnam War filters and fogs the images of World War II. Vietnam, itself so much a product of the mythos of Hollywood's war, has discredited its predecessor and the medium that projected it. "I can't help thinking of the kids who got wiped out by seventeen years of war movies before coming to Vietnam to get wiped out for good," mused journalist Michael Herr in *Dispatches*. "We'd all seen too many war movies, stayed too long in Television City, years of media glut had made certain connections difficult." In the antiwar agit-doc *Hearts and Minds* (1974), the final image is the explosive climax from *Bataan* (1943)— in the Vietnam context, a bloodthirsty freeze-frame of American machismo, violence, and imperialism. When crippled Vietnam veteran Ron Kovic in *Born on the Fourth of July* (1989), book and movie, bellows "They lied to us!," the antecedent is as much the makers of Hollywood movies as Washington policy.

The thickets of aesthetic disregard, historiographical condescension, theoretical obfuscation, and Vietnam backfire have blocked entry into the true nature of Hollywood's war work. To visit the era through the medium of motion pictures, to backtrack to a preparodic perspective before narratives had hardened into predictability and metaphors calcified into cliché, is to perceive a wider spectrum of colors within this black-and-white world. For "the present emergency," the Hollywood studio system took emergency measures and creative initiative. Like other industries forced to improvise under the gun, its shop was retooled and its products redesigned. Another four-year sampling might match the artistry of Hollywood's wartime output, but at no other time was the motion picture industry more deliberately engaged in documenting, and making, American history.

Like a vintage movie program, this inquiry into Hollywood and American culture has a double feature (albeit both unwind simultaneously). The first is archaeological: to resurrect and reclaim the motion picture world of 1941–45. An act of cultural-historical excavation, it traces Hollywood's transition from peacetime entertainment to wartime engagement, from the studied avoidance of message-mongering to a forthright commitment to information-heavy and value-laden cinema. The shift in tone and temper is verified by an interpretive survey of the war-minded motion picture work of the day—military education and civilian orientation, combat films, homefront melodramas, wartime comedies, martial musicals, and the newsreels, combat reports, and documentaries chronicling the frontline action.

The second purpose is argumentative. It asserts that the nature of the contract between Hollywood and American culture was rewritten during 1941–45. "For the duration" and beyond, old agreements were abrogated and new terms negotiated in the media partnership linking motion picture spectacle and motion picture spectator. The realignment clusters around five theaters of operation. By way of preview, the marquee taglines and capsule descriptions read:

Frames of Meaning: Before the war, American movies were mainly considered an amusement or an investment. A few academics dissented, arguing for a profound if intangible "sociological" influence. A more numerous legion of public guardians concurred after a fashion, railing against the movies as moral blight or religious blasphemy. Not until Hollywood enlisted as an active agent in the Second World War did the ephemeral popular art dedicated to "mere entertainment" suddenly and seriously matter—to the War Department, to the Office of War Information, to spectators made sensitive to the educational import and ideological impact of the movies. Recalibrated as a weapon of war, the mass medium that magically deployed sound and moving image, that wedded technological wonder to creative artistry, garnered the respect due the possession of potent firepower. Shocked and enlightened by the motion picture propaganda of the Nazis, obliged to obey new codes of conduct and send out life-and-death messages, the motion picture industry became the preeminent transmitter of wartime policy and a lightning rod for public discourse. The unique, unprecedented alliance between Washington and Hollywood generated not only new kinds of movies but a new attitude toward them. Hereafter, popular art and cultural meaning, mass communications and national politics, would be intimately aligned and commonly acknowledged in American culture.

Casting Decisions and Screen Credit: The assimilationist credo of the war years found vibrant expression and visible confirmation on the Hollywood screen. As a social glue for a pluralistic culture, American movies had always been something of an ethnic and ecumenical melting pot: classical Hollywood cinema might be flippantly defined as a Jewish-owned business selling Roman Catholic theology to Protestant America. When the struggle against the master racists of the Third Reich forced a recognition of the unseemly domestic parallels, a rich assortment of exotic new elements were added to the motion picture mix. The cast of Hollywood characters expanded to embrace Americans traditionally sidestepped and overlooked, ridiculed and demeaned. The sight and celebration of the heretofore invisible or lampooned granted a cinematic validation—and impetus—to a civil rights revolution in the making.

Technical Advising: For an America remade by war, Hollywood served as a guide to the new order. The movies were not the main vehicles for change, but they carried the news and softened the shock of the new. Amid the political transformations and cultural dislocations of 1941–45 (the centralization of state power, the creation of complex techno-bureaucracies, the flesh-and-blood casualties of war), Hollywood promised continuity alongside the transformations, permanence beneath the reorientation of values. A mass communications industry with a human face and familiar landscape, the studio system memorialized a bygone era even as it segued America into the future.

The Image Ascendant: The war years witnessed the culmination of a trend percolating since the first exhibition of moving images in 1895: the transition from a rational, print-based culture to an impressionistic motion picture world. In 1941–45 a linear, bookbound mentality was displaced by a movie-mediated vision. Moving images became the new alphabet, the hieroglyphics of meaning and memory for American culture.

Motion Picture Records: The privileged medium for America at war came to be the chief custodian of the legacy. The massive warehouse of moving-image documentation and dramatization that came out of the Second World War comprises a comprehensive and spectacular archival record. No accurate measure exists of the sheer quantity of film exposed during 1941–45, but military photographic units and the Hollywood trade press took it for granted that the Second World War was the most thoroughly documented event in human history. It probably remains the event most thoroughly documented via the medium of celluloid motion pictures. Through countless postwar compilations and reenactments, Hollywood preserved, embroidered, and recollected the motion picture record of 1941–45. For America after 1945 the vision of the present and expectations for the future would be filtered through the wartime motion picture record.

As a final directional addendum, and at the risk of milking a metaphor dry, the archaeological/argumentative presentations are meant to receive coequal billing. Hopefully, readers restless with one feature will be compensated by the other half of the program.

All the above presupposes an imaginative engagement that takes the past on its own terms and the films on theirs; that respects the perceptions and acknowledges the perceptiveness of the wartime generation; and that trusts that the search for meaning in history through film, though elusive, is not illusory. Fortunately, the means of access encourage the passage. The wartime features and newsreel clips of classical Hollywood retain their power to move, to inform, to bind the present spectator in sympathy with the experience of the past. A few rules of engagement, rough outlines of conduct—not inviolable commands—may smooth the way.

First, the wartime generation was every bit as cognizant of the limitations of art as the present one, and quite a bit sharper-eyed to celluloid evasion and Hollywood convention. A nation that had one in ten citizens in uniform, that received thousands of telegrams per month containing regrettable information from Secretary of War Henry Stimson, knew well the gulf between war on film and war on the field. For soldier and civilian alike, public responses ran the full range of aesthetic reaction, from utter credulity to ironic distance. Playing against expectations, one GI moviegoer wrote the motion picture trade press to report that soldiers harbored an intense paternal affection for child actress Margaret O'Brien, who as a reminder of home moved the men deeply. In 1945 war correspondent Ernie Pyle, aboard a flattop off the coast of Japan, recorded the less sentimental reactions of a squadron of cheerful cynics:

> They showed a movie for the first time in three or four days. It was a western called *The Lights of Old Santa Fe,* with a regulation hero and villain and runaway horses and shootin' and everything. Those fliers received it the way modern audiences receive *The Drunkard.* We almost hissed the villain off the screen. We booed at all underhand business, we cheered all good deeds, and we whistled and clapped when the hero took the girl in his arms.

In like manner, for the film version of Pyle's *Here Is Your War,* a collection of dispatches from the front published in 1943, the GI's reporter gave strict instructions for his own screen incarnation. "He must weigh in the neighborhood of 112 pounds and look anaemic. He must not be glamorized or have any love interest in the picture," Pyle ordered. "He must write on a typewriter and absolutely never be shown with a pencil or notebook." Producer Lester Cowan abided by Pyle's wishes and cast the wispy Burgess Meredith, recently discharged from the Army for sinus trouble, as his surrogate in United Artists's *The Story of G.I. Joe.* On June 9, 1945, in Okinawa, Cowan also saw to it that another of the reporter's demands (that the film's premiere be held "wherever Ernie Pyle happens to be") was honored—though by then, with Pyle killed by a sniper's bullet on Ie Shima, the gesture was a posthumous tribute.

Deglamourizing combat: Burgess Meredith fits the role of war correspondent Ernie Pyle in *The Story of G.I. Joe* (1945).

The rift between emotional sustenance and enemy fire is well chronicled in the "Mail Call" pages of *Yank,* the Army weekly. The unsolicited film criticism of GI correspondents records a consistent attention to and insight into what a staff writer distinguished as *"The War"* and "Hollywood's war." Toward the latter, troops expressed by turns raw disgust and tolerant bemusement. "When I see Japs once again portrayed as comic opera characters, thick skulled and insanely egotistical, I am inclined to walk out [of the theater]," wrote a combat veteran. Other soldiers savored the irony. "Occasionally," remarked a mordant private first class, "a soldier's girlfriend does not work in a war plant where is manufactured the weapon the soldier is armed with or the airplane he flies." A GI in Sicily demurred: "In fact, I think Warner Brothers produces a better war all around." Whether overseas or on the homefront, American audiences knew what Hollywood was about and Hollywood knew they knew. In producer Sam Goldwyn's popular musical comedy *Up in Arms* (1944), a troop ship sailing to the Pacific theater is bedecked with a bevy of curvaceous nurses who picnic midship in shorts, sunbathe, and play a buoyant game of volleyball. Two soldiers, a grizzled sergeant and a young GI, appreciatively check out the action from an upper deck. "We never had anything like this in the last war," says the disbelieving NCO. "Sergeant," responds his companion wearily, "we don't have anything like it in *this war* either."

Second, an era surfeited with images tends to forget the esteemed status of cinema at a time when celluloid projection in a public space was the sole source of moving pictures. Before television and the global transmission of a 24-hour flow of images—images of all kinds, received and retrievable with an ease that has made the modern spectator both more visually attuned and less cinematically alert— motion pictures were the mass medium of choice. The complete theatrical package available to the wartime moviegoer was known as the "staple program." It consisted of a combination of featured attractions (a prestige "A" picture perhaps preceded by an abbreviated, low-budget "B"—the original "double bill") in tandem with some variation of newsreel, cartoon, travelogue, featurette, serial, singalong, and previews of coming attractions ("trailers"). In 1944 the Department of Commerce estimated that fully eighty cents of every dollar spent on "spectator amusement," a category including theater, concerts, and sports, went to the motion picture industry. An audience of roughly 90 million per week attended avidly—if not quite "spellbound in darkness" then neither as jaded to visual input nor as jammed up by imagistic overload as the cable era channel surfer.

Exhibition venues and release patterns accentuated the allure of Hollywood's high-definition art. The "Academy ratio" width-to-height dimensions of the wartime screen (1.33 to 1) made for a smaller field of peripheral vision, but the size of the projected image itself was generally larger than today's multiplex rectangle; the theaters more elaborate, comfortable, and decorous. Though the palatial movie-

The mass medium of choice: an "A" picture gets the "A" treatment at New York's Astor Theater, 1941. (Courtesy of the Academy of Motion Picture Arts and Sciences)

house of legend was more the exception than the rule, few venues for exhibition housed the puny dimensions, impersonal treatment, and minimalist interiors of what Jay Leno has referred to as "the concrete bunker at the end of the mall." Nor were the movies instantly available. The lag time from a gala metropolitan premiere, to limited big city engagements, and on to small town exhibition "at popular prices" might be a year or more. Today, backed by television ad campaigns and timed cover stories in mass circulation weeklies, the saturation release of a big-budget Hollywood production reaches over two thousand "screens" simultaneously. The intricate choreography of release-pattern foreplay—ballyhoo and teasing exploitation, the momentum and rising anticipation of a movie "now playing at your local theater"—is a lost enticement.

Lost too is the universality of the once-mass medium. Television, the great usurper, had not yet eroded and fragmented the audience for the movies. Classical Hollywood cinema embraced and attracted the whole family of ambulatory Americans. In the days before precision demographics, "target groups," and overnight movie tracking, the question of who and how many saw what when is something of a statistical void. Film scholars generally agree that the standard industry estimate of anywhere from 85 to 90 million moviegoers per week is about right; the precise composition of that audience—males to females, young to old—is contestable and elusive. Though inside dopesters recognized that the young attended more frequently than the old, and females more avidly than males, the official pronouncements of the motion picture industry typically idealized a great, undifferentiated mass audience known as "the Public." Whatever the composite breakdown, the motion picture industry thought of itself as (and wartime Washington so considered it) a truly mass medium that served the broad American public, not a sexual or generational segment of same.

Along with the privileges of media rank came cultural responsibilities. The war years saw a popular art, first haltingly, soon with assurance, deal with the dislocations and transformations of wartime mobilization, the anguish of death suffered in combat and mourned on the homefront, and the awesome stakes in the conflict between totalitarianism and democracy. In grappling with "the present emergency," a singular recognition pervades wartime Hollywood: the cinematic sophistication of its audience. Already the movies presume themselves as a common frame of reference. In Dore Schary's production *I'll Be Seeing You* (1944), Zachary Morgan (Joseph Cotton), a burnt-out combat veteran on sick leave, takes newly met girlfriend Mary Marshall (Ginger Rogers), herself a prisoner on furlough, to a war movie called *Make Way for Glory*. The film-within-the-film is fictitious, but the type is real enough—a rousing, morale-building combat adventure, what the GIs called a "flag-waver." In the darkened theater, the soldier averts his eyes from the action on-screen but the soundtrack (a fusillade of rifle shots and explosives) and a lobby one-sheet (a garish portrait of charging soldiers) identifies the guts-and-glory caliber of the spectacle. As the sprightly martial music from the final credits of *Make Way for Glory* shares the soundtrack of *I'll Be Seeing You,* the couple walks through the theater lobby, where the sergeant almost trips over a symbolic trio of little boys playing soldier with toy rifles. "Was the war really like that?" asks Mary as the two stroll out the theater. "I guess so," replies the soldier. "That's funny," she rejoins. "That you should only *guess* so." In a measured, droll tone, Cotton underplays his big monologue:

Well, they have experts making those pictures. I . . . I guess that's the way they see the war—a beach a mile long and thousands of soldiers and tanks and machine guns and everything. . . . I *guess* that's the way it is.

They walk a few steps in silence and Mary ventures, "But it wasn't that way for you, huh?"

It's just a difference in size. To a guy that's in it, the war's about ten feet wide and . . . kind of empty. It's you and . . . a couple of fellows in your company maybe, maybe a couple of Japs. It's all kind of mixed up, uh, sometimes it's . . . all full of noise and sometimes it's quiet. It all depends on what you're thinking about I guess. It depends on how scared you are, how cold you are, and how wet you are. I guess if you asked a hundred guys what the war is like, they'd all give you a different answer.

The delivery—by turns halting and breathless, punctuated by repetitive equivocation—expresses not only the soldier's inability to render experience in language but Hollywood's awareness of its own

Saluting the difference between war and cinema: Joseph Cotton and Ginger Rogers at the movies in *I'll Be Seeing You* (1944). (Museum of Modern Art/Film Stills Archives)

inability to conjure with cinema the full reality of war. *I'll Be Seeing You* is no *Make Way for Glory.*

Finally, the clear-eyed pronouncements of government bureaucrats, studio executives, and military men (three of the stock villains of post-Vietnam America) invite an unhealthy skepticism. Listen to Warner Bros. production chief Jack Warner, speaking on the record, in 1943:

> Actually, if you stop to think about whether it's now or five years from now, there are pictures such as *Action in the North Atlantic* or *Air Force* or *Wake Island,* which can play anywhere, any time, merely with new introductory titles, and depict that "this is something which we all went through in 1943, and which should be a warning to you, both the public and statesman alike, so that we should never have to go through this again." That's how much a force for good the screen can be.

In the same selfless and public-spirited tones, 20th Century-Fox head Spyros Skouras pledged his unconditional support for government-sponsored Victory shorts, financial considerations notwithstanding. "The main thing is the war effort," Skouras asserted, "and what does it mean if we lose a certain portion of revenue from normal shorts releases, if we must find room for the Victory films?" Whether shown at profit, cost, or loss, they must be shown, Skouras declared, since "what else matters if we lose the war?"

To later generations bred to cynicism and suspicion, the bombast reads too ripe, the lofty sentiments a mask for self-interest and profiteering. The war years, after all, were very good to Hollywood. For homefront consumers, employed in a soaring war economy and renewing a long-dormant acquaintance with the pleasures of discretionary spending, the movies were one of the few outlets for surplus dollars. Riding the crest of a high-angle recovery from the dark days of the early Depression, Hollywood was flush with cash and sturdy in structure. "At present," boasted a front-page article in *Variety* at the close of 1943, "the industry is in the best shape it's ever been in and so strongly financed that the debacle of the Big Depression cannot repeat itself." In commercial terms World War II was a box-office windfall. In the more ephemeral currency of social prestige and cultural cachet, the motion picture industry achieved an ascendancy in American culture it was never again to recapture—a popular and prestigious art, a respected and cultivated business, an acknowledged and powerful weapon of war.

But in the front offices of the major studios, as in the rest of the nation, patriotism was seldom a refuge for scoundrels. For the moguls no less than the extras, idealism was buttressed by a more personal interest. Unlike Vietnam, this war reached into boardrooms and penetrated the highest executive levels. Jack Warner dated his bitter, premature anti-Fascism from 1936 when, wrote Warner, the studio's Berlin representative was beaten to death in a back alley by Nazi thugs. At 20th Century-Fox the Skouras brothers learned in 1943 that their nephew in Greece had been executed by the Nazis. George J. Schaefer, former RKO president and chairman of the War Activities Committee of the Motion Picture Industry, lost a son in the Normandy invasion. Joseph I. Breen, the power behind the Production Code Administration, had three sons serving overseas. During the same week in 1944, Breen received two telegrams: one son had been wounded in Normandy, another had lost a leg on Guam. The studio honor rolls and gold stars testified to the noncelluloid side of Hollywood's war work and the cost of the off-screen contributions.

A shared sense of the apocalyptic nature of what director Frank Capra called "the Great Struggle" animated the motion picture industry. Against the unifying power of the Japanese attack on Pearl Harbor and the palpable Nazi menace, tensions with the government over antitrust decrees and tax law paled. Disputes there were—with the War Production Board over the use of raw film stock; with the War Manpower Commission on the definition of an "essential worker" in an "essential activity"; with the Office of War Information on just about everything—but on the whole Hollywood's public relations matched its private intentions. Besides, no industry dominated by American Jews had to be coerced into a cinematic war against Fascism.

Perhaps too for traffickers in fantasy the lure of a real life field of endeavor exerted a special attraction. More than selfless patriotism seems at work in the scramble to action of people eager to measure combat reality against celluloid expectations. A pantheon of the best directors (Frank Capra, John Ford, John Huston, George Stevens, and William Wyler) and the most popular stars (Clark Gable, Henry Fonda, Myrna Loy, Robert Montgomery, Tyrone Power, and Jimmy Stewart) willingly put their careers on hold and themselves in harm's way. "I am thrilled to be an infinitesimal part of it," Darryl F. Zanuck confided in *Tunis Expedition,* a diary of his role in the North African campaign. Given a turn in the copilot's seat of a Flying Fortress, 20th Century-Fox's production chief could barely contain himself. "I hold the control wheel gently," rhapsodized Zanuck, in 1942 a newly commissioned colonel in the U.S. Army Signal Corps. "It all seems like a dream or a scenario I have written. I can't really believe we are flying vanguard of a mighty attacking force headed for Africa and that I am actually here in the cockpit of a Flying Fortress en route to Gibraltar."

In later years, at Academy Award tributes and saccharine "showbiz at war" compilations, the motion picture industry's unctuous self-salutes would become working definitions of kitsch. Between 1941 and 1945, however, the commitment was heartfelt and purposeful, the sacrifices a true expression of the enormity of an awesome and peculiar responsibility. The designated dream factory had never dared conjure spectacle on so huge and wondrous a scale, painted villains and heroes so sharp and larger than life. Nor had it presumed that moviemakers would be active players, not just passive recorders, in the twentieth century's greatest production. No wonder Hollywood's favorite war story has always been its own.

2 Leni Riefenstahl's Contribution to the American War Effort

The average American moviegoer is an imaginary construct, a fictional fellow or lady brought forth in the service of rhetorical exchange and cast aside when the transaction ends. Depending on the medium, contingent on the argument, the ideal spectator takes on a variety of solid shapes. Classical Hollywood's preferred version is immortalized in the Church of the Sacred Screen sequence from Preston Sturges's *Sullivan's Travels* (1941): a chain gang steals a few moments of bliss from the penal system to laugh—gratefully, uproariously—at a Walt Disney cartoon. In a less escapist mode, the literary critic Alfred Kazin sketched a meditative self-portrait in his memoir *Starting Out In the Thirties:* sitting in a theater in the fall of 1940, watching newsreels of armored tanks and heavy guns rolling off an assembly line, Kazin knew, with sudden clarity, that the Great Depression was finally over. Then as now, the movies could as easily provide transportation back to the world as away from it.

However, then, unlike now, the average American moviegoer looked at a screen world of regal status and formal parameters. Despite black clouds spewing from the Anti-trust Division of the Department of Justice, the Hollywood studio system still held a virtual monopoly on the wonder of motion picture imagery. Despite frightful newspaper headlines with overseas datelines, the Hays Office still upheld a world of moral order and just authority. With the motion picture industry holding all the cards and rigging every hand, the relationship between the movies and the moviegoer might seem one of contractual exploitation, an unequal partnership wherein the party of the first part agrees to take the party of the second part systematically to the cleaners. But the deck was never so predictably stacked, nor was the game played only for money—on either side. Also on the table were stakes of a personal and cultural kind, webs of meaning harder to count up: recreational diversion, artistic expression, emotional sustenance, public affirmation, cathartic release, dating ritual, shared communion, and solitary revelation. To presume to go behind the eyes of the past and speculate about a between-the-ears experience is to encounter the outer limits of historical reconstruction. Better then to begin with the visible and tangible—the motion picture record, circa 1941—as a window on how the average American moviegoer looked at Hollywood, how Hollywood looked at itself and its audience, and how both sides redirected their visions over the next four years. Ironically, the best opening attraction is a motion picture genius without a Hollywood portfolio.

The inverted narrative of a film noir befits the story. In the waning days of the Second World War, the Hollywood trade press gleefully reports an emblematic encounter near Kitzbühel, Austria. A battle-hardened American soldier is requisitioning the lakeside villa of a former Nazi big shot and forcibly ousting its recalcitrant occupant— Leni Riefenstahl, the Third Reich's "golden girl," the motion picture director who had made her mark by making Fascism fascinating. Outraged at the brutish treatment, Riefenstahl tearfully protests and desperately identifies herself. As the GI rousts her out the door, he can't resist a parting salvo. "Baby, I've been going to the movies for a long time and I never heard of you. And now get going. We need the house."

The soldier misspoke. By 1945 any American who had been going to the movies for a long time knew the work of Leni Riefenstahl. Her

A Mephistophelian horror: the Third Reich's most famous director sets up a shot, Nuremberg, 1934. (Spaarnestad Foto-Archief, the Netherlands)

two documentary masterpieces—*Triumph of the Will* (1935), the official record of the Nazi Party's Congress in Nuremberg in 1934, and *Olympia* (1938), a two-part chronicle of the 1936 Olympic Games in Berlin—had supplied the American screen with its most powerful and lasting images of the Nazis in full dudgeon. Spliced into newsreels, War Department orientation films, and Hollywood features, the awful beauty and repellent substance of Riefenstahl's footage gave an immortal motion picture life to the twelve-year Reich.

Like the Nuremberg rallies, filmmaking is a collaborative enterprise resisting the assignment of individual responsibility for the total production. Without the architecture and lighting of Albert Speer, the geometric arrangement of troops drilled by Heinrich Himmler and Viktor Lutze, and the generative imagination of Hitler himself, no Nazi spectacle would be picture perfect. But Riefenstahl gave the iconography and rituals of Nazism a purely cinematic vitality. Her screen vision—the exultant compositions of brawny *übermensch* and budding *Hitlerjungend,* the night-for-night glow of Teutonic bonfires and torchlit parades, the worshipful low-angle shots and natural lighting silhouetting a deific Führer—imprinted the spectacular allure of the Nazi mythos in motion picture memory.

It also brought the director to the attention of an intrigued and appalled Hollywood. Attractive, talented, and female, Riefenstahl was a charismatic celebrity who under different patronage might have been feted and fawned over. She became instead a parable for the corruption of art by power. As an enemy propagandist, only (Paul) Joseph Goebbels surpassed her in infamy and insult. Around Hollywood, Riefenstahl may actually have edged him out. Reichsminister Goebbels presided over the complete range of mass media; Riefenstahl was of the movies alone and a genuine artist of the cinema at that. For the motion picture industry, the thought of a gifted and gorgeous filmmaker willfully in liege to Hitler inspired a Mephistophelian horror.

Riefenstahl was to become a representative figure, her work a dark mirror, because in motion picture (no less than in ideological or military) terms the war pitted stark alternatives against one another.

The Nazis on screen: Geometric precision and dynamic mise-en-scène in Riefenstahl's *Triumph of the Will* (1935). (Spaarnestad Foto-Archief, the Netherlands)

"We have seen that the first act of tyranny anywhere is to make it impossible to see American films," proclaimed Charles Francis Coe, vice president and general counsel for the Motion Picture Producers and Distributors of America (MPPDA). "We know that no propaganda-laden picture can stand against American films. We know the first effect of vicious propaganda films is to empty theaters." For the motion picture industry, the media-driven dimension of the Second World War structured the order of battle. Where the American military and GI everyman faced the challenge of the Wehrmacht and the Nazi superman, the studio system took on the Reichsfilmkammer and the popular artist fought the party hack. Matters of tactics and policy—democratic persuasion versus totalitarian manipulation, entertainment versus propaganda—were reflected in a contest of creative will and personal vision—Jack Warner versus Joseph Goebbels, Frank Capra versus Leni Riefenstahl.

The films that earned Riefenstahl ill-repute also made her reputation. Although never commercially released nor readily accessible in America during the 1930s, both *Triumph of the Will* and *Olympia* were well known around Hollywood—mostly by word of mouth, occasionally by sight. Either overseas or at the Museum of Modern Art in New York, where film curator Iris Barry jealously guarded a 35mm print obtained from a German-American businessman, a select number of critics and directors had seen *Triumph of the Will*. Word of its dread impact circulated throughout the motion picture industry. Visiting Germany in 1938, director Josef von Sternberg told Riefenstahl he had caught a screening of *Triumph of the Will* at MOMA and praised it effusively. "Mädchen," he rightly predicted, "this film will make film history—it is revolutionary." Siegfried Kracauer, working on his psychohistory *From Caligari to Hitler,* also studied the film at MOMA and wrote about it in a pamphlet, "Propaganda and the Nazi War Film," issued in 1942. Like many viewers at the time and since, Kracauer's "deep feeling of uneasiness" at the "frightening spectacle" was the more acute for an aesthetic appreciation of its "sumptuous orchestration" of the elements of film grammar.

In November 1938, Riefenstahl undertook an ill-fated tour of America in order to publicize the more tolerable of her two opuses, *Olympia*, and perhaps secure it a stateside commercial release. Arriving at the docks of New York aboard the luxury liner *Europa* on November 4, she was initially cast by the American press as just another glamorous celebrity from the Continent. Photos show her bedecked in furs and jewels; captions clad the "vivacious German film actress and director" in the apparel-minded prose of the women's pages. "A handsome woman of 30, with deep auburn hair and gray-green eyes, Miss Riefenstahl was smartly dressed in a mulberry wool dress under a gray broadtail coat trimmed with silver fox. She wore a cluster of orchids." Unable to imagine a purely professional relationship between the director and the dictator, journalists insinuated a titillating dalliance with her "close friend" Chancellor Hitler.

The fashionable coverage was abruptly curtailed when news of Kristallnacht, the Nazi-orchestrated rampage of destruction against synagogues and Jewish-owned businesses on the night of November 9–10, reached the metropolitan press. The Nazis, said Riefenstahl in response to hostile questioning, would never do such a thing. Thereafter, she met with abuse and rejection from coast to coast. Although *Olympia* was screened in Chicago and Los Angeles to not unfavorable notices, its distribution prospects in the domestic market were nil. In her memoirs Riefenstahl claims that the manager of Radio City Music Hall wanted to book *Olympia* but was later dissuaded by the uproar accompanying her tour. Wherever she went, controversy and calumny followed the woman sneered at as "Hitler's honey," "der Führer's pet photographer," and "a bosom pal of Adolf Hitler."

Nowhere did Riefenstahl receive a colder shoulder than in Hollywood, where throughout the last week of November 1938 the motion picture industry shunned her and anti-Nazi leagues protested her appearances and boycotted her screenings. Only a few insensitive souls broke ranks. She spent the better part of a day with Walt Disney touring his studio and discussing *Fantasia* storyboards. The ever image-conscious Disney refused, however, to be seen in public with a personality not known for family entertainment. Less socially astute, producer Hal Roach threw a welcoming party in her honor, an ill-attended soirée conspicuously bereft of A-list glitter. "There is no room in Hollywood for Leni Riefenstahl," proclaimed ads published in the trade press by the Hollywood Anti-Nazi League for the Defense of American Democracy. True enough—but a special place was reserved for Leni Riefenstahl's footage in Hollywood's wartime films.

It was Frank Capra, years later, who presented, or re-presented, *Triumph of the Will* to an American mass audience. He first screened the film in 1942 while mulling over plans for the project that became *Why We Fight*. "It scared the hell out of me," Capra recalled. In fact he was traumatized to discover that his beloved vocation might be

Der Führer's pet photographer: Leni Riefenstahl
alone in California, 1938. (Spaarnestad Foto-Archief,
the Netherlands)

used for such unholy ends—and used so well. Thirty years later,
recollecting the screening in his autobiography, Capra still sounded
spooked. "The film was the ominous prelude to Hitler's holocaust of
hate," he wrote. "Satan himself couldn't have devised a more blood-
chilling super-spectacle." Personally affronted and morally chal-
lenged, the director seems to have been compelled to tear the footage to shreds, to cut the Nazis down to size on the editing table and
restore honor to the art debased by Riefenstahl. At first resisted by
a non-movie-minded military, Capra's strategy of defacing the polished images of Nazism soon became standard practice. *Triumph of
the Will,* which screenwriter Philip Dunne called "so valuable a
source of Nazi material to all the American war-film agencies," was

in such demand that various branches of the War Department squabbled incessantly over priority access to MOMA's print and a second print confiscated by the United States Customs Service.

Hollywood studios were no less eager to obtain segments of *Triumph of the Will* to add impact and cutaway shots to war-themed melodramas. At MOMA Iris Barry initially balked at putting the museum's archives at the disposal of commercial features, explaining that "we have only one print being run here constantly for government officials, army, etc." With an archivist's sense of priority and possession, Barry wrote Nelson Rockefeller at the Office of Inter-American Affairs to voice her "strong feeling that it would be most improper for the Museum to supply enemy film in its care for use for commercial purposes." In the same spirit of shortsighted farsightedness, she also expressed concern regarding MOMA's "position after the war in regard to claims that conceivably might be made against the Museum by the German government and/or German film production companies involved." Barry relented only when Rockefeller interceded on behalf of the studios.

Drawn on as "library footage" by the newsreels, incorporated and recast throughout Capra's *Why We Fight* (1942–45) series, utilized as exposition and transition in *Hitler's Children* (1942) and *Mission to Moscow* (1943), *Triumph of the Will* was a consistent source of negative inspiration. It furnished the signature images of Nazism on the American screen even as it conferred a certain stylistic influence. *Hitler's Children,* a salaciously advertised and immensely popular proto-exploitation film, is downright fetishistic in its cultivation of swastika iconography and SS S&M. In low-angle two-shots of a uniformed Nazi in a loving clinch with his democratic girlfriend, the camera's awed gaze embraces some of the will to power the film's own dialogue condemns.

For Riefenstahl, meanwhile, the fortunes of war and antipathy from Reichsminister Goebbels thwarted further artistic development. At the very time Frank Capra's 834th Photo Signal Detachment and the Hollywood studios were making her work the American-approved, American-filtered version of the Nazis on screen, the director herself had fallen precipitously out of favor. Throughout the war, she stood on the propaganda sidelines, an absence that in Hollywood sparked the revealing rumor that she had been "liquidated."

But though Riefenstahl was missing in action, *Triumph of the Will* commanded center stage for the duration. By war's end its images were likely better known in America than in Germany. The postwar denouement confirms the film's popularity and persistence. While public screenings of *Triumph of the Will* were banned for nearly fifty years throughout much of Europe (and can still spark a picket line in formerly occupied countries), its archival contribution to wartime America was taken up enthusiastically and extended throughout the 1950s and 1960s in feature films and television documentaries. Standardized by recurrent usage, impossible to eradicate, Riefenstahl's images entered the select chambers of the American movie memory. In Stanley Kramer's *Judgment at Nuremberg* (1961), a crusty trial judge (played by Spencer Tracy) walks through the vacant Nuremberg Youth Stadium, now deserted but still haunted by the ghosts of rallies past. As Tracy gazes around the arena, up at the seats and across the field, the soundtrack mixes shouts of "Heil!" with the joyous call-and-response duet between *volk* and *führer*. Kramer did not need to screen a single frame of Riefenstahl's film for character and spectator alike to replay *Triumph of the Will* in the mind's eye.

Before the usurpation and containment, however, Riefenstahl's striking formal brilliance and Goebbels's sinister mass communications dexterity unnerved the motion picture industry at war. Just as the aura of battlefield invincibility surrounded the Wehrmacht, the cunning effectiveness of Nazi propaganda, particularly the exploitation of the art of cinema, suffused Goebbels's Reich Ministry for Popular Enlightenment and Propaganda. Understandably, Hollywood was at first uneasy about the matchup. On the propaganda canvas, after all, it was fighting out of its class. As unofficial and unselfconscious propagators of American culture, studio system filmmakers were the preeminent world champions; as official and conscious propagandists for the state, they were rank amateurs. When Army Chief of Staff George C. Marshall ordered Frank Capra to make what became the *Why We Fight* series, the ace director balked: "General Marshall, it's only fair to tell you that I have never before made a single documentary film. In fact, I've never even been near anybody that's made one." By common agreement the Nazis enjoyed a competitive edge on their own field and possessed what an intimidated *Variety* reporter called "the slickest propaganda regimentation extant."

Moreover, in a town where making documentaries was an esoteric practice, "propaganda" was a dirty word. Discredited in the American tradition by the hysterical Hun-baiting of the Creel Committee

Pictures in the mind's eye: Spencer Tracy walks through a haunted stadium in *Judgment at Nuremberg* (1961). (Museum of Modern Art/Film Stills Archive)

during World War I—a reputation now reinforced by the work of the Nazis—a designation once descriptive had become pejorative. In an address to the Chicago Rotary Club in 1943, War Activities Committee vice chairman Francis S. Harmon expressed the common sense: "I suppose the rank and file of people associate 'propaganda' either with outright falsehood or with something that is being put over by devious methods." To one Hollywood artist, the already legendary director John Ford, the very word was anathema. Working in the Office of Strategic Services under Ford, lately put on active duty as a lieutenant commander in the Navy, film editor Robert Parrish was assigned to work on the combat report, *The Battle of Midway* (September 1942). Did Ford have in mind a propaganda picture, inquired Parrish? "Ford looked at me a long time, looked away and looked back at me," recalled Parrish, himself a petty officer second class. "Then he lit his pipe, which usually took about two minutes. This time it seemed more like two hours. Finally, he said, 'How do you spell that word?' I spelled it for him and he said, 'Don't you ever let me hear you use that word again in my presence as long as you're under my command.' " Whatever the incidental ideological impact, American movies had been produced in service to a studio, not the state, and American moviemakers had mainly thought of themselves as doing a "job of work," not of political indoctrination.

In Hollywood's eyes, Riefenstahl's documentaries set the standard for a sustained celluloid assault directed by the Reichsfilmkammer, the coordinating board that in 1937 took full control of the German motion picture industry. In 1943 *American Cinematographer* conjured a frightening portrait of the machine works behind the cinematic blitzkrieg:

> Dr Goebbels converted the Ufa Studio at Neubabelsberg—one of the largest and finest in the world—into an assembly plant for making propaganda for Nazism. Directors, technicians, and artists were put to work, three shifts a day, twenty four hours per day, grinding out films that glorified the Nazi ideals of the Super-race, of devotion to the State, and of hatred for the rest of the world. Shooting and production schedules were cut in half, sets were made to do double duty. Ufa's fourteen sound stages, twenty-one cutting rooms, and five private theaters hummed with day and night activity.

Rolling off the production line were "topnotch battle films" showcasing the relentless Nazis in action-packed combat and glorious victory. In 1942 *Variety* shamefully acknowledged that American pictures of war production plants and troop training "look very pallid against shots of hard hitting Nazi tanks and Panzer divisions overcoming United Nations fighters on various fronts."

Like a viral infection, Nazi films "softened up" and intimidated targets of opportunity, making democratic countries susceptible to Axis invasion by weakening the immune system of potential victims. Besides *Triumph of the Will* and special nation-specific segments of *Olympia*, Ufa newsreels and Reichsfilmkammer documentaries such as *Der Feldzug in Polen* (*The Campaign in Poland*) (1939) and *Sieg im Westen* (*Victory in the West*) (1940) presaged and assisted Nazi expansionism. "These films were shown to gatherings of foreign diplomats in practically every country in Europe, always prior to Nazi invasion," warned the *Hollywood Reporter* in 1942. "Several weeks before the Nazi invasion of Yugoslavia and Greece these films were shown before high dignitaries of the two victims. Goering himself reportedly showed King Boris of Bulgaria many reels of Nazi conquests before that Balkan country signed on with the Axis." According to discomforting reports, the Nazis devoted no less than two full divisions of men "assigned strictly to obtaining a motion picture version of the war," which then got an expert "Nazified treatment" in postproduction. In *Divide and Conquer* (August 1942), a Warner Bros. short utilizing captured enemy footage (not to be confused with Capra's *Why We Fight* entry of the same name), Nazi propaganda is accorded a plaguelike capacity to poison the polis with "mental confusion, indecisiveness, and panic."

Lacy W. Kastner of the overseas branch of the Office of War Information frankly acknowledged the propaganda gap. During extensive travels in prewar Europe, Kastner "saw and studied the screen technique of the Germans" and publicly, in 1942, praised it as superlative. "Sometimes after I came away from seeing one of those Nazi propaganda films, I was so impressed by the technical excellence of the picture that I had to remember it was Hitler we were fighting." Ruefully observing how the Allied screen suffered by comparison, Siegfried Kracauer was also discouragingly blunt. "Owing to [the traditions of German cinema], the Nazis knew how to use the three film media—commentary, visuals, and sound. With a pronounced feeling for editing, they exploited each medium to the full, so that the total effect frequently resulted from the blending of different meanings in different media. Such polyphonic handling is not often found in democratic war films." When the Motion Picture Society for the Americas and the Office of Inter-American Affairs presented "Two Evenings of German Propaganda Films, 1934–1941" at Hollywood's Filmarte Theater in 1943, industry producers, directors, and writers packed the auditorium. The propaganda neophytes came to learn from the master race.

Hollywood had nowhere else to turn for instruction. From Washington, studio professionals could expect little in the way of practical guidance. The state's entry into the motion picture business was as new as the industry's induction into the purposes of the state. In comparison to KINO and Ufa, the movie-making agencies under totalitarian regimes Leninist and Fascist, the American motion picture industry was conspicuously free of legal constraints and state-financed competition. As regulators and manipulators, the U.S. government had left cinema unfettered, untapped, and ill-considered. "Films are a field in which I am only dimly acquainted," Elmer Davis guilelessly confessed upon his appointment as director of the Office of War Information in June 1942. "I have no ideas at all as yet as to the part they should play in the war effort." Lowell Mellett, head of the OWI's Bureau of Motion Pictures (BMP), was equally vague on specifics and even shorter on tact. During a tour of a studio sound-stage, he remarked to his executive guides that some of their movies had not been good for the war effort. Asked what titles he had in mind, the government official in charge of liaison with the motion picture industry replied, "I just can't mention the pictures, as I don't see many pictures. I'm too busy." Col. Kirke B. Lawton, a former law-yer heading the Army Pictorial Service at least knew his limitations. "I can operate [my division] as an executive here in Washington, but as for making pictures, I know nothing about it," he admitted. "To take a man who knows nothing about the industry, who knows noth-ing about the research end, and send him out there [to Hollywood] would be like sending me out there." Against the confirmed cineastes and frustrated auteurs of the Third Reich, the officials of the OWI and the War Department come off as visual illiterates.

During the course of the war, more in spite of government guid-ance than because of it, Hollywood filmmakers settled on an anti-Axis strategy suited to a mediawise and cinematically sophisticated cul-ture. It was not a coordinated campaign or a rigorously enforced set of axioms; it was a commonsense recognition by popular artists of the background and values of an audience they had long been wed-ded to. By way of direct countermeasures, one line of attack con-fronted and rebutted Axis ideology. The other flank waged a subtler media-centered campaign that offered instruction in mass commu-nications and propaganda techniques. Throughout both movements, Hollywood deployed the weapons it handled best, juxtaposing its own grammar and imagery with the enemy's cinematic vision of himself.

The first front explicitly responded to Axis provocations. The open avowal of American values and stacked-deck responses to Axis prop-aganda determine much of the structure of wartime orientation films, Victory shorts, and the more nakedly polemical of the Hollywood features. Commentators coo over breadbasket beneficence and crow about industrial might. Forward narrative action halts for magnilo-quent declarations of democratic verities and expressive montages of heartland tapestries. Hence too the compulsive inclusion of shots of captured German and Japanese troops in the newsreels and com-bat reports, defeated and deflated would-be conquerors who now, as

RKO's narration to the Soviet documentary *Moscow Strikes Back* (1942) gloats, "seem less than supermen."

The second front was explicitly media-oriented. Audiences were educated to the ideological power of mass communications, flattered over their superior powers of apprehension, and assured of their democratic immunity to the falsehoods of Axis enticements. The appropriation and recasting of the Nazis' own widely disseminated images was the favorite guerrilla tactic. Redrawn to Allied specifications, hijacked enemy propaganda films supplied the raw material for the most clever and effective of American countermeasures. Announcing the screening of a reedited German film of the North African campaign, the London edition of the *Stars and Stripes* was airily nonchalant. "Sponsored by Goebbels, the movie is entitled *Invincible*. Reservations may be obtained by telephone." In the combat report *The Enemy Strikes* (March 1945), seized German footage of Field Marshal Gerd von Rundstedt's offensive during the Battle of the Bulge was recast for the domestic purpose of extinguishing homefront complacency. The Reichsfilmkammer film within the War Department film shows grimly determined Nazi soldiers smoking American cigarettes. The commentator expounds: "Germans smoked Camels and Chesterfields robbed from American dead and the Nazi cameraman filmed it to amuse and reassure the moviegoers of Munich and Berlin." Not all the hijacking was so somber. Circulated stateside by the newsreels beginning on January 15, 1942, the British import *Lambeth Walk* (1941), a two-minute travesty of *Triumph of the Will,* featured rewound and sped-up goosesteppers marching in time to a jaunty dancehall melody.

The native invulnerability to the clumsy enticements of Axis propagandists was a constant transmedia motif. Radio, the living room medium of the day, came in for special scrutiny. Americans had logged too many hours before Philco and RCA furniture to be suckered by overseas transmissions beneath the standards and subtlety of the stateside commercial networks. "Every night soldiers [in the Russell Islands] are entertained by what they call 'The Zero Hour,' a variety program beamed in this direction by the Nips from Tokyo," reported *Yank* in 1943. The article then sardonically listed a series of accented teasers:

> "How would you boys on Guadalcanal like a cold beer?"
> "You men in New Guinea, your girls at home are running around with defense workers."

"How would you men in the Russell Islands like to sink your teeth into a juicy steak?"

"American soldiers listen to this crap with good humor," the Army weekly cracked. "They even get a kick out of it." In a more serious, analytic tone, *Yank* noted that "sometimes Jap radio takes on the peculiar propaganda technique of trying to persuade our soldiers that the Japs are pushovers for our side"—a lure more insidious than the sensory deprivations of booze, babes, and beef. Back on the homefront, "rumor clinics" interpreted verbal sabotage and traced defeatist and divisive talk back to Axis propaganda broadcasts. In 1944, with the ready approval of the OWI and the War Department, San Francisco radio station KYA began rebroadcasting selections from Tokyo Rose and her friends. Afterward, network news commentators and military experts analyzed her psychological ploys.

Fancying itself a more prestigious and technically complex medium, Hollywood cinema assumed a condescending and professorial tone when addressing its poor relations in mass communications. Look, the screen seemed to say, see how amateurish are the tricks, how easily exposed are the secrets, of these lesser media, so prone to manipulation and cheap effects: rely on the movies to open your eyes. By depicting the careful attention the Axis lavished on mass communications, laying bare the techniques and disrupting the presentation, wartime films illustrated how to see (and hear) through doctored photos, forged documents, and deceitful broadcasting.

Shockingly, the motion picture industry's chief media rival was especially inclined to treachery. Hissing in accented English, radio broadcasters from Tokyo to Berlin chortled over fictional battlefield victories and cast seeds of psychological discord over the air. Fortunately, radio transmissions were susceptible to celluloid exposure and democratic disruptions. Both *Once Upon a Honeymoon* (1942) and *Hitler's Children* include scenes in which live radio broadcasts are sabotaged to the consternation of Goebbels-like overseers. The fraudulence of Axis propaganda in print had only to be seen, not heard, to reveal its bold-faced prevarications. Flashbacking to the prewar innocence of undergraduate life at Texas A&M, Walter Wanger's *We've Never Been Licked* (1943) relies solely on twenty-twenty hindsight when a newspaper headline from late 1938 comes into focus: " 'Germany Wants World Understanding and Peace'—Hitler." In *This Land Is Mine* (1943), directed by temporary exile Jean Renoir from a Dudley Nichols screenplay, the testimony is mute and the image speaks for itself. No shot is fired when the Nazis raise the swastika over an occupied French village, and no commentary is needed except the cold presentation of the Nazi truth: a propaganda poster ("Citizens! Trust the German Soldier") and a collaborationist newspaper with the headline "Hitler Speaks for United Europe."

Yet the danger of duplicity and misapprehension lurked also in the noblest of the media. In Axis hands the movies lied at twenty-four frames a second. During Darryl F. Zanuck's speculative courtroom drama *The Purple Heart* (1944), a Japanese prosecutor (Richard Loo) screens bogus motion picture evidence to a kangaroo court sitting in judgment of American POWs falsely accused of bombing civilian targets. In a darkened courtroom, he projects apparently authentic newsreel pictures of the bloody aftermath of the Doolittle Raid on Tokyo. As the prosecutor enunciates a deceptive voice-over ("The court will notice the wreckage of the Daijingu Shrine and the many civilian causalities"), forescreen, in the press gallery, a sympathetic newspaper correspondent objects. "That is not an actual air raid," he rasps sotto voce. "Those pictures were made during an air raid drill—before Japan was even at war. You know, we were all there!"

Perhaps the most polished inquiry into high-definition deception occurred in a lowbrow subgenre of wartime cinema. Released on the heels of *Hitler's Children* and exploited in like manner, RKO's anti-Japanese melodrama *Behind the Rising Sun* (1943) elaborately exposes the full scope of ideological awareness and mass communications smarts in Hollywood countermeasures. Its extended lesson in visual propaganda warrants a shot-by-shot breakdown; a plot summary may, or may not, provide necessary background orientation. In prewar Japan, Taro (Tom Neal), the handsome, Cornell-educated scion of Japan's sole surviving liberal patrician, returns to his militaristic homeland. He secures altruistic but self-fulfilling employment with the engineering firm of *gaijin* businessman O'Hara (Don Douglas) and embraces Western-style romantic love in the shape of the company's pretty Japanese secretary, Tama (Margo). But when Taro is drafted into the Imperial Army, he reverts to type as an occupying officer in ravaged China. One day he confronts an old acquaintance from his assimilationist time in Tokyo, a woman reporter who has been pushed, slapped, and insulted by guffawing soldiers under his command. She complains futilely to the now insensitive and fully

Lying at twenty-four frames per second: a Japanese prosecutor (Richard Loo) manipulates the medium in *The Purple Heart* (1944).

Samurai-encoded Taro. At this point, the camera "matches" Taro's eyeline to initiate a deft cinematic exposure of Axis propaganda technique. As the sequence unwinds, the spectator receives a full education in the manipulation of the medium and the unreliability of the photographic image.

The exposé begins with what will be a repeated "core image," a medium shot of friendly Japanese troops handing out food packages to grateful Chinese civilians. In the course of the sequence, *Behind the Rising Sun* systematically reveals the reality behind a photographic image initially beheld and falsely perceived:

1. Taro (his eyeline gazing screen right)
2. From Taro's perspective, friendly Japanese soldiers hand out provisions to grateful Chinese women and children.
3. Taro (now holding a pocket camera). He sets up his photograph and takes a snapshot of the generous Japanese soldiers distributing food.

4. The core image—(2) above—constructed from Taro's perspective. The soundtrack mixes in the "click" of a snapshot being taken, and the screen freezes. The camera pulls back on the fixed, photographed image of Japanese soldiers giving out goods to reveal a hand holding what has now become a still photograph.
5. Back in Tokyo (in flash-forwarded, nonparallel action), Mr. O'Hara, the American businessman, and Tama, the girl back home, contemplate the snapshot:

TAMA: "You see, Mr. O'Hara? They're really very nice to the Chinese children, aren't they?"
O'HARA: (Scrutinizing the core image, skeptically): "... Certainly seems so."

After some talk about Taro and his family, Tama picks up the photograph again and gazes down at it.

6. The camera pulls in to a precise rendering of the core shot (shots 2 and 4 above) and "starts up" sound and action, flashbacking to the previous, China-set tableau. The reanimated Japanese troops continue to give out provisions to lines of smiling Chinese children. A girl grabs her package, pauses face-forward (before walking out of frame) and looks at what she has been given. Cut to:
7. Tight close-up of package label: "Imperial Japanese OPIUM monopoly."
8. Cut back to core set up. Frowning Chinese girl approaches Japanese troops.
9. Girl pushes package back into soldier's hands.

JAPANESE SOLDIER: "What's this?"
CHINESE GIRL: "We don't use opium here!"

10. Japanese Soldier: "You will eat what we give you—or you will not eat at all! Do you understand?" (Whereupon the Japanese soldier pushes the Chinese girl into oncoming traffic)

Eschewing verbal narration, with a slick cinematic dexterity suited to a fast lesson in photographic sleight of hand, *Behind the Rising Sun* delivers its media message in purely visual terms.

Clearly, the supreme magicians of screen propaganda no longer resided in the Ufa Studio at Neubabelsberg. Whatever anxieties the Reichsfilmkammer blitzkrieg and Riefenstahl triumphs had fostered in Hollywood at the onset of war had turned to serene confidence once the battle was truly joined. Capra's *Why We Fight* series alone had outmaneuvered and outstripped the once-feared "Nazified treatments" of the "slickest propaganda regimentation extant." By midwar, evidence of the heightened mass communications smarts of American culture was daily visible on any motion picture screen—even in the unlikely precincts of *Behind the Rising Sun*.

The lately perfected dexterity on the American side had one unforeseen consequence. If the medium qua medium invited manipulation and deception, the potential for misapprehension could not be intrinsic to Axis cinema alone. Therefore, while the educational program in the treacherous techniques of enemy cinema proceeded apace, reassurances needed to be offered about the good intentions and fair dealing of Hollywood cinema. As an expression of trust and openness, the motion picture industry stopped safeguarding some its own secrets. Hollywood's trademark "invisible style," the studio system aesthetic that concealed the guiding hand of the filmmaker, was made visible for all to see. Increasingly after 1941, the newsreels, documentary shorts, and government information films spotlighted behind-the-scenes glimpses of Hollywood production and detailed reports on the techniques of motion picture photography, especially combat camerawork shot under fire. Feature films too began incorporating moments of instructive self-reflexivity. In *Pilot No. 5* (1943) a demagogic state governor rehearses a newsreel appearance with cameramen-cum-henchmen. Seated at his desk, oozing an affected homespun touch, he begins his on-camera presentation. The newsreel cameramen coach him to arise from his seat more slowly: "Remember, we have to pan up with you." During the subsequent take, the demagogue complies and a reverse shot reviews the lesson in film grammar by showing the newsreel cameras panning up. Contrasting the American with the Axis approach (and making generous use of the first-person plural), Lowell Mellett asserted the propaganda difference at the 1943 Academy Awards ceremony. "We have not sought to mesmerize the American people through the play of light and shadow upon their eyes and sound upon their ears," Mellett explained to the artists who devised the strategy. "We have not sought to goosestep the American soul."

Far from having a mesmerized gaze or a goosestepped soul, the average American moviegoer circa 1945 had acquired a more alert, attuned, and skeptical eye than the circa 1941 model. Graduating from the four-year curriculum in motion picture technique and propagandistic persuasion was the first generation of moving-image spectators as accustomed to education as entertainment, as prepared for critical engagement as for cultural diversion. Axis cinema, endowed elsewhere with an almost hypnotic power of persuasion, could rightly be marked as crudely obvious and transparently deceptive to the discerning American whose Hollywood-trained vision was sharp enough to spot the con. "You are up to his tricks," Warner Bros.'s *Divide and Conquer* assures. "You can see through his technique." As for the deprived foreigners and occupied peoples who suffered prolonged exposure to the Reichsfilmkammer blight, the motion picture industry prescribed a predictable refresher course: its own features. As the *Hollywood Reporter* bragged: "Military authorities and OWI men are convinced that American films are the most important means of disintoxicating people in areas formerly occupied by the enemy from Axis propaganda and re-educating them to the knowledge of the free world and free people from which they have been cut off." In selected cases the suspicion that should be accorded all images might be suspended.

Production Codes

Although less iron-fisted than the grip of the Reichsfilmkammer, Hollywood too worked under guiding hands—or rather an assortment of fingers reaching into production to mold the movies into prescribed shape. Some of the agents that left their mark were known quantities, such as the personnel of the Hays Office and the priests of the Catholic Legion of Decency, overseers whose tastes and objectives were long-standing and well understood. In contrast, the wartime regulators commissioned to monitor and motivate the motion picture industry during 1941–45 dispensed a totally different kind of directional guidance. Their interest in motion picture dialogue, characters, plots, and themes marked the most elaborate and concentrated attempt by the American government to harness cinema for its own ends.

The familiar and unquestioned oversight authority in Hollywood was the Production Code Administration (PCA), also known as the Hays Office, a voluntary system of self-regulation administered by the

Motion Picture Producers and Distributors of America (MPPDA) and enforced with vigor since 1934. The man at the helm was not titular head Will H. Hays but Joseph I. Breen, a Jesuit-educated and industry-wise workhorse whose stern brand of Irish Catholicism provided the theological grounding for the Production Code. A tabletlike list of moral injunctions in imperative syntax, the Code was the catechism against which the movies were measured. No classical Hollywood film escaped bureaucratic passage through the Hays Office or achieved wide commercial release without its imprimatur. The Code seal of approval remains the single best certification of classical Hollywood status.

If the immediate political purpose of the Code was to circumvent the threat of federal censorship, and the immediate economic purpose to forestall boycotts by the public-spirited or clerically congregated, the main cultural function was to assert moral order and vindicate lawful authority. The restrictions on the exposure of skin, the utterance of slang or blasphemy, the sanitizing of violence, and the other often-ridiculed markers of Code influence are mainly diversions. The squabbles between producers and Breen tended to be over minor fissures—prohibited language, the contours of a silhouette, the erotic implications of a fade-out—not over the consequential content and the ultimate message—that the guilty are punished, virtue is rewarded, and the providence of God and the legitimacy of government is upheld. Tensions rumbled up from beneath the Code-smoothed surface, but the ground of moral order was steady in classical Hollywood cinema.

After Pearl Harbor, the Code's role as cultural arbiter was shared and jostled by a new order of regulatory authority more faithful to the interests of the state than the church. Breen, a man notoriously jealous of his turf, at first expressed no fear of usurpation from government interlopers. The outbreak of world war, he told an apparently stunned reporter in 1942, was of no consequence to his office. The Code's standard practice concerning war and military films, which Breen simply pledged to continue, required that producers supply five copies of each script to the Secretary of War or Navy together with a "specific description of military locations, equipment, personnel or operations for filming of which permission is sought." Following the initial okay, a finished print was screened for final approval by the PCA before public exhibition. "The war simply does not affect the Code or its application," Breen claimed with a straight face. "It has raised no issues or questions that were not present and covered by the Code in peace time."

In a sense Breen was right. Attentive to and restrictive on matters of morality and propriety, the Code was silent on crucial war-specific lessons. In 1942 Breen issued a lengthy memorandum that bluntly outlined the boundaries of his jurisdiction. "The function of the Production Code is not to create authenticity or realism. The Code cannot be sufficiently elastic to accommodate itself to the impulse of the individual to be any of these things. The Code is the chart. It is the collateral which guarantees our public trust," he declared. One line from the memo, startling in historical context, sums up Breen's perspective: "*The function of the Code is not to be patriotic; it is to be moral.*"

Theoretically, then, Hollywood movies might remain true to the Code and yet contribute little to the war effort. The most famous celluloid sacrifice of wartime Hollywood cinema—the end of *Casablanca* (1942), when cynical Rick puts his beloved Ilsa on a plane with Victor Laslo, hero of the Czechoslovakian underground—is a case in point. "The power of *Casablanca*'s ending," film historian Robert B. Ray points out, "derived from the coincidence of ideological need (to send the woman away) with official morality." That is, the film needs Rick to stick his neck out and commit to the Allied cause at the same time it needs to respect the sanctity of the bonds of matrimony. In a purely Code-driven universe, it is impossible to imagine Rick running off with Ilsa and leaving her lawful husband on a North African runway. Yet it is quite plausible to concoct a Code-sealed scenario in which Victor dies gallantly to leave the field clear for an end-reel clinch between the romantic leads. Even in a nation at war, the charter of the Production Code remained taste and morality, not domestic policy and national security. Breen himself broke up the spheres of influence into three parts. "It is bad *taste* to show drunk men or soldiers in unsavory situations," he said. "It is bad *policy* to show scenes of any kind that might give aid to the enemy. As for those that give *military information,* there is no need to comment about that." Freshly commissioned tasks of cultural instruction—the new breed of heroism, the abnegation of self, the value of cooperative enterprise, the appreciation of Allied efforts, the contributions of women, the unity of "Americans All"—were quite literally not Breen's department.

Washington willingly begat the agencies and bureaucrats to fill the regulatory vacuum. In the forced and not always happy partnership between the state and the studios, the two sides frequently spatted and exchanged recriminations. Postwar memoirs are replete with stories of energetic Hollywood go-getters knocking heads against dense military "brasshats" and intrusive civilian suits. But the disputes were tactical and temperamental, never over ultimate purpose. Pressed into alliance, the incompatible couple worked together fairly smoothly for common ends.

Wartime cooperation between the state and the studios actually predated the date of infamy. On June 5, 1940, industry representatives formed the Motion Picture Committee Cooperating for the National Defense, through which the studios produced twenty-five defense-related short subjects and twelve trailers for Army recruitment. The committee cajoled exhibitors into screening civil defense and informational shorts such as the Tennessee Valley Authority's *Power for Defense* (February 1941), the Civilian Conservation Corps' *Army in Overalls* (June 1941), and the Office of Emergency Management's *Bomber* (October 1941). From these bureaucratic beginnings came the multitiered, intercoordinated network of government-industry agencies and committees that coordinated Hollywood's war effort. From Hollywood's side, the most important intermediary was the renamed and expanded War Activities Committee of the Motion Picture Industry (WAC).

More controversial and avowedly interventionist than the defense-minded shorts was a modest prewar cycle of anti-Nazi feature films produced on the studios' own initiative. With the progressive decline and by 1938 virtual elimination of the German market for Hollywood product, the external constraint of overseas profits no longer hindered public expressions of private loathing. From this vantage, the anti-Nazi films of 1939–41 were but the overdue rejoinder from an industry that, more than most, had no reason to be quiescent in the face of Fascism. A cluster of three concurrent and interrelated events in late 1938 also sparked the industry's atypical move away from the apolitical: (1) the galvanizing incitement of Leni Riefenstahl's visit to Hollywood; (2) the announcement by Warner Bros. of production plans for the anti-Nazi melodrama *Confessions of a Nazi Spy,* the first real shot across the bow; and (3) the meeting of a vanguard group of studio notables calling themselves "the Committee of 56," which was convened at Edward G. Robinson's house to promote anti-Nazi action within the industry. Singling out the trailblazing *Confessions of a Nazi Spy,* committee member Groucho Marx delivered one of his few publicly recorded straight lines: "I want to propose a toast to Warners—the only studio with any guts."

Motivated by the closing of the Continental market and sincere anti-Nazism, the industry ventured boldly into oppositional action not only in the docu-dramatic *Confessions of a Nazi Spy* (1939) but also in roman'·c melodramas such as *The Mortal Storm* (1940) and *The Man I Married* (1940). The colonial propensity for Anglophilia, dormant since the rise to political power of the Irish-American, revived in the face of the Nazi onslaught and the status of Great Britain as the sole European outlet for English-language films. Stiff-upper-lipped and admirably resolute British filled some of the best films in the legendary 1939 vintage, such as MGM's *Goodbye Mr. Chips* and RKO's *Gunga Din.* Like FDR, Warner Bros. tilted discernibly toward the English. In *They Died with Their Boots On* (1941) General Custer (Errol Flynn) pauses before riding down into the Little Big Horn and gives the British military observer at his side the chance to escape his last stand. Refusing to abandon an ally under duress, the Englishman replies with the dramaturgical equivalent of presidential envoy Harry Hopkins's biblical promise to the besieged British the same year: "Whither thou goest I will go."

Not all Americans held to the Hopkins–Warner Bros. line. In September 1941 the isolationist anti-Semite Gerald Nye (R–N.D.) initiated an investigation into "Moving Picture Screen and Radio Propaganda" by the Senate Subcommittee on Interstate Commerce. "Unquestionably there are in Hollywood today, engaged by the motion picture industry, those who are naturally far more interested in the fate of their homelands than they are in the fortunes of the United States," warned Nye. "I would myself call it the most potent and dangerous 'fifth column' in our country." Nye named an eclectic blacklist of fifth-columnist films, including the British import *Convoy* (1940), Charles Chaplin's *The Great Dictator* (1940), *Flight Command* (1940), *Escape* (1940), *That Hamilton Woman* (1941), *Man Hunt* (1941), and three from the worst offender, Warner Bros., *Confessions of a Nazi Spy, Underground* (1941), and *Sergeant York* (1941).

Emboldened by a dawning sense of inevitable engagement, the motion picture industry, usually so timorous in the face of government scrutiny or public opprobrium, played smart, seized the offensive, and roundly outpointed the opposition. The MPPDA hired Wendell

L. Willkie, the Republican presidential candidate in 1940 and an un-assailable figure of moderation and respectability, to represent studio interests before Congress. Willkie baldly testified that a Senate inquiry into "whether or not the motion picture industry as a whole and its leading executives as individuals are opposed to the Nazi dictatorship in Germany" was totally unnecessary because they *were* opposed to Hitler. "We make no pretense of friendliness to Nazi Germany nor to the objectives and goals of this ruthless dictatorship. We abhor everything which Hitler represents." Willkie calculated that, of the 1,100 Hollywood movies produced in the two years since the outbreak of the European war, only some fifty had war-related themes. However, "some of these fifty, we are glad to admit, do portray Nazism for what it is—a cruel, lustful, ruthless, and cynical force."

Willkie was followed on the industry side by Harry M. Warner, president of Warner Bros. Warner was equally forthright ("I abhor and detest every principle and practice of the Nazi movement"), unrepentant ("*Sergeant York* is a factual portrait of the life of one of the great heroes of the last war. If that is propaganda, we plead guilty"), and contemptuous of accusers who had not done their homework ("These witnesses have not seen these pictures, so I cannot imagine how they can judge them"). Fox's Darryl F. Zanuck delivered the knockout blow. In a sly set of disarming opening remarks, he mentioned his smalltown roots in Wahoo, Nebraska, referred joshingly to his overseas service in the Great War (where he rose to "the rank of private first class,") and, for Nye's benefit, listed his impeccably gentile credentials ("My parents and grandparents were regular attendants and lifelong members of the Methodist Church"). With rising passion, the former screenwriter testified, literally now, to a creed that bespoke the inseparable bond between America and Hollywood. After invoking Ma Joad's "We're the people" peroration from the John Ford–directed, Zanuck-produced *The Grapes of Wrath* (1940), Zanuck declared:

> I look back and I recall picture after picture, pictures so strong and powerful that they sold the American way of life not only to America but to the entire world. They sold it so strongly that when dictators took over Italy and Germany, what did Hitler and his flunky, Mussolini, do? The first thing they did was ban our pictures, throw us out. They wanted no part of the American way of life.

Too busy to go to the movies: Lowell Mellett (*center*), Coordinator of Government Films and soon-to-be head of the Office of War Information's Bureau of Motion Pictures, during a January 1942 visit to Hollywood. With Mellett are (*left to right*): Y. Frank Freeman, chairman of the War Activities Group; Clark Gable, chairman of the Actors Committee of the Hollywood Victory Committee; Charles Boyer, member of the Actors Committee; and Edward Arnold, president of the Screen Actors Committee. (Quigley Photo Archive/ Georgetown University)

The senate gallery erupted in applause, Sen. Ernest McFarland (D–Ariz.) called Zanuck's speech "the best I have ever heard," and chairman Bennett C. Clark (D–Mo.) adjourned the hearings later that day—permanently as it turned out. After Pearl Harbor and throughout the next four years, industry executives took no little pleasure in recalling the "war propaganda" hearings as a sorry example of congressional dimwittedness before Hollywood prescience.

On December 18, 1941, President Roosevelt officially called Hollywood to war and formally recognized the wartime role of cinema with the appointment of Lowell Mellett, then director of the Office of Government Reports, as Coordinator of Government Films. In June

1942 an executive order created the Office of War Information (OWI) under the directorship of former CBS news analyst Elmer Davis, to gather "all varied Government press and information services under one leadership." Mellett's office then became the Bureau of Motion Pictures (BMP), which until 1943 acted as the main civilian liaison and contact point between Washington and Hollywood. In the summer of that year Congress, wary that the faith the agency was promulgating was as pro-FDR as anti-Axis, cut the OWI's domestic budget and gutted the BMP. The agency that some senators derisively referred to as "Mellett's Madhouse" was out of the motion picture production business and consigned to advisory status. Hollywood thereupon assumed major responsibility for domestic production of war information shorts and screen bulletins to the homefront.

Despite a copious paper trail of OWI cables and War Department memos, the exact nature of government involvement in the motion picture industry—even the precise nexus of authority—is sometimes difficult to appreciate and locate. Certainly the footprints of government agents are often too clumsy and club-footed to escape detection. In *I'll Be Seeing You* (1944), two old duffers lug their golf clubs off a bus onto a driving range, observing that public transportation truly *is* as convenient as a private vehicle and, besides, it conserves gasoline. In the same spirit, *The Human Comedy* (1943) abruptly freezes its forward motion to praise a convenient encampment of United Nations Allies participating in a roadside folk festival. However, broadly speaking, Breen's tripartite division corresponds to three centers of authority: morality (the Production Code Administration), wartime policy (the Office of War Information), and military security (the War Department). Keeping the chain of command loose and the centers of power fuzzy suited the purpose of government and industry alike. "It is not possible, of course, to write a set of hard and fast rules to govern an undertaking of this kind," said Nelson Poynter of the BMP's Hollywood office. "There are so many intangibles, so many variables, that personal discussion, conference, and comparing of viewpoints is necessary if results are to be obtained swiftly and without confusion."

Thus gentlemen's agreements and word-of-mouth accommodations influenced production decisions as much as the printed directives of the OWI. In January 1943 *Motion Picture Herald* published an extensive, two-part summation of government "suggestions to producers for film treatment" that expressed the elusive nature of the

Hollywood-Washington arrangement. The first section of the summary included an eye-glazing litany of OWI hobbyhorses ("clarify confusion regarding Lend Lease," "depict adjustment of lives to the 24-hour schedule of working shifts," "picture curtailment of pleasure spending in favor of War Bond purchase and payment of taxes as offsets against inflation"). The second part listed Axis propaganda lines to be dispelled ("that wealthy men in the democracies engineered the war and are running it on a platform of profit above patriotism," "that the American Government's policy with respect to Latin-American countries is camouflage for imperialism"). The magazine concluded its propaganda roundup with a revelatory qualification:

> Neither of the foregoing summaries is derived *verbatim* from any official documentation of OWI policy and neither is complete, for there is no point of completeness save from day to day in the development of the nation's war program and the OWI problem of dealing with it. The summaries do portray in essence, however, the OWI counsel proffered producers.

The "essence" of the relationship between Hollywood and Washington was in the air not on paper.

Of course the government's right to control and censor news and dramatic material related to matters of military secrecy and national security was unequivocal. Under a 1917 Espionage Act reinvoked on December 7, Army and Navy censorship of the newsreels (in effect "semiofficially" for some time) was given the force of law. Moreover, the rules of the game in 1941–45—the limits to what was permissible and mentionable—were restrictively self-regulating. To a later journalistic ethos, the media seem astonishingly compliant. The unspoken codes of conduct were more discreet, the internal mechanisms of media-government relations more accommodating. Speaking to the press upon his return from a USO tour of Italy in 1944, actor Fredric March ventured a mild criticism of Army policy. A military press officer stepped forward and said "that will have to be stricken from the record," and it was.

But excepting matters of national security, the government's claim on the industry was as much cultural as legal. The tangible compulsions of power meshed with the ephemeral force of moral suasion. For the first- and second-generation Americans who ran the studios, the foreign-born directors who spoke with thick accents, and the actors whose real names did not end in Anglo-Saxon suffixes, celebrity stature and financial success did not necessarily dispel feelings of cultural marginality. The need to prove patriotism—to do not only one's share but a little more—energized the Hollywood community. Another seduction was the status that came with being on easy terms with political power and high-ranking military officers, men vested with the kind of authority before which one's grandparents had quaked. Whether dining with "his good friend" Gen. H. H. ("Hap") Arnold or receiving a late-night phone call from FDR, Jack Warner was only too happy to heed a gentlemanly request and order up *The Rear Gunner* (April 1943) for Army Air Force recruitment or *Mission to Moscow* (1943) for Soviet-American relations. The binding power of the common cause and the fear of public censure cemented the open willingness to cooperate.

On board of their own accord, the motion picture industry preferred suggestive "cues" and "amicable supervision," not preemptive dictates. The looming bludgeon of legal compulsion notwithstanding, both parties wanted to avoid the onus of federal censorship or precedent-setting incursions into Hollywood prerogatives. In calling the motion picture to service in the days after Pearl Harbor, FDR stated flatly that the government assumed no coercive authority. "I want no censorship of the motion picture; I want no restrictions placed thereon which will impair the usefulness of the film other than those very necessary restrictions which the dictates of safety make imperative." It was a declaration the motion picture industry cited repeatedly in the next four years. For Hollywood the constant frustration was not that the government presumed a measure of control and censorship, but that the levels of bureaucracy and the multiplicity of concerned agencies crossed signals, mixed messages, and generally mucked up the works.

The flash point for government-industry relations was Mellett's Bureau of Motion Pictures, which reviewed Hollywood films, coordinated the release of Victory film shorts with WAC, and issued advice on the government's special interest in themes and subject matter. The advice took a variety of forms, including private conversations, speeches to motion picture guilds and associations, vague pronouncements from Mellett or his underlings, and informational memos and booklets. The most widely circulated axiom guidebook was a fifty-page loose-leaf brochure called "Government Information Manual for the Motion Picture Industry," which concluded with specific OWI suggestions for full-length features. Favored BMP topics were the less heralded and hence less cinematic and remunerative aspects of the war effort, such as the importance of a unified command on a worldwide scale and the unassuming heroism of the humdrum branches of the service. Coupled with the search for unfallowed narrative ground, nudging from the BMP inspired dutiful paeans to wartime warriors who wielded weapons besides guns. Warner Bros.'s *Heroes without Uniforms* (1942) praised the Merchant Marine; Universal's *Corvettes in Action* (1942) was "the first spectacular picture of our Atlantic life-line patrol!"; Paramount's *Minesweeper* (1943) declared that "the men who sweep the sea are sweeping the screen with thrills!"; and Republic's *The Fighting Seabees* (1944) paid tribute to the Civilian Construction Brigade. For all that, to the stern eyes of the film analysts at the BMP, Hollywood was all too liable to be Hollywood. "The emphasis in the entire industry," lectured a 1942 report, "is still too much on the exciting blood-and-thunder aspect of the war and too little on the equally important problems arising in civilian life and dealing with basic issues of the war and peace to come."

The recurrent problem in government-industry relations was that Washington was not at all sure what it wanted from Hollywood and when it did know what it wanted it was incapable of telling Hollywood how to achieve it. The actual "job of work"—the creation of narratives, characters, and tropes to dramatize vividly and visually wartime policy—was beyond the ken of the government's agents. After the fact, OWI film analysts officiously sat in judgment of the on-screen result. During production, they were altogether useless in getting the result up on screen. Typical was the presumption and prescriptions of Nelson Poynter, then assistant coordinator for government film, in a speech to the Hollywood Writers Mobilization in 1942. "It is easier to glorify the Air Corps than the Infantry. It is easier to portray on screen Great Britain's struggle than that of the Chinese or the Russians, who are on the front line of this war," lectured Poynter. Referring to the year's most successful homefront melodrama, he admonished the screenwriters to "give us a *Mrs. Miniver* of China or Russia, making clear our common interest with the Russians or Chinese in this struggle." A ten-page screen treatment detailing how Hollywood might cook up a Chinese *Mrs. Miniver* was not forthcoming.

The intrusive presence and hectoring memos of the BMP desk jockeys taxed the patience and tested the tolerance of Hollywood professionals. "The OWI has entrusted the full sweep of war power to gentlemen with no previous film experience," marveled producer Walter Wanger. Martin Quigley, the influential editor of *Motion Picture Herald*, offered a sharp rebuke to OWI bureaucrats "who are even now [1943] not gaining practical experience, and who are constantly torn between a wonderment as to what makes the wheels go around and an urge to apply a monkey wrench as a show of professional capacity." Heartily resented was the Hollywood branch of the BMP, under the resident directorship of the aforementioned Nelson Poynter. Annoyingly keen on suggesting topics the government felt worthy of feature film treatment, never shy about displaying his lack of motion picture expertise, Poynter addressed producer and screenwriter associations, notified studios of government interest in film treatments, and even sat in on "as many as fifteen story conferences a week." Hollywood had a sardonic name for the pushy cues emanating from his office: "poynters."

For reasons of professional pride and legal precedent, the motion picture industry wanted at least the appearance of voluntary cooperation. Nicholas M. Schenck, president of Loews, Inc., insisted that "the industry's cooperation and the services of the Bureau of Motion Pictures have been on a purely voluntary basis." In his official communications, Mellett was careful to speak of "the motion picture industry's voluntary cooperation" and the "mutual judgment" about any alterations in film content. Nonetheless, cooperation with his office was described as "uniform not to say unanimous." In 1942 Sam Goldwyn immediately complied with a request from Mellett to withdraw from circulation his recently rereleased production, *The Real Glory* (1939). The prewar adventure, set in the Philippines in 1898, portrayed the native Morros tribesmen as bloodthirsty guerrillas opposing benevolent American colonists at the very moment the Morros were being praised by General MacArthur as heroic freedom fighters repelling malevolent Japanese invaders.

The alacrity bespeaks a relationship of subservience, but Schenck and Mellett were not entirely disingenuous in exchanging their mutual regards. In late 1942 Mellett issued a memorandum requesting preliminary screenplay review of all Hollywood features, including the military films previously the exclusive bailiwick of the War Department. Smelling a power grab and the prospect of prior restraint, the motion picture industry rebelled. "The producers of motion pictures will not take this move, trial balloon or otherwise, sitting down," blustered an unusually angry front-page feature in the *Hollywood Reporter*. "They see in Mellett's request the probable first move for a control of the writing and production of motion pictures — a Government censorship — and they will fight any such move to the industry's death, if necessary." Responding with an exculpatory statement, Mellett explained that regardless of the nature of the OWI review process:

> there is a clear understanding on the part of the producers that they are completely free to disregard any of our views or suggestions; that we have no authority enabling us to force our views upon them and have never desired any such authority. In effect our cooperation is largely one of keeping producers informed of wartime problems and conscious of possible implications of proposed pictures or details of pictures.

More maladroitly, Elmer Davis tried to cool the firestorm. "Hollywood is a very excitable place and they're quite imaginative out there," he told a press conference. "We propose to make suggestions to the studios and they can make changes if any of our ideas seem suitable to them, but we exercise no compulsion over the picture companies." Though the studios soon agreed to clear military-themed material with the OWI, they continued to balk at submitting scenarios lacking an armed forces angle. On March 15, 1943, after months of bad feeling and public wrangling, the OWI accepted a studio-proposed compromise which, though complying with the OWI request for inspection of military-themed scenarios, pledged to "continue the relationship between OWI and the motion picture industry on a voluntary basis." The dispute was finessed in intentionally elliptical language:

> The War Department and the producers shall continue to deal with each other exactly in the manner they did prior to the arrangement described in [the Mellett] memorandum, without the requirement of consulting and advising with OWI. The respective producers will simultaneously with, or prior to, their submission of title, story, outline, shooting script and completed film to the War Department make the same submission to OWI. If OWI wishes to make any recommendations or give advice concerning the title, script, or picture in any instance it will offer its recommendation and advice to the producer of the picture, which will receive and give consideration to the same. If consultation appears advisable, it will take place between OWI and producer.

In other words, the producers felt compelled to do what they insisted the government could not compel them to do.

Competing with the OWI civilians was the military, which as a whole and in its separate branches naturally had agenda of its own. Saving matters of military security, itself an elastic concept when invoked by martinet colonels, the uniformed services had no official power of censorship over studio productions. They needed none: at a time when America's fighting forces were esteemed and unassailable, a public expression of disapproval alone could wilt production plans or redirect narratives. Moreover, since the Army and the Navy departments possessed the means of verisimilitude for films with a military background, each exerted control by providing (or threatening to withhold) essential technical advice, equipment, facilities, locations, and personnel. Thus a contemplated version of *The Court Martial of Billy Mitchell* was stillborn because the studios knew that the Army would refuse to participate in its own villainization. "The filming of General Mitchell's life at this time," an Army spokesman said evenly, "would not serve the best interest of the country." As a concession to wartime exigencies and the production surge in war-themed films, both the Army and the Navy stationed special liaison officers in Hollywood to expedite the review process, two of the choicer duty assignments of the Second World War.

The last important layer of government oversight was the Office of Censorship, also authorized by the 1917 Espionage Law. The Office of Censorship's special responsibility was to clear incoming foreign films and to approve outgoing domestic films for foreign export. According to chief censor Byron Price, "As in all other phases of censorship, the boards will ask one basic question: 'Will this material be of value to the enemy?'"

In theory, this meant shots of shipyard and railroad backgrounds, war production plants and military installations, coastlines and strategic positions, and new aircraft or weaponry. In practice, it meant a whole range of considerations that had less to do with national security than international sensitivities. The Office of Censorship quickly expanded the scope of its concerns from matters of military significance to those of political delicacy. It took an intense interest in "scenes of labor, class, or other disturbances . . . which might be distorted into enemy propaganda." Among the films banned from export in 1942 for their amenity to distortion were MGM's *Panama Hattie* (for portraying the armed forces in too comic a light), Warner Bros.'s *Juke Girl* (for scenes depicting a threatened lynching of a white man), and Producers Releasing Corporation's *City of Silent Men* (ditto). Another unsavory disturbance erupted in *Tomorrow the World* (1944), in which American parents attempt to de-program their adoptive Hitler youth. It was denied an export license for being "too sympathetic to the Nazis." If an American family is unable to cope with a single Nazi-indoctrinated youngster, then what would be the prospect of handling millions of the little monsters in Germany after the war? (Incidentally, an unforeseen consequence of Office of Censorship prohibitions was generic. The dearth of background shots, exterior locations, and panoramic establishing shots in movies from the war years spurred the emergence of film noir—the dark, confined spaces of urban life: one reason the railroad yard in *Double Indemnity* (1944) is a night-for-night obscurity.)

A special annoyance was the Office of Censorship's prohibition against the "derogatory picturization or presentation of nationals of United nations and of the neutral countries." For the duration at least, foreigners were no longer funny folk with ridiculous accents and incongruous customs. The stock ethnic lowlives and sinister foreign villains who had always freely stumbled and slithered across the screen were suddenly receiving blanket disapproval. Stereotypical or negative portrayals that might give offense to overseas allies, potential allies, or the anti-Axis underground hit the cutting room floor. "As far as the screen is concerned," the *Hollywood Reporter* commented acerbically, "there are no heels, jerks, or inferior characters any place in the world except in the Axis countries and the United States."

Besides the regular employment of character actors specializing in bogus accents, the government-mandated sensitivity affected the production of whole film series. In 1942 Republic Pictures announced it was shelving plans for *Fu Manchu Strikes Back* "out of deference to the Chinese people." The oriental villain had long stuck in the craw of Chinese-Americans, and the studio's move was lavishly praised. After a calmer consideration of the box-office returns on the immensely profitable series, however, the wily occidentals at Republic hit on the expedient of simply "cleaning up" Fu Manchu and making him the enemy of the Japanese. (In the end, the new Fu didn't fly, although Republic did issue a feature-length version of the 1940 serial *Drums of Fu Manchu* in 1943.)

What really distinguished the Office of Censorship from rival oversight agencies was its unequivocal state-sanctioned power to hit the motion picture industry where it hurt most. With many once-lucrative foreign markets closed, the leave to grant or deny a Hollywood film an export license was an intimidating constraint. Foreign markets for "A" pictures accounted for approximately 40 to 50 percent of what was typically received in domestic rentals, which could translate into an even heftier percentage of a producer's net profits. Furthermore, unlike the OWI and the military, the Office of Censorship didn't consult with studios before or during production. Any needed alterations in film content were postproduction and hence more costly. Finally, in contrast to the instinctive resistance to official intrusions into the domestic market, producers were more prone to defer to the judgment of the government in matters of foreign policy and the overseas reception of Hollywood pictures. Unlike the OWI, the Office of Censorship need not bother overmuch with talk of "mutual cooperation" and "amicable supervision."

The cluttered overgrowth of film-interested agencies exacerbated the difficulty of complying with open-ended criteria. Functions were duplicated, jurisdictions overlapped, and directives contradicted each other. The overseas branch of the OWI was perceived in Hollywood as "a separately contained but identically motivated advance guard of the Office of Censorship," yet the decision of the one was no guarantee of agreement with the other. Similarly, if the Army, Navy, or another government department had an expertise or supervisory authority over a particular film, the Office of Censorship required written approval from the agency in question before rendering its judgment—a judgment in no way binding on the Office of Censorship. A locale or theme involving Central and South America was considered the fiefdom of Nelson Rockefeller, heading yet another government agency as Coordinator of Inter-American Affairs, but was also subject to the usual oversight from the OWI and the Office of Censorship. No less than the Hollywood studios, the government agencies were left to anticipate or preempt potential flare-ups among themselves. At the overseas branch of the OWI in 1943 former Hollywood screenwriter Robert Riskin was put in the Kafkaesque, not Capraesque, situation of banning the darkly demagogic *Meet John Doe* (1941) as "unsuitable for foreign screens at this time." Riskin, Frank Capra's longtime collaborator, had written the film.

Labyrinthine bureaucracy, divergent regulatory concerns, and erratic enforcement made for some tortuous entanglements. In 1943 *Cowboy Commandos*, the current issue of Monogram's "Range Bust-ers" serial, got roped into an interagency brushfire. The OWI recommended that the original villains (German-accented Nazi spies) be changed to native-born Americans with Nazi ideology on the grounds that the accented portrayals might offend German-Americans or friendly foreigners of Teutonic origin. Monogram complied, whereupon the Office of Censorship's Los Angeles Board of Review rejected the film for export on the grounds that overseas audiences might view the American West as a haven for Axis sympathizers. Only after rereviews by both agencies and postproduction dialogue changes was the film cleared for foreign distribution. To track the regulatory input and gauge the results, the studios appointed in-house overseers to monitor what was going into their own movies.

Little wonder that the government sometimes had as much trouble figuring out its policies as Hollywood. In late 1943, at the height of a controversy over the depiction of enemy depredations, Ulric Bell, chief motion picture liaison in the Los Angeles–based branch of the OWI, was upset to read in the *Hollywood Reporter* that George A. Barnes of the OWI's Washington office had stated "atrocity movies" didn't concern the OWI. "For your information, this has highly confused the motion picture industry," Bell wired his colleague. "Please pull yourself together." When intragovernment confusion only intensified, Bell sent a plaintive teletype to the home office:

> Situation here far more serious than you seem to realize and piecemeal advice will not suffice. Have known nothing about complete ban [on atrocity material by the Office of Censorship] that you say existed for year. Besides Office of Censorship and Navy and Marine Corps under contrary policy. We can continue to warn studios against atrocity material but it is difficult to overcome lack of government coordination.

Likewise, after V-E Day the Office of Censorship cleared for export the *Hitlerjungen* adoption story *Tomorrow the World,* but the OWI, which controlled the actual shipping docks for overseas distribution, simply refused to load the film for transport.

Meanwhile, despite all the freshly inscribed commandments from agents of the state, the basic tenets of the durable Production Code emerged relatively unscathed. "The war years were among the least controversial in Production Code history," concluded Leonard J. Leff and Jerold L. Simmons, two film historians on intimate terms with the PCA archives. Just as the clarity of the moral contest against the

Axis was a sturdy reinforcer of the Code's larger purpose, the Second World War lent itself well to the official Irish-Catholic view of life—suffering, sacrifice, and long stretches of compulsory chastity.

Joseph Breen surely retained his peremptory impact on Hollywood production. As government bureaucrats bickered, he continued his calm, efficient, and steadfast application of Production Code regulations to war-minded scenarios. His administrative authority was bolstered by professional competence. Unlike Mellett's men, Breen and his able, sharp-eyed staff knew the grammar of cinema and the business of moviemaking. They could tell producers not just what was prohibited by the Code but how to negotiate their way around the Code. Part collaborator, part censor, Breen would suggest alternative tacks and helpfully "flag" scenes he thought might ultimately run afoul of what he called the "political censors" in Washington. While adamantly refusing to compromise standards and violate the letter of his law, he maintained his prewar practice of guiding producers up to the very edges of Code acceptability before pulling them back to safe ground.

One of the inviolable laws of Breen's moral universe was the dogmatic distinction between the ambiguity of "suggestion" and the explicitness of "depiction." Images that would be unacceptable if shown on screen, he instructed, might be permissible if conjured by implication. "We remind you again that in spite of the fact that this is a war story, we cannot approve scenes of unacceptable gruesomeness," he told the producers of the homicidal combat film *Gung Ho!* (1943), before drawing a precise roadmap for PCA approval: "The suggestion that this Jap officer is scalded to death is unacceptable. We recommend that you omit the showing of 'steam' and the officer's 'screams' leaving merely the suggestion that he has been killed by the sterilization itself."

Producers who figured that scenes of enemy sadism, dramatized under the guise of propagandistic exposé, might be permitted wider Code latitude were soon disabused of the notion. Advertising one-sheets to the contrary, the torture sequences in RKO's exploitation twinpack *Hitler's Children* (1942) and *Behind the Rising Sun* (1943) tamely complied with the Code's demand for off-screen implication. Cautioning that "there must, of course, be no unacceptable exposure of Anna's person in this scene where the blouse is ripped off her back when she is being lashed," the PCA passed the sensational flagellation scene from *Hitler's Children* because the actual application of leather to flesh was suggestively rendered through the soundtrack report of a cracking whip. Similarly, for the depiction of the torment of the female victim in *Behind the Rising Sun,* Breen ordered that "the torturing of Sara should be suggested and not shown. The business of the fountain pen being run under her fingernails is unacceptably gruesome and could not be approved."

Still, two factors converged to push against the outer walls of Joseph Breen's moral universe. First, pressure from rival forms of mass communications—radio broadcasts, wire service reports and photographs, and the graphic photojournalism of *Life* magazine—drove the American screen to admit war-related material of equivalent explicitness. Second, official government policy was less stringent than the Code and in some points contradicted it. A mid-1943 conference among the President, Army chiefs, and the OWI's Elmer Davis fleshed out a guiding principle: that the war should be seen "as a struggle rather than as a series of triumphs." Common sense dictated a measure of frankness and the bearing of bad news. Given the growing bluntness of newspaper and radio coverage, the hard knowledge of returning veterans, and official OWI policy itself, the PCA's discretion in matters of earthy vernacular and its sanitized vision of violence and death were derided as outmoded and criticized as deceptive even at the time. In manners if never in message, the Code's framework underwent some visible modifications.

The built-in contradiction between the Code's tradition of churchly discretion and the OWI's policy of blunt notification was exposed when what was good for morale collided with what was morally good. Like Breen, Will Hays insisted that it would be "culpable dereliction" to regard the war as "an excuse for abandoning the principles of the Code or relaxing its administration." Applying the prewar standards, his office peremptorily demanded the deletion of language like "hell," "damn," and "bastard" from the feature-length *March of Time* documentary *We Are the Marines* (1943). The *March of Time* appealed the ruling, arguing that "to destroy the natural speech used under stress of battle conditions is an unnecessary action resulting in unrealistic portrayal of American fighting men." Ultimately, the Code agreed to make a two-thirds compromise. "We went through 'hell' to save 'damn,' and only as it applies to this one picture," joked Charles Francis Coe. The MPPDA vice president then turned serious: "That does not mean that it will be permitted in other pictures. We voted to uphold the Production Code, but we relaxed

Joseph Breen's moral universe: while the suggestive whipping sequence in *Hitler's Children* (1942) passed muster, the explicit torture sequence in *Behind the Rising Sun* (1943) was deemed "unacceptably gruesome." (Courtesy of the Academy of Motion Picture Arts and Sciences)

its provisions in this case because of the nature of the scene in which the words were used." As for "bastard," Coe promised that it would remain illegitimate. In the most ridiculed example of the Code's tender ears, Noel Coward's *In Which We Serve* (1942), a British import, was held up from American release for seventeen words: ten "damns," two "hells," two "Gods," two "bastards," and one "lousy." Playwright Lillian Hellman scoffed at such skittishness. When the Code demanded punishment for the killer of the Nazi agent at the climax of *Watch on the Rhine* (1943), she responded with a note that inquired whether "the Hays Office was aware that killing Nazis was now a matter of national policy." The scene remained intact.

The Code's level of tolerance for suggestions of sex and exposures of skin is roughly indicated by the fact that the title of stripper Gypsy Rose Lee's best-selling *The G-String Murders* had to be changed to *Lady of Burlesque* (1943) in the film version. The Second World War never prevented Breen from hearing double entendres in single entendre dialogue and from seeing through the devices of designing directors. Suspicious of the immodest attire of actress Ann Rutherford in *Happy Land* (1943), Breen demanded advance pictures of her two costume changes for inspection. Twentieth Century-Fox sent over two cleverly shot still photographs of Rutherford in an evening gown and a bathing suit. The cinematically astute censor responded:

> [Both outfits] seem to us to be cut too low over the breasts. When these stills were taken, the camera was evidently placed rather low, which, of course, minimizes this exposure, but it is our impression that with a higher camera set up, such as would normally be used, the result would be undue exposure in certain scenes, which we might have to ask to be deleted.

Where glimpses of the body and discussions of sex remained corsetted, a slight loosening of restrictions was apparent in the newsreels and documentaries. Cautions against venereal disease, as the *March of Time* maturely noted, could now be spoken from the theatrical screen. Nudity, totally prohibited by the Code, edged into sight in a documentary context and if male. In the combat reports, GI backsides were exposed during scenes of jungle bathing. However, the Code continued to restrict less medicinal and more prurient outbreaks of errant civilian sexuality. The most lascivious testing of Code strictures was Howard Hughes's flaunting of Jane Russell in *The Outlaw* (1943), a notorious case that actually confirms the Code's wartime grip. The intensely scrutinized and wrangled-over film received its Code seal before the war; it was briefly released during the war (in 1943 at a single San Francisco theater). However, it was only *after* the war that Hughes presumed to defy the authority of the Production Code—first, with an incitefully vulgar advertising campaign accompanying the 1946 rerelease, and second, with legal action when Breen revoked his original approval. Hollywood aside, the most prudish example of skin-deep censorship was the widely circulated tale of the illustrated GI whose captain ordered him to ink in a skirt on a tattoo of a nude dancer.

Violence, not sex, inspired the more substantive and visible shift in standards. Prior to the war, Fox Movietone News had abided by an in-house policy of never showing a dead body. Under the Code too combat was quite literally bloodless. War's full fury and gruesomeness—shrieks of terror and torment, pools of blood, the evisceration and dismemberment that accompanies the impact of sophisticated weaponry on the human frame—never reached the homefront screen. But gradually, incrementally, spurred on by *Life* and newspaper wirephotos, the newsreels and combat documentaries exposed a measure of the human ravages of war. Wounded GIs, in the field or in hospital beds, fallen soldiers draped by blanket or canvas, and (in the later war years) American servicemen shot dead on beachheads were glimpses of mortality incompatible with the Code's commandments. Only war and the wishes of FDR himself suspended the rules.

Farther from home, enemy dead were laid out with an unprecedented explicitness. Combat reports lingered over enemy corpses with an unblinking satisfaction. Feature films were also allowed an extra measure of clinical detail if the victim were Axis and especially if that victim were Japanese. For access to such images, homefront audiences clashed with their moral guardians. Workers in a Detroit war factory protested resentfully when local censors cut the atrocity footage from *Ravaged Earth* (1942). Paramount profited from a Brian Donlevy–narrated version of the Soviet documentary *The City That Stopped Hitler—Heroic Stalingrad* (1943) despite a "B" rating from the Legion of Decency "on the grounds it incites to hatred and is extremely gruesome." The guardians themselves seldom saw eye to eye. Documentaries that cleared the Code were sometimes pared down by state censorship boards. Pennsylvania's Board of Censorship deleted shots of hanging corpses from *The Battle of Russia*

(1943), an official government entry in the *Why We Fight* series and approved for commercial release by the Code. Seeing too much blood in a classic montage, the Ohio Board of Censors demanded the elimination of Eisenstein's Odessa Steps sequence from Artkino's compilation film *The Russian Story* (1943).

Although War Department combat reports released through WAC were not subject to Hays Office review, the military accepted the Code's moral authority if not its official oversight. "The Army, of course, conforms to the tenets of good taste in the editing of motion pictures of documentary importance," explained Col. Curtis Mitchell, head of the Pictorial Section of the War Department's Bureau of Public Relations. "Thus, the Army subscribes without the compulsion to do so." Under the auspices of the Army Signal Corps or the Navy Photographic Unit, a documentary context and a war-approved purpose legitimized once unscreenable images. The advertising for *With the Marines at Tarawa* (March 1944)—"the real thing at last—no punches pulled, no gory details omitted"—took full advantage of the leeway.

The newsreels benefited in turn. If audiences had seen or were going to see the gory details in Army Signal Corps footage, it made little sense to proscribe the same footage elsewhere. Nonetheless, part of the Tarawa and Makin Island footage passed by the War Department and the Hays Office was voluntarily withheld by the newsreels themselves as "too grim." Whereas newsreels and commercial documentaries were subject to Code censorship, their status as journalism accorded both forms greater latitude than film entertainment. Like the War Department's combat reports, the news-oriented and war-themed context shielded potentially inadmissible images. The Hays Office censored none of the concentration camp or atrocity footage supplied to the commercial newsreels in May 1945, but that same month it refused a Code seal to *Atrocities*. Also known as *We Accuse* and comprised of captured German newsreels and donated Russian material, the documentary was rejected mainly because it delivered what it promised and used the word "damn." The relentlessness of the horror imagery, compiled in the context of an exploitation feature, not in Army Signal Corps footage supplied to the newsreels, delegitimized the project. Even material that cleared all the higher echelon hurdles might stumble upon tampering in the projection booth itself. A few theater managers exerted in-house censorship and cut the concentration camp reels entirely from their staple program. The material from Buchenwald, explained the manager of Radio City Music Hall, was "too gruesome to be shown at a family theater."

In sum, then, producers who previously answered alone to the Production Code Administration, according to Joseph Breen, now had to withstand close-quarter interference from OWI officials, military liaisons, and genuine government censors. Yet having proven dexterous in circumventing the spirit if not the letter of the Code, Hollywood was constrained but not unduly stifled by the wartime regulators. In 1947, when asked by the House Committee on Un-American Activities to gauge the degree of government influence in MGM's wartime production schedule, Louis B. Mayer was contemptuously vague: "So much happened in that period, coming and going. They had an office out there—War Information, I think they called themselves." The Bureau of Motion Pictures was suffered politely rather than obeyed unquestioningly; the relationship with the War and Navy departments was one of cozy symbiosis; the Office of Censorship restrictions were insufferable but not insurmountable. Hollywood filmmakers had always worked under the strictures of studio control, had always had to pass muster under the Code and maneuver through local censorship boards. No one thought of the director as an autonomous auteur, and everyone knew the nature of hierarchy. Finally, any balanced appraisal of the impact of Washington on Hollywood should consider that government bureaucrats and desk-bound colonels might not easily intimidate the likes of Harry Cohn, Jack Warner, Darryl F. Zanuck, and Louis B. Mayer, still less the people who worked for them.

CHAPTER 4 Government Work

According to the final report of the War Activities Committee (WAC), some 7,000 studio employees or about "one-third of the men normally employed in the motion picture industry" entered the military during the Second World War. Like the name directors and movie stars who signed up or received greetings, most of the cinematographers, sound men, technicians and craftsmen who operated cameras, worked boom mikes, wired soundstages, and constructed sets found themselves doing in uniform what they had done on the backlot. Though the scatterbrained displacement of civilian job skills by Army personnel officers was a reliable fount of dry humor, the assignment of a military occupational specialty (MOS) was usually destiny for the duration. More often than not, a motion picture expertise was matched to a fitting branch of the armed services, such as the Navy Photographic Unit or the Army Signal Corps—or, if serving in a civilian capacity, one of the agencies within the Office of War Information was the likely berth.

The liaison between Hollywood and Washington was a distinctly American and democratic arrangement, a mesh of public policy and private initiative, state need and business enterprise. In the alliance of talented personnel and the exploitation of tangible resources, Washington surely got the better deal. Unschooled in production realities and cinematic technique, civilian bureaucrats and uniformed "brasshats" often just didn't know how to deploy the talent at their command. Unlike the moguls, they had little eye for technical quality and visual invention. The ironic catchphrase that studio system personnel coined during the Second World War—"good enough for government work"—slighted not the significance of the work but the competence of the government to evaluate it.

Whether done at the behest of the Office of War Information or the War Department, whether produced under pressure or under contract, Hollywood's government work encompassed three main functions engaging two distinct audiences. In a serviceable separation, Will Hays delineated the trinity of responsibilities as educational, inspirational, and recreational. The educational and inspirational films were each conceived for separate target audiences—military servicemen on the one side, and homefront civilians on the other. The recreational films—that is, normal Hollywood shorts and features—made no distinction.

Like all Hollywood genres, the categories intermingle promiscuously. A military film conceived and produced exclusively for GIs might later be deemed appropriate for commercial release to civilian theaters. Saving what Walt Disney referred to as the "secret stuff," the boundary between a training film and a film that warranted civilian exhibition was hazy. *Safeguarding Military Secrets* (January 1942), made for GIs, was distributed commercially by RKO and became the first Army training film released to the general public. Likewise, *Wings Up* (May 1943), a War Department film about the Army Air Force's Officer Candidate School, received a general release on the strength of a narration from OCS graduate Clark Gable. From the opposite direction, a commercial Hollywood feature might find its way into a military classroom. Jack Warner boasted that his company's 1940 bio-pic, *Dr. Ehrlich's Magic Bullet,* trimmed down to "just the biological stuff," was the only film approved by the Surgeon General for VD education in the U.S. Army.

Bridging education and inspiration was the "incentive film" aimed at a special category of homefront civilians—workers in war pro-

A motion picture military occupational specialty: shooting an Army training film at the Signal Corps Photographic Center in Astoria, New York, 1942. (National Archives)

duction plants. An advertisement for Kodak film explained the rationale: "In good part, production depends on workers' enthusiasm. Thrilling movies of our weapons in action spur workers to greater effort. In these incentive films they can see *their* tanks, *their* planes, *their* guns blaze into action on the fighting fronts . . . the final test of their handiwork." Overseen by the Navy's Industrial Incentive Division and nicknamed the "smokestack circuit," the program screened 16mm exhortations to an audience estimated at 3,500,000 monthly. "Theirs is not the realm of plush seats, air conditioning, and festooned balustrade," wrote an enthused observer in the educational magazine *Business Screen,* but of "factory aisles, locker rooms, and cafeterias." For workers in shipbuilding plants, *Full Speed Ahead* (1944) dramatized the submarine menace to convoys and *December 7th* (1943) documented the herculean task of salvaging sunken ships. "The philosophy behind the employment of the incentive films," explained Rear Adm. C. H. Woodward, chief of the Navy's Industrial Incentive Division, "is that the worker who sees them can project himself on the screen and obtain a better, fuller understanding of the job ahead of him." And a measure of perspective: *The Arm Behind the Army* (1942) compares the self-regulated resourcefulness and motivation of the American worker to the ruthless oversight and automaton-like slave labor of the Nazis.

The production of training films for servicemen (also known as pedagogical or "nuts and bolts" films) called for the closest cooperation between the War Department and the studios. The full range of Hollywood technical talent was recruited for the mammoth task of acquainting GIs with the arcane skills of modern warfare, "everything from *The Tank Platoon in the Attack* to *The Operation of the Quartermaster Mobile Laundry,"* as one Signal Corps officer expressed it. Screen animation taught aircraft identification and explained top-secret mechanisms; huge topographical set designs familiarized bomber crews with the contours and skylines of target territory; and projected images of enemy aircraft simulated aerial combat for gunners. Branches of the armed forces designated the necessary productions and, first through the Research Council of the Academy of Motion Picture Arts and Sciences and later independently, contracted the labor to the Hollywood studios. Meanwhile the Army's facilities at the Signal Corps Photographic Center in Astoria, New York, Fort Monmouth, New Jersey, and Wright Field, Ohio, together with the Army Air Force's First Motion Picture Unit in Culver City, produced their own in-house training films with crews of Hollywood draftees.

Generally made on a standard contract basis, the training films were an essential if unromantic aspect of the studios' wartime record. But as in so many areas of Hollywood-related service, the perfunctory production of the nuts and bolts films drew scrutiny and generated controversy. In February 1943 the Senate Special Committee Investigating the National Defense Program, chaired by Harry S. Truman (D–Mo.), held a mean-spirited inquiry into Army training-film contracts and the commissioning of motion picture personnel by the Army Signal Corps. Darryl F. Zanuck—perhaps because of his spirited defense of the industry before the Senate in its untimely investigation of "moving picture screen propaganda" three months before Pearl Harbor, certainly because of his insuperable high profile—was the target of opportunity. Derided by the press as a "Hollywood colonel," Zanuck found his motives, patriotism, and effectiveness questioned by the U.S. Senate. The Academy's Research Council, which Zanuck chaired, was responsible for channeling War Department scenarios to member studios for production. There were no formal contracts as such, just an understanding that, if the Army was satisfied with the final product, it would purchase the film "off the shelf." Since the commercial market for titles like *Military Courtesy and Customs of the Service* and *The 240mm Howitzer, Service of the Piece* was negligible, the arrangement fell in a gray area between an unspoken obligation and a quid pro quo. The senators implied that Zanuck had favored 20th Century-Fox with the choicer assignments, a dark insinuation of financial malfeasance and war profiteering. They also questioned why the Army contracted out training films to Hollywood when it retained its own production facilities at Astoria, Fort Monmouth, and Wright Field.

The military rose to Zanuck's—and its own—defense. Col. Kirke B. Lawton, chief of the Army Pictorial Section, submitted documents that showed not only that Fox hadn't been favored but that the studios actually *lost* money on the training films. "They don't charge production, overhead, or salaries of men working on shorts," Lawton testified. "These films were coming in between four and five thousand dollars a reel. We knew if they put in all the charges which they are allowed to by law, we would be paying around $7000." The Army relied on the studios for the simple reason that Hollywood did the best job of work. Said Lawton: "No matter how you write the scenario, they can make the film." Under grilling by the committee's chief counsel, Hugh Fulton, Lawton tried to explain to politicians unversed in auteurism the bargain the Army got by employing top-of-the-line directorial talent at less than scale wages:

> *Colonel Lawton:* . . . when you set up an accounting system for production of a training film in the Army where you are using a George Cukor as a director for $50 dollars a month, and try to compare that with making—
> *Mr. Fulton* (interposing): Who?

Unlike the director of *Holiday* (1938) and *The Philadelphia Story* (1939), Darryl F. Zanuck was a name the committee recognized. Fulton implied that Zanuck, who despite an active-duty commission as Lieutenant Colonel had retained his position at Fox and the $50,000 annual salary that went with it, may have had "divided loyalties."

Lawton testified to the "remarkable job" done by Fox's production head:

> Darryl Zanuck is invaluable to us because he can go to any company executive where a film is lagging and tell them to "get on your bicycles." The Chief Signal Officer needs just such a man to get the films out, one, good, and two, as fast as you can get 'em. . . . He's a go-getter, the equal of which I have not seen in the motion picture industry or anywhere else.

That April, Under Secretary of War Robert P. Patterson reiterated the assessment and praised Zanuck's "courage, energy, patriotism, and accomplishment." Though admitting that Zanuck's retention of the chairmanship of the Academy's Research Council and his office at 20th Century-Fox was "unwise" for a commissioned military officer, Patterson stuck by his man. "He has made a heavy personal financial sacrifice," Patterson pointed out. "I do not believe he is subject to any personal criticism or censure." Nonetheless, the Army readily acceded to Zanuck's request to go on inactive duty after May 31, 1943. Patterson had also earlier reformed the system of training-film procurement. After December 15, 1942, the production of training films was arranged through direct contractual relations between the War Department and the designated producer.

Testimony before the Truman committee revealed that the Army had not rejected a single training film from the Hollywood studios. "These people are past masters in this business," Colonel Lawton pointed out. "It is inconceivable to me that we could walk into a place that good that couldn't make the type of film we want, the 'nut and bolt' film. They can make any films they want to make."

Though weapons ordnance and dress regulations were subject matter of less than hypnotic intensity, the professional habits of a movie-making lifetime were hard to break. Arid assembly-disassembly demonstrations were enlivened by background music, crisp and witty narration, and even bits of incidental comedy. At first the armed forces pedagogues were not amused. At a paper delivered to the Society of Motion Picture Engineers in 1942, Lt. William Exton, Jr. sternly explained the difference between the whimsical Hollywood short subject and the serious military training film. The latter was typically played several times by the instructor in each training session and diversionary material "looks silly the second time around." Postproduction "sweetening" detracted from the severe business of instruction. "This is a gross abuse of the principle of a training film," Exton lectured. "A training film should be regarded as a textbook. . . . There is no obligation on the part of a textbook to be amusing or ingratiating."

But the deployment of the unique qualities of the medium was hardly sweetening; it was substance. A listless commentator droning on during a static long take was no improvement over a bored lieutenant before a blackboard. Elements of film style emphasized and visually imprinted important lessons. Inseparable from cinematic artistry was the evocation of combat emotions—suspense, fear, doubt, and exhilaration. In September 1942, when the Army decided it required a series of films on "precombat conditioning" and "battlefield psychosis," it turned instinctively to Hollywood "where the facilities and experienced personnel of the American motion picture industry could bring to these films the realism and dramatization which we required." The result was the influential *Fighting Men* series (1942–43), devoted mainly to the psychological pressures of warfare. *Baptism of Fire* took a soldier through first engagement to first blood; *Kill or Be Killed* taught the nasty nonrules of hand-to-hand fighting; and *On Your Own* showed how to endure isolation.

Capt. Edmund North of the Signal Corps Photographic Center articulated the reigning aesthetic of the *Fighting Men* series: "There has been no attempt made in this series to be inspirational. War has not been painted as a delightful or glorious experience, but simply and straightforwardly as the cold, grim, scientific business that it is." In the blunt entry *How To Get Killed in One Easy Lesson,* a GI crawls through the jungle—no background music, no voice-over orientation—and the camera catches his gun's glint in the sunlight. A long shot shows an enemy sniper picking up the light. He takes his own long shot, and the GI lies dead. The lesson is taught without a word of narration.

Initially skeptical, the military came to appreciate and imitate the studio style. With the production of the *Army-Navy Screen Magazine* (1943–45), the armed services brandished that proud banner of major studio status, the flagship featurette. Billed as being to *Yank* magazine what the *March of Time* was to *Time,* the biweekly "pictorial report from all fronts" was a compilation of straight reportage, snippets of education, and clips of celebrity shenanigans. Distributed exclusively to GIs and unmonitored by the Production Code Administration, it assumed a unisexual audience of selfsame predicament and indelicate sensibility. Except for the khaki-colored filter on existence and the minor trespasses against Hays, however, the *Army-Navy Screen Magazine* might have wedged itself undetected into the staple program of any theater in America. Truly, Hollywood had showed the Army, wrote Colonel Lawton in 1944, "how to make a training movie or an educational subject which will hold the interest of the soldier by means of a story, the introduction of standard GI characters, the use of varied methods of presentation, and the employment of emotional techniques." Interpersonal dialogue and human intercourse was unavoidable if GIs were to dodge another kind of shot. John Ford's *Sex Hygiene* (1941) blended an elliptical romance of procurement with graphic medical photos of the ravages of syphilis. "I think it made its point and helped a lot of young kids," Ford later commented. "I looked at it and threw up." *Three Cadets* (1943) was another venereal disease film that one commentator called "the most coldly unromantic love story ever brought to the screen."

Intrinsically pleasing to the eye, unbound by the laws of physics, and accessible to microscopic reality, animation was a wonderfully malleable educational medium. The corollary to cartoonist Max Fleischer's dictum ("If it can happen in real life, it's not animation") is that if it can't be photographed in real life, it can be rendered in animation. Theoretical physics, molecular biology, and aircraft and cruiser identification invaded a screen plane traditionally occupied by talking mice and flying elephants. In *Enemy Bacteria* (1942) — a title as military as medicinal — florid streptococci invade the GI interior. Army Air Force trainees were taught aerodynamics by Thrust ("a little fellow who propels the plane on its way"), Gravity ("a lazy chap who loves to sleep in a hammock suspended beneath an airplane"), and Drag ("a lad who paints that balloon in the air while he hangs on to the plane's tail, holding it back").

For the dramatization of potentially fatal mistakes the expendability and immortality of animated nitwits was surefire instruction/entertainment. Among cartoon cretins, none was detonated more regularly or inventively than Private Snafu, the hangdog mascot of the *Army-Navy Screen Magazine*. Animated by Tex Avery's unit at Warner Bros. and voiced by Mel Blanc, Snafu sounded like Bugs Bunny but had none of the rabbit's alert intelligence or madcap ingenuity. Tirelessly serving the war effort as a bad example, Private Snafu lived up to his name (a recently coined acronym for bureaucratic bungling and military incompetence): Situation Normal, All Fouled (or Fucked)

Up). In his premiere escapade, *Spies* (1943), Snafu is seduced by an Axis Mata Hari with a radio transmitter in her D-cups and a typewriter in her garter. Unaware of her underwear, he spills the beans on a troop deployment and winds up blown to hell. In *Fighting Tools* (1943) Snafu allows his M-1 rifle to malfunction, his machine gun to overheat, his artillery piece to deteriorate, and his jeep battery to run down. By instructive contrast, the animated enemy is a muscular giant who towers over the runt GI and exploits his every blunder. Blown up again, a stark naked Snafu lands in a Nazi prison camp and via dissolve metamorphoses into a horse's ass.

The flesh-colored exposure of the private's parts broke with normative cartoon convention. As Code-free animation screened to an all-male audience, the Snafu series was far more verbally and visually vulgar than its Looney Tunes–Merrie Melodies cousins. "It's so cold it would freeze the nuts off a jeep," comments the narrator of *Homefront* (1943), an episode that finds Snafu in Alaska griping about sheltered civilians in the lower forty-eight. The opening of *Rumors* (1943) is set in a latrine, where Snafu and a buddy, seated side by side, exchange scuttlebutt.

The animators at Disney Studios were the elite cartoon corps. They worked on hundreds of instructional films and designed insignias for over 16,000 military units. Silhouette fuselages of aircraft and warships taught friend from foe to gunners and artillery crews. Bomb sights, radar, and other top-secret equipment were painstakingly storyboarded and carefully guarded. "Creative personnel accustomed to wracking their brains for a new switch on some problem near and dear to Donald Duck's personality found themselves commissioned to explain to men at Navy training bases all aspects of the functioning and maintenance of the gyroscope and its relation to the over-all functioning of an aerial torpedo," recalled a Disney employee. In 1943, 94 percent of Disney's work was war-related. Sandbags and antiaircraft guns surrounded the only Hollywood studio to be designated a "key war production plant" and "essential industry."

At war in the field, the high-definition medium was an invaluable intelligence agent for aerial reconnaissance, battle damage assessment, and cultural analysis. The expository scenes of Hollywood combat films measure the progressive importance of photographic intelligence gathering: the illustrated maps and hand-drawn diagrams of 1941–43 give way to detailed still photographs and frame enlargements in 1943–45. For intelligence of both a tactical and psychologi-

Visual identification and expert orientation: the intelligence gleaned from aerial photo␣␣␣␣␣␣ is charted by Gen. Claire Chenault (Raymond Massey) in *God Is My Co-Pilot* (1945).

cal nature, captured enemy film was a vivid text and Rorschach test. Episode no. 15 of the *Army-Navy Screen Magazine* (1943) features an extended sequence entitled "Seized from the Japs," which consists purely of captured footage and interpretative voice-over. "This is seized Japanese film," declares the commentator. "Captured film helps us to piece together the character of the enemy." One conclusion: "They're smaller than we are, but they make the toughest and most brutal enemy in modern warfare."

In a remark more noteworthy as a reflection of official enthusiasm than rank-and-file results, Colonel Lawton asserted that "a soldier during his training period looks eagerly to instruction in procedure, thanks to the employment of Hollywood technique." From the hundreds of "pedagogical films" produced each year, the Army claimed "that men can learn in three weeks though proper use of instructional film what would otherwise take thirteen weeks to learn."

What American educators learned was the value of film as a standard tool of classroom pedagogy. Hands-on experience eroded the mystery of 16mm equipment, and repeated exposure to filmic instruction dissipated escapist expectations. The war gave civilian teachers a "broadly enlarged vision of the scope of [film's] usefulness" as a way "to provide broad social orientation and to disseminate important information," wrote Charles F. Hoban in *Movies That Teach,* a 1946 guidebook that popularized reliance on film in the classroom. In postwar America few high schools, commercial businesses, and civic or church groups were so backward as to be without a 16mm projector and a shelf of government-made educational films. Hollywood chalked up what it called "the celluloid blackboard" as one of its main wartime contributions.

WHY WE FIGHT

Training films told how; orientation films explained why. Recalling his own boredom and frustrations in World War I, the farsighted Army Chief of Staff George C. Marshall gave morale a high military priority and accorded the movies a vital role in its maintenance. General Marshall's stance bucked military tradition and congressional sentiment. Old-line officers groused about "mollycoddling," and tightwad politicians fulminated over the wasteful frivolity of a movie-minded War Department. "I want our generals to put their time in winning battles rather than fighting psychological warfare," fumed Sen. Rufus C. Holman (R–Oreg.). "Does the administration have the nerve to say that our fighting men don't know why they're fighting this war?" But Marshall insisted on men motivated and knowledgeable about the democratic cause. Military education was never just a matter of force-fed information and rote recitation but of nurtured incentive and felt commitment.

The most widely seen and influential of the government orientation films was Frank Capra's *Why We Fight* series, made under the aegis of the Special Services Branch and, after September 1, 1943, the Army Pictorial Service. In his factually suspect but culturally fascinating autobiography, *The Name Above the Title,* Capra tells how in early 1942, as a newly minted Army major, he was ushered into the Pentagon office of General Marshall and told to produce a series of documentaries articulating the American stake in the war against Fascism. Never having directed a documentary before, Capra demurred. Marshall eyed him evenly and said, "I have never been Chief of Staff before. Thousands of Americans have never had their legs shot off before. Boys are commanding ships today, who a year ago had never seen the ocean before." Chastened, the major promised, "I'll make the best damned documentary films ever made."

Capra was as good as his word. The War Department orientation films produced under his supervision at the 834th Photo Signal Detachment—notably the seven-part *Why We Fight* series (1942–45), as well as *Know Your Ally: Britain* (1943), *The Negro Soldier* (1944), *Tunisian Victory* (1944), *Know Your Enemy: Germany* (1945), and *Know Your Enemy: Japan* (1945)—became enduring testimonies to American power and purpose during the Second World War. More than any other government moviemaking, *Why We Fight* was decisive in impact. It not only vividly clarified the official line on present policy; it retrospectively ordered the past and set a course for the future. As a wartime historian and director of postwar policy, Frank Capra was there at the creation. In his own way too he was among the "wise men" who helped shape American action on the world stage.

Of course Capra had produced political films for years. A classic

The architects of *Why We Fight:* Gen. George C. Marshall and director Frank Capra plan a revolution in screen education, 1942. (Courtesy of the Academy of Motion Picture Arts and Sciences)

American success story himself—from penniless Sicilian immigrant to Hollywood raja—he professed an unshakable faith in the traditional verities of hard work, straight dealing, and patriotic duty. His name above the title promised an unabashed embrace of sentimental humor and democratic heroes, of common men and women with an uncommon capacity for greatness. Highbrow critics called it "Capracorn," but his Columbia Pictures classics—*It Happened One Night* (1934), *Mr. Deeds Goes to Town* (1936), and *Mr. Smith Goes to Washington* (1939)—raised the spirits and restored the faith of a people hurt and hard-up from the Great Depression.

So at least is the official story. But like Mark Twain, another heartland hero whose folksy humor masked a hard heart, Capra always had an eye for the darker kernels in the American grain. Chicanery and comradery rode together on the bus in *It Happened One Night,* greed and intolerance beset the "pixilated" philanthropy of Longfellow Deeds in *Mr. Deeds Goes to Town,* and political corruption and brutal suppression nearly brought down Jeffersonian idealism in *Mr. Smith Goes to Washington.* By the time of *Meet John Doe* (1941) the gloomy undertow had engulfed the surface optimism: democratic citizens became totalitarian masses; the fourth estate was a nest of deceit; and the common man seemed doomed in a mean and manipulated society. *Why We Fight* elaborates on these last themes.

Capra tackled his military assignment with the same aggressive tenacity that had given Harry Cohn fits at Columbia Pictures. He didn't so much move from entertainment to orientation as use the means of the one for the ends of the other. Capra reasoned that he first had to engage the attention of a captive audience of GIs before he could begin teaching the Army's bewildering curriculum of geopolitics, military strategy, political ideology, and world history. Each film had to be packed with essential information yet possess compelling narrative thrust and visual interest. "There are no rules in filmmaking, only sins," was Capra's credo. "And the cardinal sin is dullness."

Prelude to War (1942), the first entry in the *Why We Fight* series, thus tells an intriguing story of how unobserved events in far-flung locales can reach out, puncture fortress America, and disrupt private lives. World War II begins not in Poland in 1939 or at Pearl Harbor in 1941, but in Manchuria on September 18, 1931. "Remember that date," orders narrator Walter Huston, "a date we should remember as well as December 7, 1941, for on that date in 1931 the war we are

Propaganda reversal: Frank Capra hijacks a Nazi lesson for the purpose of Allied orientation in *Prelude to War* (1942). (Museum of Modern Art/Film Stills Archive)

now fighting began." The macromeaning in the microscopic was a consistent motif of wartime orientation. Midway was not a speck in the Pacific but "our front yard," Iwo Jima "not just eight square miles of rock" but a vital forward base. The direct impact of obscure and distant happenings—on homefront conveniences, on the fate of blood relatives—penetrated American provincialism and planted the ground for the international outlook and interventionist impulses of the postwar era.

The textbook information fortified the inspirational, morale-building function. The title *Why We Fight* was a declaration, not a question. Over and over, the films say, this is not just a war *against* Axis villainy but *for* liberty, equality, and security. The series does not always live up to its own high-minded purposes. Jingoism and vitriol drip from sections of the commentary. The Germans are "ruthless automatons" genetically predisposed to barbarity, the Japanese bloodthirsty simians bred to treachery. But to a degree remarkable given the wartime context, the films speak calmly and eloquently to the aspirations of a free people opposing the forces of evil, to the postwar hopes for a better world.

The grammar of cinema served both ends. Capra's tactic of choice was to hijack the Nazis' own images. "One of Hitler's chief secret weapons has been the films," Capra asserted in 1942. "We will now turn that weapon against him." Since little Allied ammunition was in storage, the director was making a virtue of necessity. American newsreels and the *March of Time* had long been shut out from independent coverage of Germany's internal affairs. In the wake of Kristallnacht in November 1938, a special meeting of newsreel executives expressed eagerness to "call the attention of filmgoers to the current persecutions in Nazi Germany," but reported "an insurmountable barrier . . . namely, the dearth of film footage available to make a vigorous impression on the public." Lacking ample stores of authentic American-shot footage, Capra drew on inauthentic German footage. Taking material from Ufa newsreels, captured enemy combat reports, and Reichsfilmkammer propaganda films, he exposed Nazi pageantry to a scathing, democratic vision. Above all, he compulsively scavenged *Triumph of the Will*. Filtered through Capra's lens, Riefenstahl's paean to Nazism becomes a real-life horror show. The images are left untouched, but the context projects another picture. The lockstep discipline of the SA stormtroopers becomes robotic simplicity, the grand parade of *Hitlerjungen* evokes a march of lemmings to oblivion. Riefenstahl's Nazis are not denied their power, only their affirming mythos.

Against the industrial light and magic of the MTV era, the level of animation in the Capra series seems a bit primitive, the visual symbolism a trifle obvious. Arrows thrust their way into maps of Poland, tentacled arms lunge out from Japan and engulf Pacific archipelagoes, rivers of black ink spread over the European continent, and little black swastikas metamorphose into Nazi vermin. However, the orchestration of visual variation and celluloid legerdemain—maps, diagrams, optical printing and double exposures, archival footage both documentary and dramatic, and specially filmed reenactments—was unprecedented. Never before had the entire panoply of cinematic devices been put to such concerted and seamless instructional use.

Capra's undiluted view of Nazism was stern stuff. Some in official Washington thought that to show American GIs Riefenstahl's triumphal images might foster defeatism by reinforcing the myth of Nazi invincibility. Capra, however, refused to patronize, or jeopardize, the men being sent into battle. After a private screening of *Prelude to*

War, President Roosevelt agreed: if the films were clear on *why* we fight, they also had to be forthright about *who* we fight. Make no mistake, the Axis powers would be no pushovers. The enemy soldier should be looked upon as a vicious gangster—skillful, dedicated, and deadly as a cobra.

Capra did not direct the War Department films in the manner of a Hollywood auteur. Rather he presided as executive producer and chief idea man over an ever-growing collaborative effort that drew upon a studio's worth of skilled artists and technicians. Still, like the shots of the Liberty Bell bracketing each film, the Capra tone and spirit rings out everywhere—in the plucky resistance of London subway dwellers to the Nazi blitz in *The Battle of Britain,* in the sturdy Russian folk beating back the Wehrmacht in *The Battle of Russia,* in the constant juxtaposition of the average citizen-soldier against the ruthless Nazi *übermensch.* As always in a Capra film, democracy's best defense is its not-so-secret weapon, the common people.

By mid-1943 the War Department had in place an elaborate GI film program, virtually its own studio system of production, distribution, and exhibition. An approximation of the staple program of the civilian theaters, the "GI movies" included a newsreel, an animated short, and the *Army-Navy Screen Magazine.* If screened in an educational context during training, the feature part of the program might be one of the *Why We Fight* series; if screened after hours as recreation, it would likely be a Hollywood feature.

The centrality of the movies for the military is well reflected in the sheer scale of the effort devoted to bringing films to soldiers on the battle front—transporting the generators, projectors, and skilled personnel needed for exhibition in rugged and still-insecure theaters of war. Hollywood producers and the trade press never tired of repeating what General Eisenhower said (or was reported to have said): that next to guns and ammunition what "the boys need most is movies and more movies." By 1945 the Army Overseas Motion Picture Service estimated that there were some 2,400 picture shows nightly in the European and Mediterranean area alone. At one time the island of Guadalcanal hosted more than sixty separate shows per night. In language that might have been written by a studio flack, the *Stars and Stripes* reported "movies are the mightiest anti-boredom weapon the Army has. GIs in the wilds, who don't often get the chance to see a movie, jostle an hour before showtime for the best seats, sometimes refusing to let the projectionist go until he's shown every reel he's

Moving up with the movies: a GI on New Guinea
gets welcome news, 1944. (National Archives)

carrying." Nor did the military neglect soldiers beyond the range of
effective command. In a trade agreement arranged through the World
Alliance of the YMCA, the Allies and Germany exchanged films for
their respective prisoners of war. Since war-themed Hollywood fare
was unacceptable to the Nazi circuit, innocuous comedies, westerns,
and musicals comprised the carefully chosen and selectively edited
attractions. Potentially troublesome sequences—as in the musical
Nice Girl (1941) when Deanna Durbin sings "There'll Always Be an
England"—were deleted from the POW prints prior to shipment to
Germany.

The logistics of Army motion picture exhibition was the responsibility of the Special Services Branch, which handled what the WAC
called "beachhead bijous" and "foxhole premieres," while in the
Navy shipboard practice tended to shanghai any sailor with a mod-
icum of technical ability for on-deck projection duties. At its most
rustic the exhibition facilities consisted of a single 16mm projector

against canvas in jungle clearings or onto the turrets of the big guns aboard a destroyer. Though as early as mid-1943 permanent installations in the European theater were being equipped with 35mm projection, screening facilities in the Pacific theater fell well short of state of the art. Monsoon rains forced intermissions in open-air venues bordered by palms and bombarded by mosquitoes. Perhaps not so curiously, the distance from home, the desperation for diversion, and the difference from hometown exhibition seems to have invested the Pacific theater screenings with a dreamy vividness in GI memory. The unit historian for a photo reconnaissance group stationed in New Caledonia sketched a pensive portrait of the only show in town. "Moving pictures were shown on fair evenings," he recollected. "Fair evenings being any that did not result in a flood. The men would lie on the hillside and listen to the evening broadcast of news before the show. The most popular song was nostalgic—'I'm Dreaming of a White Christmas.'"

The "moving up" of the movies to troops at the front held a dual strategic and psychological significance. Besides providing diversion to combat-weary soldiers, the projection of Hollywood movies was a kind of "all clear" signal trumpeting the arrival of the Americans and the firmness of military control. "Up on Bouganville I attended an Army movie that was being screened less than *two miles* from the enemy lines!" enthused a grateful GI in the South Pacific, who praised Special Services for having "their first movie going in our Bouganville beachhead less than a week after they landed there, and within [the same] week there were seven movies showing." Another soldier wrote the trade press to confirm that "on Peleliu the Special Services officer had the screen set up the same day we moved off the front lines." The military and the motion picture industry each had good reason to boast of the speed and efficiency with which screenings were set up: the one because it demonstrated that a contested battlefield had been secured, the other because it proved the movies were vital to the nourishment of all good Americans.

And not just Americans. In both the European and Pacific theaters, moviegoing soldiers reported instances of enemy troops being within hearing distance of a film's soundtrack and applauding the celluloid performances. More remarkable stories circulated about enemy troops succumbing to the lure of Hollywood and watching the Army's open-air screenings from treetops or (unlikely as it sounds) of sneaking into the movies and watching a film with the GI audience. In the

Open air screenings: rustic exhibition for a stateside military audience, 1942.
(National Archives)

Marianas, an Army lieutenant on guard during an outdoor show came
across an unmanned Japanese machine gun trained on the screening
area. The show was stopped and the machine gun crew, eleven Japanese in all, was discovered among the audience and taken prisoner.

VICTORY FILMS

On homefront turf, the relationship between Hollywood and Washington was less cordial and businesslike. Over the moviegoing public,
the motion picture industry held a proprietary interest and the presumption of expert credentials. To requisition an exhibitor's precious screen time for overlong and soporific pronouncements contributed little to the war effort and less to the box office. Informing
and orienting an uncaptive civilian audience required special enticements, tricks of the trade unknown to the War Department or OWI.

The commercial failure of the early government-produced and military-minded orientation films confirmed the difference between being ordered to go to a movie and paying to see one. *The World at War* (1942), produced by the Bureau of Motion Pictures (BMP) and publicized as the United States government's "first officially sponsored feature length motion picture," was released with high hopes and ripe ballyhoo. But despite voyeuristic taglines ("from sources available only to our Government! from secret film archives! from enemy films obtained at risk of life!"), the picture was a turkey not even wartime patriotism made palatable. "Those who liked education on the screen enjoyed it—the others walked out," snarled a disappointed smalltown exhibitor. "In spite of the fact that this is free of charge I lost money running it," complained a fellow showman. "This is a well done feature showing the development of the war from way back, and those who saw it praised it highly, but I cannot get them in for this type of show."

Likewise, the commercial release of *Prelude to War* was botched both in timing (May 27, 1943, and hopelessly out of date) and running time (54 mins.). Encouraged by overpolite congressional and industry comment at advance screenings, the Army decided to release the first of the *Why We Fight* series into the marketplace. Bypassing the BMP, which opposed the domestic exhibition as an unwarranted incursion into their civilian franchise, the Army arranged distribution via WAC. It supplied 150 prints and a testimonial from Under Secretary of War Robert Patterson: "This is a picture every patriotic American should see." WAC urged exhibitors to book the film with a guilt-inducing ad featuring a dead serviceman, arms outstretched, and the question: "Mister, can you spare 55 minutes of screen time?"

Though *Prelude to War* was offered free of charge to exhibitors, at nearly an hour in length it took up a major chunk of coveted screen time. It was so tardy and redundant that Capra's landmark documentary garnered a quick and unequivocal commercial demise. The planned release of the next two films in the *Why We Fight* series, *The Nazis Strike* (1942) and *Divide and Conquer* (1943), was scuttled. Only an edited version of *The Battle of Russia* (1943) and the last in the series, *War Comes to America* (1945), were released to civilian theaters, the one as a sop to Allied solidarity and Russophile pressure, the other as a final admonition to homefront vigilance. "I guess I've lost my box office touch," Capra shrugged. Though the entries in the series circulated widely in war plants as incentive films, the War Department thereafter shifted its theatrical ambitions away from lengthy orientation films and toward timely and action-packed combat reports.

Meanwhile, the BMP coordinated the distribution and production of a regular program of civilian-targeted films. In the first year of the war, the homefront orientation came in two versions. Comprising one type was a group of shorts produced by a variety of concerned government agencies, often the BMP itself (a category officially designated "Victory Films"). The second type was the studio-made short produced at the behest of the BMP or the War Department (dubbed the "America Speaks" series). The initial arrangement between the BMP and the studios called for each to produce twenty-six information shorts, or one OWI-approved film per week for 1942. The difference between the government-made reels and the Hollywood shorts was in expertise and tone rather than purpose. The OWI-BMP's *Salvage* (October 1942) and Paramount's *The Aldrich Family Gets in the Scrap* (April 1943) both exhort Americans to conserve precious war materials, one through documentary style information and admonition, the other through vignettes acted out by the homespun serialized family.

After Congress refused to renew funding for a production arm for the BMP in June 1943, the studios assumed responsibility for most of the war orientation shorts distributed by WAC and screened in commercial theaters. The cooperation between the studios, distributors, WAC, and the government made for novel combinations and lengthy credits. *Something You Didn't Eat* (June 1945), a Disney-made short on the need for a balanced diet, was prefaced with a mouthful of acknowledgments:

> The Office of War Information, through the facilities of the War Activities Committee of the Motion Picture Industry, presents a Walt Disney Production on behalf of the War Food Administration and distributed by Warner Brothers Picture Corp., in Technicolor and copyrighted by Walt Disney Incorporated.

Whether made by the OWI and distributed by WAC, or produced by the studios and distributed via their usual outlets, the wartime shorts were known in common parlance as "Victory films" or "Victory shorts." Generally running no longer than two reels (20 mins.), they were distinct from the training and orientation films made for armed services personnel and from the full-length "recreational and inspirational" features made in the normal course of Hollywood production. Falling just outside the "Victory film" rubric but serving largely the same purposes were two- and three-minute "community sings" of patriotic songs (wherein audiences followed a bouncing ball across anti-Axis anthems), "briefies" (one- or two-minute announcements from government officials or pleas from celebrities for war charities), and OWI film bulletins attached to the newsreels.

In temper the Victory films were crash-course instruction in wartime purpose and guideposts for civilian participation. *Frying Pan to Firing Line* (September 1942) and *Let's Share and Play Square* (October 1943) called for conservation and salvage efforts; *Farmer at War* (March 1943) and *Glamour Girls of '43* (September 1943) praised homefront heroes and heroines in agriculture and industry; *Japanese Relocation* (November 1942) and *Why of Wartime Taxes* (March 1944) explained disturbing and unpleasant government policies. An exceptionally stolid entry such as *Right of Way* (April 1943), "a simple direct, pictorial explanation for traffic delays," was a cue for popcorn or a smoke, but occasionally the Victory films played better than the regular program offerings. *Winning Your Wings* (May 1942), a ten-minute recruiting short for the Army Air Force featuring Lt. James Stewart, got more enthusiastic word of mouth than its accompanying features.

The circulation of the Victory films was as rapid and widespread as priority restrictions on cargo and transportation allowed. In 1943 WAC vice chairman Francis S. Harmon described a distribution network that was close to saturation. "Both speed and complete national coverage have been attained for the screen's war information," Harmon reported. "Whereas eighteen to twenty-four *months* are required for a commercial feature to complete its run, only eighteen to twenty-four *weeks* are now required for one of these war information reels to appear on more than fourteen thousand screens. And it should be said in passing that less than a dozen commercial releases per year ever reach fourteen thousand screens." For more urgent information or exhortation, OWI film bulletins were sent out with the newsreels, which circulated nationwide in four to six weeks.

Virtually all the nation's exhibitors (a number that hovered around 16,500 throughout the war years) donated screen time for WAC-approved films, with any profits generated going to war relief or emergency charities. In the very early months of the war, a few exhibitors left the Victory shorts in film cans or played them only during sparsely attended matinees. Fearing government intervention and genuinely outraged, WAC personnel quickly put in place an enforcement system to monitor and police the exhibition of war shorts. "It is not a matter of shorts fitting into a theater's schedule," warned a WAC spokesman in March 1942, "but of the scheduling made to fit the shorts." The next month a WAC survey found that 94 percent of theaters were playing a government short at every performance daily.

Early on, FDR recognized the special importance of the moviehouse in American culture and publicly endorsed it as a "necessary and beneficial part of the war effort." In many American towns, the local Bijou was more of a locus for community than the church or city hall. As such, theaters were natural places to disseminate information, sell war bonds, hold rallies, solicit money for charities, and collect scarce goods for the war effort. In the main, exhibitors took to their task with relish: for once they, not the glamorous production end of the business, were on the front lines (and the front page). Honed by decades of pumping up flat films, the ballyhoo talent of theatermen adapted itself readily to war promotion. Theater fronts and marquees linked patriotic displays with movie publicity while in lobbies huge cardboard caricatures of Hitler and Tojo provided tempting targets for passing fists and feet. Theaters doubled as official stations for the collection of scrap, shellac, silk stockings, and other wartime materials. Responding to a call by FDR for scrap rubber, exhibitors inaugurated special "scrap screenings" and "rubber matinees" that granted admission for a pound of aluminum or an old tire. Taglines assured moviegoers that "every scrap matinee puts steel through the Axis heart."

Less vicarious was the financial punch theaters brought to war-related salesmanship and solicitation. As the Minuteman logo imprinted on the closing frame of wartime films reminded patrons, outlets for the sale of war bonds were in the lobbies of most of the nation's theaters. On-screen appeals for charities such as China Relief, the Red Cross, and the Army and Navy Emergency Relief, collected by ushers prior to the staple program or after the screened appeal, aimed to loosen the pockets of a homefront enjoying leisure and sweets while others served and starved. Exhibitors donated "annie oakleys" (free movie passes, so called because a hole was punched in the tickets to prevent resale) and at night offered their theater interiors for emergency shelter for soldiers in transit. Each

Offerings at the ticket window: under an Andy Hardy poster, the Los Angeles branch of the Woodcraft Rangers do their bit in a Victory Book Drive, April 1943. (Quigley Photo Archive/Georgetown University)

year the major studios and exhibitors backed huge war-loan campaigns, offering free admissions with the sale of bonds, pledging fixed sums, and sponsoring competitions. The New York premiere of Warner Bros.'s *Yankee Doodle Dandy* (1942) made the purchase of a war bond requisite for admission and netted $5,750,000 in sales. The same company earmarked all the proceeds from *This Is the Army* (1943) for the Army-Navy Relief. More businesslike, 20th Century-Fox's *Winged Victory* (1944) concocted a profit-sharing plan for the same charity. "Up to now, our efforts have been morale building, public relations, and similar more-or-less intangible activities," said Oscar Doob, a theaterman from Loews who was chairman of WAC's publicity committee. "The drive to raise dollars, to keep the war chest filled, providing money to maintain fighting men at the front and pay for their fighting machines—that sort of drive is tangible, practical, and worthy of American showmen." The worthiest and most showmanlike drive of all may have been the "plasma premiere" for *Three Russian Girls* (1944), during which a Cincinnati exhibitor opened his doors to donors of half a pint of blood to the Red Cross.

What is more difficult to recapture is the sense of the moviehouse as a communal space with discrete conventions of deportment and manners. The practice of "community sings," of strangers bursting into song accompanying filmed sheet music and Kate Smith, already seems the cultural rite of an alien tribe. Although moviegoing decorum was more inhibited and polite than the boorishness of television-age patronage, participatory zeal and backtalk were actively encouraged by cartoons and shorts. In Walt Disney's enormously popular call-and-response cartoon, *Der Fuehrer's Face* (December 1942), Donald Duck incited audiences to sing "Heil!" right in the Führer's face, or at least his Technicolor caricature. Cheers and applause greeted newsreels of Allied victories or clips of enemy planes careening into the sea.

Not all expressions were so vociferous. On D-Day, theater managers stopped their programs, announced the invasion news, and led audiences in the national anthem. For most in the crowd, it was a reprise. In the late 1930s exhibitors had begun adding "The Star Spangled Banner" to the top of the staple program; Pearl Harbor made the practice all but universal. Soldiers and small boys came to attention, women put their hands over their hearts, most sang along, and everyone stood. In the pre–Warren Court era, a biblical interlude might also complement a patriotic outpouring. For momentous and bracing news on the order of D-Day, the death of FDR, V-E Day, and V-J Day, managers-turned-deacons led audiences-turned-congregations in recitations of the Twenty-third Psalm or the Lord's Prayer. In victory or crisis, the moviehouse provided a ritual space for remembrance and celebration, medleys of hymns and patriotic songs, even moments of prayer and silent contemplation.

CHAPTER  **5** Genre
Work

The most potent weapon of war in Hollywood's arsenal was its stock in trade, the feature-length commercial film. Even at a time when the state went into production as never before, when so many studio players on the first string had gone into uniform, it was the private industry of artists off the government payroll, a civilian auxiliary dressed "in mufti," who did the better portion of war-related work. As ever, American culture was more satisfyingly nourished by popular entertainment than state propaganda.

Hollywood and Washington alike perceived the role for commercial features in two ways, disagreeing somewhat on the respective weight. The first was manifest: to be inspirational, to deploy the movies to rally the faithful and embolden the fearful. "The fact that no other medium is so adapted to the task of building and sustaining morale on both the fighting and home fronts readily attests to the motion picture's essentiality," affirmed Chester Bahn of the *Film Daily*. To underscore the linkage, industry executives commandeered a rich assortment of martial metaphors to militarize their mission. Hollywood closed ranks, marshaled its army of artists and technicians, and enlisted for the duration. "Marching as a unit," sounded off Will Hays, "the American motion industry accepted its responsibilities in war and took up its position on the whole width of the front." Industry officials loved to point out that the chemical ingredients of film—nitric acid, sulphuric acid, methyl alcohol, and cotton liners—were the same as for making smokeless gunpowder.

Smoking out the elements of classical Hollywood cinema discloses a volatility all its own. The raw material was the genre film. Peering into the animal memory of mankind, Carl Jung saw myth as "the history we already know." Genre is the movie we've already seen. In the age of the image, the visual landscapes, narrative conventions, and thematic concerns that comprise westerns, gangster films, screwball comedies, and familial melodramas make up generic clusters of a nearly genetic immediacy. Within the familiar tropes and tales of the genre film, the aspirations, tensions, and contradictions of American culture work themselves out as art.

The meaning of any genre—the clash of savagery and civilization in the western, the repulsion and attraction of the brutal gangster, the erotic lure and deadly consequences of the film noir femme fatale—is a study in contradictions. After film critic Robin Wood synthesized a list of twelve dominant qualities of classical Hollywood cinema, he quickly concluded it was "inherently riddled with hopeless contradictions and unresolvable tensions." The work of Hollywood genre is to make the body of American culture whole, to reconcile the tensions in the push and pull, affirmations and negations, of expressive art. The surface meanings of Hollywood narratives (to say nothing of the subsurface) send out contrary messages that allow critics interpretative sweep and audiences the luxury of having it both ways. Not surprisingly, the two vintage motion pictures every sentient American knows by heart—*The Wizard of Oz* (1939) and *It's a Wonderful Life* (1946)—perform the work with staggering virtuosity. In televised cultural rites held every year, at Thanksgiving and Christmas respectively, viewers are assured that "there's no place like home" when every celluloid detail testifies to the fact that monochromic Kansas is a barren wilderness and there's really no place like Technicolored Oz, that a life spent in dark frustration and forced sacrifice is actually quite wonderful. The work of genre is to convey and resolve the "dreams and dead ends" of American culture efficiently, movingly, and surreptitiously.

The distinctive genre work of 1941–45 wasn't a whole new project of cultural creation. It built on a foundation common to the movies and the national myths—asserting them when serviceable, adapting them when possible, and creating new ones when absolutely necessary. The structure that emerged did not spring from a blueprint drawn up by calculating government officials working in collusion with compliant studio heads. It was more like a spontaneous barn raising: born of common purpose, jerryrigged, but sturdy withal. Part of the enterprise was in the restoration of past genres, part the construction of entirely new wings. First, the ground had to be cleared.

PRELUDE TO WAR FILMS

In 1917, disgusted by the war fever gripping America, the critic Randolph Bourne reminded his countrymen that "the real enemy is War not imperial Germany." The heady hurrahs and ardent patriotism of the early months of the American entry into the European maelstrom not only crushed progressive hopes for pan-national socialism but worse still had found artists and intellectuals willingly succumbing to the war mania. "There is work to be done," Bourne warned, "to prevent this war of ours from passing into popular mythology as a holy crusade." Bourne himself—dead in 1918 of another fever, the influenza pandemic—never lived to hear his solitary voice of dissent become the common chorus. Yet no sooner was the Armistice signed than Bourne's work was taken up by historians, writers, and filmmakers. From 1918 until the eve of the Second World War, the popular mythology of the Great War—memoirs, novels, stage plays, and movies—derided the Wilsonian idealism and debunked the holy crusade.

The motion picture industry followed the course of Bourne's weak-willed artists: during the war, a willing participant; after the war, a penitent erasing its own complicity. Where the war years from 1914 to 1918 had witnessed the embryonic medium's formal entry into the art of war, the retrospective films of the interwar years from 1919 to 1939 projected the futility of combat and the nobility of pacifism. The Great War was seldom a preferred subject for film treatment much less the direct celebration later engendered by the Second World War. The carnage was so brutal and senseless, the outcome so shattering and disorienting, that it resisted celluloid rehabilitation. Hollywood never engineered the raw materials of the Great War—destruction, death, and disillusionment—into the scaffolding for durable generic construction—reconciliation, reassurance, affirmation. On screen, the main lesson of the "War to End All Wars" was to end all wars.

During the Great War itself, government policy blended an instinctive awareness that cinema and war were natural mates with a suspicion that the new medium was combustible and liable to misfire. A special government agency headed by a former muckraker named George Creel was charged with overseeing propaganda activities. Officially designated the Committee on Public Information (CPI), the agency was better known by the name of its energetic leader, the Creel Committee. As director of the first official U.S. propaganda agency, Creel started from scratch on the process he preferred to call "advertising" and a task he likened to the missionary's work of "carrying the gospel of Americanism to every corner of the globe."

Persuasion and debate were the province of classical rhetoric, but the Creel Committee took prophetic cognizance of the moving image. "At the very outset," recalled Creel in his memoirs, "it was obvious that the motion picture had to be placed on the same plane of importance as the written or spoken word." Or rather a different plane: the Creel Committee rigidly regulated the official motion pictures of combat reaching the homefront. It served as the sole authorized center for the distribution of official Army and Navy footage, material that had already been thoroughly "combed" by the War Department. Like still photographers, motion picture makers either needed special CPI permits prior to shooting or clearance from CPI censors "in regard to the admissibility of pictures that are taken without permits." The looming preeminence of the new medium was foretold in an official communication that acknowledged the necessity for speed and priority treatment: "Motion picture films will receive immediate consideration, and will be returned with the written approval of the Committee or with suggestions concerning changes that may be desirable."

From the very beginning the military also knew that war on film called for special handling. Neither freelancers nor representatives from private newsreel companies were allowed on the field of battle.

A. P. Waxman, a cameraman for the Photographic Division of the U.S. Army Signal Corps, recalled that while civilian reporters from the press were accredited as War News Correspondents, only soldiers from the Signal Corps were permitted "to cover the photographic side of the war. Their material—newsreels and stills—were [then] furnished to the newsreels."

In addition to a weekly Official War Preview produced with England, France, and Italy, the Creel Committee issued three feature-length films during the Great War—*Pershing's Crusaders* (May 1918), *America's Answer (to the Hun)* (August 1918), and *Under Four Flags* (November 1918). Billed as "the first official American war picture," *Pershing's Invaders* tied the American Expeditionary Force to a medieval crusade. One-sheet illustrations showed knightly horsemen shadowing the mounted general and his troops; intertitles assumed Victorian cadences: "Belgium! Her feet are placed mid Death and Desolation but Honor crowns her brow!" or "German arrogance casts its shadow on America when the Deutschland rises like a serpent in our harbors." Documenting the mobilization of "an Army of eleven million," *America's Answer (to the Hun)* updated the imagery and lure. Like the first, it boasted photography taken by the Army Signal Corps, including blurry glimpses of an artillery barrage and antiseptic footage of doughboys convalescing in "a temporary hospital in which there seems to be more happiness than pain." Huge one-sheets advertising *America's Answer* placed moving imagery up front. A blood-red illustration by Frank Fancher shows a cameraman in outline against the bombed-out skeleton of a town. The motto in the lower left reads "pro patria" ("for country"). Prior to commercially arranged distribution, the Creel Committee films were given promotional screenings "under the auspices of the U.S. government" in the big cities.

Despite Creel's avowed elevation of film to a plane of equality with speech and print, cinema was low medium in his communications trinity. With media as much as morality, the outlook of the Creel Committee was Victorian. In his official report to Congress and in his memoir *How We Advertised America*, Creel warms not to the motion picture (he takes pride mainly in the fact that the Division of Films made money) but to older, precedent media such as speeches, posters, and leaflets. Above all, Creel lavishes praise on his "Four Minute Men," a nationwide network of some 75,000 volunteer speakers, drawn from the zealous and public-spirited in local communities.

Coordinated by the CPI and speaking with the authority of the U.S. government, the Four Minute Men exhorted and instructed the home-front, often at movie theaters between one- and two-reelers. For a generation that respected and responded to public speaking, that still taught declamation and memorization in grade schools, the Four Minute Men were highly effective mediums for channeling public service announcements. "History should, and will, pay high tribute to the Four Minute Men," enthused Creel, "an organization unique in world annals, and as effective in the battle at home as was the onward rush of Pershing's heroes at St. Michiel." With vaudevillian ruthless-ness, Creel gave bores and blowhards the hook "whenever a speaker failed to hold his audience or injected a note of partisanship or else proved himself lacking in restraint or good manners."

The declamations of the Four Minute Men were the last gasps of oratory in the age of the image. Uttered or written, words were still the weapons of choice, the privileged medium of public discourse. Two decades later, official pronouncements and patriotic exhorta-tions were delivered from the screen, not the podium. By 1941 no American motion picture audience would have permitted the inter-ruption of a celluloid star by a corporeal neighbor.

The verbal orientation from above notwithstanding, the Great War created a ravenous market for moving pictures of mobilization and combat. Early newsreels ("the weeklies") and screen magazines re-ported back from the front with the promise of *War As It Really Is* (1916) and *The Horrors of War* (1916). Not infrequently, the attacking soldiers were a throng of extras dodging explosions set off by tech-nicians, a brazen violation of the boundary between news and drama that was almost unknown in the next war.

The moving picture record of the Great War—the documentary footage of trench warfare over there and doughboys scrambling over the top—is not large. Difficulties with the preservation of raw stock and the development of exposed negatives, cumbersome and primi-tive camera equipment, and stringent military restrictions all limited the scope of the camera eye. According to film historian Terry Ram-saye, "the military and naval authorities of the First World War knew nothing of the motion picture, saw no utility in it and did as little about it as convenient." Shortly after the Armistice, while working for the Treasury Department's War Loan campaign, Ramsaye claimed to have "examined every foot of U.S. military film after the Armistice and with difficulty found enough usable, competent negative to make up a five-reel newsreel out of the whole war." By 1944 John G. Bradley, head of the Motion Picture Division of the National Archives, estimated that only one-sixth of the footage taken of World War I was still extant. The screen memory of the Great War projects few moving images; in the mind's eye, no-man's-land is a still picture.

The incipient relationship between war and cinema, government design and commercial exigencies, set only a rough pattern for the next great war. The time was too brief (April 1917 to November 1918) and the protean medium too fragile to permit an accumulation of experience and wisdom. "World War I," adjudged Terry Ramsaye in the midst of its sequel, "was over before the military learned what to do about the motion picture."

By contrast, the motion picture business learned a lot about turning war into movies. Limiting itself to a consideration of "outstanding films," a trade survey of motion picture content traced the rising tide of war-on-screen. "The early years of the war, prior to America's entry, found the screen offering less than 10 per cent of war coloration, with but two war subjects in the 1914–1915 period, none during 1915–1916, and eight in 1916–1917." In 1917–18, however, Hollywood produced twenty-three major war films, or 26 percent of a total of eighty-nine productions. Moreover, "in 1918, from September through December, the proportion rose. There were 15 war pictures among the 35 listed or 43 per cent of the total for that period." For the first time also fiction films incorporated frontline footage into narratives for purposes of authenticity and impact, notably in D. W. Griffith's *Hearts of the World* (1918). Anti-German melodramas featuring a marauding Rupert Julian or a monocled Erich von Stroheim ("the man you love to hate," salivated taglines) dominate the archival record. Even by the standards of 1917–18, *Escaping the Hun, To Hell with the Kaiser!* and *The Kaiser, the Beast of Berlin,* where frothing Huns violate Belgian virgins and defenestrate squalling infants, were crudely fantastical. They served to discredit not only the portrayal of war on screen but the whole enterprise of cinematic propaganda.

After the Armistice, during the interwar period that witnessed the consolidation of studio-system dominance and the full flowering of motion picture art, Hollywood atoned for its excesses. The memory of the Great War, preserved, distorted, and measured by Hollywood film before 1941, contrasts strikingly with subsequent recollections. Picturesque violence aside, the retrospective Great War film produced *prior* to World War II was elegiac in tone, pacifist in purpose, and cynical in perspective. Like the poetry of Ezra Pound, the memoirs of e.e. cummings, and the fiction of Ernest Hemingway, the films make a separate peace.

The first of the antiwar epics, MGM's *The Big Parade,* held its gala premiere at Grauman's Egyptian Theatre on November 11, 1925, a widely covered event that foretold a perennial difficulty in deeming war simultaneously intolerable as experience and irresistible as spectacle. In the days when full stage shows served as prologue to major motion pictures, Grauman's devised a pageant entitled "Memories of 1918" to precede the premiere screening. Featuring a medley of martial tunes, a series of posed "historical tableaux," and an elaborate "danse militaire" (twenty-four chorus girls doing "a high-stepping, kicking, dancing military routine"), the original preshow extravaganza climaxed on a telling miscalculation. A reporter from *Variety* described the last moments of the live warm-up:

> For the finale, "The Unknown Soldier" was the tableau on the opening performance. It had a catafalque with two soldiers guarding the flag-draped bier in the shadows of the Capital at Washington. It was beautiful and impressive but for a climax held the audience in reverence on account of [the] forceful impressiveness of the symbol it conveyed, with the result it did not leave such a pleasant taste in the mouth of the patrons for the beginning of the picture, as well as denying them their commendation to Grauman for his wonderful achievement. [That is, to applaud would have been disrespectful.]

That bad taste in the collective mouth was the bitter fruit of the late war, a funereal memory evoked all too vividly by the military pageant within a pageant. For successive performances, the showstopper was made more palatable. After the initial misstep, the flag-draped catafalque was taken out, "with the Presentation of the Colors of the Allies" being used to close the show and "get the big applause the presentation deserved."

Thus primed, audiences for *The Big Parade* saw the cinematic equivalent of the disillusioning literature, a wasteland of meaningless death yoked uncertainly to conventional romance. Director King Vidor's stated intent was to deglamorize warfare. Like Stephen Crane in *The Red Badge of Courage,* he sought to depict war from the mud of the trenches instead of the chambers of the General Staff. Matinee idol John Gilbert plays James Apperson, the wealthy scion of a mill owner, who enlists in a flurry of nationalistic fervor and oedipal re-

The legacy of the not-so-Great War: a wounded veteran (John Gilbert) returns to a callow homefront in MGM's *The Big Parade* (1925).

bellion. In the Army he mixes with the lower orders, Bull (Tom O'Brien), a beefy Irish bartender, and Slim (Karl Dane), a lanky, tobacco-chewing ironworker. All learn that no one wins in the patriot's game. Karl and Bull die bloody deaths and James returns home missing a leg. James learns too that the enemy soldiers on the other side of the concertina wire are his kinsmen. Sharing a cigarette with a dying German, James sees an enemy transformed into a man no different from himself.

The bestial Hun was suddenly a fraternal friend—sometimes literally so. In John Ford's *Four Sons* (1928) an American soldier hears the chilling cries of a German moaning "mutterchen" across no-man's-land. "I guess they gots mothers too," admits a doughboy in intertitle. Unable to stand the lament, a Yank goes over the top to offer the Hun comfort. A beautiful tracking shot follows the Samaritan's course through the mist and wire, to the source of the sound, his enemy, his real-life brother.

The next landmark antiwar film arose from Eric Maria Remarque's international bestseller, *All Quiet on the Western Front*. Originally published in German in 1928, the worldwide success of *Im Westen Nichts Neues* was extraordinary not only because it gave the enemy a human face but because Americans were so disposed to recognize it as their own. In Universal-International's $1,200,000 adaptation, directed by Lewis Milestone and released in 1930, the avuncular scrounger Katczinsky (Louis Wolheim) suggests a diplomatic solution to war. "You should take all the kings and their cabinets and their generals, put 'em in the center [of a big field] dressed in their underpants and let 'em fight it out with clubs." His fellow troops, and Depression audiences, grumbled their assent.

All Quiet on the Western Front begins in sound and fury. Massing troops and blaring martial music drown out a high school professor's lecture. What looks at first like ironic commentary, the frenzy of war smothering the voice of learning, is in fact complicity not juxtaposition. The teacher exhorts his young charges to be "gay heroes" for the fatherland, to enlist as one in the name of patriotism and school spirit. In a dizzying Eisensteinian montage of close-ups, the boys jump to the bait.

Exploiting the comparative freedom of expression in the pre-Code era, *All Quiet on the Western Front* shoots down the transcendence of storybook battle with the flatulence of ground-level reality. The raw recruits are beset by hunger, rats, lice, and loss of sphincter control. Stringing concertina wire, enduring endless artillery bombardments, marching into machine guns, fighting hand-to-hand and killing up close, the homeroom class is shot, shelled, and blasted apart. The horror is relieved by a few incidents of low comedy, dalliance, and an uncomfortable home leave, but the rule is inexorable and inevitable death: files of pack-laden troops mowed down by withering machine gun fire; the noise, smoke, and chaos of forward assault; the lunar landscape of the no-man's-land. As Armistice negotiations drag on, the hero (Lew Ayres)—or rather protagonist—is killed by a sniper while reaching over the parapets to touch a butterfly. A double exposure reprises the earnest young faces marching off to war over another kind of no-man's-land, a graveyard filled with white crosses, row on row.

Only in aerial combat, with its man-to-man jousts and chivalrous conventions, might the Great War evoke romantic dreams. Alone among the mechanical innovations in the technology of war, the biplane was a vehicle for high adventure, tests of personal mettle, and noble rivalries. The spirit of the old glory soars in Paramount's barn-

Cannon fodder: German schoolboys jump to the bait in Universal's *All Quiet on the Western Front* (1930).

storming *Wings* (1927), the first Best Picture Oscar winner. "They gave me *Wings* because I was the only director who had been a flyer, in action," helmsman William Wellman recalled to silent film historian Kevin Brownlow, decades later. "I was the only one who knew what it was all about." If so, memory and myth were in perfect sync. An intertitle announces the entrance to an Aviation Examination Station: "Here was a door that only the bravest of the brave dared open—a path of glory mounting to the stars." The pilots on both sides are all "game" and suitably sportsmanlike. When the American's machine gun jams in mid-duel, his German opponent ceases fire and salutes jauntily for "there was chivalry among these knights of the air." A convoluted romantic triangle and Clara Bow's unrequited love for her dim hometown sweetheart ground the action interminably, but as is not unusual in Great War territory the boy-girl stuff is less passionate than the boy-boy stuff. Jack (Charles "Buddy" Rogers) and David (Richard Arlen) spat, reconcile, and wind up in each other's arms in a homoerotic deathbed clinch complete with caresses and kisses. Despite his ordeal and the addition of gray streaks to his hair, the callow Jack (or maybe Rogers's shallow performance) seems unaffected by war. Back home, he and Clara Bow wind up in a less heartfelt but more orthodox heterosexual union. Even in the flighty *Wings,* though, Great War death is swift and merciless. In a brief turn that brought him to prominence, a virile and charismatic Gary Cooper plays a dashing pilot who casually goes aloft for a practice flight and just as casually crashes to his death.

Similarly, Howard Hughes's *Hell's Angels* (1930) taxis when in earthbound melodrama and takes off only in the clouds, especially in a spectacular, climactic dogfight. An authentic blockbuster, brought in at an alleged cost of $4 million and the lives of three stunt pilots, the film is as oxymoronic as its title. Monte Routledge (James Hall), an unprincipled cad, and his brother Roy (Ben Lyon), an idealistic stiff, join the Royal Flying Corps, one through thoughtless impulse, the other through patriotic duty. A true bounder, Monte has no fidelity to abstract codes and conventions. Caught in the arms of a Prussian officer's wife and challenged to a duel, he packs his bags and cheerfully, hilariously, skips out on the dawn appointment. Roy covers for his ignoble brother, but his stout-hearted faith in the purity of nation and the honor of women is at least half wrong. Roy's gossamer platinum blonde fiancée (Jean Harlow) is a faithless party girl only too willing to "slip into something more comfortable" for worldly wise Monte, who sees through more than her negligee. So wrong about the occupant of one pedestal, idealistic Roy remains unshaken in his devotion to God and country. In the end, he shoots his brother Monte rather than permit him to reveal military secrets. The last of the Victorian heroes, Roy then faces a firing squad.

Paramount's *The Eagle and the Hawk* (1933) well captures the gallantry of combat and the knightly codes of behavior regulating the airborne jousts of the Great War: the rules of combat; a stylish salute between enemies; a toast to fallen opponents. After the newly arrived gunner Crocker (Cary Grant) machineguns a defenseless German parachuting to earth, his comrades back at the canteen shun him. "I don't get it," he says reasonably enough. "This is war. I'm hired to kill the enemy. And there ain't no book of rules about that. Every one I put away means one less to kill me. That's my job and I'm doing it." "It's like shooting a man in the back," he's told. "Nobody does it, that's all." "A gentleman's agreement, old chap." Not that compliance to the rulebook confers any meaning on the game. Polo-playing Jerry

Young (Fredric March) enlists as a Royal Flying Corps pilot for the "sport in it," but in short order five of his gunners are killed in combat. Their lives, like their names in chalk on the squadron's blackboard, are erased with the sweep of a hand. Boyish exhilaration turns to stale existentialism as Young finds himself "chauffeur to a graveyard."

A rainswept, noirish film, *The Eagle and the Hawk* features an extraordinary performance by Fredric March as the burnt-out pilot (with what was not then called the thousand-yard stare). Haunted by guilt and tormented by nightmares, he plays a "shining example" of the heroic flying ace, saying all the right words about courage and country but betrayed by his hollow eyes and halting tones. At a binge in his honor, he finally snaps, drinks to the health of the Germans, and rips off his chestful of medals. "I got these for killing kids. They're all chunks of torn flesh and broken bones and blood!" Raising his glass in mock tribute and flinging it across the room, he makes a bitter toast. "I give you war!" The World War I flying ace then walks to his quarters and puts a gun to his head. It is left to Crocker to restore the myth. The next morning he takes his friend's body up in their plane and fakes a gallant death for him. The ship's emblem, a skeletal grim reaper, dissolves into a memorial plaque that prints the legend of a man "who gallantly gave his life in aerial combat to save the world for democracy." The reality is that war is suicide, the patriotic cause a sham.

Undeniably, stoic gallantry and dashing disillusionment has a romance of its own. Many of the Great War films ricochet from celebration to condemnation to commemoration. While the narratives proclaim peace among nations and the horrors of war, the visuals entice with the allure of spectacle. The soundtracks also trumpet a rousing call to arms. As the dialogue enunciates futility, the mix of music and sound screams out the thrill of combat. In the climactic bombardment and dogfight to *Hell's Angels,* the war film first discovered and creatively deployed the art of synchronous sound. Like the ambiance of the gangster film, itself being born at Warner Bros. with *Little Caesar* (1930) and *The Public Enemy* (1931), the cinematic imagination of war requires a sense besides sight. In *Wings* the wild blue yonder is silent or symphonic; in *Hell's Angels* it is jarringly mechanical, a cacophony of loud, percussive buzzings and blasts. The memorable finale, in which a score of biplanes buzz and swoop at each other like angry mosquitoes, is as much an aural as visual spectacle.

The sudden blasts of explosions, the calibrated hum of the propellers, the fits and starts of engines divebombing and stalling out, and the staccato rat-tat-tat of machine guns complete the sensory bombardment.

Keeping in tune with the technical advance, and underscoring the integral role of sound, MGM rereleased *The Big Parade* in 1931 with a specially recorded soundtrack. The revamped exploitation campaign for the antiwar classic was keyed entirely to the new technology and bent on drowning out the original thematic tonalities. "*The Big Parade* is back . . . with the old thrills doubled by the addition of sound," read the ad sheets, which also promised:

> —When the big guns of *The Big Parade* flash, they will roar as well.
> —When the airplanes hover over the laboring trucks, stretching toward a war-torn horizon, their thunder will hurl itself from the scene.
> —And when Karl Dane launches the tobacco juice that puts out the candle—it will sizzle too!

Though the original music score for the film, performed by a full orchestra, was also on the track, it was the impact of engines and ordnance—not strings and woodwinds—that turned up the volume of war on screen.

In other war-themed locales, the tonal register remained a mournful dirge throughout the 1930s. Off the battlefield, over here, veterans of the Great War trod their way through social conditions only slightly less murderous than trench warfare. Gassed or not, ex-doughboys were permanently blighted by their service and thoughtlessly betrayed by the homefront. In eruptions of Warner Bros. "social consciousness," their run of bad luck taxed the sadistic imaginations of stables of screenwriters. Ex-servicemen were unjustly condemned to hellish chain gangs, (*I Am a Fugitive from a Chain Gang*, 1932), unjustly imprisoned in state penitentiaries (*Heroes for Sale*, 1933), or shamefully deserted by an ungrateful nation (the "forgotten man" number in *Gold Diggers of 1933*).

Descending to earth and moving forward in time, *Wings* director William Wellman depicted the homefront legacy of the Great War in *Heroes for Sale*. Made in the aftermath of the violent eviction of the Bonus Expeditionary Force from Washington, D.C., on July 28, 1932, the film traces the preternatural bad luck streak of veteran Tom Holmes (Richard Barthelemess). Wellman opens with an aviator's eye view of the land war, a majestic overhead shot that pulls back and pivots up. The camera follows the troops over the top into a long shot of a no-man's-land of parapets, concertina wire, and shell holes. Left for dead on the field of battle, Holmes is rescued by German medical workers, their humanity another defiance of the Hun-as-beast propaganda. During convalescence he becomes hooked on morphine, and after the Armistice his addiction gets him fired from his bank teller job. "It's time to stop beating the drum and waving the flag," snaps an unsympathetic bank president. A torrent of ill fortune rains down. Tom is sent to a narcotics farm and his mother dies from the shock; he tries to stop a labor riot, and his wife is killed in the confusion; he is unjustly sent to prison for five years; he is run out of town by federal agents and harassed by local police. On the bum, herded into a boxcar by brutish cops and hired thugs, he erupts, "Who you calling reds and hoboes? We're ex-servicemen!" An abrupt New Deal finale ("At least it's stopped raining") erases neither the despair of the Great Depression nor the legacy of the Great War.

The doom of the battlefield and the gloom of the homefront were the dominant shadings until the very eve of the Second World War. Hollywood conjured a few frivolous and glorious marches off to war, such as the alternately zany and grim *What Price Glory?* (1926) and, on the eve of a mythic turnabout, the Hibernian frolic *The Fighting 69th* (1940). Unlike Europeans, the relatively unscathed Americans might sustain a portion of the grand illusion. More often, though, whether in *The Lost Patrol* (1934) or *The Dawn Patrol* (both the 1930 original and the 1938 remake), men at war were wiped out one by one. MGM's *They Gave Him a Gun* (1937) occupies the center of gravity. A product of the most glamorous and politically conservative of the studios, it opens with a merchants-of-death montage tracing the manufacture of a firearm in a humming munitions factory. The sequence might have been lifted whole from outtakes from the Soviet Union's Dziga Vertov Group. The film charts the progress of a peaceful hayseed turned into a trained killer by the U.S. military. Urged to bayonet the abdomen of a dummy by his bloodthirsty drill sergeant, the raw recruit faints dead away, but soon he itches to get off the target range and demonstrate his sharpshooting skills on flesh and blood. In battle he passes his test, picking off a German machine gun crew one by one, including a soldier who raises his arms in surrender. Stateside, he puts his expertise to work as a gangster until he is hunted down and killed in a hail of civilian bullets. His former drill sergeant, now a police sergeant, moans that "this was one of my boys." "He was your star pupil," spits out an embittered pal. As late as 1939, a *March of Time* retrospective on Hollywood history matter-of-factly referred to *All Quiet on the Western Front* as the "greatest of war pictures." By definition, war movies were antiwar movies.

SERGEANT YORK

The creation of a new mythos for the Second World War began with the de-mythologizing of the First World War. Hollywood had to recast the Great War as a reasonable national enterprise, not as the crazy slaughterhouse depicted in literature and film for the previous twenty years. Despair, meaninglessness, pacifism—the dominant legacy of the suicide of Europe—had to be erased, rejected, or re-vamped.

Outright obliteration was a prerequisite. In early 1942 both *All Quiet on the Western Front* and *The Eagle and the Hawk* were reissued, apparently under the impression that one war with Germany was as good as another. A line-up consisting of a newsreel showing scenes of a smoldering Pearl Harbor with the commentator snarling "Look at these pictures and get mad and stay mad!" followed by the paci-fistic *All Quiet on the Western Front* (billed now as "the timeliest pic-ture ever made!") comprised an unstable staple program. Exhibitors "not cognizant of the violently anti-war character" of the films re-ceived protests from befuddled moviegoers. The untimely reissues were called to the attention of the OWI and hastily withdrawn.

A World War I film that was really about World War II better fit the bill. *Sergeant York* (released July 2, 1941), the immensely popular Warner Bros. bio-pic of the Great War's most famous American hero, rehabilitated the war movie. As played by Gary Cooper and inter-preted by director Howard Hawks, Sergeant York undergoes a So-cratic crisis between private conscience and patriotic duty before decisively committing himself to the ways of war. The genre work of the film is twofold: (1) to re-mythologize World War I as a national crusade worthy of admiration, and (2) to reconcile the conflict be-tween state (patriotism) and church (morality).

The casting of Cooper, an icon of quiet frontier determination, made the recasting go more smoothly. York/Cooper incarnates a high school pageant's worth of folk heroes. Like Daniel Boone, he hunts in the Tennessee valley; like Abraham Lincoln, the tall, lanky westerner splits rails; like the Jefferson yeoman, he stands proud behind his plow, and like Ben Franklin he records his pennies earned and saved on a daily calendar. In the film's best-remembered scene (one whose signature gesture was mimicked by a generation of schoolboys), York competes at a backwoods turkey shoot. The keen eye and steady hand of the frontiersman is matched by his native guile. Setting up to aim, York wets his thumb, dabs the sight of his longrifle, and gobbles like a turkey. The bird looks up from behind a log and—crack!—York nails him.

The patriotic inheritance is preliminary to a more prophetic passage. York's story follows the course of a spiritual autobiography rather than a war memoir, contemplates the grace of God rather than grace under pressure. As the ghosts of Americans past cast their shadow on York, so does the religious fervor of the Great Awakening. Away from the shooting range, York is aimless, a wild and alcoholic youth. The town preacher, whose service York's gun-shooting gang interrupts at the beginning of the film, counsels the boy to follow the Good Book and to "wrestle with Satan." The love of a good woman seems to put him on the right track, but when frustrated in his attempt to buy the rich "bottom land" he wants to farm, York goes on a violent bender. Drunk, he vows revenge and rides home through a nighttime thunderstorm with murder in mind. He experiences the most schematic of Damascus moments after a bolt of lightning strikes, stunning his mule and blasting apart his rifle barrel. From afar, the glow of the preacher's church beckons and York, transported, joins the congregation in singing "That Old Time Religion." By accepting Christ, York (and *Sergeant York*) completes the first stage of a reformation.

Embodying both an American and biblical mythos, Boone of Kentucky and Saul of Tarsus, York can serve country and church—until America's entry into World War I. Taking his own Bible lessons to heart, the converted backwoodsman files for conscientious objector status, but the local draft board refuses to certify his charismatic church as a deferrable religion. Reluctantly, he surrenders his body to the state, keeping his soul to himself. At boot camp, however, the white-haired preacher who has been York's mentor is supplanted by an alternative patriarch, a white-haired Army major. The military man gives the still-waffling York a book of American history to balance his Bible study and a weekend pass to mull things over back in Tennessee. Alone on a mountaintop with his dog and photographed in monumental silhouette, York endures a dark night of the soul before a divine wind blows his Bible to the proper passage: "Render unto Caesar the things that are Caesar's and to God the things that are God's." In good Hollywood fashion, the conflict between state and church, patriotism and conscience, is not so much settled by decision as smoothed over by denial.

The re-creation of York's Congressional Medal of Honor–winning assault, in which he single-handedly killed twenty-three Germans and captured 132, takes up only the last act. It is a measure of the difference between classical Hollywood cinema and its present-day descendent that a film about the most decorated hero of the Great War spends less than a fifth of its screen time in actual combat. Ideologically if not biographically, *Sergeant York* might well have ended after the second divine intervention on the mountaintop. As an ancillary marketing tactic, a hardcover edition of York's 1922 autobiography was reissued. The dust jacket illustrates not violent destruction but religious reflection, featuring York/Cooper in saintly contemplation on a Tennessee mountaintop. The combat, depicted as just another turkey shoot, is followed by York's ticker-tape reception in New York, a thunderous welcome on a scale not seen again until Charles Lindbergh returned from France in 1927.

Released and ballyhooed in a manner befitting a prestigious "A" picture—that is, an exclusive New York premiere followed by selected big-city openings—*Sergeant York* went into wide distribution "at popular prices" on July 4, 1942, and garnered more than 22,000 bookings (including repeats) by fall of 1943. According to several Selective Service Boards, pacifist ministers and conscientious objectors lost their qualms about combat duty after viewing the film. The comparison is enlightening. In 1917 God's chosen medium was the Bible; in 1941, the movies.

Sergeant York washed clean over the memory of the Great War, but its singular protagonist was the wrong agent for the next assignment. The main reason for York's heroic stature and spontaneous popularity was not his personal courage but the cultural resonance of his act. York was a solitary, ruggedly individualistic hero in a war of assembly-line destruction and mass death. Marksmanship, his vaunted military skill, was itself a throwback to a time when precision and bull's eyes meant something on the field of battle. (As in horseshoes, close *counts* in grenades.) Even in his time, as a twentieth-

Redirecting allegiances: Howard Hawks (*seated under the key light*) orchestrates Gary Cooper's spiritual transformation in *Sergeant York* (1941). (Museum of Modern Art/Film Stills Archive)

century warrior, York was an anachronism. The hyperbole of his heroism—one lone man killing and capturing so many—spoke to an abiding American faith in the value of personal initiative in a war of anonymous cannon fodder (hence too the ecstatic reception of lone eagle Lindbergh in the wake of so many sitting ducks). For the Second World War, solo acts like York and Lindbergh had to be harnessed to the team, the crew, the corps.

WARNER BROS.'S *AIR FORCE*

Where *Sergeant York* celebrated the one-man show, the combat films of the war years pay tribute to the disciplined component part. Bearing the names of battle sites, battle stations, and branches of the armed services, the very titles repudiate surnames: *Wake Island, Eagle Squadron, Flying Tigers, Aerial Gunner, Top Sergeant, Bombardier, Air Force, The Navy Comes Through, Marine Raiders, The Fighting Seabees, Guadalcanal Diary, Destination Tokyo, Objective, Burma!,* and so on. The featured warriors are not mythic frontiersmen but regular guys, not legends in their time but average Joes. "No," read a tagline for *Air Force,* "they're no 'master race,' these boys from up the street, U.S.A. . . . ." This war, the soldier-citizen-spectator is told again and again, requires a new breed of hero, one who like the complex machines of war he keeps aflight cannot work unless all pistons fire in tempo. As film historian Jeanine Basinger demonstrates in her exhaustive study *The World War II Combat Film,* the real champion of the genre is the combat unit, the crew of demographically dispersed characters with complementary occupational specialties. In World War II the showoff, the loner, and the outlaw accept military discipline, repress personal desires, and sign on for choral contribution in the service of the nation.

The new heroes rode onto a wholly new field of action. The decisive battleground of the Second World War was not properly a ground at all. Hollywood waited until 1945 to produce *The Story of G.I. Joe,* the first major film celebrating the Army infantry and the GI dogface, a favored figure of postwar combat films. Instead, soaring titles and sky-bound narratives blanketed the marquee firmament of 1941–45. Advertising taglines reflect the celestial fixation. Universal's featurette *Cavalcade of Aviation* (1941) was "an exploitation feature timed for the minute"; *Flight Lieutenant* (1942) was "made to order for an air-minded world"; and Universal's quasi-documentary *Eagle Squadron* (1942) accrued record-breaking rerelease engagements. In service to the latest machine technology of war, the most intensive and original genre work took place in the air, within a fuselage.

Unhappily, however, the modern air war arrived with sparse mythological precedent. Unlike the man-to-man jousts of the Great War, the flying fortress bombing runs—the quality of the courage, the skills of the warrior, and the nature of the mission—required that a new mythos be created from the ground up. Though well suited to narrative ordering and tailor-made for visual spectacle, airborne warfare called for a painstaking reorientation of values.

The practice of aerial bombardment itself presented a nettlesome problem. The recent past had universally adjudged it a barbarian tactic beyond the pale of civilized nations. Just as the most famous painting of the 1930s was Picasso's terrorized *Guernica,* the most famous newsreel image was a shot of a burned Chinese baby crying in the ruins of bombed-out Shanghai South Station. For most Americans, however, the swift attitudinal turnabout can be evoked with a place name. Pearl Harbor—and the hardening of the heart of a nation at war—deflected moral qualms. In wartime cinema, news of the Japanese attack is the all-purpose epiphany, the *zeroes ex machina* that in the space of a radio bulletin renders all clear, gives direction to drift, and postpones for the duration a too-exquisite sensitivity to the welfare of enemy populations.

For the conscience-stricken, the commentaries of the combat reports and the dialogue of Hollywood bomber films pointedly designate bombing targets as military not civilian. After a bombs-away sequence, reverse shots show chemical factories and armaments plants irrupting into fireballs as an identifying sign ("Deutsch Chemische") crumbles into the rubble. Pinpoint accuracy and special delivery was guaranteed in *Passage to Marseille* (1944) when waist gunner Humphrey Bogart tosses a message in a bottle out of his low-flying bomber and into the front yard of his French wife. When American bombs do happen to stray off course, a divine hand guides their destination. In *Uncertain Glory* (1944) unrepentant French criminal Jean Picard (Errol Flynn) is moments away from a date with the guillotine. Targeted at an adjacent military installation, errant American bombs blast apart the prison yard, allowing Flynn to escape and sacrifice himself in a more serviceably Gaelic manner.

The removal of embedded popular heroes and the installation of credible replacements was a more culturally sensitive task. Free agents and laconic daredevils, the screen idols of the past, flew few hours of air time after 1941. In accord with the burdens of leadership in a complicated war, the aerial knight of the Great War gave way to the mature perspective and calm intelligence of the bomber pilot and his well-oiled crew. Trouble was, the necessity of personal sacrifice and the value of communitarian purpose were not exactly main currents in American thought. The native self-made man made an unlikely candidate for selfless devotion. The cheeky newspaperman, the lonesome cowboy, the private detective, the single-minded inventor, even the will to power of the urban gangster strike chords unsounded by the rewards of group solidarity and communal work. The solo hero was so deeply ingrained in the American tradition that Hollywood, which had done its share of the planting, had trouble uprooting him.

Thunder Birds (1942) illustrates the lingering legacy of the old model. Returning to the aerial arena, Lafayette Flying Corps veteran William Wellman still embraces the flight mentality of the Great War. In this Technicolor tribute to fighter pilots and Gene Tierney's crimson lips, flight school instructor and former World War I pilot Preston Foster takes a paternal interest in a young Britisher trying to gain his wings. The lad suffers from a dizziness syndrome that causes him to fail repeatedly in his solo flying attempts. The narrative hinges on the travails of that one young pilot, with the flight teacher refusing to wash him ôut despite the fact that he has clearly not cut it. The time and effort expended, the organizational attention lavished on one man, and the teacher's personal stake in his success (the boy is the son of an old Lafayette Escadrille comrade) defies military logic and sabotages the construction of a new aerial mythos. In the contrived finale, the teacher resorts to shock therapy. Parachuting out of an instruction plane during the crucial examination flight, he leaves his student copilot to master his fear or crash. With its already dated biplanes, barnstorming stunt flying, and grandstanding gestures, *Thunder Birds* is one war out of date.

Though suffering less acutely from a Great War cultural lag, Warner Bros.'s *Desperate Journey* (1942) has also not yet caught up to the war at hand. A fast-paced Raoul Walsh action adventure, this early wartime entry briskly introduces the Anglo-American alliance within the space of sixty seconds: Canadian (Arthur Kennedy), American (Ronald Reagan), Britisher (Ronald Sinclair), Anglo-Irishman (Alan Hale), and Australian (Errol Flynn). However, as the Anglocentricity signals, *Desperate Journey* represents a transitional phase between a past mythos and a present one. After successfully completing their bombing run over German railway lines, the Allied bomber crew is shot down and captured by the Nazis. They escape and blitz their way through four hundred miles of enemy territory, stealing Göring's staff car, overpowering and outsmarting a succession of Nazi guards, and detouring for a side trip of improvisational sabotage. The behind-the-lines havoc ends when the surviving crew members (featured stars Flynn, Reagan, and Kennedy) hijack a captured British bomber and fly back over the Channel.

Laden with low comedy from Warner's utility backfielder Alan Hale and a brush with romance in the figure of a beautiful resistance heroine, *Desperate Journey* is wildly unlikely and cloyingly juvenile. Unlike *Thunder Birds,* however, this transitional film seems aware of the adult chore before it. Walsh and company seem to know that Errol Flynn, playing his usual strutting self, should be put in his place, but they can't quite bring themselves to do it. Flynn is an independent Aussie pilot who resents assignment to the cooperative bomber squadron instead of the individualistic fighter command. "Keeping the Australians in the bombers!" he gripes. "Well, if that isn't typical brass hat idiocy. The Australians are fighting men—we're not truck drivers." Though the escaping crew possesses vital strategic information (the location of underground Messerschmitt factories), Flynn cavalierly suggests a side trip to blow up a chemical plant where the Germans manufacture incendiary bombs. His fellow crewmen follow their leader, literally rubbing their hands together at the prospect of a really big explosion. A solemn Arthur Kennedy is the sole voice of mature reason in the boys' club. "That's always been a secondary objective," he argues. "But our information on these Messerschmitt factories is important. . . . We haven't got the right to risk our getting back on side issues. Weigh the values." Flynn and Reagan accuse him of taking the fun out of war. In a close-up that commands respect and attention, Kennedy delivers a not-yet-familiar lesson:

> Fun? I didn't get into this war for fun, or adventure, or because it was expected of me. I got in because it was a hard, dirty job that has to be done before I can go back to doing what I liked—before a hundred million other people can get back to doing what they liked. It's no bright game to me. It's a job—a job that has to be done as rapidly and efficiently as possible.

Kennedy's unassailable logic and workmanlike approach fail to persuade his fellows, who successfully pull off a satisfyingly explosive guerrilla raid. Flynn later concedes that the Kennedy line of argument was tactically correct, but the narrative exacts no penalty for his defiance of military necessity. *Desperate Journey* knows what it must say, but Hollywood has not yet found a way to integrate wartime words into wartime drama. In 1942 it was still possible to be in like Errol Flynn rather than in line with Arthur Kennedy.

The Flynn-like independent streak in American GIs had serious military consequences for manpower allocation and military occupation specialities. The Army Air Force reported little trouble recruiting pilots because, as Hollywood had consistently taught, pilots got the glory and the girl. The sexual compensation was promised officially by the Army Air Force itself in *Winning Your Wings*. Lt. Jimmy Stewart eyes the camera confidentially and drawls that, well, it isn't strictly in the manual, but "the effect those shiny little wings have on a gal— it's phenomenal"—whereupon winged crewmen walk onto a dance floor and draw pretty women like honey. As a recruiting device for pilots, *Winning Your Wings* was all too effective. Inundated with candidates for the cockpit, the service was sorely in need of bombardiers, navigators, crew chiefs, and gunners.

A famous Hollywood anecdote, too often told to be totally unreliable and too perfect to be totally unembellished, records the genesis of a generic revolution. In the executive dining room at the Warner Bros. studio in Burbank, Jack Warner tells Army Air Force head Gen. H. H. ("Hap") Arnold that his studio will do whatever it can to help the war effort. Veteran trade reporter Barney Oldfield recalled the general's "seemingly guileless" suggestion to the script doctors at Warner Bros.:

> Well, there is something you can do. We are up to our necks in pilot applications, can get more than we will ever need. But gunners, navigators, crew chiefs, ground crews—there, we're in trouble. Every kid thinks he has to be a pilot or he's nothing. We need some way to put some glamour in these other jobs to put a flight team together. Maybe films would be the way to do it.

Led by Warner Bros., Hollywood gave close-ups or full-length tributes to every member of the bomber crew line-up. In the U.S. Army Air Force-via-Warner Bros. featurette *The Rear Gunner* (April 1943), the diminutive Pee Wee (Lt. Burgess Meredith) learns the pivotal value of his battle station. Tucked securely in place as tail gunner, Pee Wee finds an acceptance and stature he never knew on the ground. "Gee," says the B-24 pilot (Ronald Reagan), "I hope those gunners can keep those Zeros off my tail." After a forced landing, Pee Wee saves crew and craft by blasting a strafing Zero out of the sky. Sharply directed, emphasizing not only the potency of 50-caliber support but classroom instruction in ballistics and trajectory, *The Rear Gunner* features a gorgeous night-for-night spectacle on a firing range lit by tracer bullets. Less compellingly, Paramount's *Aerial Gunner* (1943) sent out the same message at feature length.

Moving up the fuselage, *Bombardier* (1943) unloaded its generic payload by elevating the title appellation to a rank higher than the pilot himself. Relegated to being a mere "taxi driver to take the bombardier to his mission," the chauffeur pilot (Randolph Scott) initially resents taking orders from the backseat bombardier (Eddie Albert), but in the course of training he gains the insight to accept his position *on* the team not *as* the team. He also loses out in the romantic competition for a blonde, the real talisman of heroic stature and hierarchical placement. Inexplicably, no Hollywood feature entitled *Navigator* was produced, but the navigator is always granted essential status in the aircrew films. In *Wings Up,* he is the weak link who botches the completion of a vital bombing mission. In *Winged Victory* (1944) a seasoned officer tells a class of cadets "you'll feel that bombardiers and navigators are the most important part of the Air Force—and you'll be right."

Like each member of the crew, each model of aircraft got its place on the screen, though the B-17 Flying Fortress (1943's *Air Force* and 1944's *The Memphis Belle*) and the B-25 (1944's *Thirty Seconds Over Tokyo*) tended to get top billing. By late 1944 the War Department

New hero, same reward: blonde Ann Shirley moves away from pilot Randolph Scott (*right*) to bombardier Eddie Albert (*left*) in RKO's *Bombardier* (1943).

allowed that "the B-17s have been effectively dramatized," but noti-fied the studios that "it would be of considerable value to the morale of the B-24 crews" to have a feature-length picture celebrating the Consolidated Liberator. When a suitable star vehicle was not imme-diately forthcoming, the War Department featured the B-24 in its own production, the combat report *Target Tokyo* (May 1945).

Concocting likely narratives and creating resonant tropes for the airborne genre work sparked a forced creativity replete with strained metaphors. In the OWI-BMP Victory film *Mission Accomplished: The Story of a Flying Fortress* (1943) the combat team is "ten men blending together like a good jazz band"; in *Winning Your Wings,* it is "as closely coordinated as a precision watch." Sports were a wellspring of reference. Baseball and football metaphors ("hand off the ball," "lay down a sacrifice bunt," "set up the defense," "wait your turn at bat") sweep through the instructional dialogue. In *Flying Tigers* (1942) a "one man team" receives a sideline lecture: "You're not the first ball carrier that didn't appreciate his interference." Overween-ing and inapt as the playing field references sometime were, Holly-wood screenwriters had few other popular traditions to draw on. Sports are one of the few cultural arenas in which American males willingly acknowledge the value of cooperative enterprise.

The morally absolved, combat-coordinated, and expert-approved way to victory through air power is charted definitively in *Air Force* (released February 4, 1943), another Howard Hawks film for Warner Bros. In Hawks, auteurist sensibility matched wartime necessity. A loving celebrant of men in groups and machines in flight, his personal vision saw eye to eye with the needs of the Army Air Force.

The skywriting in two earlier Hawks works, *Ceiling Zero* (1935) and *Only Angels Have Wings* (1939), sketched much of the tone and con-tour of the World War II air film. Though the field of action and the payload is nonmilitary (both films are set in the formulative days of the civilian postal service), the airborne brotherhood is in full flower. The males deliver the mail in a romance of fraternal bonding that witnesses the absorption of independent action into corporate and cooperative solidarity. The Hawksian pilots embody professional skill, stoic endurance, and existential machismo. When a brother pi-lot crashes to his death in *Only Angels Have Wings,* his friends sit down to eat the man's steak. Grief, loyalty, courage, love, fear all are unspoken emotions, for men don't talk about such things. In a later age, Tom Wolfe would christen this enduring Hawksian-Hemingway-esque mythos "the brotherhood of the right stuff."

Air Force recruits the mail carriers of the 1930s for a military cargo. In wartime, the silent bond of brotherhood is not enough; aboard the B-17 *Mary-Ann* the unspoken codes and values must be articulated and dramatized. To wit, that dedication to cause and craft means the forfeiture of personal desire and independent action. Mucking up the defensive line is gunner Winoki (John Garfield), an embittered wash-out from flight school. Within the Army Air Force, complains Winoki, the pilot is king, the crew mere pawns. Like Sergeant York, Gunner Winoki must undergo a conversion but one of culture not religion. His Damascus experience is the lightning bolt of Pearl Harbor. Trans-formed, Winoki climbs aboard and the simpatico crew operates smoothly. Each component gets his place in the sun—the youthful but paternal pilot who attends to the psychological integration of his men, the navigator who finds Wake Island, the gunners who protect the vessel fore and aft, the crew chief who repairs and sustains the ship, the radioman who communicates the location of a Japanese task force, and the bombardier who targets same. Visually (the nav-igator works under a picture of his father, an ace from the Lafayette Escadrille and a Great War ghost who must be exorcised), cinemat-ically (group portraits not close-ups), and narratively (after the pilot dies, a replacement part is inserted in the cockpit and the damaged *Mary-Ann* continues to soar), the singular hero of *Air Force* is the air crew.

Around Hollywood's air-minded world the only really permissible form of self-assertion was the noble act of self-annihilation. If a pilot were critically wounded and his craft beyond salvage, a grand ges-ture might precede a terminal exit. Allied kamikaze attacks climax a striking number of aerial careers. In *Flying Tigers, Pilot No. 5, A Guy Named Joe,* and *The North Star,* pilots in blazing aircraft nosedive into ships, convoys, or bridges as a final flaming act of courage. Save for last-ditch suicides, however, private flights and the settlement of per-sonal scores were forbidden. Whatever the provocation, no matter how powerful the emotional pull, the war came first. Elsewhere, ab-ject self-sacrifice (a virtue Hollywood once confined mainly to long-suffering mothers in women's melodramas), became a transgeneric sine qua non. In *Edge of Darkness* (1943), the guerrilla fighter played by Errol Flynn grits his teeth and relinquishes the right to avenge a

The airborne combat unit: ensemble acting, group shots, and team playing create the composite hero of *Air Force* (1943). (Museum of Modern Art/Film Stills Archive)

girlfriend ravished by the Nazis. In *The Fighting Seabees* (1944), the construction crew that defies military authority and goes off half-cocked botches the Big Picture strategy. In *Bataan* (1943) and *They Were Expendable* (1945), officers whose every masculine instinct tells them to stay behind with their men must leave and escape to safety. In *Casablanca* (1942) Rick surrenders Ilsa. The stars who bit their lips and swallowed their pride were often the swaggering swains and taciturn outsiders of the 1930s—Flynn, the rakish egoist; Bogart and Garfield, the urban loners; and John Wayne, the brawling cowboy. So unsettling and unfamiliar is the transfiguration that the films perversely work against their own message. In *Edge of Darkness,* the girl's father erupts in rage and kills the Nazi rapist. In *Air Force*, would-be pilot Winoki gets his turn in the cockpit. And Rick and Ilsa will always have Paris.

THE WAR DEPARTMENT'S AIR FORCE

Although Warner Bros. seemed to possess exclusive film rights to the air war, the War Department also staked a legitimate claim to the territory. In a series of combat reports distributed to commercial theaters through the War Activities Committee, the Army Air Force provided an official documentary record of aerial warfare, air crew cooperation, and relentless bombardment. The military's aerial genre work, if not the screen faces and film grain, was virtually indistinguishable from Hollywood's. It stood to reason: the narratives and the directors overlapped. The natural trajectory of the bombing run—preparation, take off, cruising, climactic release, return—neatly parallels the five-act formula of classical dramaturgy; the officers in charge were also motion picture stalwarts. Unsurprisingly, then, in John Huston's *Report from the Aleutians* (July 1943) and William Wyler's *The Memphis Belle* (April 1944), the War Department's Air Force proved thematically consistent with Warner Bros.'s *Air Force*.

Huston's *Report from the Aleutians* is the more placid and ponderous of the two dispatches. Addressed directly to "you Americans here at home," it begins by orienting audiences to military strategy through an illustrated graphic. The narration provides some particularly extensive meteorological background about the "cold air masses" and "cyclonic disturbances" that sweep west to east across the Pacific and provide atmospheric cover for the invading Japanese. Huston then makes an Aleutian report that bears all the markings of an allusive screen treatment.

Huston's chosen mission is something of a milk run. His B-17 faces no opposition and drops its payload over the barren Kiska Island to little seeming effect. But the danger of war and the dexterity of Hollywood's government work is rendered in a sly cinematic ambush. As planes touch down on a puddle-drenched runway, a lilting, whimsical music score accompanies each landing. Suddenly, uncued by the lulling soundtrack, a plane careens and crashes, a body is taken away, and a rainbow-lit burial follows.

The War Department/Warner Bros. symbiosis: newly commissioned Lt. Col. Jack L. Warner (*left*), producer Hal B. Wallis and location chief W. L. Guthrie ("in mufti"), and a quartet of Army Air Force colonels on the set of the color short *Men of the Sky* (July 1942). (Quigley Photo Archive/Georgetown University)

The weakness of the military mission, however, does not foreclose the generic mission. A narrative voice-over carefully explains the difference between the fighter pilot and the bomber pilot. Praising the "split-second judgement, inspiration, daring" of the former, Huston asserts that "a monument ought to be put up to that pre-war fraternity of high school speed maniacs, for out of their ranks our fighter pilots are largely drawn." But the heroic hierarchy becomes clear by comparison:

> The aerial pilot is a different breed than your fighter pilot. Where the fighter is reckless and inspired, the bomber pilot is responsible, determined. Because of the size and imponderability of his ship, there are no last minute decisions for him. And besides the big intricate costly piece of machinery that a heavy bomber is, he has the lives of six or eight others on his mind.

Report from the Aleutians is notable also for finally persuading the War Department that Hollywood knew whereof it spoke when it came to the moviegoing taste of the American public. At four reels, the film was too long to receive enthusiastic acceptance from exhibitors jealous of screen time and audiences impatient with overlong war films. The OWI wanted the film cut to two reels (approximately twenty minutes), the standard running time for a featurette. Unpersuaded, the military insisted on the four-reel version. In a letter of protest to Maj. Gen. Alexander Surles, chief of Army public relations, the OWI's Palmer Hoyt argued "we feel the purpose of war information would be better served if a large part of the public were able to see the 16-minute picture than if a small part of the public were able to see the full picture which runs approximately 45 minutes." His reasoning was impeccable, but the military was implacable. Released in long form, the film garnered lukewarm response and a mere 3,554 playdates.

Wyler's *The Memphis Belle,* an Army Signal Corps film following an

Hollywood auteurs in uniform *(shown left to right)*: Lt. Col. William Wyler, Lt. Col. Sy Bartlett, Maj. John Huston, and Col. Anatole Litvak during ceremonies at March Field, California. Huston and Litvak are being congratulated upon receiving the Legion of Merit. (Quigley Photo Archive/Georgetown University)

eponymous B-17 from the Eighth Air Force, is graced not only with the narrative unity of the bombing run but with a terrific dramatic hook: this is the twenty-fifth and final mission for the crew of the *Memphis Belle*. The best of the aerial combat reports, it is fraught with danger, mystery, and tension. The course of action mapped out in reality, the thematics lift off in documentary art.

The crew is introduced on the airfield, the mission explained on a blackboard, and a fast montage surveys the colorful insignias and feminine mascots that decorate the B-17 fuselages. Slowly, the heavy bomber takes off and soars over the fields of England, an island transformed into one "giant airfield." As the *Memphis Belle* gains altitude and closes in for formation, the camera sweeps the skies, catches the plexiglass reflections of clouds and planes, and tilts upward to display the formation's streaks in the cloudy, icy sky.

With the fortresses safely aloft and flying to their targets, the film's forward progress backtracks for an exegesis of the squadron's assignment. The bombing mission is a complicated and awesome undertaking that involves a thousand planes in three main groups, one of which is purely diversionary. A series of color illustrations (maps of continental Europe, colored arrows tracing the flight plan, figures indicating air defense, targets, and enemy fighters) explains the mission in meticulous detail. The intricate lesson in bombing tactics is impossible to master with a single viewing, but its purpose is not to teach but to impress, to insure that the spectator recognizes the coherence of the sortie and appreciates its wonderful, chessboard coordination. Like the crew, dodging flak, flying the bombing run, and firing at attacking fighters, homefront audiences discern a larger meaning in the isolated actions of the *Memphis Belle*. Not incidentally, the narrative voice-over insists upon the military nature and strategic import of the targets below: submarine pens, docks, armaments factories. As in the bombs-away sequence that climaxes *Air Force,* a shot/reverse-shot pattern locks in spectator identification: (1) bombardier looks in sights, (2) wide aerial view of target, and (3) back to bombardier in sights. The devastating rain of bombs then floats silently down, white puffs on a map.

The trip back to England is spectacular. As enemy planes fly into frame from all angles, point-of-view shots through the ring sights of 50-caliber machine guns render the perspective and capture the thrill of aerial sharpshooting. In a riveting slice of high aerial drama, a B–17 spirals upside down helplessly out of control. Two parachuting fig-

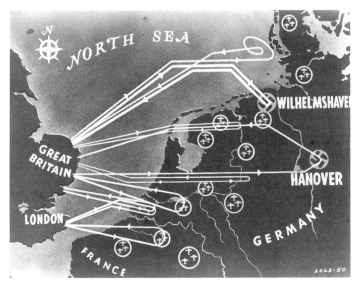

Mapping strategy: in bewildering detail an extended sequence plots the plan of attack in *The Memphis Belle* (1944). (Museum of Modern Art/Film Stills Archive)

ures pop out of the careening fortress; the breathless exclamations of the *Memphis Belle* crew ("get out of there guys!") over the interphone fill the soundtrack. (The interphone dialogue is a postproduction reconstruction. The racket of the engines and guns on board made sound-on-sound recording impossible. Wyler himself went partially deaf from the noise.)

After the action centerpiece, Wyler crosscuts to the second-unit work, to the parallel action of the men back at the airfield "sweating out the mission." The ground crews pace, play, and brood until, one by one, the planes come in for landings or—in the case of a few—do not come back. The director takes the Hawksian approach to filming flight (nothing is more exciting than a plane landing or taking off) and the Hitchcockian approach to suspense (a bomb that doesn't go off is better than a bomb that does). After a few torn and sputtering B-17s come in on a wing and a prayer, one of the very last planes to return is the *Memphis Belle,* "the one everybody is pulling for."

The Memphis Belle was wisely exploited as a commercial attraction in its own right, getting equal billing with "A" features and acclaim from exhibitors for its "unusual box office appeal." The film was well enough known to create its own real-life stars. In *Target Tokyo,* the combat report on the first superfortress mission over Japan, the narrator introduces some of the crew of the lead ship, including pilot Robert Morgan and bombardier Vince Evans. "Remember them?" prompts the voice of Ronald Reagan. "They were the pilot and bombardier who flew twenty-five missions over Germany in a B-17 called the *Memphis Belle.*"

Amidst all the steady navigation and coordinated flight plans of the Hollywood feature film and the military combat report, only one motion picture broke formation. Neither Warner Bros. nor the War Department produced so curious an air-minded artifact as Walt Disney's elaborate primer-cum-polemic *Victory Through Air Power* (1943). Based on Alexander P. de Seversky's popular book and dedicated to "Billy Mitchell and the gallant airmen of America," it argues for the forcefully applied use of air power, especially bombers, to blast the enemy into submission and smithereens. A remarkable, offbeat project, *Victory Through Air Power* is nothing less than a private studio memorandum telling the government how to wage war.

Seversky talks directly into the camera while animated vignettes

Airborne armageddon: Disney animation illustrates the prospect of homefront bombardment in *Victory Through Air Power* (1943). (Museum of Modern Art/Film Stills Archive)

in a melange of styles—cartoon caricature and realistic rendering—
illustrate aviation history and military tactics. Lent an offshore sophistication and professorial air by his Russian accent, Seversky is
very good on screen—passionate but not overbearing, complex but
lucid. He assaults the "outmoded military thinking" of the "earthbound mind," including tactical decisions being formulated by the
War Department at that very moment. On an illustrated map of Germany, a pulsating wheel symbolizes the power of Hitler's machine
and the tactical leverage granted to the enemy in land warfare. "As
long as we fight on the surface of the earth," argues Seversky, "Hitler
has all the advantages." In the Pacific theater also "some still cling
to the island by island approach," a tactic that raises the specter of
a costly war of attrition dragging on to 1948 and beyond. Seversky
looks piercingly into the camera and declares:

> As soon as the airplanes which are already on the drafting boards
> of all the warring nations take to the air, there will not be a single
> spot on the face of the earth immune from overhead attack. The
> enormous flying range and destructive power of these planes will
> transform the entire surface of our planet into a battlefield. The
> distinctions between soldiers and civilians will be erased. And I
> believe it is only a matter or time before we here in America will
> suffer our share of civilian casualties.

The official response to Seversky's dire warnings and unsolicited
stratagems was sullen. The government found turnabout unfair play.
Washington could tell Hollywood how to make movies, but Hollywood could not tell Washington how to wage war. OWI film analyst
Barbara Deming snidely put down "Seversky's own pet plan for winning the war" and wrote that, for all the animated creativity, the art
direction was "in the long run cheesy," the color "a bit sleazy," and
the end result "dubious." Audiences too were dubious, less because
of antipathy to the message than to the irregular tone (from whimsy
to vengeance) and the odd array of cinematic styles (from newsreel
to animation, from broad caricature to realistic portraiture). A box-
office report from a disgruntled exhibitor explains why *Victory
Through Air Power* remains one Walt Disney production not rereleased every seven years. "People went out saying it was the damnd-
est thing they ever saw and they didn't wait until it was over, either."
In fairness to Seversky, the stateside walkouts reflect less on the dramatic power of his screen message than its immediate pertinence.

Voices of authority: Alexander de Seversky, a prototype of
the war-born "expert," explains it all in *Victory Through Air
Power* (1943). (Museum of Modern Art/Film Stills Archive)

Under Disney sponsorship in American theaters, he was playing to
the wrong crowd. The prospect of imminent obliteration from the
sky was a portent that other populations, in other venues, had better
reason to heed.

Seversky did however articulate one universal truth of the Second
World War. Arguing from the general proposition, he introduced himself as the logical corollary: "And so warfare becomes everybody's
business. All of us must understand the strategy of war. No longer
should it be a mystery open only to military minds." That is, if modern war was "everybody's business," a mystery that all must understand, professional help was essential to full comprehension. The line
of argument in *Victory Through Air Power* hinges not on aerial bombardment but on Seversky himself. He is the prototype of "the
expert," a newly born and recurrent figure in wartime films. The calm,
knowing voice of the expert explains the complexities of modern war
and cushions the shock of the new. Sometimes cloaked in the dis-
embodied baritone of the off-camera commentator, just as often
speaking directly from the screen behind an ordered desk or in front
of maps and precision instruments, the expert clears the way through
a thicket of war-related information. (The expert is readily distin-

guishable from the teacher in that the expert imparts lessons his listeners attend to avidly.) In *The Memphis Belle* a squadron of flyers listen in dead earnest as their briefing officer outlines the mission. As the camera pans the rapt faces and intensive note taking, the commentator observes: "Not so long ago you were sitting like this in a college or high school classroom, not listening too hard, perhaps even a little sleepy. *But you listen here.*"

Close attention was being paid elsewhere as well. Few wartime experts gained a greater measure of cultural authority than the motion picture screen. Between 1941 and 1945 the medium whose guiding aesthetic was the invisible style, and whose standard business practice was to send messages through Western Union, committed itself to the flagrant transmission of cultural values. Hollywood wiped out the film memory of the Great War and conjured a unique mythos to serve and sustain the Great Struggle. In line with wartime necessity, the most specialized and urgent genre work was in the sky and, like the vessels in *Air Force* and *The Memphis Belle,* was as cinematically as aerodynamically sound.

CHAPTER **6** Properly
Directed
Hatred

In *Communiqué,* the in-house weekly of the Hollywood Writers Mobilization, Nelson Poynter was asked, "Is it true that the Office of War Information does not want pictures which will promote hatred of the Japanese and Nazis?" "No," replied the OWI's Hollywood chief. "Properly directed hatred is of vital importance to the war effort." Poynter helpfully elaborated:

> The Office of War Information wishes only to insure that hatred will not be directed either at Hitler, Mussolini, Tojo or a small group of Fascist leaders as personalized enemies on the one hand, or at the whole German, Japanese, or Italian people on the other hand. Hatred of the militaristic *system* which governs the Axis countries and of those responsible for its furtherance definitely should be promoted.

The official promotion of a deadly sin was not to be entered into without misgivings. Having assumed moral superiority to the enemy, America could not wholeheartedly embrace his Big Lies and loathsome bigotries. After complaints about unduly venomous lyrics and choreography, Warner Bros. felt obliged to reshoot the grand finale for Irving Berlin's patriotic musical *This Is the Army* (1943). The original closing was a Berlin number called "Dressed Up to Kill" in which a choral multitude of grim-faced soldiers sing out bloody murder and point bayonets at the camera. Upon reflection the studio allowed that the performance was "not symbolic of the humane manner in which the United States has waged war" and substituted a revamped version called "Dressed Up to Win." In a thoughtful paper delivered to the fall 1942 meeting of the Society of Motion Picture Engineers, John G. Bradley of the National Archives argued that Americans might well "cringe at the thought of organized and propagandized hate." He continued: "Organized love of country? That doesn't sound so bad. Righteous anger organized for action? That is understandable. But organized hate? That is a hard concept even to put down on paper."

Harder still to put up on the screen. The OWI wanted an ideology not an individual to be the Hollywood villain, a policy good in theory but bad as theater. On stage and in film, a magnetic villain—the hissable embodiment of evil, the vestibule for audience hatred—is more charismatically compelling than a considered analysis of totalitarian structure. Rather than delving into the banality of evil, *The North Star* (1943) opts for Nazi doctors sucking Russian children dry to supply blood transfusions for wounded German soldiers. Instead of decrying the hypocrisy of Japan's Co-Prosperity Sphere, *The Fighting Seabees* (1944) has John Wayne scream about "Tojo's bug-eyed monkeys."

The OWI harbored a deep suspicion of the American tendency to perceive political problems in personal terms. To make the lone dictator the embodiment of all that was evil in the enemy, to hold him alone solely responsible for the system and nation, risked the abatement of ardor if the human representative happened to get wiped out. For official purposes, World War II was not about bad guys like Hitler and Hirohito but a bad body politic. "Americans, the theory is, will be better haters—and thus better fighters and workers—if they are not beclouded with the false idea that the enemy is a bunch of poor misguided people, who deserve more pity than bullets and bombs," explained *Variety*. "In the event that Hitler should die or be killed, Americans must not be led to believe their job is over."

Just as the OWI doted on collective villainy, it preferred group heroism. An OWI film analyst praised the lately sensitized *This Is the Army* because of "the representation the film gives of the American soldier, the unnamed soldier, of whom there are hundreds in the cast.

This composite soldier is, against the competition of those of his comrades who do individual stunts, and against the competition of Hollywood actors in blazing technicolor, the star of the show. And that is as it should be." The chorus, not the matinee idol, was supposed to take center stage.

On a deeper level, the OWI distinctions dodged the thorny question of the relationship between the totalitarian system and the inhabitants who were either (1) under its heel or (2) wearing the boots. Taking the first option, *The Hitler Gang* (1944) portrayed the rise of the Third Reich as a mobsterlike usurpation of power. The Society for the Prevention of World War III, a group whose advisory council included author William L. Shirer and the Great War propagandist George Creel, scorned the notion of a duped demos. In the words of the so-far-successful society:

> We consider *The Hitler Gang* not only a bad picture but a very dangerous one. Germany—not only the Hitler gang—has occupied and oppressed most of the European continent. Millions of German soldiers are still fighting like lions. The German people are still united behind its Führer—and Hollywood dares to show us this childlike picture of "a gang that stole a nation."

Noting the difficulties inherent in explaining the difference between Nazis and Germans, *Variety* wondered whether the latter should be portrayed "either as villains, dupes, or innocent bystanders in the greatest slaughter in history."

The proper direction of hatred was a tactical consideration; the quality of hatred and the means to incite it were aesthetic problems. Recent experience set a poor precedent. The anti-Hun hysteria and carefree jingoism of the Creel Committee had left a strong residual cynicism about official regimentations of patriotic fervor. What other warring nation would have sanctioned a satire on the order of Preston Sturges's *Hail the Conquering Hero* (1944), a free-for-all farce that scathingly punctured the pomposity of homefront flag-waving? The present war called for a more mature and intelligent appreciation of the enemy, the nature of modern warfare, and the enormous sacrifices required of all.

The realization preceded its fulfillment. In the early days of the war, with the government offering little practical advice and the industry in unfamiliar waters, no coherent strategy guided the temper of the Hollywood feature film. The new agenda for popular entertain-

"Not only a bad picture but a dangerous one": Robert Weston played der Führer as a salacious mobster in Paramount's *The Hitler Gang* (1944).

ment raised vexatious questions: Did the celebration of American prowess and industrial strength inadvertently breed a dangerous over-confidence? Did footage of enemy atrocities and depredations inspire or disgust the homefront? What was the best way to portray the Nazis on screen—as goosestepping buffoons or calculating supermen? A misstep on either side left Hollywood open to the most dreaded terms of wartime opprobrium: *complacency* (if too light) or *defeatism* (if too heavy).

As a breach of taste and tactics, the lampoon-the-*übermensch* model quickly disqualified itself. In cartoons or comedy shorts, the triviality of the form granted the license to exaggerate. To let loose and spray a raspberry in der Führer's face or to launch a loony send-up of the Axis powers (and the top of the bill) in *Tokio Jokio* and *Confusions of a Nutzy Spy* was perfectly permissible and violently hilarious in a six-minute format. Likewise, low budgeters took the low road with impunity. Hal Roach's 44-minute quickie *The Devil with Hitler* (1942) concocts a Dantesque duel between the Third Reich's overlord and the ruler of the netherworld (with the former edging out the latter in venality); a sequel, *That Nazty Nuisance* (1943), features Hitler, Mussolini, and the Japanese dictator "Suki Yaki" shipwrecked on the mythical land of "No-room." Also beneath contempt were the unintentional comedies, such as the below Poverty Row production *Hitler—Dead or Alive* (1942), wherein three paroled convicts from Alcatraz try to collect on a businessman's $1 million offer for the head of der Führer.

Higher up the production line, standards were tougher. In *The Wife Takes a Flyer* (1942), a madcap frolic through Nazi-occupied Holland with topliners Franchot Tone and Joan Bennett slapsticking it to heil-Hitlering straight men, comic relief exceeded the bounds of wartime propriety. Within the more elaborate and respectable enterprise of the "A" picture, the indecency of playing the Nazis for laughs, joshing about concentration camps, and staging pratfalls for the Gestapo struck the OWI, sundry commentators, and not a few spectators as frivolous and shameful. The more serious form needed to take Fascism more seriously.

Significantly, Hollywood's two enduring anti-Nazi satires, Charlie Chaplin's *The Great Dictator* (1940) and Ernst Lubitsch's *To Be or Not To Be* (1942), were prewar concepts. Both take a qualified laugh line on the Nazis, poking fun at the strutting pomposity of the humorless leaders while insisting on a high seriousness in ultimate intention. *The Great Dictator* escaped critical misfortune through good timing; *To Be or Not To Be* had the bad luck to arrive punctually at the worst possible moment. Always a film category unto himself, Chaplin turned to geopolitical subject matter too early to run afoul of the serious demeanor of America at war. Released October 15, 1940, *The Great Dictator* could be laughed at with disinterested appreciation—even if the unsettling sight of the global pop icon suited up as his evil doppelgänger and the sounds of the suddenly preachy Tramp tended to foreclose the comedy. Released in March 1942, *To Be or Not To Be* landed directly on the cultural fault line that broke open in December 1941. Over the long haul Lubitsch's film has weathered time better than Chaplin's, but in early 1942 its elegant style and two-toned manner was last season's fashion.

To Be or Not To Be came to market two months after the death of star Carole Lombard and amidst humiliating news of American re-treats in the Pacific. Its reception then (and since) well reflects how laughter flows most freely from a secure vantage. A sly black comedy about acting, adultery, and the invasion of Poland, Lubitsch's classic-in-retrospect was emphatically not the kind of screen treatment of the enemy that was suited to the moment. The plot miscasts the Nazis as sustained comic foils in a literal theater of war. The famous actor Joseph Tura (Jack Benny) is the ham playing Hamlet while his actress wife Maria (Lombard) plays backstage with a dashing young pilot (Robert Stack). When Nazi tanks barrel into the theatrical world, the troupe improvises an elaborate scheme of disguise and decep-tion, double dealing and double entendre. Tura impersonates a Nazi commandant ("So they call me 'Concentration Camp' Erhardt," chuckles the flattered lunkhead), and Mrs. Tura is patriotically willing to represent Polish culture to the Nazis but only "in a more suitable dress." The gags are topnotch and telling. A Hitler lookalike disposes of troublesome Nazis through the witty expedient of ordering them out of an airplane. Without hesitation, the soldiers yell "Heil!," salute, and jump.

Lubitsch's Nazis are not just clods but vandals. Amid the comedy is a culture in ruins. Soundstage shots of demolished storefronts and the wreckage of a once-bustling theater render the artist's horror at the destruction of the arts. But if the ill-mannered intrusion of the Nazis into a smartly sophisticated comedy of manners means the show can not go on and *Hamlet* is not to be, *To Be or Not To Be* can be. Lubitsch wanted to demonstrate that during wartime the play is *not* the thing—and yet to continue playing by the prewar rules of screen comedy.

What the Nazis did to Poland, wartime critics did to Lubitsch. A fiery *New York Times* editorial by Lyman Beecher Stowe blasted the film: "I say that people who present to us on the screen or otherwise, a fool's paradise, however innocently, are as dangerous as the most dangerous Fifth Columnist." Melchior Lengyel, who wrote the story on which *To Be or Not To Be* was based, replied that "Nazis and Fascists are essentially humorless creatures," and thus the comedian was uniquely equipped to puncture their poise. Better to manhandle the master race with laughter and ridicule, argued Lengyel, than to "put wind into the Nazis' sails by saturating the public with the im-pression of their power and invincibility." But wit, irony, black hu-mor, even the choice of so painfully equivocal a Shakespearian in-

Lampooning the Nazis: Carole Lombard, Sig Rumann, and Hitler lookalike Tom Dugan in Ernst Lubitsch's ill-timed comedy of manners, *To Be or Not To Be* (1942). (Museum of Modern Art/Film Stills Archive)

terrogative, was out of tune with a time that knew not only the question but the answer.

The other famous, though not as long-lived, marker of the initial confusion over how to play the Nazis for comedy is Leo McCarey's *Once Upon a Honeymoon* (1942), an uneven (not to say bizarre) tradeoff between humorous and serious business. Like Lubitsch, McCarey vaults abruptly from 1930s screwball comedy, the genre of the past, to wartime melodrama, the genre of the present. Upon entry into uncharted generic territory, his sense of direction deserts him.

The plot follows the invasive course of Baron von Luber (Walter Slezak, Hollywood's perennial Nazi autocrat) and his American wife, former burlesque showgirl Katie O'Hara (Ginger Rogers), who is operating under an assumed name and hightone accent. Radio broadcaster Patrick O'Toole (Cary Grant) knows the baron is a Nazi agent provocateur and first-rate fifth columnist because whenever the newlyweds visit a European country—Austria, Czechoslovakia, Poland, and so on—it immediately succumbs to Nazi domination.

GRANT: I've been getting my war news by following your honeymoon trail. Tell me, where did the Baron plan on taking you from here?

ROGERS: To Norway, where we'll be houseguests of the Quislings. Ever hear of them?

Cary and Ginger flirt and crack wise (he takes her measurements in a cutesy dress-fitting scene; she outdrinks him in a slurring tête-à-tête), but the periodic intrusions of actual newsreel footage—the Wehrmacht storming through the streets of Vienna; Ufa clips of the Nazis in Paris (including the jarring low-angle shot of Hitler towering victoriously over Paris, dwarfing even the Eiffel Tower in backframe)—flattens any screwball effervescence. At one point, McCarey seems to know the mixture has fizzled. Two uniformed SS men interrupt a whimsical exchange between Grant and Rogers in a bombed-out warehouse in Warsaw. Walking over a pile of bricks, one of the SS men stumbles and falls on his ass. The pratfall timing is off; the clowning is overlong. After his fellow goosestepper berates him in (untranslated) German, Grant stands up and says, "Look, fella, he's right. Don't keep doing that—that isn't funny."

Less funny still, the two Gestapo cutups then discover a "Juden"-stamped passport in Ginger's possession (she having magnanimously traded her American passport to a Jewish chambermaid and her two children). Taken into Nazi custody ("Now they think we're Jewish—this could be serious!"), the couple are placed in a concentration camp. The camp scene, in which Grant's brightly lit sparkle and Rogers's backlit tresses shimmer among the huddled and bearded inmates, is foggy and forlorn. Obviously, narrative dexterity will save hero and heroine, but what, Grant inquires (gesturing around him), about these other people in the camp? The next morning, Grant and Rogers confront two doors. Behind one, Nazi doctors perform sterilization procedures. At the last minute, the couple are directed away from the surgical chamber and through the second door, where awaits an American counsel. The reprieved and relieved pair, having escaped infertility or worse, breathlessly embrace him.

The failure to appreciate the humor in the comic antics and close shaves in *Once Upon a Honeymoon* is not a product of historical hindsight. "There are some very strong feelings and subjects covered in the plot," wrote the OWI film analyst, "particularly the heavy tragedy of the Jewish concentration camp into which we are thrust after a

Misfired screwball comedy: Cary Grant and Ginger Rogers playing
for laughs in Leo McCarey's *Once Upon a Honeymoon* (1942).

comedy scene, and one doesn't have time to assimilate the implications of the scene in order to realize its import." An exhibitor's report
spoke to the impact of current events on comedy: "All depends on
whether the war news puts the public in the mood for seeing the
Nazis triumphed over by Ginger Rogers and Cary Grant being coy
and none too bright."

Discordant though the tone shifts in *The Great Dictator, To Be or
Not To Be,* and *Once Upon a Honeymoon* may be, the comedies
squarely face the music in one sense. Unlike the bulk of anti-Nazi
melodramas and thrillers, they present the Jews as the Nazi's chosen
victims. Chaplin's adorable everyman is no longer just anybody; he
is a persecuted Jew. Lubitsch gives a Jewish extra (played by rabbin-
ically typed character actor Felix Bressart) the chance to recite the
"Hath not a Jew eyes?" speech from *The Merchant of Venice,* and
McCarey depicts the Nuremberg laws, deportation, incarceration,
and the prospect of forced sterilization. Weighed against the comedies, wartime melodramas are all too discreet on the Jewish question.

In an influential front-page editorial in *Variety,* Professor Robert

Gessner, chairman of the Department of Motion Pictures at New York University and a former Warner Bros. scriptwriter, launched a broadside that helped squelch the Nazi-filled funfests. "The ugly fact is that we are in danger of losing the war because the American public is not awake to the menace of Fascism," asserted Gessner. "We know that the Nazis are not Keystone Kops. This war is no Mack Sennett chase. So why make it one on celluloid? . . . We must give the Gestapo the respect that we would give a rattlesnake." John Grierson, Canadian film commissioner and overseer of the documentary *World in Action* series, agreed, advising Hollywood to explain "perhaps grimly at times, that the enemy is a bitter foe and that we must toughen up and fight him with every available weapon."

Yet the reptilian adversary must not be too slippery and invincible else foster defeatism. Ultimately, the Nazis had to be defanged. In the British import *Forty-Ninth Parallel* (1941), released stateside by Columbia as *The Invaders,* a band of escaped Nazis in Canada demonstrate a disconcerting ability to outfox the entire Canadian Mounted Police force. Lowell Mellett, who read Professor Gessner's article and agreed that "there's nothing funny about the Nazis, the Gestapo, or the Axis," derailed a proposed American-set remake of *Forty-Ninth Parallel* with the observation that the film was "too much in the hokum superman idiom"—that is, too much like the Nazis' own self-image.

Better though to incur criticism for overseriousness than for undervigilance and to go overboard in portrayals of the Nazis as too superior rather than too silly. In Alfred Hitchcock's adaptation of John Steinbeck's *Lifeboat* (1944), the director proves equal to the challenge of staging a feature-length motion picture within a bathtub's worth of screen space, but the lone Nazi aboard (Walter Slezak again) is more resourceful and determined than any of the contentious Allied ballast. Likewise, in the well-named *The Master Race* (1944) one Nazi agent single-handedly subverts the American supervision of a liberated French village and, upon capture, fearlessly faces a firing squad.

By contrast, Fascist Italians were hapless understudies who possessed none of the threatening élan and menacing aptitude of the Teutonic Nazis. Two factors accounted for the conspicuous belittlement of the second element in the Axis triumvirate. First, the mythos of Italian prowess on the battlefield was not imposing. Darryl F. Zanuck's combat report *At the Front in North Africa* (March 1943) takes a cheap but revealing shot at defeated Italian forces. An intertitle reads: "Captured Italian paratroopers seem very depressed at being safely out of the war." Jump cut to: shots of joyous Italian POWs, thrilled to be out of the battle and secure in American hands, turning somersaults in the desert sand. Second, the dual power of Italian-Americans in the New Deal coalition and at the box-office window caused the OWI and Hollywood to tread lightly on Mediterranean sensibilities. Unwilling to affront stateside Americans who bristled at the epithet "Eye-tie," the Hays Office deleted anti-Italian slurs from the British import *In Which We Serve* (1942).

The Axis alignment in *Sahara* (1943) registers the difference between warm-blooded redeemable Italians and cold-blooded degenerate Germans. The sandswept combat film sets the sympathetic Italian POW Guisseppe (played by ethnic chameleon J. Carrol Naish) against a malevolent *übermensch* who stabs him, quite literally, in the back. As a makeshift squad of United Nations fighters trudges across the North African desert, Guisseppe metamorphoses smoothly from a sniveling enemy into a self-sacrificing ally. Over a report on OWI guidelines on enemy portrayals, a 1942 *Variety* headline expressed the imbalance: "Hollywood Cued on Hitler and Hirohito, but Doesn't Even Bother with Musso." Il Duce himself was mainly a figure for ripe ridicule, not the fear and respect grudgingly allowed his German sponsor. "I think Hitler is God and Mussolini is only his prophet," opines a smirking Guisseppe in *Sahara*. Also, for sheer strutting caricature, it was hard to surpass Mussolini's own newsreel appearances.

Eventually the government and the motion picture industry arrived at an ideal that mediated between Gestapo bozo and invincible *übermensch*, that portrayed the enormity of the menace without discouraging resistance. An enemy portrayal might be laced with comic relief, but as RKO producer David Hempstead said, "that doesn't mean we will make fools of our enemies or underrate their cleverness." To Hempstead's way of thinking, good drama dovetailed with patriotic vigilance anyway. "No Nazi or Jap will be portrayed as a comic figure for, as well as being dangerous, that would only provide a hero or heroine with windmills against which to battle, and would kill dramatic impact."

There was never any monolithic master plan—no OWI directive with the force of law, no industry memo that set out unbreachable guidelines. It was a fine line, one that the government sometimes

The weak link in the Axis triad: an Allied soldier (Rex Ingram) has the hapless Italian enemy (J. Carrol Naish) well in hand in *Sahara* (1943).

traced vaguely, one that the industry sometimes crossed over. But by about 1943 it was something like an official line. It said that war is a serious business where people you love die, where you sacrifice your personal desires for the nation's good, where the enemy is deadly not dumb, where there is true glory but where victory exacts a price. *Casablanca, Mrs. Miniver, Air Force, Since You Went Away, Pride of the Marines,* and *They Were Expendable*—the most popular and respected films of the era—walk it steadily.

FACING THE JAPANESE

The Japanese were, in the glib phrase of the day, hordes of a different color. Though the gallery of yellow-peril imagery—inscrutable orientals, sinister warlords, two-faced servants—was ready-made for wartime propaganda, nothing, not even racism, was simple any longer. Just as portraits of the Nazi balanced due respect with ultimate triumph, portraits of the Japanese modulated racist contempt with xenophobic caution. Moreover, the racism had to be particularized and focused on Japan alone. Heretofore in the American imagination Asian peoples were an indistinguishable swarm of almond-eyed, tallow-skinned multitudes. With China a crucial ally in the Pacific, degrees of orientalism needed to be cataloged and highlighted. (In the 1930s, Pearl Buck's novels and the MGM adaptation of *The Good Earth* (1937) had sketched the outlines of intra-Asian difference by sympathetically portraying an earthy Chinese peasantry and planting the idea that not all yellow men were yellow menaces.)

John Dower's landmark study, *War without Mercy: Race and Power in the Pacific War, 1941–1945,* tracks the images projected onto the Japanese. Basically, Americans dehumanized the Pacific enemy in three schizophrenic ways: he was a fearsome monster, a contemptible insect, and sometimes both at once. Separately or together, the projections provoked an impulse toward utter extermination. In producer Walter Wanger's *Gung Ho!* (1943), the story of Col. Evan Carlson's Makin Island Raiders, the mission of the knife-wielding marines is to "kill Japs" and wipe every one from the island. The men execute mission and enemy in explicit detail, garroting, stabbing, and shooting with a joy and vividness granted special dispensation by the Code. In an instructional vignette, three apparently defeated Japanese soldiers walk up a dirt road waving a white flag. "I feel like riddling them anyway," says a stern machinegunner. His companion, a former minister of the gospel, does the Christian thing and walks out to accept their surrender. The Japanese, in a jujitsu-like sneak attack, conjure up a concealed machine gun and cut down the trusting GI. Violations of the Geneva Convention by the Japanese included the shooting of defenseless parachuters (*Flying Tigers, Air Force*), murdering POWs (*Jack London, The Purple Heart*), bombing orphans (*Bataan, God Is My Co-Pilot*); attacking clearly marked Red Cross facilities (*The Battle of Midway, The Story of Dr. Wassell*); and beating, raping, and killing women (*Behind the Rising Sun, China Sky,* and *Dragon Seed*). Despite the provocations, epithets and screen dialogue had to remain discreet. In a conventional circumlocution, the Japanese are referred to as "sons of . . . heaven."

Fire—not firepower—best suited the pestilence. The searing pain and cleansing scourge of the flamethrower was a resonant method of eradication. Incinerated in pillboxes, fried in caves, and shot down with cold-blooded deliberation, the Japanese soldier was extermi-

nated with a grim determination not even the supercilious Nazis inspired. In *Guadalcanal Diary* (1943) a squad of Japanese soldiers re-
sists an American assault from inside a cave. The marines concoct a
gasoline bomb to swing into the interior and roast the occupants.
Prior to the toss inside, a reverse shot shows the Japanese squad
huddled together (the better to visualize a cremation whose explicitness remains off-screen).

The most notorious cinematic incitement to anti-Japanese sentiment was the independently produced documentary *Ravaged Earth*
(1942), a record of the Japanese takeover of China. Filmed in 16mm
by Mark L. Moody, "a businessman with twenty-three years of experience in China," the film puts forth its amateur standing as an
argument for authenticity. Introduced by newsman Knox Manning,
the commentary makes truth (not technique) the proffered product:

> [Mark L. Moody] is not a professional cameraman as you will per-
> haps agree as you view this picture. But the very lack of a profes-
> sional touch is eloquent testimony to the sincerity of this film. As
> you see *Ravaged Earth*, we hope that you'll be kind enough to weigh
> the frankness of the subject against any lack of professional touch
> in production.

Ravaged Earth is certainly unvarnished. Grainy, blurry, and pad-
ded with stock newsreel footage, it is nonetheless a persuasive indictment of the brutality of the Imperial Japanese Army in Shanghai.
The racial taxonomy follows the pattern of enlightened Allied thinking. The Chinese are peaceful, civilized, and gentle; the Japanese are
warlike, feudal, and brutal. The atrocity footage, unprecedented in
its time, shows grisly executions, decomposed and charred corpses,
and the remains of a young man crucified alive. A horror tour through
a hospital ward forces a photographic confrontation with the cut
bodies of women and children sliced by Samurai swords, the frames
freezing on the gaping wounds of nearly severed limbs and heads.

Because Americans needed all too little encouragement in the way
of directed hatred against the Japanese, the OWI was leery of atrocity
pictures and hysterical slurs against the "mad brood of Japan." Derogatory reference or portrayal of Emperor Hirohito was forbidden
so "as not to malign religion and thus add to Japanese fanaticism"—
a warning ignored by Columbia's cartoon *Song of Victory* (1942),
which caricatured Hirohito as a baying hyena. In a memo cautioning
United Artists on *Blood on the Sun*, Ulric Bell stated: "The Japanese

Emperor should be dealt with in indirect fashion only—as a tool of Japanese militarists, not as a personal heavy." The OWI was apprehensive about anti-Japanese films not only because of well-remembered embarrassments over Great War excesses but because of a fear of enemy retaliation on Allied POWs. "The first and only request made by the U.S. government in the war so far [1943]," said Luigi Luraschi, head of the censorship department at Paramount, "was the one concerning pictures with Jap atrocity angles which, it was pointed out, might result in harmful treatment of U.S. servicemen and civilians in Jap prison camps."

A shift in atrocity-related policy came about in January 1944 when the government revealed gruesome details of the torture of American prisoners on Bataan in 1942. The news set off renewed waves of anti-Japanese hatred and signaled a surge in the aesthetics of hate. To reinvigorate flagging interest in the Pacific war and to deter complacency, atrocity material was approved if not tacitly encouraged by both the OWI and the War Department. "There will be no trouble [with atrocity scenes]," a War Department directive informed the industry, "so long as the studios use reason and don't go hog wild." Although the emperor was still supposed to remain sacrosanct, Robert E. Sherwood, head of the overseas branch of the OWI, took the same line and officially lifted the ban on atrocity films on January 31, 1944. "We assume motion picture studios will confine themselves to atrocities officially reported," Sherwood announced. He added the caveat: "Intelligent and convincing use of atrocity material will be useful . . . as a means of keeping alive understanding of our enemy and the will to defeat him. Please note, however, the words 'intelligent' and 'convincing.' Our purposes abroad will not repeat not be served by mere horror material that is beyond the bounds of credibility."

The hate revival spurred the box office of anti-Japanese films fortunate enough to be already in the pipeline. RKO's *Behind the Rising Sun* and Universal's *Gung Ho!* (both 1943) got predictable lifts, while 20th Century-Fox rushed *The Purple Heart* (1944) into release; Warner Bros., lucking out again, played up *Destination Tokyo* (1943). *Ravaged Earth* was best positioned. "This is *not* a Hollywood production," crowed the made-to-order ad campaign for the revitalized documentary, which aimed special appeals at exhibitors in the wake of the Bataan revelations: "Flash! Cash in now! This Is the Only Actual Japanese Atrocity Picture in America Today Actually Filmed at the

Scenes of the Action!" A more unlikely beneficiary was the bio-pic *Jack London* (1943), in which surprising parallels to wartime America unfold during the life of the onetime war correspondent covering the 1904–1905 Russo-Japanese war, "the first American to know the horror of a Jap detention camp!"

Depictions of the Japanese on screen were downright austere when viewed against advertising and publicity campaigns. Taglines and florid one-sheets catered to the lowest racist instincts. In the ads for *Behind the Rising Sun,* buck-toothed, nearsighted, apelike creatures hover tumescently over semiclad maidens. "Jap brutes manhandling helpless women—by official proclamation!" panted the boldfaced copy. "See why the villainous Japs have simply got to be *exterminated!*" The Alan Ladd vehicle *China* (1943) promised "the screen's No. 1 Man blasting the Japs for what they do to women. . . . Paramount is first to bring you a truly great story of the torture of this valiant land and its defenseless womanhood—and what a Yankee Ladd did about it!" A lobby display for *Betrayal from the East* featured a neon box-office mount advertising a dart game with Hirohito's head as the target and an invitation to "Slap the Jap."

Hollywood's Japanese monsters from the id are at once perversely fascinating and cringingly unwatchable. The formats designed for unbridled exaggeration—cartoons, one-sheets, lobby displays, and admats—made the worst of the opportunity. Yet the medium of cinema, itself so dependent on stereotype and caricature, also lends humanity and individuation. To follow a character and frame him, to provide him point of view and celluloid projection, to behold even an enemy can bequeath identification, validation, and sympathy. The extended running times of *Behind the Rising Sun, The Purple Heart, Blood on the Sun,* and *Betrayal from the East* cannot sustain the malignancy promised by the advertising. Seldom then was the Japanese enemy given an identifiable face, proper name, or prolonged reaction shot (Richard Loo always excepted). The two films that spend the most screen time in a Japanese milieu, *Behind the Rising Sun* and *Blood on the Sun,* each feature sympathetic Japanese characters, one of whom heroically dies. "This stand may arouse criticism from those who hold that all Japs, without exception, are evil," commented the *Hollywood Reporter* in a review of *Behind the Rising Sun* that offered a sensible perspective and germane analogy: "Such controversy can be likened to that which swept America about the Huns in World War I." In *Dragon Seed* (1944) the Japanese invaders who pillage a peaceful

Chinese village are bestial, but their actions do not justify a commensurate response. A kindly white-haired farmer (Walter Huston) flinches in horror when he beholds his guerrilla son heartlessly stick a blade into a surrendering Japanese soldier. "Must we too become as beasts?" he asks his wife during a bedside conversation. "Tonight I learned that men kill differently. I saw our third son with his knife and he came back into this house and picked up food and ate it with the blood still upon his hands. I saw that it's wrong."

The veiled humanity of the enemy was the subsurface and inadvertent message of *First Yank into Tokyo* (1945), the weirdest of the anti-Japanese films in plotline and eyeline. Released a month after Hiroshima and hastily brought up to date with bracketing by Pathé newsreel clips, the film fires off a headache-inducing constellation of conflicting meanings: racism and tolerance, narrative suppression and cinematic liberation, racial repulsion and erotic attraction. To rescue an imprisoned engineer holding vital military information, the War Department hatches a scheme to infiltrate a concentration camp on the outskirts of Tokyo. American pilot Major Ross (Tom Neal, the two-faced Taro from *Behind the Rising Sun*) volunteers to undergo radical and irreversible cosmetic surgery to turn his features Japanese. Thinking his beloved has been killed on Bataan, he has nothing to live for as a Caucasian and seeks only revenge. (The simple expedient of recruiting a Japanese-American for the mission never occurs to anybody, though a line of dialogue mentions that the major's fluency in the Japanese language and facility with native customs has been approvingly authenticated by a "Japanese-American Review Board.") Visually an enemy Japanese, emotionally an American, the madeover actor Neal is the focus of identification for spectators who must overlook his Japanese exterior to apprehend the kinsman within. Throughout, the spectator knows what neither Japanese enemy nor Allied friend gleans upon first gaze: that the face is a mask concealing the true self. Aided by a courageous Korean (Chinese-American character actor Keye Luke), who dons a mask of his own by playing a servile and dimwitted servant to deceive the racist Japanese guardsmen, Neal gains a position inside the POW camp. His prewar former college roommate (Richard Loo) happens to preside over the compound that also confines his former girlfriend (Barbara Hale), now a nurse in the camp's sick ward. Neither recognizes him, and both treat him as a subhuman—the commander for reasons of military hierarchy, the white American woman for reasons of sexual and racial hierarchy. When Neal finally unveils himself to his old love, she overcomes visceral repulsion and embraces him. Tragically, though, the outer facade of Japanese-ness dooms the all-American lovers. After rescuing his girlfriend, Neal decides to die heroically rather than live life inside a freakish frame. Race ultimately faces down romance in *First Yank into Tokyo,* a film that dramatizes the mutability of race and the endurance of romance.

AMERICANS ALL

The projection of hatred without matched a rejection of hatred within. Between 1941 and 1945 the long-standing wars at home over class, ethnicity, religion, and race were negotiated, curtailed, and denied. In official government posters and proclamations, "Americans All" closed ranks. The native melting pot, a harmonious blend of ethnic flavors and class elements, was the staple fare for all parts of the staple program. The rough egalitarianism of the military and the universality of the draft made the depiction credible; the need to unify a pluralistic and contentious people made it urgent. That the American strength-in-heterogeneity was an instant rebuff to Master Race eugenics lent the trope resonance and depth. The hyphenated Americans who got the wittiest lines, most extended screen time, and best odds for end-reel survival tended to be prominent in assimilationist success and domestic box-office influence—Irish, Italians, and Jews. But with an inclusiveness remarkable for its time, more exotic and heretofore invisible peoples—Hispanics, Asians, Native Americans, and blacks—also appear, and not always as expendable tokens.

The melting pot was the insistent theme of the combat film—fictional and documentary, ground and air. Indeed the hate-mongering *Gung Ho!* can do double duty as a declaration of brotherly love. So venomous toward the Japanese enemy, it purrs good-naturedly at a mélange of divergent ethnicities and sensibilities. A recruitment sequence efficiently introduces the calibrated quotient of Irish brogues and Southern drawls, Mediterranean flavors and Yankee airs. Dedicated to expunging every "Jap" from Makin Island, Carlson's Raiders nonetheless function as a model of OWI tolerance. Since the commanding officer (Randolph Scott) wants men who fight with the precision of "a harmonious machine," he orders his soldiers to "cast out all prejudices—racial, religious, and every other kind."

Allied intentions: the all-American combat unit welcomes Filipino membership in MGM's *Bataan* (1943).

The film helped make its title part of the language, but in 1943 it was an injunction to "work together," not a cry of homicidal enthusiasm.

The sole personal prejudice not only tolerated but sanctioned was against the unbeliever. There were no atheists in Hollywood's foxholes. Divine copilots, repentant sinners, and clumsy but heartfelt prayers spread the word that a quiet devotion to generic religiosity infused Americans All. Being in tighter with the ecclesiastical Production Code, Roman Catholics were granted special indulgence, but denominational differences and theological disputations melted away in the heat of battle. In twenty economical seconds, *Guadalcanal Diary* preached the ecumenical lesson that became holy writ for wartime cinema. The camera settles in on the deck of a transport ship in the Pacific. A religious service is in progress, packed with devout marines singing "Rock of Ages." The seemingly Protestant service is presided over by a Roman Catholic priest in full vestments, filling in for his sick Protestant colleague. Cut to a medium shot of two marines in the congregation who deliver the following exchange:

FIRST MARINE: Gee, Sammy, you sing pretty good.
SECOND MARINE: I should. My father was a cantor.

Pride of the Marines made the same point with the symbols decorating the machine gun of its Judeo-Christian heroes: a Star of David and a shamrock.

The open-armed embrace of the family of man stretched beyond American borders. Determined by theater of operation and the desire to cement Allied unity, offshore nationalities were wedged into the American combat team. Latins, Chinese, Russians, and Filipinos served alongside Midwest farmers and Brooklyn Dodger fans. Always, the boys from the plains and the peasants from the valley discover they have more than anti-Fascism in common.

Education in geography and physiognomy helped make the correct international connections. Because slanted eyes might send out crossed signals, Hollywood taught Americans to keep their yellow perils straight. Chinese and Chinese-Americans were distinguished from Japanese, and (eventually) Japanese-Americans were distinguished from Japanese enemies. Shortly after Pearl Harbor, *Life* ran

Judeo-Christianity in action: ecumenical buddies Al Schmid (John Garfield, *right*) Johnny Rivers (Anthony Caruso, *center*), and Lee Diamond (Dane Clark, *left*) in *Pride of the Marines* (1945).

an instructional spread headlined "How to Tell Japs from the Chinese." "U.S. citizens have been demonstrating a distressing ignorance on the delicate question of how to tell a Chinese from a Jap," reported the photo magazine of record. "To dispel some of the confusion" and having adduced a "rule of thumb from the anthropometric conformations that distinguish friendly Chinese from enemy alien Japs," *Life* printed mug shots of representative models of the no-longer-lookalike races. With arrows and helpful asides ("higher bridge" / "higher nose"), points on the proboscis pitted "the rational calm of tolerant realists" against the "humorless intensity of ruthless mystics."

The screen underscored the lessons of *Life*. In Sam Goldwyn's *They Got Me Covered* (1942), Bob Hope dials a phone number at random and pretends to report a kidnapping to the FBI. On the other end of the line is a grinning Chinese who babbles, "I no kidnap nobody. Only wash laundry. FBI? You want Japanese—me Chinese. Hundred percent American!" In *Mr. Blabbermouth* (August 1942), an MGM-produced Victory film attacking rumor mongers, an Asian chef alleviates any ethnic doubts by wearing a sign on his hat reading, "I am a Chinese American." From such small favors, the OWI took great encouragement. A satisfied Nelson Poynter cabled Bureau of Motion Picture chief Mellett to call his attention to *Dr. Gillespie's Criminal Case* (1943), where Dr. Lee (Keye Luke), "a young Chinese American is presented simply as a citizen, [who is] treated no different from and who has no less privilege than other Americans."

Blood on the Sun (1945) provided a trenchant lesson in cross-Asian stereotyping. James Cagney, a reporter in prewar Tokyo, plays a totally assimilated and sensitized *gaijin*. He knows judo and karate, speaks Japanese fluently, and bathes (albeit alone) in the public baths. When a woman is murdered aboard a ship anchored in Tokyo bay, Cagney spies a sinister dragon lady exiting the crime scene. The suspect woman (Sylvia Sidney) is later spotted serving tea to two Japanese politicians. "She's of mixed parentage?" inquires one. His companion nods affirmatively. "Her mother was—" "Chinese," interjects the other. Typing the Eurasian character as half Chinese not only establishes her innocence of the murder but illustrates how the face of the alien Other has been reformulated without being redesigned—a lesson taught by raising and then exorcising the specter of the Asian dragon lady. When she and Cagney fall in love, she says the match is doomed because "I'm half Chinese." "So what?" rejoins

Cagney with a color-blind casualness unimaginable a few years previous. "I'm half Irish and half Norwegian." The features of actress Sylvia Sidney (European, not Asian) mitigates the miscegenation, but *Blood on the Sun* assumes distinctions that were once a blur and approves interminglings that were once unthinkable.

To Western eyes the difference was intramural. Screen credits ignored the distinctions among Asians asserted so forcefully in the narratives. Central Casting prejudice foreclosed what should have been boon times for Asian-American actors. The few Japanese-American actors working in Hollywood were soon cast elsewhere by the War Relocation Authority, but even before internment they had refused to play the enemy in *Secret Agent of Japan* (1942). A trade reviewer with an eye for verisimilitude complained: "Some of the 'Japs' used in the pic act and look like fugitives from a Chinese hand laundry." Another trouble with cross-racial optometrics, as *Behind the Rising Sun*'s director Edward Dmytryk later cracked, was that "fake eyelids don't come cheap." Eschewing laugh lines, *Variety* spilled the truth. The reason so many Caucasian actors "impersonated Japs" in *Blood on the Sun* was "the idea that orientals don't make good actors."

Interracial coupling: James Cagney romances Sylvia Sidney in *Blood on the Sun* (1945).

Nonetheless, though the inside track was given to eyeline-adaptable occidentals like J. Carrol Naish and Walter Huston, Asians of extractions other than Japanese were more in demand than before. Reluctant initially to pass themselves off as nationals of a land despised for centuries before 1941, Chinese- and Korean-Americans such as Richard Loo and Philip Ahn sacrificed ethnic pride to contribute to the war effort as morale-enhancing Japanese villains. Loo, typed forever as the oily, overconfident, American-educated Japanese officer, gave a face to the enemy that wartime audiences—to flash back one war—loved to hate. As the lying prosecutor in *The Purple Heart,* the smirking diplomat in *Jack London,* the taunting Zero pilot in *God Is My Co-Pilot,* and the sadistic camp commandant in *First Yank into Tokyo,* he mispronounced Japanese and spat out comic balloon dialogue in Pidgin English ("O-kay, you Yankee Doodle Dandies, come and get it! Where are you gangsters? Come on up and get a load of that scrap metal you sold us!").

The best way to allay xenophobia and rehabilitate formerly threatening aliens was to transform the rest of the planet's inhabitants into proto-Americans holding democratic values. With Communist fellow-traveling a trip deemed necessary, the godless and enslaved Soviet Union under Joseph Stalin was transformed to expose a tolerant and affluent side not at all unlike the Kansas heartland. *Mission to Moscow, Song of Russia,* and *The North Star* (the three pro-Soviet melodramas of 1943 rendered retroactively impolitic by the House Committee on Un-American Activities in 1947) depict a bustling agricultural prosperity and billowing industrial might. In *Song of Russia,* symphony conductor John Meredith (Robert Taylor) takes a musical tour of a motherland replete with plush nightclubs, thriving collective farms, and salt-of-the-earth comrades who worship freely at Greek Orthodox churches. After an elaborate floor show at a grand restaurant (done up in the inimitable MGM style), Meredith surveys the boisterous, prosperous diners and marvels, "I can't get over it. Everybody seems to be having such a good time. I always thought Russians were sad and melancholy people—you know, sitting around brooding about their souls." On his beautiful companion he bestows the highest compliment. "If I didn't know I met you in Moscow, you might be an American girl!" Artkino's documentary *Moscow Strikes Back* (1942), released by Republic with a special English commentary written by Albert Maltz and narrated by Edward G. Robinson, also paints the USSR in USA hues. The 1939 May Day Parade in Red Square becomes a kind of "combined Labor Day and ring around the Maypole." When the ethnic representatives of the Socialist Republics march by in full folk dress, narrator Robinson bridges the culture gap with comments like "this is jive, Mongolian style" and "in the groove with the Uzbeks." In Hollywood's portrait of a people rustic, peaceful, and prosperous under the benevolent rule of avuncular Joseph Stalin, the romantic vision of Soviet communism finally reached the American "masses"—through the cooperation of America's most fervent capitalists.

The nation's generous embrace of ethnic differences overseas was not extended to one of its own. Decreed on February 19, 1942, by Executive Order 9066, the forced internment of 120,000 native Japanese-Americans and resident Japanese aliens on the West Coast punctured the high ideals of assimilationist OWI rhetoric. Unlike the segregation of black Americans, the internment policy was a wartime innovation, not a venerable custom. Yet the defense of the internment on screen was half-hearted and shamefaced. Even in 1942, perhaps especially in 1942, it didn't fit the mythos.

The OWI-BMP Victory film *Japanese Relocation* (November 1942) was charged with explaining and justifying the internment policy. "Following the outbreak of the present war," reads the introductory crawl, "it became necessary to transfer several thousand Japanese residents from the Pacific Coast to points in the American interior. This is an historical record of the operation as carried out by the United States Army and the War Relocation Authority." It is a record also of a singular American tragedy and the incompatibility of wartime language, verbal and visual, to contain it.

On-screen narrator Milton Eisenhower, himself the descendent of German immigrants, asserts that "our West can't become a potential combat zone" and although the government didn't "relish the job," relocation is a military necessity. The War Relocation Authority thus "determined to do the job as a real democracy should, with real consideration for the people involved." The calculated omissions, half-truths, and outright lies are refuted by the images meant to illustrate the benign intentions. During the forced-relocation sequence, no Japanese-American is given a voice or a close-up. A montage of hastily abandoned homes and huddled families with belongings in tow inevitably evokes newsreel memories of the forced "resettlements" in Europe. The narration admits the aptness of the analogy: "We hope most earnestly that our example will influence the Axis powers in the treatment of Americans who fall into their hands." The commentary protests too much ("we are protecting ourselves without violating the principles of Christian democracy") and lets the camera take in more than enough, framing glum children ("these American children of Japanese descent") and panning the bleak desert vistas of Arizona and Nevada.

In its final movement, *Japanese Relocation* recasts the forced evacuation to the desert interior in the only mythically justifiable manner—as an American journey into the frontier. The internment camps become "new pioneer communities," and the prisoners mutate into hopeful settlers entering "a land that was raw, untamed, but full of opportunity. Here they would educate their children, reclaim the desert." No forced roundup and illegal detention, the "relocation" takes its place in a long line of American immigrant experiences, another errand into the wilderness.

Where a spiritual relocation to the pioneer plains was a transparent act of cultural sleight of hand, the actual admission of Japanese-Americans into the military's ranks was no trick. The next year witnessed a striking turnabout regarding the imagined domestic threat. In 1943 the *Stars and Stripes* spoke up twice in support of Japanese-American soldiers. "As a result of the stab in the back tactics employed by the Nipponese at Pearl Harbor, all Japs have been 'suspect' in the minds of most Americans," asserted a bellwether editorial that March. "In recent months this attitude has gradually changed as the folks at home begin to realize that many American Japanese are as loyal as Americans of German and Italian descent. . . . Strange as it may seem Japanese emigrants came to America to enjoy the same privileges and opportunities that attracted millions of other immigrants. They and their children are willing to die to protect the privileges and opportunities provided by democracy, and it would be unwise to waste this loyal and intelligent manpower." *Yank,* whose Pacific correspondents seethed with loathing toward the Japanese enemy, published glowing letters by European theater GIs on Japanese-American soldiers. Released now of the need to separate out one ingredient, the melting-pot rhetoric flowed naturally and expansively. Although racist hatred of the Japanese enemy was a steady hum that regularly surged to high decibels with fresh provocation, the indiscriminate discrimination of the previous year had abated.

For Japanese-Americans no less than black Americans, the price of admission was exacted in blood. The formation of Japanese-Amer-

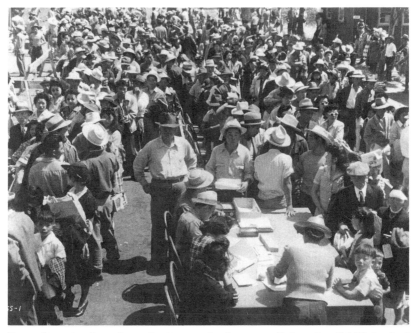

Exceptions to the ethos: the images in *Japanese Relocation* (1942) invited uncomfortable comparison to overseas "resettlements." (Museum of Modern Art/Film Stills Archive)

ican combat units in 1943 and their sterling performance under fire in Italy and Germany the next year were chronicled with appreciation and wonderment in press and newsreel reports. Episode no. 45 of the *Army-Navy Screen Magazine* (January 1945) devoted an extended segment in praise of Japanese-American combat units, focusing on the storied 442nd Regimental Combat Team, the "Go for Broke" boys. In service to the emperor, the native tenacity of the Japanese was fanaticism; in service to Uncle Sam, it was exemplary devotion to duty. Wounded Nisei, the narrator informs his GI audience in laudatory tones, pull an "AWOL in reverse" by returning to their units before completing convalescence. The segment even pokes fun at a group of befuddled Germans captured by a Japanese-American unit ("They think they're fighting Japan too!"). Likewise, both John Ford's *December 7th* (1943) and Frank Capra's *Know Your Enemy: Japan* (1945) carefully distinguish between loyal Japanese-Americans and "Japs in Japan." At the very moment tens of thousands of Japanese-

Americans were languishing in internment camps as suspect aliens, Ford's official Navy incentive film shows a Japanese-American on Hawaii taking down the sign from his shop, formally "The Banzai Cafe," and raising a new one for "The Keep 'Em Flying Cafe."

But the "Americans All" portrait included this most exotic of native elements only if properly framed and tethered. No Japanese-American walked casually into a Warner Bros. platoon or looked into the camera without a sticker that labeled him friendly. In 1943 Lt. Col. R. P. Presnel of the Signal Corps Photographic Center related a representative anecdote about an ethnic close call. Presnel explained that Army training films sought to use soldiers from the ranks, "ordinary men of all racial types," so that "the men who see the pictures will most readily identify themselves with the men on the screen."

> We were considerably embarrassed, however, on one occasion, when one of the southwestern camps supplied us with a contingent of Japanese-American soldiers to enact an important scene. They were fine fellows and good soldiers and loyal to everything American, but we did not know how the rest of the Army would take instruction from them. It happened to be a scene in which poison gas was depicted, however, and so we were able to put them all in gas masks and get away with it.

Though wartime rhetoric freely admitted "everything American," the motion picture camera was not quite ready to look all Americans straight in the eye.

CHAPTER **7** Women
Without
Men

War is traditionally an all-male club. Possession of the required member grants membership to an exclusive fraternity where a few good boys become men, callow fellows lock arms as brothers in battle, and same-sex intimacy edges out matrimonial affections. Like the ancient Greeks, the American military demands Spartan training and defines virtue in masculine terms. The embodiment of grace under pressure, under fire, is a male figure.

Modern warfare, alas, respects neither the prerogatives of gender nor the integrity of myth. Discrimination between combatant and noncombatant, frontline fighter and homefront backup, was never practiced in earnest, but in a century of aerial bombardment, chemical warfare, and fragmentation explosives it quickly became a chivalric anachronism. When America went to war, the deference due a woman was deferred for the duration.

In cinematic service to the war effort, women first needed to live down old reputations before living up to new expectations. Hollywood had traditionally held wives and mothers to be above the fray of battle, to be wiser and more spiritual than their brutish and warlike worse halves. In 1930, writing of *All Quiet on the Western Front* in *Variety*'s "To the Ladies" pages, Ruth Morris praised the salvific function of antiwar cinema with a standard sex-based fancy: "All the disarmament conferences in the world . . . will not do as much to avert the disaster [of war] as repeated showings of this film. When the next war impends, show *All Quiet* to the women of any nation—and there won't be a next war." Unfortunately, *All Quiet* was banned in Germany and Italy for unseemly peace-mongering. It fell to *Men Must Fight* (1933) to take up the ladies' dare. Set in 1940, the film predicts a second world war and posits a united matriarchal front against a pandemic outbreak of testosterone poisoning. The hero is a noble conscientious objector who follows Mom's upright pacifism before succumbing to Dad's reborn patriotism. If men must fight, said the interwar antiwar films, women must fight against such men.

But after 1941, American women had to learn to fight *in concert with* such men. Traditional configurations of the female, chiseled in granite in art, history, and law, underwent official remodeling. Yet to launch a full-scale battle of the sexes alongside the one against the Axis threatened cultural overload. Placing anti-Fascism ahead of protofeminism, Hollywood and Washington rejected a two-front war. The challenge to venerable notions of the female's nature and talents was tempered with the reassurance of a basic continuity in the sexual hierarchy.

Long before the creation of the Office of War Manpower, Hollywood had paid all due respect to American womanpower. Though granted no say in military strategy and with only supportive functions in combat, women commanded the dominant voice at the motion picture box office. Prior to the juvenilization and masculinization of the film audience in the 1950s, the accepted wisdom of the motion picture industry held that the moviegoing audience was perhaps 70 to 80 percent female and selection of pictures decisively the woman's prerogative. On dates, the boy paid for the ticket and the girl picked the movie. An article of faith bolstered by experience, the truism resisted statistical cross-examination. In 1942 pollster George Gallup conducted a survey on motion picture attendance that attempted to puncture the common perception. Noting that the problem of the sexual composition of the audience was "one of the most controversial in the motion picture industry" and that his conclusions differed "markedly from the popular tradition," Gallup went to great lengths

Swing shifts: actress Alexis Smith presses a contemporary
question about war and women. (Photofest)

in a preamble explanation to justify the reliability of his surveying
techniques. He then presented figures revealing that men actually
slightly edged out women as frequent moviegoers. Gallup concluded
that although women did seem to choose the film when moviegoers
attended in couples, "men attend the theater *alone* much more often
than do women. The net result is that in 51 cases out of every 100
the picture is chosen by the male."

Distrustful of market research and emboldened by unprecedented
wartime profits, industry veterans scoffed at the emergent breed of
market researchers. In a wry response to Gallup's statistical presumption, Lou Pollock, a former advertising and publicity manager

for Universal, articulated what remained demographic gospel throughout the war years. As a representative statement of Hollywood gender associations and a colorful example of vintage moviespeak, Pollock's rebuttal is worth quoting at length:

Had [Gallup delved a little deeper] he might have come to the following conclusions that every showman knows by heart—if he can't prove it by arithmetic:

1. The fact that in a mixed couple it will be the woman who makes the *choice* of picture to see is not half as important as the point that it is the woman who decides whether she and her man will go to a movie in the first place—any movie! It's when you have made a picture that has successfully intrigued feminine interest that the gals start hypoing their males to take them to see it.

2. The fact that more men than women may be found in a given audience indicates that men go to the movies alone—women rarely do. But not enough men go alone to keep any theater alive except the occasional action house here and there in congested downtown centers of larger cities where there are enough male drifters and time-killers to keep a grind spot running on a diet of gangster, adventurer and rawer sex fare.

Men go [virtually] everywhere alone, but women hardly anywhere outside of their shopping and beauty parlor visits. *The bulk of any successful show audience always consists of couples.*

Continuing in the ad-pub lingo that manages to demean the integrity of both sexes, Pollock summed up with a practical prescription for Doctor Gallup:

Instead of canvassing a cross-section of the whole country, simplify the job by canvassing every patron in one theater—but pick a house that is smashing its box office record. And ask the patrons why they came.

There will be men who attended alone. Probably there will be some women who attended alone. Neither means anything. The big point, if you're looking for success secrets, is that most of the house will be formed by mixed pairs, the females of which had previously announced to their males: "Let's go to see *Mrs. Miniver* tonight." Or it might have been *Rebecca* or *Yankee Doodle Dandy* or *Gone with the Wind*.

And the men said, "Okay, honey," and they stumbled along—

little suspecting that they were going to mislead a lot of bright, young statisticians into thinking that it was their idea in the first place.

Women then were classical Hollywood's prime movers, the audience most fervently courted and catered to. Enhancing their already formidable influence was the appearance of a salient war-spawned consumer category: the unescorted female. Pollock's notion of mixed-up "mixed pairs" notwithstanding, John Walsh, an exhibitor in Pittsburgh, tracked a new phenomenon at his theater. At the evening screenings, half of the young women in attendance arrived either unescorted or in clusters of five or six. In 1941–45, more than ever, the eye of the beholder was apt to be a woman's. An offhand comment by Humphrey Bogart about his unexpected appeal in *Casablanca* speaks to the dominance of the female perspective in classical Hollywood cinema (and suggests that for the bulk of the wartime audience the real sacrifice was Ilsa's, not Rick's). Perceived as an unlikely romantic lead, Bogart was asked if he thought he was adorable. "If a face like Ingrid Bergman's looks at you as though you're adorable," he replied, "everybody does."

The female gaze was not always so starry-eyed. Speculating that Fox's *Son of Fury* (1942) was "such a stick of dynamite at the box office" because the ads "featured Tyrone Power showing off his manly form in a loin cloth," *Variety* coyly reported that "the gals are shopping chiefly for men stars and they prefer them with plenty of oomph in all the right places." But though women liked to check out good-looking men, they preferred sightings set in romantic melodramas or Technicolored epics to those in grimy, all-male action adventures—as a box-office measurement of Errol Flynn in tights in *The Adventures of Robin Hood* (1938) and in fatigues in *Objective, Burma!* (1945) verifies.

The wartime glut of male-dominated combat films portended a predictable shortfall in female attendance. Transparent desperation saturates publicity ploys designed to sell fiery combat films to women, a market the ballyhoo boys and the trade press called with a mixture of condescension, regard, and bewilderment "the distaff side." Universal tried to bolster *Corvette K-225* (1943), a good-neighborly nod to the Canadian Navy, with a ladylike endorsement from Kate Smith: "All women will like this picture because American mothers, wives, and sweethearts will always remember that many American boys' lives were saved because the Canadian boys made the [Atlantic] crossing so much safer." The female-less *The Story of G.I. Joe* (1945) was billed as "the true story of every woman's fighting man." To no avail: the distaff side remained disengaged. In 1942, the year of *Wake Island, To the Shores of Tripoli,* and *Flying Tigers,* the most popular war-themed film was *Mrs. Miniver.* In 1943, the year of *Bataan, Sahara,* and *Air Force,* it was *Casablanca.*

That traditional resistance to screen violence was reinforced by intimate emotional attachments. According to exhibitors, women were staying away from war films because mothers, wives, and sisters were "not keen on being reminded of the dangers their young men were experiencing overseas." "We get walk outs on the depressing type of war films," a Midwest theater owner reported. "Women especially complain about the brutality in many war pictures. Perhaps they have sons in the service, and naturally, it brings to mind the welfare of their own flesh and blood." Naturally.

After 1941, when shortages in the labor force compelled the deployment of a neglected and suppressed national resource, Washington shared Hollywood's respect for womanpower. Urged on by the OWI and the Office of War Manpower, the motion picture industry undertook a concerted effort to recruit and inspire women and to reform and reeducate men concerning heretofore hidden female proficiencies. As today's feminist documentaries and rock music videos attest, the archival record of sisters doing it for themselves is rich in montage possibilities. Wartime newsreels and Victory films chronicled women's work in the factory, the hospital, the shipyard, and the combat zone. RKO's *This Is America* issue "Woman at Arms" (November 1942) answered the "important question millions of women are asking: What Can I Do to Help?" Warner Bros.'s special issue *Women at War* (October 1943) paid homage to the WACs. The Victory film *Glamour Girls of '43* (September 1943) showed women in aircraft factories, in vital civilian employments, and at home doing their bit. United Artists distributed the War Activities Committee's *It's Your War, Too* (April 1944), a nine-minute film dedicated to the "girls in khaki." Hollywood feature films honored women's work both of a homefront, housewifely sort (as when Claudette Colbert gets by just fine on her ration points in *Since You Went Away*), and of an overseas under fire kind (as when Veronica Lake pulls the pin on some lecherous Japanese—and herself—in *So Proudly We Hail!*).

To reconcile feminist aspirations and chauvinist shibboleths, the gender-specific genre work called for dexterous manhandling. So potentially discombobulating were the new projections that women-minded wartime cinema made certain to channel and constrain whatever revolutionary spirit it unleashed. Directing female energy and keeping the lid on sexual equity, the genre work functioned as a kind of cultural safety valve, albeit one that vented as much pent-up emotion as it shut off. Three war-born versions of American womanhood emerged.

First, traditional gender associations were reinforced and merely moved out of the domestic sphere and into the industrial workplace. The first of the officially instigated lessons in directing women's talent, the Office of Emergency Management's *Women in Defense* (December 1941), taught that "women are skillful in gauging and checking for imperfections" because their "natural skill" and "nimble fingers" are a perfect genetic match for sewing silk parachutes. The commentary, credited to Eleanor Roosevelt and spoken by Katharine Hepburn, also argues that detail work at precision instruments is "work in which women excel" due to their "constant care and alertness." Though a woman's space has changed, her place hasn't. Thus, the standard send-off in the newsreel clips and Victory shorts: the reminder that a woman's role in the home is always, really, the first line of national defense.

Second, new and challenging gender associations coexisted with old and reassuring ones in a calibrated equipoise that found men and women alike moving back and forth from one vision of the sexes to the other. Woman's wartime importance—both in her traditional role as girl, wife, and mother *and* her new wartime role as factory worker, nurse, and servicewoman—receives simultaneous affirmations. In *Tender Comrade* (1943), four women factory workers bind together in a single household. The women lecture each other on hoarding, preach democracy to their refugee housekeeper, and cope quite wonderfully without mates. Their self-reliant harmony makes a series of flashbacks (in which Ginger Rogers relives her courtship and early married life) intrusive and instructive. Rogers's prewar, prework self is petulant, dependent, and childish, a whiny and infantilized contrast to the initiative, strength, and maturity of her war-tempered character. Yet Ginger tucks herself in at night with a picture of her husband by the bedside, and she and the rest of the girls dreamily dote on tokens sent by their boys. When the newlywed husband of one of their number shows up in the living room on furlough,

Women without men (1): absent males prove no great loss to Ruth
Hussey (left) and Ginger Rogers in *Tender Comrade* (1943).

the women revert instinctively to wifely type and smother the poor
fellow in domestic solicitude.

That the two visions of the one sex were in polar opposition did
not prevent Hollywood from selling both versions. *Swing Shift Maisie*
(1943) and the assembly-line musical *Rosie the Riveter* (1944) negotiated the demands of the shop floor and the glamour of the backlot
with alacrity, the latter urging audiences to "revel with Rosie as she
welds her way to Victory in a melee of wrenches and wenches." Despite a masculine title, *Good Luck Mr. Yates* (1943) was dedicated to
alleviating the threat of gender rebellion and "glorifying the American
girl on the homefront." The advertising fused prewar expectations
with wartime exigencies:

> She's tender—and tough!
> Strong—and feminine!
> Brave—and clinging!
> At work on a ship! At work on a man!
> At work on the biggest job that ever made a soft-as-satin girl a
> tough-as-nails homefront heroine!

Frequently, such schizoid incompatibility led to irreconcilable differences. In *She's in the Army* (1942) a debutante songstress frivolously enlists in the Women's Ambulance Corps to find husky romance among the officer class. "Might mislead ambitious girls into thinking they can catch the handsome captain if they half try," cautioned a dour OWI analysis. When Congressman John Martin Costello (D–Calif.) proposed legislation to make the Women's Airforce Service Pilots (WASPs) an integral part of the Army Air Force in 1944, opponents urged wavering voters to see *Ladies Courageous* (1944), which showed the Women's Auxiliary Ferry Squadron (WAFS) as "emotionally unstable" and "more interested in their personal career than in patriotism."

The third variant forcefully declared new notions of a woman's work, place, and nature. To feminist eyes the compromises and evasions are glaringly, gratingly transparent, but during the war years the newsreel clips featuring woodcutting "lumber jills," the Victory

Gender equipoise: combat nurse Ella Raines (*left*) keeps femininity alive in *Cry "Havoc!"* (1943).

films equating glamour with gunnery, and the sight of Ginger Rogers driving a forklift were jarring and transforming revisions of a gender contract once written in stone. A big-name actress wearing a welding mask and brandishing a blowtorch could not help but melt away the pedestal image.

Perhaps the most uncompromising and schematic of the wartime gender persuaders is the Warner Bros. short *So Proudly We Serve* (September 1944), a tribute to female Marines that sets out with suffragette fervor to raise the consciousness of a blowhard male chauvinist. Sent for training as a rear seat gunner, Sgt. Tex Gordon (Warren Douglas) is nonplussed to discover his instructor is a pretty "girl sergeant" (Andrea King). Though his initial interest in her is decidedly nonballistic, she ably instructs him in both gunsight alignment and gender realignment. In a cafeteria sharing a milkshake, the two sergeants scan adjacent tables for likely female stereotypes. Tex, a self-styled expert on female "types," obnoxiously prejudges the women under the camera's gaze. The lout is invariably wrong. Montage vignettes reveal the apparently frivolous, delicate, and bookish types to be parachute packers, airplane mechanics, and trumpet players. Tex fares little better in athletic competition. On the tennis court and baseball diamond, his sergeant hammers him with power serves and low fastballs. Training ended, sensitized now to women and marksmanship alike, the aerial gunner returns to the Pacific the master of two wartime lessons. Before getting back in harness over the skies, Tex drops a significant piece of information on his ground crew: he's "married the girl." But gender equipoise cannot be regained after so lopsided a battle of the sexes. When a Zero zooms into Tex's crosshairs, the face of his spouse/instructor materializes in double exposure, whispering sweet gunnery instruction into his ear. Together, they make the score.

Clothes, the second most visible gender marker, were tailored to fit the swing shifts in job action and personal interaction. Studio wardrobe departments exchanged the formal wear and diaphanous gowns of last season's RKO musicals and Art Deco screwball comedies for form-fitting military outfits and sensible shoes. Men dressed uniformly, women dressed like men, and clotheshorses of all breeds dressed down. In *This Is the Army*, the flamboyant outerwear of urban American blacks was redesigned in a musical number called "What the Well Dressed Man in Harlem Will Wear" (answer: a uniform). Zoot suits were singled out and discouraged by the Hays Office as an expression of civilian insensitivity and extravagance. Besides being "generally associated with a hot time," the peacock pleats of the city streets represented "an irresponsible convention defining stratum of youth." Paulette Goddard's attire in *I Love a Soldier* (1944) warranted an official government fashion statement. "We believe that the sight of Miss Goddard in an approved women's welder's costume would be proof positive that such clothing need not detract from feminine charm," said Col. John Stillwell, president of the National Safety Council. Despite Goddard's sarcastic rejoinder ("Of course, he's kidding"), producer-director Mark Sandrich ordered her to wear "approved leather coveralls, steel boots, and face masks for the welding scenes"—and also covered the action with a wind machine to blow her skirt up for another scene.

When not actually wearing the pants, women were pragmatically repackaged. Wartime scarcity and sacrifice ill-suited the frills, furs, silks, and opulent outfits favored by studio costume designers with one name. "Luxury clothes are not only old fashioned, they're unpatriotic and in bad taste," announced Edith Head, chief designer at Paramount. Promising to "set a pace for economical smartness women will emulate to benefit the war effort," Head pointed to the outerwear enveloping Dorothy Lamour in *They Got Me Covered* (1942) and Betty Hutton in *The Miracle of Morgan's Creek* (1944) as wardrobes for working-girl characters that could really be worn by working girls. "The golden bathtub days of film are gone," she announced. "The average girl will remain smartly but inexpensively dressed for the duration, and the movies will mirror that trend."

If clothes make the woman, a military uniform betokened a sanctioned dominance that undermined gender subservience. On screen if not in service the outer coatings of the officer class gave women scant protection against masculine onslaughts from below. Regulations against fraternization did not deter enlisted class romeos from moving up the ranks and in on commissioned girlfriends. However, with visible signs of consumption, leisure, and gender closeted for the duration, clothes no longer provided instant biological orientation. A repeated trope of wartime cinema is a male GI accosting a woman in uniform from behind ("hey, Mac!") and getting called up short by her full-breasted front.

Hollywood women being Hollywood women, feminine vanity compelled a few actresses to wiggle out of uniform constraints. In *So Proudly We Hail!* (1943) the incorrigibly seductive Paulette Goddard braves aerial bombardment to return to her barracks to retrieve a precious black lace nightgown. More in fashion was the always exemplary Claudette Colbert, who in the same film patches together an evening dress from a white surgical gown, a girdle with a towel dyed with mercurochrome, and ruffles of two-inch bandages. The pressbook for *A Guy Named Joe* (1943) made much of the fact that Irene Dunne's single "wardrobe" had the distinction of being the smallest (numerically) "ever worn by a major star." Yet Dunne too succumbs to the appeal of apparel when her guy gives her a gift-wrapped evening dress. "Oh, Joe," she gushes. "Girl clothes!"

A higher-stakes arena for all three gender visions was the combat zone. Placing women in harm's way was not only a natural invention on the male convention but an admission of the current state of affairs. In the Great War films, whether it was Clara Bow as the ambulance driver in *Wings* (1927) or Eleanor Boardman's doughboy impersonator in *She Goes to War* (1929)—the incongruity of females in battle gear and the essential addition of boy-girl stuff was the main point. In World War II, American women—nurses, WAVEs, WAFs, and WACs—were truly in the line of fire, and their inclusion in combat situations was no tomboy fantasy.

When stationing women amidst battlefield action, the combat film leavened celebration with condescension. The title of *Five Little Ladies at War* (1943) tells much of the story. In more somber territory, ambushed expectations came to be expected. During the first reel of *Days of Glory* (1944) a guerrilla sniper picks off two German soldiers, stands up tall, and pulls back a hood to reveal—her face. The aviatrix, a screen heroine since the silent era, performed credible service in *Wings and the Woman* (1942) ("the amazing drama of the girl who refused to be a white-collar nobody—and became one of the first women in army uniform") and *Flight for Freedom* (1943), which featured Rosalind Russell as a "girl flier" sent on a "mysterious mission over Jap-mandated islands." On the ground, though, American woman warriors never attained the degree of virile prowess and equalitarian firepower of their Red Army compatriots. No domestic parallel exists to the Soviet feature *She Defends Her Country* (1943), in which a prize-winning tractor driver turns into the feared guerrilla leader "Comrade P" after her family is murdered and she is ravished by Nazi invaders.

Nurses were accommodating helpmates, nurturing Nightingales

being as unthreatening as their battlefield contributions were undeniable. The war's two big-budget female-centered combat films, *So Proudly We Hail!* and *Cry "Havoc!"* (1943), share a setting (the Philippines in the dark days of 1942) and a plot outline (nurses under fire). Unlike the boys' club, the all-girl squad was not as concerned with absorbing ethnic differences as in unifying divergent female stereotypes—the man-hungry gal, the world-weary dame, the sheltered rich girl, the cornfed sweetie, and the mother hen. Where the featured protagonist in the male combat team is torn between self-assertion and group contribution, the featured female protagonist wrestles with the conflict between duty and romance. Where men prove their mettle by suppressing aggressiveness and independence, women prove theirs by doing the exact opposite: suppressing docility and calling up reservoirs of strength and endurance. In *Cry "Havoc!"* a delicate writer reveals a sturdy backbone, a plucky lady masters aerial gunnery, and a bubbly Southern belle turns efficiently unladylike. Meanwhile, by way of gender equipoise, the stern and

Women under fire: the combat unit of *So Proudly We Hail!* (1943).

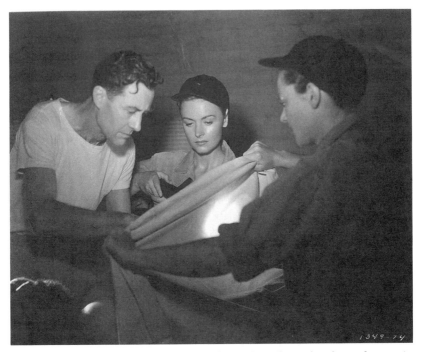

The combat nurse as madonna: Donna Reed, beatific under the male gaze in *They Were Expendable* (1945).

steady matriarchs expose underbellies of feminine vulnerability and romantic yearning—in *So Proudly We Hail!* Claudette Colbert cracks during an aerial attack and pledges to sacrifice all for love; in *Cry "Havoc!"* Margaret Sullavan's chilly exterior conceals her passion for a barely glimpsed lieutenant, secretly her beloved husband.

John Ford's *They Were Expendable* (1945) gives striking recognition to frontline women in the figure of a Bataan nurse played by Donna Reed. Under the adoring male gaze, she attends at surgery, calm and steady under bombardment. "That's a nice kind of gal to have around in wartime," admits a smitten John Wayne. "Or anytime," chimes in his buddy. After a hard day's night of medical work, the nurses, outlined in silhouette and hallowed chiaroscuro, walk back to their quarters through an underground passageway. During a quintessentially Fordian interlude, the camera stays with the nurse when her suitor is called from their loveseat by his commander. As the men talk in the background, the woman is center screen, fiddling

with his cap. Invited to dinner back at the squadron's all-male pre-
serve, she inspires devotional reverence, the sailors now a priest-
hood celebrating the nurse and all she represents.

The embodiment of "why we fight," women make appearances in
the most exclusive of male-dominated chambers. Despite the claus-
trophobic confines of a submarine, *Destination Tokyo* (1943) smuggles women aboard through photographs on desks and above bunks,
fantasy sequences, a dream sequence, and a recorded message
played at 78 rpm. In *Thirty Seconds Over Tokyo* (1944), advertised as
"the love story behind the greatest story of our time," Col. Ted Lawson's wife (Phyllis Thaxter) is mainly off-screen but always in mind.
As an animating force, women are invoked as the B-17 *Mary-Ann* in
Air Force or the tank *Lulubelle* in *Sahara,* the Betty Grable and Veronica Lake pinups that adorn barracks walls, and the letters read aloud
by lonely GIs from (and to) mothers, wives, and girls back home.

Absent a photographic or physical representation of women, a full-
blooded romantic energy courses through the bond between man
and machine. In *Winged Victory* (1944) a flyer kisses the tire of his

Men without women: John Garfield (*right*) smuggles feminine interest on board a submarine in *Destination Tokyo* (1943).

new bomber and asks, "How's my little pinup girl?" At sea the third-person feminine bestowed on ocean-going vessels reached fetishistic levels of affectionate intensity and voluptuous metaphor. In *Stand By for Action* (1943) the recommissioned destroyer the USS *Warren* is both mother ship and warm spouse to the men on board. "So this is the USS *Warren*, huh?" says the executive officer (Robert Taylor), reluctantly assigned to "the old girl." "She's a mess, isn't she?" The ship's chief yeoman and loyal mate (Walter Brennen) leaps chivalrously to her defense. "Right now she's a little like the lady that was waked out of a sound sleep in the middle of the night with her face full of cold cream and her hair done up in curlers, but you give her a chance to get prettied up, sir, and she'll give those new destroyers cards and spades in any beauty contest." Once at sea, she proves her fecundity by rescuing twenty babies and two pregnant women from a life raft. Below deck, the crew quarters double as a nursery. With the carpenter's mate acting as midwife, the pregnant women give birth, both bearing sons to a crew that to a man paces and waits like nervous husbands. And Louis de Rochemont's documentary on the exploits of an otherwise unnamed naval vessel in the Pacific theater had an inevitable sobriquet: *The Fighting Lady* (1945).

Few combat films are so mission oriented and male dominated as not to be able to pause for a poignant goodbye. As a woman gazes after the husband, boyfriend, or son going off to an uncertain fate, the classical Hollywood director invariably gives her a sustained reaction shot: the nurse pausing for a quick backward glance at her husband as she's hustled onto a departing ambulance in *Bataan;* the wife and mother who see off their respective boys in *Air Force;* or the Filipino wife of a PT-boat crewman watching from the dock in *They Were Expendable.* The feminine principle militated the violence, the crudity, and the insensitivity of men without women. Where men were expendable, women were indispensable.

WATCHING AND WAITING

No less than women's work, the status of manly endeavor underwent upheaval in wartime America. Obviously the greatest portion of public esteem still went to the hero who proved his bravery under fire on the field of battle. But in a complex war, once-simple concepts such as courage, duty, and sacrifice became blurred and the relative merits of different contributions harder to gauge. The kind of work deemed essential to the war effort—experienced factory foremen, technicians, and lab workers—was a vexatious problem in practical terms for the Office of War Manpower and in cultural ones for the studio system.

The recalibrations of courage reflected the providential blessing that, alone among the great powers, America actually had an authentic homefront, a native land that was not also a killing ground. The imaginative engagement of homefront with frontline was powerful and the reasons for emotional engagement thicker than water. Yet however intense in personal attachment, the homefront was remote from physical danger and serious discomfort. Even in a war in which one in ten were in uniform, the arsenal of democracy sheltered a civilian population who, as cultural historian John Morton Blum put it, "in most cases and at most times were fighting the war on imagination alone." The accusatory reminder—"Don't you know there's a war on?"—could only have been uttered in America.

In adjudging and ranking the contributions of frontline warrior and homefront valet, the OWI struggled mightily to encourage the identification of latter with former and to persuade Americans that in the Big Picture the factory worker, the morale builder, and the air raid warden was doing his—and her—part. "Serving their country more humbly but in the same measure as its fighting men are the American people" was how an intertitle expressed it in the *March of Time*'s "Mr. and Mrs. America" (November 1942). The Victory film *What's Your Name* (January 1945) was typical of orientation shorts paralleling "the anonymous soldier" and "the anonymous worker" who were "both doing a job that will hasten victory." Through V-Mail, salvage drives, rationing, nomenclature ("bondbardiers"), and slogans ("For every hero in a fox-hole, a hero in a bond booth"), the OWI and the popular media equated the two and encouraged linkage. Press reports from the front identified soldiers by name, rank, and hometown not only to alert editors to a local angle but to nurture vicarious participation. In *God Is My Co-Pilot* (1945) the citizens of Macon, Georgia, tally up the score of hometown ace Robert L. Scott (Dennis Morgan) and even keep something of a miniature shrine to him in a storefront window in the center of town.

Since being shot at intensifies the qualitative experience of wartime service, the aggrandizement of stateside "fighters" tightened the jaws of combat veterans. Forthright homefront warriors had the decency to blush at the equivalence. The "Mr. and Mrs. America" issue for the *March of Time* features a man writing his overseas son about the mobilization back home in Muncie, Indiana. The father describes the town's Civil Defense activities but admits "the chances of us being bombed here are pretty slim." The national attitude toward air raid wardens was a fair indication of how dire was stateside anxiety. After 1942 the nerves of Atlantic seaboard residents and Californians calmed as German U-boats disappeared and Imperial invasion became ever more implausible. Air raids and lights-out drills were abided by and practiced with decreasing vigilance. *Dixie Dugan* (1943) and the Laurel and Hardy vehicle *Air Raid Wardens* (1943) implied that self-important nincompoops were in charge of superfluous busywork (the latter despite deletions made at the request of the Office of Civilian Defense).

If monitoring compliance with brownouts was the nadir of homefront endeavor, the zenith was the skilled work that stoked the arsenal of democracy in aircraft, armaments, and shipbuilding factories. A brawny laborer towering over a cauldron of molten steel, a Promethean figure resurrected by social realists enraptured by five-year plans, made a vigorous poster boy for the Office of War Manpower. But though a short-lived spate of studio "incentive films" tried valiantly to put the poster boy into motion pictures, assembly-line labor was not conducive to feature-length romance and adventure. "Actually filmed at the famous Lockheed Vega plant!" was the pathetic boast of *Wings for the Eagle* (1942): "The first big story of Uncle Sam's Army in overalls . . . the guys and gals who keep 'em rolling to keep 'em flying!"

Few of the Hollywood films designed to celebrate "the man behind the man with the gun" wait for a whistle to blow before bolting from the workplace. In *Joe Smith, American* (1942) adventure quickly enters the life of an everyman crew chief at an aircraft plant after promotion to a top-secret position installing bombsights. Joe (Robert Young) no sooner clocks out from his first day on the new job than thugs kidnap and torture him for vital blueprint information. The tight-lipped worker endures repeated socks on the jaw by flashbacking to his all-American past before escaping and leading the cops to his captors' hide-out. In Monogram's exploitation quickie *Rubber Racketeers* (1942), war plant workers prove their industrial strength by chasing down gangsters who have turned from bootleg whiskey to black-market tires. *Gangway for Tomorrow* (1943) drops all pretense of labor-intensive intrigue. Carpooling to their defense plant job (itself a matte job), five workers flashback their personal playlets.

The passengers include a French Resistance heroine, an Indy 500 champ, a retired warden who pulled the switch to electrocute his murderer brother, a former Miss America, and an ex-hobo turned nine-to-fiver for the duration. Not one second of this paean to war labor is spent on the job.

A more productive workshop from which to instruct and extol the homefront was the genre of melodrama. Traditionally, Hollywood's two female-targeted variants, romantic melodrama and familial melodrama, had emphasized the travails of lovers and mothers to spark heightened states of emotion (the trade designation put it succinctly: "women's weepies"). During a time already replete with emotional intensity, when the stock stuff of the genre (whirlwind courtships, separations and reunions, family crises) was the common stuff of everyday experience, melodrama would seem culturally redundant (not to say temperamentally uncongenial) to OWI-approved thematics. In a genre ill-suited to elevating the national cause over the nuclear family or substituting the armed service for a lover's arms, heated emotions tend to bubble over the top and subsurface sympathies work against surface message. Yet on the evidence of production schedules and box-office returns, a female-dominated audience never wearied of the catharsis wrought by tales of beset womanhood, augmented with war-specific machinations.

By far the most popular wartime melodrama was William Wyler's *Mrs. Miniver,* the tale of a steadfast upper-middle-class family living in an English village landscaped by MGM. Filled only with the purchase of ridiculous hats, the pretty little head of Greer Garson's bourgeois housewife expands its imaginative horizons when her secure doll's house is shattered by the blitz. Like many homefront melodramas, it has a double edge. The Minivers exude such balmy bucolity that one waits expectantly for the Luftwaffe to blast them out of complacency. As war comes to a quiet corner of England, the family blossoms in maturity—husband Walter Pidgeon participates in the evacuation of the troops at Dunkirk, Garson captures a downed German flyer—and the English class system breaks down in the face of indiscriminate terror.

Director Wyler bushwhacks expectations in an instructive narrative twist, the final-act death of a second Mrs. Miniver, the beautiful young wife of the family's RAF son. As viewers of *Wings* and *The Eagle and the Hawk* well knew, the dauntless young pilot is a Great War figure doomed to a sudden death. In a vignette early on, Wyler con-

Blasted out of complacency by the Luftwaffe: the banal, pre-blitz Minivers, Mrs. (Greer Garson) and Mr. (Walter Pidgeon), in William Wyler's war-tempered melodrama *Mrs. Miniver* (1942).

firms the suspicion when the raffish flyer in *Mrs. Miniver* frolics with his little brother, zooming the child through the air like a biplane. Barely audible on the soundtrack, a foreboding musical motif plays as foreshadowing. But during the fateful dogfight over the skies of England, it is the young bride, not the callow pilot, who is killed by aerial bombardment. A Church of England minister speaks the lesson in thwarted expectations and generic reversal:

> This is not only a war of soldiers in uniform. It is a war of the people, of *all* the people, and it must be fought not only on the battlefield but in the cities and the villages, in the factories and on the farms, in the home and in the heart of every man, woman, and child who loves freedom. . . . This is the People's war. It is our war. We are the fighters. Fight it then. Fight it with all that is in us. And may God defend the right.

A beautiful red rose, the third "Mrs. Miniver," survives as a botanical symbol of British constancy. Hugely popular (winner of six Oscars, including Best Picture, Best Director for Wyler, Best Actress for Garson, and Best Supporting Actress for newcomer Teresa Wright), praised by press and officialdom alike, MGM's idealized portrait of British pluck was the cinematic echo of Edward R. Murrow's radio broadcasts during the Battle of Britain—and in its way equally influential in cementing Anglo-American solidarity. A sign of the revolution in sensibility was the advertising claim: "*Mrs. Miniver* is *The Big Parade* of *this* war!*"

The American version of disrupted domesticity wasn't as suited to domestic consumption. In *Watch on the Rhine* (1943), directed by Herman Shumlin and written by Lillian Hellman, a genteel Washington, D.C., family is "shaken out of the magnolias" when their plantation-like citadel becomes a battleground for Nazi secret agents and anti-Nazi partisans. Set in April 1940, Hellman's play is a cautionary tale of American complacency, a stern exhortation to homefront vigilance, and a smug plug for Popular Front prescience that omits reference to the Hitler-Stalin Pact interregnum. Despite Paul Lukas's forceful performance as the visionary antifascist, *Watch on the Rhine* was set in hard Stalinist concrete. Hellman's party line—the Young Pioneer children, the cold-blooded execution of a blackmailer, a doctrine that compels a father to let his children go hungry rather than dip into political funds—was more stiff-necked than the British upper crust in *Mrs. Miniver.*

The most prestigious and expensive of the homefront melodramas was David O. Selznick's *Since You Went Away* (1944), directed by John Cromwell from a screenplay "by the producer." The three-hour epic, subtitled "a panorama of the homefront" and set within the walls of "the Unconquerable Fortress: the American home . . . 1943," opens with a fluid lesson in expository brevity and icon-packed resonance. An establishing shot frames a window containing a blue star banner, the sign that a family member is serving in uniform. A dissolve then initiates entry into the interior of the home. Cromwell's camera glides over the exposed mementos of the living room. Backed with lilting musical cues, the uninterrupted shot tracks laterally from detail to detail:

1. A creased and indented leather chair, palpably empty of the household patriarch
2. A bulldog at the feet of the chair, awaiting the master

3. A military parcel ("Rush," reads the label, "Military Raincoats")
4. A day calendar (showing the date: Tuesday, January 12)
5. A crumpled War Department telegram ordering Capt. Timothy Hilton to report for duty at Camp Claiborne, Louisiana. In the foreground lies a set of car keys, monogrammed "T.H." (a possession only an American male off to war would relinquish)
6. A plaque with a tiny mounted fish and the legend "Caught by Anne & Tim Hilton on Their Wedding Trip, August 23, 1925"
7. Two bronzed baby shoes
8. A portrait showing the three females left behind, wife (Claudette Colbert) and two young daughters (Jennifer Jones and Shirley Temple)
9. The blue star banner, viewed now from the interior, while through the window a car pulls into frame, in the rain, to park in front of the house.

Claudette Colbert then enters the manless fortress to begin a year without her husband. The presence of the never-seen Captain Hilton is solidified by letters, diary entries, and little messages and presents left behind by this most conscientious of husband/fathers. In *Tender Comrade* the men are gone but not missed. In *Since You Went Away* the absent patriarch leaves an aching emotional gulf in the lives of his wife and daughters.

With a ham-handedness typical of OWI-stamped melodrama, *Since You Went Away* taught a dozen-odd lessons in proper homefront behavior. High school graduate Jennifer Jones grows up fast as a nurse's aid, and younger sister Shirley Temple pitches in by collecting salvage and selling war stamps. Not content with rationing her family's coffee and taking in a crusty old boarder, Colbert goes to work as a "lady welder." In train stations, servicemen spend their salaries on war bonds and citizens voice a willingness to be taxed 100 percent. The selfish homefront exists as a contemptible and condemned aberration. A spoiled society matron (Agnes Moorehead, in her usual thankless role) hoards, blathers, and rumor mongers before finally getting lectured, but good, by an enraged Jennifer Jones. When a businessman traveling by train complains about an unsched-

Women without men (2) (*left to right*): Jennifer Jones, Claudette Colbert, and Shirley Temple yearn for a masculine shoulder in *Since You Went Away* (1944).

uled delay because a military transport is given priority, the camera pans to an amputee in uniform.

Unlike *Mrs. Miniver, Since You Went Away* conforms to melodramatic convention not wartime contingency. All its emotional punches are telegraphed in fidelity to sentimental regulations. A doomed young flyer really is doomed. The basso leitmotif that sends a fiancé off to war signals that he will not return, and the soundtrack music is prophetic. Just before the film's intermission break, Colbert receives a War Department telegram announcing that her husband is missing in action. His uncertain fate, which hovers over the second part of the narrative, is never really uncertain. On Christmas Eve, after the maid has placed the Captain's presents (bought long ago) under the Christmas tree, Colbert answers a telephone call from the War Department. Whether from David Selznick or Henry Stimson, only good news is sent out on the night before Christmas: Pop has been found, he is coming home.

The diverse machinations of *Since You Went Away* and *Mrs. Miniver*—the telltale soundtrack tones that predictably seal the generic bond in the one and unexpectedly break it the other—put into relief the difference between melodrama warmed over by war and melodrama tempered by it. Warmed-over melodrama used the war for the purposes of the genre: to unleash wellsprings of emotion. War-tempered melodrama used generic conventions for the purposes of the war: to teach a lesson by reversing expectations. The British import *In Which We Serve* (1942), Noel Coward's restrained tribute to the Royal Navy, measures up to the difference. In giving equal time to battleship warfare and homefront connubiality, it establishes the moral and strategic equivalence of warriors at sea with those on the hearth—a lesson brought home when, as in *Mrs. Miniver,* the husband at the front, not the wife at home, receives the notice of a spouse lost to enemy action.

Romance, the "boy-girl stuff" wedged into classical Hollywood narratives whether germane or not, remained inextinguishable. The irrepressible narrative drive toward the closing kiss, clinch, or marriage worked to the detriment of most other points of interest, not excepting anti-Fascism. Though war-tempered melodrama fought gallantly against the power of love, the Hollywood heart was not wholeheartedly committed to boy-girl separations. One reason *Casablanca* endures in the popular movie memory is the aberrational decisiveness of its climax, which tackled and resolved the question of dual loyalties head on. Less indelibly, *Eagle Squadron* (1942) switches the sex roles and allows the woman to put her man off by affirming the greater importance of the war effort. When given a choice, however, even war-tempered melodrama preferred not to choose. Romantic liaisons were more often finessed or shunted aside than forthrightly repudiated. Thus though the distant figure of a handsome lieutenant is an obscure object of unrequited desire for the women without men in *Cry "Havoc!",* the film eliminates him from close-up inspection to prevent needless distraction.

A significant exception is *They Were Expendable,* John Ford's elegiac tribute to the PT-boat crews who fought, and faced defeat, in the Philippines in 1942. All the more striking for being so unobtrusive, and for being a postwar (December 20, 1945) release, the film subordinates romantic interest to military necessity. The love story between John Wayne's PT-boat captain and Donna Reed's Bataan nurse is frustratingly unresolved. Two-thirds of the way into the narrative, the couple manages a rushed, interrupted exchange over the telephone. It is the final moment the lovers share together, the last the captain (or the spectator) hears of the nurse. Only in retrospect does the emotional impact and dramatic significance of the moment accumulate as Wayne realizes that the romantic link was broken perhaps never to be retied, that he and his love exchanged final words and didn't know it at the time. Boy-girl stuff in classical Hollywood cinema need not end happily, but it needs to end coherently. In the final reel, romantic relationships are settled by union, separation, or death. Against all expectations, *They Were Expendable* totally forswears boy-girl closure.

More frequently, the bluster of breathless romance held its own against the winds of war. Milestones in secular history—the outbreak of the European war, the attack on Pearl Harbor, and the invasion of Russia—erupt inconveniently to disrupt the course of true love. In *Song of Russia* (1943), Hitler's Operation Barbarosa and Stalin's "scorched earth" policy serve mainly to keep an American symphony conductor (Robert Taylor) out of the hands of his Russian pianist wife (Susan Peters), a beauty as adept at playing Tchaikovsky

Disrupting the course of true love: Robert Taylor and Susan Peters cope with Hitler's Operation Barbarosa in *Song of Russia* (1943).

as at mixing a Molotov cocktail. For less star-crossed lovers, invasive coincidence and military purpose might work to the advantage of romantic liaison. In *This Is the Army* Ronald Reagan tries the *Casablanca* kiss off with his fiancée, a strong-willed gal who will not permit world war to excuse his breach of promise. The right to get married, she tells him, is "one of things this war is about."

THE DEAD AND THE QUICK

Hollywood melodrama was also assigned delivery duty on the harshest message from Washington: death. As the lifeblood of drama and the by-product of cinematic violence, death is always a welcome guest, a character who invigorates emotion and enlivens action. In slices of smalltown Americana, however, the sudden termination of a guiltless and sympathetic protagonist was a visitation in defiance of all Codely propriety. That the intrusion was not close at hand but a bolt from afar, announced by an impersonal Western Union telegram from the War Department or a uniformed soldier in the living room, heightened the shock and the sense of dislocation. Under the aegis of the Code, the Reaper came as the arm of justice or the wedge for sentiment. In wartime cinema, he came as he so often comes in life—grimly and unbidden.

Cinematic recovery of the departed was one consolation. With a transparent allegorical reach and cultural purpose, Hollywood fantasy and comedy conjured a witch's brew of ghosts, angels, and spirits during the war years: *Here Comes Mr. Jordan, I Married a Witch, I Married an Angel, Heaven Can Wait, The Canterville Ghost, Ghost Catchers,* and *Blithe Spirit,* among others. A more down-to-earth and consciously therapeutic variant used the ethereal to assuage the grief of families and friends left with only memories and gold stars in the windows. Dead in the narrative proper, the departed are resurrected in cinematic space—in dissolves, in scenes of paradise, in double exposures as hovering guardian angels, in heaven-bent curtain bows for the closing credits.

The Human Comedy (1943), directed by Clarence Brown from an Oscar-winning original screen treatment by William Saroyan, pretends to look death squarely in the eye, but flinches in the final face-off. Narrated by the deceased father of a Rockwellian family, the film explains that people don't really die, they just aren't around much any more (corporeally speaking). To prove the point, the posthumous patriarch materializes and hovers in screen space behind his Bible-reading wife. Mickey Rooney, the exuberant icon of smalltown impregnability, plays the Western Union delivery boy (the dreaded harbinger who rode by bicycle into neighborhoods bearing tidings no household wanted to sign for). Rooney's unenviable position allows him to glimpse the emotional ravages of the newly widowed and to receive first word of the death of his own brother, the family's second gold star. The youngster is inconsolable until his deceased brother's best army buddy arrives in town as a fraternal stand-in. The coda has Rooney and the substitute sibling walk inside the family home followed by the ectoplasmic dissolves of the two dead men in the family.

More poignant is the laconically titled *Happy Land* (1943), directed by Irving Pichel from a MacKinlay Kantor novel. Again the telegram deliverer, a girl this time, rides her bike up to a homefront door with the dreaded words from Secretary of War Stimson. Visually telescoping the moment of stark comprehension, a tight close-up focuses on the cold typeface. Killed in action is the son of a beloved smalltown druggist (Don Ameche). The death blow sucks the life out of the father. Awakened by this wrenching earthbound pain, Ameche's departed grandfather (the benign character actor Harry Carey) returns to earth and guides the disconsolate father in flashback through the passages of his son's life—the boy's birth, first day of school, first crush, true love, and enlistment. The ending is similar to *The Human Comedy* but less glib. On furlough, one of the son's shipmates pays a courtesy visit to the pharmacist. After a few quiet words about the dead son, they share a glass of elderberry wine in somber consecration (formerly the ritual of father and son). The toast provides some solace and promises endurance, but there is no neat epiphany, no Hollywood "happyend" for *Happy Land*.

Closer to home—too close to home for some—was *The Sullivans* (1944). The all-too-true sacrifice of the Sullivan family was hyperbolic cruelty at once horrifying in enormity and consoling by comparison. In November 1942 five brothers from one Iowa family died when their ship, the USS *Juneau*, was sunk by the Japanese fleet. The obliteration of an entire male line of the Sullivans provoked a ritualistic outpouring of national mourning. A generation before, the Great War melodrama *Four Sons* had inspired a widely repeated comment about the thin line between tragedy and comedy: to wit, if the successive heart-

War Department death knells: Don Ameche receives the Western Union telegram in *Happy Land* (1943) while Navy emissary Ward Bond delivers the grim news personally in *The Sullivans* (1944).

break of the mother's loss were extended to a fifth son, laughter would be the only response to what was transformed by excess into a farce. Apparently not. Although the publicity surrounding the bereaved Sullivans had its share of ghoulish bad taste (studio agents rushed to Iowa for exclusive story rights, and Mrs. Sullivan reportedly insisted that no one but James Cagney should play her eldest son), the film is no farce. Every moment of screen time—from the baptisms of five baby boys, through a childhood fraught with scrapes and close calls, on to enlistment and duty call—is mercilessly heartbreaking.

Foreknowledge of the Sullivan brothers' fate casts a pallor over every gesture, every expression of childhood joy and filial spirit. The emotional apogee is a ruthlessly premeditated and devastatingly effective cinematic wallop. In childhood, the five boys race to the top of a water tower to wave farewell to their father, a railroad brakeman, as his train pulls out of town. A short lifetime later, after a Navy officer personally delivers news of the boys' deaths, Mr. Sullivan (Thomas Mitchell) returns to work, ashen-faced and beyond grief, and takes up his place on the train. As the locomotive rolls down the tracks, he gazes up to the water tower. Repeating the grammar of the earlier sequence, the camera holds on a shot of the tower, now painfully empty of the smiling, waving boys. Tears and audible bouts of sobbing regularly accompanied wartime melodrama, but that moment at the end of *The Sullivans* incited grief of a near hysterical dimension in some theaters. The visitation was too cruel, the obliteration too total, to sustain any talk of Providence and images of afterlife. The closing credits, in which the five boys march into soundstage heaven and wave farewell to a fade-out, was only a reminder of the gulf between cinematic recovery and irretrievable loss.

Some homefront audiences were put off by the unfamiliar presumption of an entertainment medium opening fresh wounds and intruding into moments of private heartbreak. To an Ohio theater owner *Happy Land* was "a slow draggy thing." "The son gets killed in the end," said the bewildered exhibitor. "I don't get it." Ad-pub agents also sometimes didn't get it. "Invite all gold star mothers to be your guests at the opening!" read an "exploitip" for *The Sullivans,* at whose New York premiere Mrs. Sullivan herself sold war bonds in the theater lobby. Against the impact of a War Department death notice, David O. Selznick at least harbored few illusions about the

Alive in cinematic space: Spencer Tracy (*center, background*) is the guardian angel watching over unknowing protégé Van Johnson (*center foreground, right*) in *A Guy Named Joe* (1943).

healing powers of fantasy. A touching moment in *Since You Went Away* shows moviegoers watching a newsreel trumpeting the arrival of a hometown hero. A middle-aged man arises and leaves his seat. As the newsreel recounts a joyous welcome in backframe, he walks up the theater aisle, his face stricken, a black mourning band on his arm.

The restrained whimsy and modulated sentiment of *A Guy Named Joe* struck a more consoling balance. Directed by Victor Fleming and written by Dalton Trumbo, it is a one-of-kind mesh of the sentimental, the explosive, and the celestial. Joe (Spencer Tracy), a reckless bomber pilot, heroically dies on a reconnaissance mission. In dry-iced heaven, a deific commander dispatches him earthward to serve as guardian angel/mentor for a young pilot in training (Van Johnson). Joe guides the rookie in the ways of flight and romance with his own former love (Irene Dunne). As the girl learns to love a new guy and get over the old one, Joe learns to displace his romantic possession

("That's my girl") to paternal protectiveness over the couple ("That's my girl—and that's my boy"). Like *The Human Comedy, Happy Land,* and *The Sullivans, A Guy Named Joe* offered the assurance that the departed are still alive—in memory, in heaven—and granted guilty survivors the leave to get on with their lives.

CHAPTER 8

Keep 'Em
Laughing

Ill-cast as pallbearers of death, Hollywood filmmakers took avidly to a less funereal project: escapist uplift, the business—nay, the duty now—of providing healthy diversion from the field of service and surcease from the cares and woes of life outside the theater. "In my humble opinion," opined director Archie Mayo in 1942, "motion pictures can best serve our fighting men and our civilians by building up morale to the tune of comedies, which, for a moment, give us contrast to this crisis that is upon us." "Keep 'em laughing," a slogan suggested by none other than Eleanor Roosevelt, became the shorthand motto for the diversionary "recreational" function of wartime cinema. It was said that soldiers craved "the three L's"—laughs, lookers, and letters—and the movies could deliver two out of the three and make kith and kin feel mighty guilty about not mailing off the third.

"Valuable as a temporary release of the high tension under which ordinary life exists today, the motion picture is vital under the added strain of war," Will Hays proclaimed. "Not only is it recording history, not only is it aiding directly through information and visual instruction, but it admittedly is an essential factor in relaxing nerves too tightly stretched and in strengthening morale." Hays's notion of celluloid therapy was taken up by Alex Gottlieb, an executive at Universal. "There are going to be plenty of sick people in the audience— people who have lost a husband, son, brother, or boyfriend—who will want and very much need the healing unguent of laughter," said the producer of seven Abbott and Costello comedies. Gottlieb pledged to continue doing his part "in making their burdens seem lighter for a couple of hours by concentrating on features that will enable the customers temporarily to forget their woes." The medicinal metaphor was stretched to literal treatment in "bedside motion picture shows." The Surgeon General of the Army obligingly asserted "that the mental relaxation and diversion afforded by the simple entertainment of motion pictures have a very desirable effect on the mental and physical welfare of the sick and injured."

Not all remedies soothed the national psyche with the same felicity. In the year after Pearl Harbor, curiosity and generic novelty assured the box-office viability of the combat film and war-tempered melodrama. By early 1943, however, motion picture exhibitors, the branch of the industry closest to the public, were sending back word that war-themed films were commercially languid and that escapist fare was the big money maker. "Overwhelmingly preponderant exhibitor opinion holds that the theater is vastly overfed with war pictures and themes of stress and strife," reported a "tide of letters" in response to an inquiry from *Motion Picture Herald*. "The preponderant demand is for entertainment and entertainment of the sort that puts aside the cares of these war worn days, when every day fills the lives of the millions with intense emotional concern." After a war newsreel, a war briefie, a Victory short, and a combat report, audiences were understandably unwilling to face a feature-length war film. For their part, exhibitors were unwilling to face disgruntled patrons or empty seats. "With the flood of war dramas and the flow of 'war shorts' the exhibitor is continually confronted with conflicts and problems," complained a theaterman from the Prudential Circuit on the Eastern seaboard. "All too often there is an embarrassing situation where the service of the national cause, and our commitments [to the War Activities Committee], demand that we show 'war shorts' in a program which has been inevitably overloaded with war, and sometimes for weeks."

The studio heads were of two minds. Motion picture executives backed the war film for patriotic reasons and, if the bottom line was never damned, it was not the sole consideration. Studios acceded to audience taste by spicing up war-themed films with more boy-girl stuff, musical interludes, and comedy, but they were not about to jettison the most visible if less profitable evidence of war-related endeavor. For Harry Warner, president or Warner Bros., recalcitrant exhibitors were tantamount to fifth columnists. "Any arbitrary exclusion of war films, either to satisfy a small appeaser element or for personal reasons without regard to the general public interest, is equivalent to sabotage," Warner told a meeting of home office executives. He then spat out the acid remark: "We would hate to be known as the company that made the most successful musical film of this great war for freedom."

The call for escapist fare from one section of the gallery could not be denounced as homefront complacency or exhibitor greed. Soldiers were typically unreceptive to and often downright contemptuous of Hollywood's rousing combat films. In training, raw recruits voiced a predilection for war films; combat veterans barely tolerated them. "Send more escapist films," a soldier in the South Pacific ordered. "We know about the war." Sitting among an unruly GI audience during a certifiable "flag-waver," an embarrassed *Variety* correspondent reported the derisive response to what the men called "go-git-'ems" and explained one reason why. "There are catcalls for war pictures which reveal all too clearly that the writers did their soldiering or sailing in the neighborhood of Sunset Boulevard." Another survey of the armed forces reported a decisive preference for westerns, musicals, and exotic fantasies. "At the top of the list detailing what the Marines *don't* want to see on the screen are 'flag wavers' or war films." Offered two Hollywood versions of the tropical Pacific, GIs chose the sarong-clad "savage excitements and dangers untamed of a forbidden island paradise!" in *White Savage* (1943) and *Tahiti Honey* (1943) over the bullet-ridden terrain of *Wake Island* (1942) and *Corregidor* (1943). Trade ads cited the wishes of an audience even higher up the ranks. "Entertainment is always a national asset," President Roosevelt told the National Conference of the Entertainment Industry for War Activities in 1943. "Invaluable in time of peace, it is indispensable in wartime."

In 1943 Paramount's executive producer B. G. ("Buddy") De Sylva announced his studio was putting the brakes on war films. "Recent preview cards show that patrons are keen for escapist movies, and they obviously believe that, after an arduous day working in munitions plants and other defense industries, they deserve a few hours of surcease from the war." The other major studios, even Warner Bros., followed suit, curtailing production of all-male combat adventures and changing the tenor of war-themed films. After 1943, war films modulated their violence and expanded introspective moments of melodramatic register. Originally slated to end in fiery violence, *Song of Russia*, "taking heed of the signs," eliminated a combat climax from the final edit. *The Sullivans* pared its war footage down to four minutes. In the bomber crew film *Winged Victory* nary a shot is fired in anger.

Faced with a backlog of war movies, publicity departments scrambled to disguise militarist content. Billy Wilder's *Five Graves to Cairo* (1943) was generically recast from a war movie about the North African campaign to a thriller about Germany's legendary Desert Fox, a "sensational *Rommel*odrama." In 1943 a planned bio-pic of a more despised Nazi, *Dr. Paul Joseph Goebbels,* was announced as emphatically "not a war picture . . . but a story that tells the heartbreaking ordeals of a girl who defied Goebbels because she loved another man." *A WAVE, a WAC, and a Marine* (1944) belied its uniformed title with taglines that promised "no battle scenes, no message, just barrels of fun and jive to make you happy you're alive."

Conversely, less the imputation of frivolous irrelevance besmirch escapist fare, movies with absolutely nothing to do with the war per se claimed a submerged martial significance. "Are we fighting for this too? Yes!" asked and answered the teaser for the effervescent *Claudia* (1943). Ernst Lubitsch's *Heaven Can Wait* (1943) put forth humor as a vital national resource: "What's this got to do with winning the war? Plenty! A nation that can laugh is a nation that can win." "No message, no mission, no misfortune," was the alliterative assurance of *Lady of Burlesque* (1943), just "music, mystery, and mirth." After 1943 some exhibitors frankly declared moratoriums on war film programming and unapologetically publicized special no-war double features. "Not a hint of war in the whole program," promised RKO of its 1944 twin bill, *This Is the Life / Ghost Catchers*. What Marxist critics condemned as the narcotic lull of mass culture, studio publicists embraced as a patriotic duty. An all-purpose tagline caught the spirit:

"Keep 'em laughing . . . and you'll keep 'em working . . . fighting . . . WINNING!"

Pledges of mindlessness notwithstanding, Hollywood's self-defined escapism was mindful of the war. No less than the straight-faced genres, wartime comedies—high and low, screwball or slap-stick—worked for the OWI and genuflected to culturally approved codes of conduct. In the musical comedy *Private Buckeroo* (1942) good Americans rush down to the recruitment center on the morning of December 8 and underage patriots try desperately to scam the draft board and enlist. But since true laughing matter demands the suspension of natural law and moral convention, comedy offers a safe haven to act out the impermissible and utter the unspeakable. Within the comedy zone, the fear of dying and the reluctance to serve the great cause surfaces in the spaces between the laughter.

Swollen with millions of incorrigible civilians, the military was the favored stage for burlesques of all sorts. Certainly the joshing never crossed over into a full-scale offensive against the armed forces, the Allied cause, or the spirit of the American fighting man. Wartime serv-ice comedies balance a howl against military life with a hymn of praise. The formula surely conforms to regulations. An unpleasant martinet (a screeching top sergeant, a by-the-book junior officer) is the nemesis of a misfit inductee who inflicts zany chaos on barracks, parade ground, and military propriety. A court martial looms but the inductee is rescued and the martinet foiled by a higher ranking and wiser commander who recognizes an exploitable military resource in the inductee's creative vigor and initiative. Typically the bumbler winds up an accidental hero, and always his clumsiness and chican-ery fall well short of a serious imputation against the courage and commitment of the average GI. *See Here, Private Hargrove* (1944) halts the high jinks when chiseler Keenan Wynn temporarily persuades the maladroit but patriotic PFC played by Robert Walker to secure a cushy rear-echelon job to avoid combat duty. Like the derisive but dependable Willie and Joe in Bill Mauldin's cartoons for the *Stars and Stripes,* the dialogue and the stock situations aired common GI gripes and targeted inane and arcane military procedure in a manner alter-nately whimsical and sardonic.

Although both Donald Duck and Daffy Duck got into the avoid-the-selective-service act, the most animated screen coward was Bob ("I'll hold your coat") Hope. An indefatigable USO entertainer, Hope played an unabashed yellow in and out of olive drab. In *Caught in the*

The service comedy: Eddie Bracken and Bob Hope think the Army is just another racket in *Caught in the Draft* (1941). (Museum of Modern Art/Film Stills Archive)

Draft (1941) he is a vain movie actor ("More blood," he tells his makeup man, "Make me more heroic") who tries to avoid conscription by courting a colonel's daughter (Dorothy Lamour) who "looks like Dorothy Lamour with clothes on." Trembling at the sound of gunfire, fainting at the sight of blood, Hope acts out natural if culturally incorrect impulses while tossing off side-of-the-mouth wisecracks. In *They Got Me Covered* (1942), his reflex reaction to a siren signaling "lights out" in peaceful Washington, D.C., is: "We're trapped! Let's surrender." Teamed with pseudonemesis Bing Crosby in a pair of movies on the road to anywhere but a combat zone, Hope bolted like a gazelle at the threat of physical danger or the prospect of sacrifice without profit.

Writer-director Preston Sturges, Paramount's ace satirist and pioneer multi-hyphenate, contrived two seriously deranged wartime comedies. To a 1942 trade press inquiry on the role of Hollywood at war, the director responded like a master of misdirection ("I don't think there should be the slightest difference in the type of picture made") and then made two back-to-back satires irreverent to the point of blasphemy. Of all the virtuoso practitioners of screwball comedy, Sturges alone adapted the madcap style to the substance of the Second World War. In *The Miracle of Morgan's Creek* and *Hail the Conquering Hero* (both 1944), doubts about homefront constancy percolate to the surface in the person of atonic actor Eddie Bracken, who plays a stuttering "unwilling civilian" afflicted in turn with high blood pressure and chronic hay fever.

In *The Miracle of Morgan's Creek,* the less than immaculate conception of smalltown party girl Trudy Kockenlocker (Betty Hutton) is pregnant with meaning. An all too willing "girl behind the man with the gun," Kockenlocker devotes herself to troop morale until she becomes pregnant by a soldier, very much missing in action the morning after, whose name she can't quite recall. The only available husband is the nasally neurasthenic Norval Jones (Bracken), who flunks his induction physicals due to cold sweats and hallucinations ("the spots!"). Norval volunteers for paternity and Trudy's delicate condition bears fruit as sextuplet sons (a "platoon of boys" trumpets a newspaper headline). Norval gains a National Guard commission in the bargain, earning what the Draft Board denied him: six tokens of potency, seven counting Trudy.

Hail the Conquering Hero, Sturges's follow-up send-up of hero worship and homefront venality, drips cynicism about the holiest and hoariest wartime verities—patriotism, the girl back home, and, astonishingly, motherhood. Rejected by the Marine Corps, Woodrow Lafayette Pershing Truesmith (Bracken) is nursing his disappointment in a bar when six authentic Marine heroes from Guadalcanal take him under their wing. The leathernecks lend him uniform, medals, and alibi and forcibly accompany the frantically resistant Woodrow to a hometown welcome worthy of a hero. In the living room of the Truesmith home, Woodrow's mother keeps a shrine to her deceased husband, a posthumous Medal of Honor recipient and a debilitating oedipal burden for his effete son. Stoked by the fertile imagination of a gruff sergeant (William Demarest), Woodrow's ersatz battlefield exploits grow in magnificence and his dilemma of deception spirals out of control. Sturges placated OWI anxieties with glimpses of a truly upright homefront—the grocer who brings by priority goods for the troops, the townsfolk who protest "business as usual" with a war on, and the war bond posters adorning background wall space. Too, Sturges's portrait of the Marines is *semper fidelis* to the best mythos of the Corps. But the distance between homefront and frontline is never washed over. Local businessmen and politicians are cupidity and avarice in action; the Guadalcanal veterans include a shell-shocked goofball whose nightmares are real enough. After a ritual of public humiliation and confession, Woodrow wins the fickle homefront girl and the keys to City Hall. The Marines ride out of town enveloped by the steam of a locomotive, a misty-eyed tableau that dissolves into a still image of the shrine to Woodrow's father. The final frame of the film kneels before the altar of the god it has wantonly desecrated.

As romantic competition Eddie Bracken was hard to take seri-

Forced induction: Eddie Bracken (*aloft*) in Preston Sturges's comedy on thin ice, *Hail the Conquering Hero* (1944).

ously, but in merely broaching the suspicion that (unlike the Marines) homefront girls were not always faithful, Sturges treaded on thin ice. "It was actually the enormous risks I took with my pictures, skating right up to the edge of nonacceptance, that paid off so handsomely," the director later remarked. Hollywood might remind women of the lack of homefront men, but it had better assure overseas men that homefront heroes were not cutting in on their action. Sturges ingenues excepted, girls back home were virtuous, steadfast, and sat under the apple tree, as the Andrews Sisters sang, with no one else; wives were Hindu-like in devotion. Faithlessness on the homefront was punished with providential swiftness. In *Tender Comrade* (1943) a homefront wife gets dolled up to step out on her husband, a sailor stationed in the Pacific. As her date arrives, a radio bulletin announces his ship has sunk. Immune to the attentions of the dashing, flirtatious, and available Joseph Cotton, Claudette Colbert set the conjugal standard in *Since You Went Away* (1944).

A different sort of romantic problem beset women. On screen and on the street, the dearth of prime-ribbed leading men that reflected the disappearance of available suitors in the population at large was a shortage at least as worrisome as nylons or coffee. Not for nothing did Columbia title one of its women's pictures *City Without Men* (1943). The age differential between screen couples spread to encompass the upper registers of middle-aged masculinity, a pairing of blossoming female ingenues with what the trade press labeled "a few name guys of indeterminate age whose physical charms fall within that rather disquieting state known as 'well-preserved.' " The matchups were chronologically lopsided or physically unlikely even when they worked: Spencer Tracy and Irene Dunne (*A Guy Named Joe*, 1943), Humphrey Bogart and Lauren Bacall (*To Have and Have Not*, 1944), Charles Laughton and Maureen O'Hara (*This Land Is Mine,* 1943), Edward G. Robinson and anybody.

For homefront men the enticement of a statistical advantage in romance was tempered by the trepidation of a hunter suddenly made fair game. In *The More the Merrier* (1943), ostensibly about the housing shortage but really about the escort shortage, a lone male endures wolf whistles, catcalls, and a pinch on the behind as he walks a gauntlet of man-hungry female workers. The number crunch ("eight gals to every fella" in male-depleted Washington, D.C.) left a skittish Joel McCrea wilting under the ravenous gaze of a gaggle of female admirers. Stretching the statistics further ("Where the men are one to ten a gal's gotta be good! No wonder no man is safe after dark!"), *Government Gal* (1943) shared the District of Columbia locale and escort-evaporation theme.

Setting laugh lines to music took off some of the edge. As the escapist genre of choice, the Hollywood musical competed and overlapped with comedy. In the later war years musicals flooded the market—over a hundred by one count. Since no genre called a total ceasefire on war work, musicals coordinated OWI steps into the choreography no matter how ungainly the promenade. The nostalgic turn-of-the-century setting and home fires of Vincente Minnelli's *Meet Me in St. Louis* (1944) is an Arthur Freed unit evocation of FDR's Four Freedoms, while the contemporaneous uptown glitz of *Cover Girl* (1944) detours for some song and dance on a flatbed truck full of grateful GIs. As a means of acknowledging the war and escaping from it, the service-set musical was the most serviceable multipurpose compromise of convenience. Military barracks and parade grounds became staging areas for comedy, melodrama, or music by troops-turned-troupes. In *This Is the Army* (1943) and *Up in Arms* (1944), well-drilled choruses burst into song, dance, and drag. At the box office, comedy and choreography in uniform regularly outperformed combat. In 1944 the success of *See Here, Private Hargrove* and *Up in Arms* outdid *The Purple Heart, Cry "Havoc!",* and the "weightier war pictures."

The militarist musical was an ideal place to recognize the contributions of an essential homefront industry Hollywood needed no urging from the OWI to recognize: itself. Cavalcade productions depicted the common touch of celebrities eagerly rolling up their sleeves to bus tables, empty ashtrays, wash dishes, or just listen sympathetically to a lonely GI talk about the girl back home while dancing with a leggy contract player. *Star Spangled Rhythm* (1942), *Stage Door Canteen* (1943), and *Hollywood Canteen* (1944) march battalions of big-name stars through uniform-thick clientele with dialogue that begins when a friendly celebrity asks "And where are you from, soldier?" or a wide-eyed GI bleats "Say, isn't that Helen Hayes?" Tributes to the USO's "soldiers in greasepaint" took a backstage format in *Follow the Boys* (1944), "the first picture to demonstrate the heroic job that has been accomplished by the motion picture and all branches of show business on behalf of the war effort," and *Four Jills in a Jeep* (1944), a laundered account of a USO tour through England and North Africa by Kay Francis, Carole Landis, Martha Raye, and Mitzi Mayfair.

One wartime industry Hollywood loved to celebrate: celebrity servants (*left to right*) Jack Carson, Jane Wyman, John Garfield, and Bette Davis mixing it up with starstruck GIs in *Hollywood Canteen* (1944).

True to form, Hollywood was never more unctuous than at work on itself. Expressing a rankled vox populi, a GI in India complained of the "cheap back patting and self-glorification on the part of the film people at the expense of the dignity and stature of the American soldier." The GI and several "fellow sufferers" had walked out on *Hollywood Canteen* because "we couldn't stomach the portrayal of our good level-headed mature American soldiers as simple gullible fools, so awe-stricken by the sight and presence of screen queens that they can only gulp and mutter stupidly, 'oh, golly,' and repeat inanely to all and sundry, 'I kissed Joan Leslie.' "

CAUGHT IN THE DRAFT

For not a few Americans the sprightly "keep 'em laughing" front smacked of sunshine patriotism. A hotbed of suspect morals and silken privilege, Hollywood never enjoyed the presumption of stalwart purpose and pure motives lent the more tangible and less glamorous wartime industries. It also labored under nasty prejudices. In September 1941 the Senate hearings on Motion Picture Screen and Radio Propaganda assailed Hollywood in vocabulary leavened with anti-Semitism. During the war the imputation was muted but not unmuttered. In 1942 Melvyn Douglas was smeared by Congressman Leland Ford (R–Calif.), who darkly reminded constituents that the actor's real name was Hesselberg. The next year the Truman Committee's inquiry into accusations of military-industry malfeasance gratuitously impugned producer Darryl F. Zanuck and director Anatole Litvak. "I don't believe in these fellows backing out," said Truman upon learning of Zanuck's request to be put on inactive service. "I think he is an officer in the Army under an emergency and I think he should stay there." Sen. Ralph O. Brewster (R–Maine) was concerned about Litvak's commission in the Army Signal Corps because the Russian-born director of *Confessions of a Nazi Spy* (1939) was a naturalized American citizen. "So recently a convert to Americanism was not a particularly happy selection unless your talent was considerably exhausted," Brewster informed Under Secretary of War Robert P. Patterson. "You could use somewhat more seasoned citizens."

Besides the halls of Congress, insinuations against motion picture experts with soft California jobs filled newspaper editorials and barroom conversations. In 1942 *Yank* published a scathing commentary:

> In Hollywood, they are working like dogs to win their war. They come back from camp shows, U.S.O. benefits, bond drives, sweating from the effort they have put into it. They compliment each other on how they wowed them. They pat each other on the back, and say, "Of course we're doing our part. We are specialists, and here is where we belong. Our work is important. We are doing as much as the boys on the fighting fronts." Then they go home, take a quick dip in their swimming pools, and rest up for a week before the next camp show comes along.

In this atmosphere, motion picture manpower allocation and celebrity status was fraught with cultural danger. Public relations collided with production realities over the issues of priority ratings and draft classification—of the studio system as an essential industry, of its workers as deferrable specialists. Lowell Mellett summed up the OWI's position in a letter to Gen. Lewis Hershey, head of the Selective Service:

Celebrity mobilization: Greer Garson maps out her War Bond tour in September 1942. (National Archives)

> As a *civilian* activity, I believe the industry is essential to the national health, safety, and interest, through the maintenance of the national morale. As a *war* activity I believe the industry is essential to the production of training and instructional films for the armed forces as well as educational and information films for the civilian population.

Given the fusillade of cheap shots, however, studio executives and union leaders were reluctant to ask (publicly) for special privileges but aware that without expert technicians and artists they could neither build morale nor provide diversion.

In February 1942 General Hershey ruled "that the motion picture industry is an activity essential in certain instances to the national health, safety, and interest and in other instances to war production." Essential, it turned out, did not mean deferrable. Though circumscribed in cast and aimed mainly at technical workers, Hersey's ruling met with widespread criticism. Demagogic politicians and tabloid editorialists decried "Hollywood Colonels" when the famous names enlisted and denigrated "the Culver City Commandos" fighting "the Battle of Beverly Hills" when they didn't.

The controversy over the retention of able-bodied, draft-age male talent, especially for leading men whose screen persona was keyed to courage and strength, was a pure case of double jeopardy. Responding to Hershey's initial ruling, the Screen Actors Guild issued a statement of tactical demurral. "[SAG] does not agree with [special] classification. It believes actors and everyone else should be subject to the same rules for the draft as the rest of the country." MPPDA Vice President Y. Frank Freeman concurred: "There can be no thought of requesting blanket deferments." They needn't have protested too much. "We agree that the production of motion pictures is essential, but we have not yet been given any clearcut equivalent that there is a shortage of qualified actors to meet the need of the film industry for morale building," said Louis Levene of the Office of War Manpower, adding pointedly: "There will be no general deferments until we are so convinced."

Yet how does Hollywood make quality entertainment to divert a war-weary nation without professional actors? How does it keep a war-conscious audience from wondering why this virile fellow isn't in uniform? *Variety* claimed the "big problem that faced the industry was not getting deferments but in keeping topnotch people," that too many irreplaceable talents had already enlisted, and that others had "talked of joining up either to avoid being considered as slackers or because they consider film production futile and uninteresting compared with playing in real-life productions."

As public creatures, Hollywood personnel were subjected to an intensity of scrutiny not accorded cardholders in the United Auto Workers. Soon after vegetarian Lew Ayres, the popular star of MGM's *Dr. Kildare* series, filed for conscientious objector status, his on-screen image was hissed off screen and his then current film, *Dr. Kildare's Victory* (1941), was dropped by exhibitors. At public appearances, stars were liable to be confronted with a blunt accusation: "Why aren't you in uniform?" "The stumbling block is the failure of the public to appreciate the value of actors," acknowledged General Hershey. "The public is willing to accept certain things, such as work in a war plant as essential. It fails to accept other things, even though they too may be important." The Selective Service head invoked the sliding scale of wartime contribution with a rhetorical question: "Are mothers content to have their sons go into battle in North Africa and Guadalcanal while musicians stay at home and play instruments?"

Basically, no. Short of visible infirmity and legal blindness, draft deferments were viewed with knowing looks or unveiled suspicion. Flat feet, bad vision, and sinus trouble were dodges not diseases— the hernia and arthritis of bandleader Kay Kyser, the bad back of Orson Welles, the perforated eardrum that exempted Frank Sinatra became bywords for the selective service granted the rich and famous. The apparently fit crooner Sinatra—certainly fit enough to ignite the not-so-subliminal passions of hordes of swooning young females—was far and away the privileged object of homefront desire most heartily despised by frontline fighters. "It is not too much to say that by the end of the war Sinatra had become the most hated man in the Army, Navy, Air Corps, and Marine Corps," wrote historian William Manchester in 1973, easily calling up the bile he had felt thirty years earlier. "Like the bobby soxers, Frankiephobes in uniform saw in the Voice a symbol: to them he stood for all available civilians." Besides a few desultory USO appearances, Sinatra's singular contribution to the Four Freedoms was made in RKO's widely screened nonprofit featurette, *The House I Live In* (July 1945). In song and talk, he voices the evils of anti-Semitism to back-alley boys in need of a dulcet lesson in religious tolerance.

One of the few available male actors of the right age and body type to prosper free of insinuation was Van Johnson. A vigorous but nondescript male ingenue who gained by default plum roles as the uniformed hero in *A Guy Named Joe*, *Two Girls and a Sailor* (1944), and *Thirty Seconds Over Tokyo* (1944), Johnson was insulated from excoriation by public awareness of his nearly fatal automobile accident in 1943. But for the unhospitalized, moments of exculpation and explanation were inserted into showbiz-sensitive scenarios to assuage audience suspicions. In *Follow the Boys* former vaudeville dancer and musical star Tony West (George Raft) tries to enlist the day after Pearl Harbor but is rejected because of an old knee injury. "Incidentally, Captain," the crestfallen hoofer tells his recruiting officer, "I'd rather nobody knew I was turned down." The postcredit crawl in Kay Kyser's cavalcade USO musical *Around the World* (1943) sounds overly defensive: "To every battle front where men and women of the United Nations fight—civilians from all walks of life are contributing their honest efforts to the struggle. Among these, the brightest stars of Hollywood and Broadway do their bit." Again, comedy was the one zone where bright stars might admit their bit was hardly hardship duty. In the resonantly titled *Mr. Lucky* (1943), noncombat-ant actor Cary Grant plays a roguish gambler who assumes the iden-tity of a dead friend to scam the draft board. While trying to seduce war-relief worker Laraine Day into allowing him to operate a gambling casino at her charity ball, he finds himself in line for a blood donation and some suggestive dialogue:

> DAY: If you're so interested in serving a cause, why don't you join the Army?
> GRANT (passing over his phony draft card and shrugging, resigned): 4-F.
> DAY: You look 1-A to me.
> GRANT: Thanks. You don't look so bad yourself.

Dreading the stigma of "slackerism," some able-bodied screen ac-tors were said to be "frankly ashamed to continue appearing in public in civvies while fellow Americans were sweltering in blood in the streaming jungles of the South Pacific and elsewhere." In 1942 Tyrone Power and Henry Fonda depleted the shrinking ranks of leading men by enlisting in the Marines Corps and Navy, respectively. Clark Ga-ble—heartbroken over the war-related death of Carole Lombard and humiliated to stand on the soundstage sidelines—turned down a per-sonal appeal from FDR and enlisted as an Army private at age 42. "I have no interest in acting as long as the war is going on," he an-nounced prior to his secret swearing-in ceremony on August 12, 1942. "And I am not looking for a commission."

Not until the epochal drafting of Elvis Presley in 1958 did the Army have in its ranks so exhaustively chronicled a GI as Clark Gable. In cold military terms, some said Gable was more trouble than he was worth. Civilians besieged his every station; soldiers broke ranks to ask for autographs. On guard duty on the Florida coastline, Gable was confronted with fifteen hundred females who turned up to gawk. At Pueblo Air Base, where the now-commissioned actor took ad-vanced training, a sign was posted: "The officers and Lieutenant Ga-ble will appreciate it if the public will not interfere with his heavy training program and will treat him just as another member of the armed forces. He will not be available for any appearances and can-not be reached by phone."

Gable's voluntary demotion from screen royalty to government issue and his self-reliant ascension up the ranks, especially with-

Clark Gable in the real thing: "You're not particularly interested in how you look." (National Archives)

standing the rigors of OCS at middle age, was widely admired by GIs. So was his grace under the dual pressure of publicity and the Luft-waffe. At the Pentagon, Gable was asked the difference between motion picture combat and bombing missions over Germany. "There is no comparison," he told the press. "In the real thing you're not particularly interested in how you look."

Wartime audiences, however, were very interested in how stars looked in the real thing. Gable himself is the true subject of the Victory film *Wings Up* (May 1943), an Army Air Force production about the Officer Candidate School. In a droll narration Gable reveals that he too has walked parade and stood retreat, gotten "gigged" for sloppy housekeeping, and endured military discipline. Describing demerits received and punishment endured, Gable filters the OCS experience through his own personality. "I got that [many demerits]," he remarks. "It was summer in Florida when I went through this [punishment]." Best of all, when an inductee is shorn of his moustache, the narrator blurts out, "I know how you feel, Mister." In Gable's case, any logistical hassle was repaid in representational power.

For the merging of screen image with war record, Gable's only competition was Jimmy Stewart. Where Gable was an unattainable dreamboat for the starstruck fan—think of Judy Garland singing "Dear Mr. Gable (You Made Me Love You)" to his 8-by-10 in *Broadway Melody of 1938*—Stewart's modest ways and common touch blended seamlessly into the ranks. "Jimmy Stewart, in or out of uniform, clung to the spirit of his small-town American background," read a contemporaneous hagiography. "He grew up like millions of other boys—went to public school, dropped a hook in the creek of a summer, joined the Boy Scouts, fell in love and out again." In the Stewart-hosted Victory film *Winning Your Wings* (May 1942), the sashaying drawl, open-faced sincerity, and stalwart American carriage of Jefferson Smith/Jimmy Stewart creates a union of art and myth as awesome as anything in Leni Riefenstahl. Taxiing in at the controls of a plane, Stewart steps out of the cockpit, looks at the camera in mock surprise, and fixes his gaze on the spectator. "Well, hello," he says in his heartland tonalities. "Gee, looks like I'm back in the movies again, doesn't it?"

Enlisting in the Army Air Corps in March 1941, Stewart said little to the press and went about fulfilling cinematic expectations. The first motion picture star to do active combat flying in the European theater, he moved up on merit. In turn a squadron commander, operations chief, and combat-wing chief of staff, Stewart commanded bombing raids, led his division in bombing efficiency, and shepherded his outfit though fourteen missions over enemy territory. When he won the Air Medal with Oak Leaf Cluster in 1943 and the Distinguished Flying Cross the next year, the usual mutterings about overquick promotion and special rewards to pampered celebrities went unsounded. The picture-perfect transition of the "one-time screen star" into the "proud living symbol of the entire motion picture industry's men in uniform" survived press hyperbole and public skepticism. Characteristically, the man who was the authentic war hero came home to play his most memorable screen role as the man who stayed behind in Frank Capra's *It's a Wonderful Life* (1946).

Studio press agents made certain that stars in uniform (or near uniforms) were kept constantly before the public eye in publicity shots, newsreel clips, and Victory shorts. The War Activities Committee distributed *A Message from Lt. Tyrone Power* (November 1944),

All Star Bond Rally (April 1945), and *Hollywood Victory Caravan* (November 1945). The *March of Time* weighed in with issues on "Show-business at War" (May 1943) and "Upbeat in Music" (December 1943). Universal distributed a ten-minute Army Signal Corps film on theaters on the battlefront, *Movies at War* (June 1944), and Columbia released the featurette *Hollywood in Uniform* (August 1943). Behind the screen too, the recognizable intonations of actors and actresses narrated almost all the widely screened Victory shorts and publicly released War Department films.

Not that selfless devotion to duty was the unanimous rule in the Screen Actors Guild any more than in the United Mine Workers. Besides the standard intimations of mortality, *Variety* noted that many stars "didn't want to reveal to the public that romantic leads were often prosaic benedicts in real life or that many a swashbuckling cinematic hero was 4-F in the Army though 1-A on the screen." Not until early 1943, when MGM asked the Los Angeles Draft Board to reclassify Mickey Rooney's 1-A status on the grounds he was an "essential worker" in an "essential industry," did a studio request that an actor be exempted from military service to perform backlot duty. The argument that Rooney was more valuable playing Andy Hardy than GI Joe makes a certain kind of sense, but not the kind to be readily appreciated from a troop ship. Rooney was shortly reevaluated 4-F due to high blood pressure and a heart murmur only to be rereclassified in 1944 and inducted as a private.

Of course Hollywood rank had its privileges. Secretary of the Navy Frank Knox gave Robert Taylor time to complete *Song of Russia,* and FDR's own confidential assistant Harry Hopkins personally decommissioned Lt. Burgess Meredith so the actor might play Ernie Pyle in *The Story of G.I. Joe.* Keeping his humor, writer-director Garson Kanin expressed a sensible attitude that, by and large, came to dictate military policy in regard to motion picture inductees: "For my part, I hope to be assigned to some film unit because I happen to be better with a camera than I am with a gun. I've tried both."

WAR TIMING

Any laughter Hollywood brought to its stressed-out audience was returned with interest. Probably the most sincere and full-throated chortling of the war years came from studio executives on their way to the bank. The usual showbusiness went on, it turned out, not in spite of the war but spurred on by it. In 1939 average weekly attendance at the nation's theaters was a robust 85 million. By 1945 the audience for motion pictures reached levels of devotional fervor never to be regained: 95 million Americans each week went to the movies. "It is axiomatic that you can open a can of sardines and people will stand in line," cracked inside dopesters. Following movie-marked money always leads down a circuitous path, but trade press tallies indicate domestic box-office gross rose from $1 billion in 1939 to $1.5 billion in 1945. Reckoning in wartime inflation and increased amusement taxes on the one hand and creative bookkeeping and short counts of the house on the other, windfall profits all around seems a balanced appraisal. The *Hollywood Reporter* was frankly flummoxed by the unparalleled good fortune in the midst of a world aflame. "The sale of tickets at the nation's box offices is unbelievable," enthused a front-page story in 1942. "Nothing approximating the amounts now being sold ever hit this business before. Good and bad pictures seemingly get the same audience draw; star values help but the lack of them seemingly presents little difference. What exhibitors judge as poor attractions turn out to be hits and they can't figure it out." With the industry's knack of finding a dark cloud among box-office silver, the paper offered one cautionary note: "Business has developed so alarmingly in most centers that there is actually a seat shortage in most every spot."

The sweet smell of success didn't mean a curtailment of the work of advertising, publicity, and exploitation. In fact the war created terrific opportunities for ancillary marketing. Timing was critical. A film dramatizing a topical and intriguing war-themed occurrence garnered a concomitant box-office boost, especially if no newsreel footage had documented the event. For the commerce-minded, the true value of Fritz Lang's *Hangmen Also Die!* (1943) lay in its having gotten "the jump on other studios rushing into production films based on the Czech blood-bath that followed the assassination of Rheinhardt Heydrich." In September 1944, Britain lifted its blackout; by November 1944, Producers Releasing Corporation was advertising *When the Lights Go On Again,* "a title that expresses the hope of millions." The most auspicious wartime movie-timing was Warner Bros.'s *Casablanca*, whose release hit the crest of the publicity wave accompanying the North African campaign and the conference between Churchill and Roosevelt in the title city. Implying a special relationship with War Department strategists, Harry Warner gloated: "Remember that [*Casablanca*] was completed and ready weeks before our forces invaded North Africa and that, almost on the heels of the first invasion barge to touch African soil with our soldiers, it was on the screen, helping in its definite way to interpret the action for you, to explain Vichy France to you."

Both Warner Bros. and 20th Century-Fox hoped for a similar invasion synchronicity with melodramas of Norwegian-set resistance, *Edge of Darkness* (1943) and *The Moon Is Down* (1943), respectively. Banking on the south of France, Paramount plotted *Marseilles* in summer 1943 and, anticipating the liberation of Paris, prepared *Till We Meet Again* (1944). *The Hitler Gang* (1944) linked itself to the attempted assassination of Hitler on July 20, 1944. The premature *Appointment in Berlin* (1943) aimed for punctuality in a 1945 rerelease, and *Hotel Berlin* (1945) arrived on schedule the same year. Ads for *The Master Race* (1944) prepared for a looming eventuality: "a shock warning to all the world to beware of the Germans *after the war!*"

With the Allied invasion of Europe approaching, Hollywood looked forward to the end of the war in two senses. The first *in medias bellum* postwar film, Columbia's *None Shall Escape* (released February 3, 1944), envisioned a war crimes tribunal in which a Nazi officer is tried for the bombing of Warsaw. In June 1944 producer Walter Wanger announced that "post-war is now" and asserted that "the most urgent homefront problems to be dealt with by screen and press are veterans' rehabilitation, post-war employment, housing, interracial friction, and education. The number one problem for the people of the United States is the reincorporation into our national life of the men and women of the armed forces." Although the proliferation of social-problem films waited until the war was really over, a modest number of 1943–45 features dealt with veterans' readjustment problems while the military was still under fire.

The more somber and therapeutic variants were called "psychiatricals." In *The Fallen Sparrow* (1943) John Garfield plays a veteran of the Spanish Civil War tormented by flashbacks of torture, a thin allegory for the anticipated influx of afflicted GIs. The next year, allegory was dispensed with for the psychoneurotic Pacific theater veteran played by Joseph Cotton in *I'll Be Seeing You.* The veteran's scars were facial and the resolution fantastical in John Cromwell's lachrymose *The Enchanted Cottage* (1945), a melodrama that failed to realize how half a million men wounded in action can undermine belief in magical potions or miracle cures.

Most of the Hollywood rehabilitation films both during and after the Second World War recognized that, for the blinded and crippled men and their sympathetic but anxious women, endurance, adaptation, and readjustment was an ongoing drama promising no climactic restoration of sight or mobility. In *Pride of the Marines* (1945) the susceptible John Garfield plays embittered hero Al Schmid, a blinded Marine who becomes reconciled to, if not completely cured of, his condition. *Thirty Seconds Over Tokyo* (1944) veers away from the conventions of the combat film to examine the physical pain, emotional torment, and conjugal complications of wounded pilot Ted Lawson (Van Johnson), who loses a leg to gangrene. The most wrenching of the rehabilitation films was John Huston's unblinking documentary for the War Department, *Let There Be Light* (1946). A primer on the psychological ravages of combat (catatonia, spasms, hysteria), it records the Army's attempts to rebuild whole personalities from the shards left after battle. Despite a coda that gives hope of future readjustment, the anguish and trauma of Huston's visibly shattered witnesses seem well beyond the restorative powers of polite and concerned surgeons, shrinks, or any other war-bred expert. With too much revealed and too little resolved, it was deemed a violation of the patients' privacy by the War Department and withheld from public screening.

A sideline beneficiary of the demand for newsworthy topicality was the independent documentary. Prior to the war Arthur L. Mayer, owner and operator of New York's Rialto Theater, noted that the "documentary" label was a "damning designation." "Commercial picture circles were scarcely aware of the existence of such films," wrote Mayer in 1944. "I recall on one occasion that an inexperienced salesman described one of my pictures as a documentary. The prospective smalltown customer to whom he was talking replied: 'The folks hereabouts are used to getting their pictures on *fillum*, and they don't like 'em no other way.'"

With war news daily surpassing in drama and excitement the boldest fiction, and with newsreel coverage granted a wider Code latitude than entertainment, the documentary feature became a readily marketable commodity for the first time since the silent era. Against the gloss of soundstage production, it offered the drama of amateur-shot reality and the vicarious danger of production under fire. The two-reel Warners short *The Unconquered Peoples* (1942) promised smuggled footage from occupied Europe and the United Artists release of Rey Scott's *Kukan: The Battle Cry of China* (1942) urged "SEE—the incredible film that was smuggled past the Japanese, in bamboo poles!" Distributors reported that the major circuits, which had consistently refused to play documentaries before December 7, were now gobbling them up.

The Eastern front provided some of the best material. In the year after Pearl Harbor, imports from the Soviet Union provided spectacular footage and victorious images when American films possessed precious little of either. RKO edited *The Bombing of Moscow* (1942) into a one-reeler, Republic added a soundtrack and commentary to *Moscow Strikes Back* (1942), and Paramount picked up the Soviet Union's *The City That Stopped Hitler—Heroic Stalingrad* (1943). By 1942 the number of theaters playing Soviet documentaries ballooned from a prewar dozen to over 200, with bookings of some shorts going as high as 2,000. In the next two years, Artkino released more than fifty war-related features and shorts into the American market. This was the more impressive because some of the films distributed by Artkino were played in the original Russian. Not until late 1942 was a wartime Soviet drama imported stateside with prerecorded English dialogue, though an inadvertent connotation was gained in translation: *In the Rear of the Enemy*.

Whether selling documentary or entertainment, motion picture strategists plotting exploitable topicality always had to think about nine months ahead, the average time period between conception and delivery for an "A" picture. The advertising campaign for *Back to Bataan* (1945) is a casebook of war-related production foresight and publicity tie-ins. Conceived in the wake of wartime history both filmic and factual (MGM's 1943 *Bataan* and the retreat of American forces from the Philippines) and trusting to the fulfillment of General MacArthur's pledge that American forces *shall* return, it asserted timeliness and verisimilitude with expository newsreel footage of the liberation of POW camps on Luzon. Leon J. Bamberger, the sales promotion manager for RKO, oversaw an elaborate and multilevel publicity plan that consciously built on (and intentionally conflated) the military campaign with the exploitation campaign. The advertising kit listed the names of liberated GIs who appeared in the authentic newsreel clips used in the film. Exhibitors were instructed to "take

special note of persons herewith that belong to [your] neighborhoods and try for personal appearances, and the attendance of relatives and neighbors at the opening of the picture." The mesh of film
and history was intense and insistent:

> Note that the *Back to Bataan* copy in this campaign stresses the
> tempo of the photopic itself, and is a parallel to the daily news
> breaks that highlight the sensational activities of the Filipino guer-
> rillas. These facts make the ad copy of very live topical impact dur-
> ing the run of *Back to Bataan*, besides tying in with RKO Radio's far
> flung exploitation that includes living testimony from fighting men
> who went through experiences on Luzon similar to those depicted
> in the ads and photoplay.

The ever-present danger to timely "photopics" was the threat of
being overtaken by events and rendered instantly outmoded. Therefore rather than risk production on an uncertain future, war films
often looked backward to the sure past. Retrospective and commemorative, they depict events leading up to the war (often inching to a
Pearl Harbor epiphany in the first act), settled battles (Wake Island,
Corregidor, Bataan), or conflicts of indeterminate temporality.

The hindsighted perspective generated a uniquely gifted protagonist: the journalist, businessman, or warrior who against the unruffled indifference and invincible ignorance of his fellow countrymen
foresees the Fascist tide on the horizon. A hectoring postcredit crawl
for *Watch on the Rhine* (1943) reminds that "some men, ordinary men,
not prophets" saw the Nazi blitzkrieg coming. "They had fought it
from the beginning and they understood it. We are most deeply in
their debt." Newspaper columnist Drew Pearson appears at the beginning of *Betrayal from the East* to offer exposition and self-congrat-
ulation:

> *Betrayal from the East* is a true story. Nobody could have made it
> up. It really happened. I know. As a newspaperman I saw it happen-
> ing. I did what I could to help assemble some of the facts in the files
> of G-2, military intelligence. But that's not important [however]
> there were a few in the year 1941 that saw the smoke [signals] and
> wondered.

Pearson's prescience was as nothing compared to the clairvoyance
of a journalistic predecessor who covered the Russo-Japanese war.
In *Jack London* (1943) the ruddy naturalist (played by Milo O'Shea)

witnesses the massacre of Russian POWs by chuckling elements of the Japanese Army, circa 1903. London tries to warn Americans of the barbarity and imperial ambitions of the Japanese, but a complacent newspaper editor refuses to publish his visionary articles on the yellow peril.

Looking forward in time, the preferred outcome was to keep ahead of—or better, on top of—events. As an exploitation tie-in, the most closely guarded secret of the European theater held seductive box-office potential. In 1943, without a trace of irony, RKO's vice president Charles W. Koerner wistfully speculated that his studio "would certainly like to have a war picture synchronized as to locale and release with the coming invasion of the Continent." Another scheme from RKO wryly appreciated the humor in ad-pub priorities. In an exploitation stunt for *Hitler's Children* (1942), the studio pretended to seek insurance coverage "against the possibility of Schikelgruber's abdication before the film is in release" on the grounds that "the sudden collapse of Nazi Germany would cause material harm to the commercial bookings." Yet for all the meticulous marketing calibrations, the exigencies of war still disrupted production plans and exploitation ploys. Placing the bottom line firmly above ground zero, the *Film Daily* looked back on 1945: "Fragments of the atomic bomb found their mark on the Broadway and Hollywood scene, disintegrating production plans for war-themed story material which will now gather dust on the property shelf."

CHAPTER **9** The

Negro

Soldier

At the level of epidermis, wartime tolerance reached its limits. Ethnic, religious, even gender bias buckled under the pressure of "the present emergency," expanding participation and refashioning stereotypes. Racism was more resilient. In the Deep South a stern Jim Crow system ruled; elsewhere separatist practice was more idiosyncratic, but sensibilities were only marginally less antagonistic. A survey on American racial attitudes by the Office of War Information found prejudice firmly ingrained North and South. "Whites overwhelmingly endorse segregation," read the 1943 report, which recorded a special aversion to interracial dining: a full 99 percent of white Southerners and 76 percent of white Northerners demanded segregated restaurants. In line with the civilian command, the military segregated GIs by race, relegated black units to service and support work, and "as far as practicable" assured that "colored officers would not command white officers." In truth the quarantine was more than skin deep. For reasons the Surgeon General allowed were "not biologically convincing" but "psychologically important in America," the Red Cross and the Armed Forces classified blood plasma by race as well as type.

Against the racial reality, the rhetoric and symbology of wartime unity—lofty language from the OWI, the Four Freedoms promised by President Roosevelt, melting-pot posters of "Americans All"— advanced a color-blind equality that forced a perceptible transformation in the medium defined by visual presentations in black and white. Having to combine egalitarian principles with exclusionary practices, wartime cinema radiates internal contradictions and schizophrenic impulses. In *Somewhere I'll Find You* (1942) newsman Clark Gable directly challenges the Surgeon General's bloodlines when he cables back from Bataan that white men and brown men have fought and bled together—and that "the blood was the same color." In terms of race, American culture no longer had its stories straight.

Accorded a measure of scrutiny now due all things media, the presentation of black Americans on the motion picture screen was an arena of special attention and expanding influence for a renascent civil rights movement. Calculatingly equating "Deutschland and Dixieland," "Hitlerism abroad with Hitlerism at home," the Negro press and the National Association for the Advancement of Colored People (NAACP) exploited wartime exigencies to advance their cause in the entertainment industry and to improve the lot of black actors on screen. Just as the preferred persuasive technique of the antebellum slave narrative was to cast the light of Christian ideals on the darkness of the peculiar institution, the wartime civil rights movement turned OWI-approved rhetoric back to domestic shores and made the American dilemma Hollywood's.

A raw nerve since the birth of the movies, the image of blacks in classical Hollywood cinema is an inventory of ugly stereotypes. D. W. Griffith's *The Birth of a Nation* (1915), a landmark of American cinema and a close-up look at the national pathology, is the earliest, most infamous entry. In Griffith's unreconstructed vision, a virginal Southern belle leaps to her death rather than fall victim to a black rapist before a heroic Ku Klux Klan gallops to the rescue of a way of life ravaged by radical Republicans and mad mulattos. Yet the breadth of Griffith's plantation lunacy was exceptional. Neither magnetic villains nor erotic menaces, blacks were more likely to be degraded by domestication than granted the potency of demonization. Friendly retainers and loyal servants in the form of grinning, toothy

Toms and chubby, squealing Jemimas fill the limited cast credits. In 1944, New York Public Library researcher C. D. Reddick undertook a rough survey of one hundred films that portrayed black Americans. Reddick reckoned that a full 75 percent were anti-Negro, 13 percent neutral at best, and only 12 percent affirmative.

As the size of Reddick's sample indicates, the main rule was not a confederacy of Negro dunces but a conspiracy of silence. In Hollywood's field of vision, blacks were invisible—out of the white world, off the screen. Dozens of representative films from the 1920s and 1930s and near-complete genres—gangster films, westerns, screwball comedies—can be projected without exposing a single black face. When the "social consciousness" films of the Great Depression grappled with a racially charged issue, only half the complexion was in place. In the antilynching melodramas *Fury* (1936) and *They Won't Forget* (1937), the victims of vigilante justice are white. In *Black Legion* (1936), the hooded and robed xenophobes standing in for the Ku Klux Klan take out their vengeance on folksy Eastern Europeans and assimilated Irishmen.

In front of the screen no less than on it, black Americans were ignored or cordoned off. Motion picture theaters were segregated, sometimes totally so in the case of all-black venues called "race houses," sometimes in sections, with black patrons typically relegated to balconies ("Jim Crow roosts" to the Negro press, "nigger heaven" to almost everyone else). On the margins of the motion picture industry, a so-called specialty market supplied some 450 "Negro Houses" with independently produced material featuring all-black casts. The Negro circuit also played Hollywood features, though usually months or years after they went into wide release at popular prices. In *Hail! Hail! Rock 'n' Roll!* (1987), the documentary bio-pic of Chuck Berry, one of the artist's rare moments of racial resentment occurs when he stands in front of the ornate Fox Theater in St. Louis and recalls how as a child he and his father were refused entry to a recently released "A" picture, *A Tale of Two Cities* (1935). Still bruised by the memory, Berry rasps, "It took *two years* to come to our theater in our neighborhood."

In July 1942 Walter White, secretary and chief executive officer of the NAACP, decided to hold the annual convention of the organization in Los Angeles, the better to lobby the motion picture industry. Producers Walter Wanger and Darryl F. Zanuck hosted a luncheon for White and Wendell L. Willkie at the 20th Century-Fox lot, a fete attended by some seventy industry powerbrokers. Demanding a "better break" in "this important medium for molding public opinion," both speakers forcefully expressed the deep offense black Americans took at racist stereotypes, something that had honestly not occurred to many of Hollywood's self-styled progressives. White told his dining companions that "restrictions of Negroes to roles with rolling eyes, chattering teeth, always scared of ghosts, or of portrayals of none-too-bright servants perpetuates a stereotype which is doing the Negro infinite harm." However, giving black actors bigger and more dignified parts in racial isolation, a kind of separate but equal access to screen space, was not the point. The ultimate goal, in the words of *The Crisis,* the official monthly of the NAACP, was the incorporation of "Negroes naturally and easily in a script in parts which are not stereotyped." A cinematic integration that would assert and prefigure social integration was the reason blacks kept wary attention on Hollywood.

The domestic pressure from the civil rights movement was abetted by the international situation. The knowledge that moviegoers overseas might be offended by Jim Crow America was an Allied impetus to reform—as was the squirming discomfort many white Americans felt when viewing stateside Sambo caricatures from foreign soil. The Office of Censorship lent compulsive force to the attitudinal metamorphosis. Ironically, the prohibitions against the "derogatory picturization or presentation" of nationals of the United Nations accrued to the benefit of American blacks, themselves nationals of a prominent member nation. One unrepentant screenwriter lamented the loss of the old-time minstrel routines: "All pictures must present only the best aspects of American life if an export license is required. The Negro must not be funny nor afraid of haunted houses. It might vex the people of North Africa."

The color of money added texture to the call of conscience. In Hollywood no less than Washington, black Americans found new influence in the convergence of idealism and economic power. The prosperity of black factory workers infused a segment of "the Public" left conspicuously untapped by the studio system. In 1943 Hollywood began allotting sizable advertising budgets to Negro publications and hiring special publicity agencies to exploit the exotic but tempting market estimated at upwards of 15 million moviegoers. With this emergent audience in mind, and with hopes of crossing over to a white audience that had long accepted blacks as performers, 20th

The NAACP comes to Hollywood's dinner (*left to right*): William Goetz, Walter Wanger, Wendell Wilkie, Col. Darryl F. Zanuck, Walter White, and Will H. Hays attend the epochal luncheon given July 18, 1942, at 20th Century-Fox. (Quigley Photo Archive/Georgetown University)

Century-Fox and MGM each produced moderately budgeted all-black musicals in 1943, *Stormy Weather* and *Cabin in the Sky* respectively. They were the first such studio ventures since Warner Bros.'s *The Green Pastures* (1936).

Both films occupy that peculiar never-never land of the all-black musical, a realm where black life mirrors white life but never intrudes into it. A segregated landscape will simply not support two shades of Americans without collapsing under the weight of the off-screen atmosphere. As a heaven-set fantasy, *Cabin in the Sky* purports to be nothing other than transcendental (though it holds out the unholy specter of a celestial afterlife as membership-exclusive as the earth below). By contrast, *Stormy Weather* locates itself in a twentieth-century history that gives the lie to a monochromic celluloid vista. Playing an unlikely love interest for Lena Horne, dancer Bill "Bojangles" Robinson reminisces about his showbiz career and flashbacks musical interludes from Horne, Fats Waller, Cab Calloway, and a showstopping pas de deux by the acrobatic Nicholas Brothers. The performance highlights are bracketed by two recognitions of black contributions to two American world wars—a newsreel clip of returning black veterans of World War I, and a present-day stage show performed to entertain black soldiers about to embark overseas. Not a single white face violates the black milieu. Performing in a Broadway musical, the all-black cast, bankrolled by black financiers and producers, plays for an audience that applauds and cheers wildly, an audience that on Broadway can only be white. The conventional "cut away" reaction shot showing the appreciative crowd never comes. Better to violate cinematic grammar than disrupt the narrative conceit.

Though Hollywood convention and wartime necessity made for a complex hybrid, new spaces for interracial mingling opened up during 1941–45 as never before. Traditionally in classical Hollywood cinema, the arenas of unrestricted access were presocial, antisocial, or offshore. In the easy integration of Hal Roach's Little Rascals, the two-steps between Shirley Temple and Bill "Bojangles" Robinson, and the multiethnic Boy Rangers in *Mr. Smith Goes to Washington* (1939), childhood suspended the rules of Jim Crow. Likewise, on chain gangs and in big houses, behind the iron bars of prison, hardened convicts enjoyed a freedom of loose association unknown in civil society. Finally, in adventures in Africa and romance in the South Seas, foreign locales tolerated a casual mix and match. During the war, such overseas theaters of operation hosted a goodly share of integrationist action. In the jungle, the desert, and the smoky interiors of Rick's Cafe, Hollywood projected racial pluralism onto a landscape beyond American borders. *Casablanca, Bataan, Sahara*—the titles bespeak the geographical displacement of a national dilemma too close to home to address on native soil. The subsurface meaning surfaces in the most transparent metaphor: *Lifeboat*, which casts adrift a microcosm of mankind (racist *übermensch* Walter Slezak, Czech-American John Hodiak, hard-bitten belle Tallulah Bankhead, black steward Canada Lee, and lumpenprole William Bendix) to float the family of man in the same boat.

Above all, in the combat zone, under duress, removed from the codes and morality of civilian life, normal hierarchies and social customs broke down. As a sturdy gunner in *Bataan* (1943), Kenneth Spencer conforms to prewar type in prayer and song, but he is an integral member of the ragtag squad of defenders, shirtless and pow-

Americans All in the same boat: Director Alfred Hitchcock kept John Steinbeck's metaphor above sea level in *Lifeboat* (1944).

erful, a committed fighter. In *Sahara* (1943) Rex Ingram played a gallant Sudanese sergeant who confronts a Nazi officer/Jim Crow surrogate. When the master racist snarls in German that he does not
want to be touched by a member of an "inferior race," Humphrey
Bogart delivers a sensitivity lesson from screenwriter and future Hollywood Ten ringleader John Howard Lawson. "Tell him not to worry
about [the sergeant's] being black," commands Bogart. "It won't
come off on his pretty uniform." In a replay of the Joe Louis–Max
Schmeling fight of 1938, Ingram beats up the Nazi and puts him out
for the count in the desert sand. On behalf of the NAACP, Roy Wilkens
publicly commended Columbia for the "outstanding contribution" of
Sahara and praised MGM's *Bataan* as "a film that shows how superfluous racial and religious problems are when common danger is
faced."

The main barrier to equal treatment of blacks in the combat film
was the unequal treatment of blacks in the military services. The
traditions of the Armed Forces upheld unique variations on racist

exclusion, notably the Navy's relegation of blacks to the Steward's Branch, the Marine Corps's refusal to commission a single black officer, and the Army Air Force's denial to blacks of membership in bomber crews. Working against racist policy, however, was a wider military ethos advancing a faceless, classless, rank equality. The efforts to reconcile uniform treatment of men called government issues, identified by serial numbers, and saluted for their service stripes with the special treatment imported from civilian custom was an exercise in contradiction captured in the oxymoronic phrase describing official War Department policy: "segregation without discrimination."

Blacks in uniform overcame the limitations beginning on December 7, 1941, when Dorris Miller, a Navy messman, manned an antiaircraft gun during the Japanese attack on Pearl Harbor. That Miller was not trained for gunnery, and that the white press and the Navy were less than forthcoming with news of his action, indicates the initial reluctance of wartime America to salute its black patriots. At a well-publicized ceremony in 1942, however, Miller was awarded the Navy Cross for heroism; the next year he died in action in the Pacific. The inevitable screen recognition was inevitably compromised. In *Crash Dive* (1943), in a role modeled on Miller, Ben Carter plays a dignified and heroic . . . messman. *Variety* correctly noted that the responsibility for Carter's lowly status in the ranks was "the Navy's not Hollywood's."

Where blacks might be persuasively recruited in extremis for shoulder-to-shoulder duty in the grounded combat film, the interracial diversity of the jungle, desert, or ocean was unknown in the air, an amphitheater of specialized skills and racist exclusion. No integrated ensemble was permitted aboard the airborne combat film. Until 1943 the Army Air Force considered the technical skills and athletic reflexes demanded of manned flight beyond the native capacity of black Americans (hence the special importance the Negro press attached to the 99th Pursuit Squadron and the Air War College at Tuskegee). In the Army Air Force documentary *Report from the Aleutians* (July 1943) the segregated skies break through when narrator John Huston speaks of the cooperative tolerance demanded inside a Flying Fortress. "A bomber crew is a team and the longer it's together the better the team works"—even if you don't happen to like "the color of a guy's hair." Hair?

Beginning in the summer of 1944, during the campaign for FDR's fourth term, the military made (on paper) substantive concessions that were to set the pattern for the postwar integration of the Armed Forces finally ordered by President Truman in July 1948. In the same spirit, the military leadership demonstrated an awareness of the importance of motion pictures as a means to soothe black anger and spur morale. "Movies [newsreels] of [black] troops in action would help," suggested Assistant Secretary of War John L. McCloy during a meeting of the Advisory Committee on Negro Troop Policies in 1944, a suggestion that Gen. Benjamin O. Davis, the highest-ranking black American in the military, quickly picked up on and interpreted: "Releasing the facts of [black] troops on movies would do a lot *without saying anything.*" Such silent signals might be sent over the heads of municipal censors. In a cinematic validation that would not have been lost on a color-conscious spectator, *December 7th* (1943), John Ford's semidocumentary for the Navy, inserts a staged shot of a black sailor manning a machine gun. The scene is an overt nod to Dorris Miller, the real-life Pearl Harbor hero. In John Huston's War Department documentary *Let There Be Light* (1946) the Army's neuropsychiatric treatment center is either totally integrated or (as tellingly) presented as so.

The most notable official response was *The Negro Soldier* (released April 13, 1944), directed by Stuart Heisler under Frank Capra's supervision. In its time the War Department film was a ground-breaking recognition not only of black contributions to American history but of the urgent problem of interracial friction within the supposedly united services. The theme—the contribution of black Americans to the war effort—was already conventional enough. It had in fact been preceded a few months earlier by Toddy Pictures's *Fighting Americans* (1944), the first feature-length treatment of the black contribution to the war effort. But where *Fighting Americans* was independently produced and aimed at the race houses, *The Negro Soldier* was government-sponsored and aimed at a biracial audience (to encourage the one and educate the other). Made at the order of General Marshall, it was required viewing for all GIs.

The framing device for *The Negro Soldier* is a black church service presided over by a preacher, played by "technical adviser" Carlton Moss. Moss speaks standard English with perfect enunciation and leads his congregation not through Negro spirituals but a montage of black American history. In depicting the honored pageant of proud achievement, the film leaves unspoken the more contentious racial

Cinematic recognition: black American soldiers man the big guns in the War Department's *The Negro Soldier* (1944). (Museum of Modern Art/Film Stills Archive)

interludes in American history (chattel slavery, the Civil War, Reconstruction, and lynchings). As in *Sahara*, the Joe Louis–Max Schmeling fight is again called up as *mano a mano* metonomy for the forthcoming "battle in a far greater arena." (Louis, former heavyweight boxing champ and current Army sergeant, bore a weighty burden as the Negro soldier's representative screen figure. Featured regularly in the newsreels, he was also recruited for role-model duty in the Warner Bros./Irving Berlin musical *This Is the Army*.) When the preacher reads from the racist invective of *Mein Kampf,* language whose florid venom could readily be heard in American accents in 1944, a montage of group reaction shots and tight close-ups records the inscrutable features of members of the congregation. They listen intently but impassively, forcing the spectator to first identify and then provide the correct moral response. Save for "the Negro angle," the rest of the film is a standard orientation to Army life. No matter: nothing *The Negro Soldier* said or showed matched its significance as a tangible gesture.

The normally suspicious Negro press praised *The Negro Soldier* lavishly. Though hardly oblivious to its compromises and omissions, black critics and audiences knew that the film was the kind of effort they could not but encourage, especially since its release was virtually concurrent with a firestorm over racist comments by Secretary of War Stimson, who in a letter to Congressman Hamilton Fish (R–N.Y.) implied that blacks were simply too dumb for combat leadership. Sitting down to a private screening in New York, author Richard Wright prepared a list of thirteen faults that he fully expected to check off one by one as the film unspooled. When the lights went up, his list was unmarked. In the *New Jersey Afro-American,* critic Michael Carter confided to his black readers a poignant reassurance: "it will not embarrass you."

Reflecting both the growing influence of black pressure groups and the seriousness with which the military viewed interracial incidents,

What the well-dressed man in Harlem will wear: Sgt. Joe Louis (*front row, left*) answers the musical question in *This Is the Army* (1943). (Museum of Modern Art/Film Stills Archive)

the government insisted that *The Negro Soldier* get a commercial release through the War Activities Committee. General Davis, whom FDR appointed as inspector and adviser "in connection with matters pertaining to the various colored units in the service," personally attended to its distribution and with the assistance of Jack Warner strong-armed exhibitors into playing the 55-minute feature. WAC made up forty 35mm prints, and by July 1944 some three hundred 16mm prints were also in circulation. Despite suppression by censorship boards in the South, the film played widely to what was its real target audience—not the Negro soldier but the white civilian. "Our concept of 'proper distribution' is not merely to Negro-attended houses, but in predominantly white-attended theaters as well," wrote the film reviewer for the *Pittsburgh Courier.* "Granting that showings in race houses will be of tremendous moral value, the success or failure of the planned message will depend largely upon white patrons seeing the film." A curious hindrance held up the release of *The Negro Soldier* when Jack Goldberg, president of The Negro Marches On, Inc., a production company serving the "specialty market," brought a lawsuit against the War Department. Goldberg, with official encouragement, had produced a similar film entitled *We've Come a Long, Long Way.* Hearing of the upcoming release of *The Negro Soldier,* he charged the government with unfair competition against private enterprise. Goldberg lost the case when a federal court ruled that interference with the distribution of *The Negro Soldier* "would seriously interfere with the war effort and program of the war."

Like the military, Hollywood inched forward in the treatment of blacks, though producers were still capable of astonishing blunders. MGM floated the idea for a remake of *Uncle Tom's Cabin,* with Lena Horne mentioned for the role of Eliza, but backed off in the face of icy protests from, among others, Vice President Henry A. Wallace. Another borderline miscalculation was MGM's *Tennessee Johnson* (1942), originally to be an orthodox Dixie-eye-view of radical Republicans and the impeachment of the seventeenth president. Word of the project leaked in the *Daily Worker,* and the Negro press, liberal organizations, and actors unions lodged vigorous protest against MGM. Walter White personally expressed his concerns in a letter to Louis B. Mayer and the OWI mediated nervously between civil rights groups and the studio. MGM ended up spending $250,000 to reshoot scenes to make the film "less objectionable." Cartoon and low-budget fare also lagged behind the "A"-level productions more liable to attract public attention and critical comment. Warner Bros.'s blackface Merrie Melody *Coal Black and De Sebben Dwarfs* (December 1942) is probably the most appalling throwback.

Motion pictures set during the Civil War could not but lay bare sectarian and racial divisions. Defeated in battle, the Confederates had captured the cultural mythos with a romantic vision of sabers and magnolias, of a noble cause and a chivalric world gone with the wind. No Hollywood films more infuriated black Americans than *The Birth of a Nation* and *Gone with the Wind* (1939), which between them rewrote the war and its aftermath. In 1942 a contemplated remake of *The Birth of a Nation* was abandoned under OWI influence, and a planned theatrical run for the original film at a downtown Baltimore theater was rescinded due to NAACP objections. In 1944 David O. Selznick announced a musical remake of *Gone with the Wind* and learned how much had changed since 1939. Protests and adverse commentary forced a cancellation of the project. What is more significant than the motion picture industry's initial obliviousness to potential flashpoints is its subsequent hasty backpedaling. During the war, for the first time, civil rights protests decisively influenced production and distribution plans. Of the two films that most deeply incited the antipathy of black Americans, both were unremakeable and one was unreleasable.

More progressive sensitivities were early evident in John Huston's *In This Our Life* (1942), a sultry melodrama in which self-serving belle Bette Davis eyes a black clerk and unjustly accuses him of a hit-and-run killing she has committed. Dignified and articulate, the clerk (Ernest Anderson) realizes the futility of challenging the word of a white woman in a country where "police don't listen to no colored boy." The clerk, who is studying to be a lawyer, shares his career ambitions with a sympathetic and encouraging Olivia de Haviland, playing the good sister to Davis's jezebel. When a restrained Hattie McDaniel, as the clerk's mother, confirms her son's alibi, not for a minute does de Haviland doubt the word of the black servant in deference to her white sibling. A liberal lawyer forces Davis to confront Anderson behind the bars of the town jail. As she lies baldly to his face and suggests *he* confess, director Huston frames the clerk behind bars and in the reverse shot frames Davis through the bars from the clerk's entrapped perspective. A thunderstruck reviewer for the Negro press may not have been hyperbolic in calling Anderson's sympathetic role "the first decent part that has ever been given a colored actor in any major motion picture."

With good intentions and little subtlety, Hollywood injected color-coded moments into wartime scenarios, and the Negro press duly noted the small steps forward. *Guadalcanal Diary* (1943) pauses for a black sailor to be pulled on-screen to identify a convoy for landlubber marines. The most popular film of 1944, Leo McCarey's *Going My Way* (1944), met with grateful approval for a seemingly seamless choral contribution. As just another member of the street gang collared by Bing Crosby and saved by song, a black youngster takes a solo on "Swinging on a Star." In the same year, Hattie McDaniel continued a personality shift from abject house servant to dignified homefront contributor in *Since You Went Away*. A black judge, conspicuous among the World Court Tribunal in *None Shall Escape* (1944), was also espied and applauded. However, the presence of the black preacher at the lynching in *The Ox-Bow Incident* (1943) served mainly as an unsettling reminder of the more usual position of black Americans at such proceedings.

In pace with the Allied cause, the image of blacks on screen advanced steadily. Hollywood's Popular Front–bred progressives, now riding with the political tide rather than against it, pressed the advantage. In a widely quoted article published in the *Negro Digest*, screenwriter Dalton Trumbo lectured his colleagues on screen stereotypes. "We have made tarts of his daughters, crap shooters of his sons, obsequious Uncle Toms of his fathers, superstitious and grotesque crones of his mothers, strutting peacocks of his successful men, psalm singing mountebanks of his priests and Barnum and Bailey sideshows of his religion." In May 1944 the Entertainment Industry Emergency Committee passed a "declaration of principles," written by Maxwell Anderson, Lillian Hellman, and Peter Lyon, which condemned racist stereotyping, called for an end to discrimination against the Negro artist, and demanded Hollywood work "for a just, serious treatment of the Negro on the screen."

Admittedly, the progress was sometimes more a virtue of omission than commission. The American Red Cross agreed to delete scenes of clowning black soldiers from the Victory film *At His Side* (January 1944) after the NAACP objected. In *God Is My Co-Pilot* (1945) the black retainer of a southern family tells his young charge, the future fighter pilot, about the divine hand that must guide the godly pilot. Granting black men religious insight at the expense of masculine dignity was a convention older than Harriet Beecher Stowe, but the portrayal is notable for what it *doesn't* do—no open-mouthed "Tomming," simpering dialect, shuffling locomotion, or other signs of Sambo.

So venerable and reliable a stock figure was not, however, to be surrendered utterly or transformed immediately. A smalltown exhibitor in Missouri reported a number of walkouts on the moralistic *Cabin in the Sky* because "my folks want their Negroes to sing and dance and have fun." Yet even when Sambo persists, increments of evolutionary development are detectable. Set after the model of Jack Benny's popular sidekick, Eddie "Rochester" Anderson, the black servant is more verbally adroit, prone to backtalk, and certain in footing. He is as likely to deliver the punchline as to be the punchline. In *Pillow to Post* (1945), character actor Willie Best, a perennial Sambo figure, plays Lucille, a shuffling/mumbling porter whose very name emasculates him. Nonetheless, his controlling intelligence and point of view filter key plot developments in the strained comedy. To a stodgy colonel, Lucille reveals the face behind his Sambo mask. The officer informs the too-deferential servant that "everyone in the Army isn't a general." "No, suh," replies the not-so-dimwit, "but you'd be surprised how my tips increased since I started calling everyone 'General.' " A few years earlier, a sophisticated mainstream comedy like *The Palm Beach Story* (1942) could still play wide-eyed porters for cheap laughs, the vaunted writer-director Preston Sturges as oblivious as his white audience to the offense. No more. *Pride of the Marines* (1945) registers the change when a well-spoken black porter approaches two Marine heroes and tells them what an honor it was to have had them aboard his train. The men shake hands all around in mutual respect. When one of the soldiers offers the porter a dollar tip, he waves the bill away.

Some white viewers too seem to have opened their eyes. In 1945 a soldier "somewhere in the Pacific" wrote *Variety* to protest "a perfect example of bad taste at its worst," a Merrie Melodies relic called *Sunday Go to Meeting Time*. "A great many people now are working to bring about a better understanding between the white and colored people, but this cartoon served only to make the colored race look ridiculous." Warner Bros. quickly apologized, blaming the vagaries of distribution and explaining that the cartoon had been made years earlier. Against that record and in that context, C. D. Reddick conceded, "Generally speaking, from the Negro angle, the films have improved."

With so long a time of leaving so much unspoken and unseen, the sudden lurch into sensitivity was not without missteps. In 1944–45 the Springfield Plan, an educational program developed by the Springfield, Massachusetts, school council to teach youngsters interracial tolerance, received widespread national publicity as a model for the construction of a harmonious postwar America. Warner Bros. released a public-spirited short, *It Happened in Springfield* (April 1945), that a few years earlier might have been praised for its progressive social consciousness. After four years of relative frankness about American prejudice, however, its concealments and duplicities were sneered at. Warner Bros. ignored both anti-Semitism and Jim Crow to expose the plight of another perennial victim of nativist intolerance and discrimination: the Scandinavian.

The most reprehensible screen-related exclusion of black Americans was in the newsreels. The Writers War Board calculated that only three newsreel clips involving Negro troops had been shown in U.S. theaters during the entire year of 1943. One showed a Negro soldier guarding a chicken coop, another showed a jitterbug contest in Australia. Only the third, a story on the 99th Pursuit Squadron, was a credit to the race. The board's survey of six hundred newsreel clips covering the year 1944 found minorities featured in only eighteen instances. Outraged, the Negro press and the NAACP detected a willful conspiracy of exclusion. The calculated cuts were a "scheme to keep from white America the news that the Negro minority is doing its part in the war," charged *The Crisis* in an editorial condemnation of what it labeled "a dastardly trick as mean as any perpetrated against the race." Shots of Eisenhower and FDR reviewing black troops at the Cairo and Teheran conference in 1943, present in the original footage supplied by the Army Signal Corps, never reached the commercial newsreel programs. As the *New Jersey Afro-American* pointed out, the omissions were not properly editorial: "In their zeal to delete the scenes showing colored troops, the movie companies sacrificed the best shot of the President and General Eisenhower chatting in the jeep because colored soldiers were in the background."

Pathé and Paramount denied the charge but heeded the point. In February 1944 the *Pittsburgh Courier,* the most widely circulated and influential of the black newsweeklies, noted that Paramount News, "reacting to sharp criticism," had begun "the inclusion of Negro subject matter in its newsreels" with a segment on black WACs on parade and paratroopers in training. During the last year of the war, the newsreels made a visible effort to incorporate segments on black troops and to include them in pans of American GIs. In October 1944, Universal Newsreel featured a segment on the 92nd Division showing black troops launching artillery, firing weapons, and receiving a boisterous welcome from liberated Europeans. At the end of the clip, Gen. Mark Clark awards Purple Hearts to "heroes who have shed their blood for America." The past mistreatment and the later shift was caught in a backhanded compliment from *The Crisis*. "The newsreels have been notorious for omitting our men, a fact only accentuated by the splendid release in October [1944] showing the 92nd division in Italy." Unbeknownst to the home offices, however, municipal censors in the South routinely cut newsreel segments featuring Negro troops.

The All-American Newsreel filled some of the information gap. A weekly issue founded in 1942, it was seen regularly in 365 of the estimated 450 Negro houses, plus some seventy military theaters operated by the Army Motion Picture Service (itself an indication of how widespread were segregated base facilities). Citing an OWI survey reporting that 85 percent of Negroes in five large cities got most of their news not from the Negro press but from the All-American News, producer E. M. Glucksman claimed a weekly audience of four million. A full one-third of its footage was devoted to Negro participation in the war—participation that until the exploits of the 99th Pursuit Squadron in 1943 and gradual, grudging deployment of black divisions such as the 92nd and 93rd in 1944, had to emphasize mundane clips of drills, parades, and training. The All-American News made extensive use of Armed Forces material, and its comprehensive coverage of war-related Negro activities provided an easy check on the five commercial companies.

Any egalitarian impulse in Hollywood cinema ran up against vigilant resistance from guardians of Jim Crow. Sensitive to regional peculiarities in the marketplace, Hollywood sometimes deferred in advance and deleted contestable scenes from release prints designated for the South. An obvious red flag like *In This Our Life* received considered attention and considerable attenuation before its Southern distribution. After the Detroit race riots of June 1943, scenes of whites and blacks dancing together—that is, sharing a dance floor—were deleted from *Stage Door Canteen* in the prints distributed in the South. Alert for breaches of social conduct, municipal censors in Southern cities refused to pass films whose black characters defied Uncle Remus subservience, whose scenes were considered integrationist, or whose black performers were deemed uppity. The border state of Tennessee possessed some of the sharpest eyes and tensest sensitivities. Knoxville censored a scene in the *March of Time*'s "Youth in Crisis" (November 1943) featuring an interracial roundtable discussion. The notoriously scissor-happy Motion Picture Board of Censors in Memphis cut Cab Calloway and his band from *Sensations of 1945* (1944) and Lena Horne from *Broadway Rhythm* (1944). Invisible editing was not the Southern style. A musical interlude showcasing Louis Armstrong and his band in *Pillow to Post* was abruptly eliminated. In the film, Ida Lupino and two suitors enter a nightclub advertising "Louis Armstrong for this week only." Once inside—no Armstrong.

The mind of the South being open to shades of meaning as well as color, the discrimination was never indiscriminate. Minstrels and mammies passed muster, but not men and women. Thus, though Lena Horne was snipped from *Broadway Rhythm*, the singer Hazel Scott escaped intact—doubtless because the one was more erotically arousing to the white imagination, the other more traditionally gospel. In a manner quite different from Joe Louis, Horne was an attractive role model whose selection as a *Yank* pinup girl in December 1943 confirmed her crossover sex appeal.

If the specter of equality permeated an entire project, the film would be banned outright. Branding the inimitable Eddie "Rochester" Anderson as "inimicable to the public welfare," Memphis forbade local release of *Brewster's Millions* (1945) because Jack Benny's bête noire had "too familiar a way about him." "The picture presents too much social equality and racial mixture," explained chief censor Lloyd T. Binford. "We don't have any trouble with racial problems down here, and we don't intend to encourage any by showing movies like this." Actually, what Binford may really have objected to was not Anderson's familiarity toward whites but the familiarity of the white players, including blonde June Havoc, toward him—the unconscious and easy touching, level eye contact, and person-to-person discussions. Not least, *Brewster's Millions* pointedly defines Anderson's character as a naval veteran of the Pacific war.

A seat at the table or still in the back of the coach? Eddie "Rochester" Anderson and the cast of *Brewster's Millions* (1945).

In theaters outside of Memphis, moviegoers no longer seemed quite so willing to suffer Southern-style censorship in silence. A letter from a former motion picture worker, printed on the front page of *Variety* in the days after victory in Europe, expresses not only the place of the movies in the recreational life of the war generation but traces the distance at least some Americans had traveled since Pearl Harbor. The correspondent, a staff sergeant in Germany whose back issues of *Variety* had just caught up with him, was steaming mad over what he called the "asinine, stupid, Hitleristic" banning of *Brewster's Millions*. The movie-minded sergeant composed a representative anecdote:

> Last night, still sizzling over the incident, I went to a nearby German beerhall that had been converted by the American Special Service into a theater. Yes, you guessed it. The film was *Brewster's Millions*. Now, it so happens that in the American Army, such theaters are attended by any Allied soldier in uniform. But the important thing was, that in 1,500 soldiers present, there was a cross-section of

Americana. There were not only soldiers from N.Y.C., Brooklyn, Chicago, and Los Angeles but from Memphis and all points South. There were Jew and Gentile, Negro and White, Catholic and Protestant but most of all . . . *Americans*.

Having called off the Warner Bros. platoon, he moves to the plot complication:

> During the performance, the projector broke down. What made it rather unusual was that it wasn't for just five minutes or even 10, but for 52 minutes. Yes, I timed it. During all this tedious wait, with the picture better than three-fourths finished and the hour growing pretty late, this being the 9 p.m. show, not a man left the theatre. How do I know? Well, I purposely stood near the exit so that I could note just such a thing or any other incident. However, the only thing that happened during the long wait was that various GIs made various and sundry remarks, all unprintable and in various and sundry American dialects that covered America from Maine to California, as to the ability, or lack of same, of the two GI operators who would pick such an inopportune time to let the machine go on the blink.

Finally, the inspiring OWI-shaded admonition:

> Now please don't feel that I'm writing to you because I feel that this was any history-making incident. I'm writing in the hope that the Hon. Lloyd T. Binford, of the Memphis Binfords, can in some way hear of this and get wise to the fact that the Americans of all colors, nationalities, and sections, who teamed against Hitler, paying the inevitable price in blood and death, just ain't gonna like the idea of some guy back home spouting off such Hitlerisms as hizzoner. Also, to throw a "good going" directly at [producer] Edward Small, who believes in presenting all peoples as the human beings that they are, in spite of the fact that he may lose a few bucks in the South because a small minority believe that "a man is good enough to die for his country but not good enough to be shown dying for it."

Shut out totally from Southern distribution was the most resounding of all cinematic calls for interracial equality, the *March of Time*'s "Americans All" (July 1944). Before the war, so forthright an integrationist plea would have been unthinkable. In fact it was. In January 1941, in an atmosphere of defense mobilization that saw also an influx of desperate European refugees, the *March of Time* had issued a nearly identically titled entry, "Americans All!" The difference in focus and spirit between the prewar exclamatory "Americans All!" and the declarative wartime "Americans All" is a sensitive barometer of historical change. The subject of the first issue is the immigrant, the theme tolerance. The unspoken (but not unscreened) beneficiary is the refugee European, in particular the Jew fleeing Nazism. The association is made explicit in a shot of a Jewish dinner blessing and in the commentary condemnation of the German-American bund as anti-Semitic. Though the approving narration tilts noticeably toward the less swarthy European immigrant groups (Irish, Germans, Scandinavians, and Eastern Europeans), the impulse is assimilationist and generous. Significantly too the narration is careful to distinguish between "loyal and peaceful Japanese-Americans" and alleged Japanese naval reservists working undercover in the California fishing fleet. American blacks, however, are never mentioned, implied, or shown. In a prewar call for national unity, race is not just a subject too hot to handle; it is totally off the mass cultural radar.

Less than four years later, race dominates the screen space. In the second "Americans All" the voice-over commentary and the eloquent filmed spokesmen forcefully advocate integration and equality. The whole tenor and direction of the issue, which begins with several pro forma pleas for religious tolerance among Catholic, Protestant, and Jew, moves toward and confronts directly the crucial problem. A Roman Catholic priest reads a pastoral letter against racism, a Southern newspaper editorialist calls for an end to Jim Crow ridership, and an Episcopalian minister proclaims equality from the pulpit. Most compellingly, blacks and whites mix socially and cinematically. They sit in equality around conference tables, on rostrums, and in classrooms. The polemical call for equality was as dynamic and uncompromising as the visual one. Over a newsreel montage of black troops marching in column, jumping from airplanes, and trekking through Pacific jungles, the authoritative voice of Westbrook Van Voorhis asserts:

> In the midst of a war which is demanding the utmost of American manpower and resources, the United States has called for and has received in full measure the help of the Negro. In the Armed Services are more than half a million colored men and women who accept the same hard training and discipline, and are subject to the same dangers as the whites. Many Southerners are aware of the injustice of denying to the Negro the rights of American citizenship

while expecting him to shoulder its ultimate responsibility—that of defending his country with his life.

Unlike its predecessor, "Americans All" lived up to its name. For once, too, the signature sign-off of the series—"Time Marches On!"—was a portent of forward progress and the marches to come.

CHAPTER **10** The
Real
War

In 1939, one of Hollywood's best years and Europe's worst, motion pictures were neither the privileged medium of record nor the main source of breaking news. Against the speed and scope of radio, magazines, and newspapers, the sluggish arrival and shallow quality of on-screen reportage rated with surface mail delivery in timeliness and tabloid headlines in depth. Even the unique attractions of moving imagery faced fierce and more accomplished competition from the pictorial weeklies, most famously the expressive photojournalism of *Life* and its second-tier imitation, *Look*. As a reliable chronicler of current events or a comprehensive index to the historical record, the motion picture screen ceded the field to broadcasting and print. For a medium that had always thrived on conjuring fantasy, capturing reality was a marginal enterprise.

Yet of all the media journalism that brought the war home—the written dispatches of Ernie Pyle, the radio broadcasts of Edward R. Murrow, the combat photography of Robert Capa—the motion pic-

ture coverage had the most powerful impact and lasting consequences. When cinema went under fire with the rest of the world, the
real images of war surpassed, spectacularly, the Hollywood imaginations of disaster. The real war may never have gotten on the screen
any more than in the books, but the motion picture record was close
enough to the referent to recast the experience of spectatorship and
to expand the domain of motion picture art. Where Hollywood entertainment had once asked only a willing suspension of disbelief,
the wartime documentary demanded a constant awareness of real
danger, real life, real death. The dividing lines are never absolute—
documentaries entertain and entertainment documents—but every
spectator can attest to the perceptual and experiential difference between on-screen fiction and on-screen reality. In *Air Force* (1943),
when waist gunner George Tobias cheerfully called out "One fried
Jap going down!," audiences laughed and applauded. In the combat
report *Fury in the Pacific* (March 1945), when footage showed flamethrowers frying Japanese soldiers in pillboxes and caves, they sat
silent and grim.

The real motion pictures of America at war came in two main versions: the commercial newsreel and the official combat report. Numerous nonfiction shorts, screen magazines, and independent documentaries also crowded a market where, for the first time in Hollywood history, the presentation of real life became a true alternative
to the narrative feature film. If "reality," as Vladimir Nabokov observed on the road through postwar America, is "one of the few
words that mean nothing without quotes," then "documentary reality" requires twice the metaphysical caution: an appreciation for the
tricks of the motion picture medium and a background in the truths
of the historical moment. But even punctuated by these qualifica-
tions, the artful documentation on screen was faithful testimony to
an awful reality. By 1945, and ever after, it would be for America the
most compelling evidence of the history and meaning of the Second
World War.

NEWS OF THE DAY

The moving-image news of the day was projected by the newsreel—
descendent of the newspaper, ancestor of the television nightly

news, and archival treasure of the future. Five commercial newsreels provided a smorgasbord overview of current but not breaking news, a lineup of headlines, human interest stories, cheesecake, and sports highlights. Issued twice weekly, running about eight minutes in length, Paramount News, 20th Century-Fox's Movietone News, RKO-Pathé News, MGM's News of the Day, and Universal Newsreel played subservient accompaniment to featured attractions in tandem with cartoons, travelogues, serials, singalongs, and previews of coming attractions. Two-thirds of the nation's approximately 16,500 theaters included one of the five newsreels as a component part of the staple program. (In 1942 Warner Bros. briefly considered producing its own flagship newsreel, but the shortage of raw film stock, the unavailability of equipment, and the already cluttered market foreclosed the project.) When a current story was deemed worthy of expanded coverage—the kidnapping of the Lindbergh baby, the birth of the Dionne quintuplets, the Hindenberg disaster—the newsreels might release a special issue or the studios might themselves produce a short subject to supplement coverage.

Two screen magazines offering more deliberate and extended coverage on topical events were also a regular feature of the wartime program. The better known was Louis de Rochemont's the *March of Time,* "a new kind of pictorial journalism" issued "every four weeks." Usually running about twenty minutes, it was an independent feature (distributed during the war by 20th Century-Fox) and devoted to expansive treatment of a single topic—such as "Youth in Crisis" (November 1943) or "The Irish Question" (April 1944). The voice of stentorian narrator Westbrook Van Voorhis ("Time . . . *marches on!*") and the Olympian-Lucian style were sent up for the ages in the expository obituary in Orson Welles's *Citizen Kane* (1941). RKO, which lost the distribution rights for the *March of Time* in 1942, underwrote a competing screen magazine, *This Is America,* beginning in October 1942 with "Private Smith of the USA."

Taken together, studio newsreels, nonfiction shorts, and the screen magazines provided a steady stream of motion picture news and documentary styles. The quantity of the programming was generous enough to support specialty "newsreel houses" devoted exclusively to news and information. Located mainly near train stations and bus depots in major cities, they catered to news junkies and stranded travelers. Finally, it is worth remembering that like the footage the news was in black and white: beginning in 1942 a sixth news-reel, the weekly All-American News, provided "Negro-oriented" sto-ries to segregated "race houses."

For the classical Hollywood audience the appeal of newsreels was in the reel, not the news. The war's two most stunning bulletins—the attack on Pearl Harbor and the death of President Roosevelt on April 12, 1945—are archetypically radio memories. Even in the mov-ies, whether on screen or in the theater itself, the urgent news comes over the air, not at the newsstand—still less in the newsreels. A re-current tableau of the wartime film is a combat unit or a homefront enclave interrupted from their revelries or complacency by a Philco flash. Back from church or routine training, anxious listeners huddle around the radio and harken to excited voices crackling through static to interrupt normal programming. Likewise, the emotional im-pact and rhetorical power of FDR's "date which will live in infamy" address to Congress on December 8 required no visual analogue for recitation. In *Flying Tigers* (1942) the pilots listen for whole minutes to a broadcast speech whose opening cadences many Americans knew by heart.

The simultaneous arrival of information and image, of learning the breaking story on sight, is the legacy of a later communications tech-nology. The shift in media terminology captures some of the differ-ence between the cinematic experience of news and the televisual one. A whole journalistic vernacular from the 1940s has died, sur-vived only as anachronism, or changed in meaning: the "bulldog" (or late evening) edition of a newspaper, the five-star final, the extra, and the news "bulletin." The bulletin, whose etymological roots are linear (as in a papal edict or printed notice), first changed media allegiance during the 1930s to became associated with radio broadcast. In 1943 when the War Activities Committee (WAC) began a program of what were called "War Bulletins" to be appended to the regular newsreel issues, Palmer Hoyt, chief of domestic operations for the Office of War Information, explained, "This is a lightning war and the impor-tance of frequent and timely communication by government with the people of vital messages cannot be overstressed." Not exactly head-line material, the so-called OWI film bulletins featured Rosalind Rus-sell soliciting support for the Third War Loan Campaign or Betty Field telling housewives to shun the black market. Today's perception of the news bulletin—a bolt of startling, instantaneously transmitted information accompanied by images—is a televisual inheritance.

The Pearl Harbor media moment: the family huddled around the radio in *The Sullivans* (1944).

The attraction of the newsreel then was neither timeliness nor urgency but verification and coherence. War news was not a blizzard of disconnected images but a discernible pattern of intelligible movements. With maps and arrows, intertitles, capsule backgrounds, illustrative graphics, and sure narrative thrust, the newsreels explained bewildering events on remote atolls and taught geography, military strategy, and international politics to a public conscious of the importance but confused by the complexity. The newsreels made sense of the thing.

The symbiosis between the war and the newsreels began literally from day one. In a seemingly scripted coincidence, a Movietone camera crew was in Hawaii photographing background shots for 20th Century-Fox's *To the Shores of Tripoli* (released April 10, 1942). Studio cameraman Al Brick had the singular honor of making the sole commercial film record of the actual attack on December 7. The eagerly anticipated (and heavily censored) footage from Pearl Harbor was held up by the military for over two full months, not reaching screens until February 27, 1942. The scenes released showed "burning hang-ers, planes on the ground smashed by Jap bombs, the raining fire that enveloped the battleship Arizona, and pictures of the capsized Oklahoma, targetship Utah, and the wreckage of destroyers, Cassin and Downes." Following official policy, the Navy deleted "all pictures of actual combat, wounded or dead, and its forces in action." Not until December 10, 1942, were some 900 feet (roughly nine minutes) of additional footage of the attack cleared for release—to the exploitation advantage of Fox Movietone, which possessed exclusive rights to Brick's historical footage because wartime pooling agreements with the other newsreels were not in effect on December 7, 1941.

The Pearl Harbor delays and deletions typified newsreel coverage for much of the next two years. Though neither side had any illusions about who ultimately called the shots, restrictions on combat footage and postponement of its timely release pitted the newsreels squarely against the newsmakers. Editors naturally deplored the policy as antithetical to a good job of motion picture journalism. In fact, feeling that Army and Navy cameramen did not measure up to professional

Captured images: a newsreel shot of Pearl Harbor from the Japanese point of view, shown to homefront audiences in December 1942. (Courtesy of the *Stars and Stripes*)

standards, each of the civilian newsreel editors had originally wanted his own experienced photographers on the battle scene. Given their place in the chain of command, however, they had little choice but to agree to a system known in the jargon as "rota-coverage," wherein each newsreel was given duplicate material shot by pool photographers, censored by military officials, and issued through the War Department's Bureau of Public Relations. The distinctive contribution of the five companies became largely a matter of logo, editing, commentary, and the announcer's voice. Throughout the 1930s the five newsreel companies had been as intensely competitive for visual scoops as the metropolitan dailies. During the war the action was more editorial than reportorial.

Though far less restricted than in the Great War, newsreel coverage was under stringent military control. Civilian cameramen were required to wear uniforms and lived under conditions similar to commissioned officers and constraints uncongenial to roving reporters. Freedom of movement and permission to film were determined at the discretion of the military authorities. Newsreel editors acquiesced not only for patriotic reasons—no one argued for unrestricted access to combat fronts or total freedom from military censorship—but because they depended on military largess for security, information, transportation, access, and sometimes even raw stock. Assenting to the principle of military oversight, Frederick Ullman, Jr., editor of RKO-Pathé News, promised that newsreel organizations would "submit to wartime censorship, yielding to the judgement of military experts as to what war scenes may or may not be released." However, editors vehemently objected to capricious applications and pointless impediments. Although the newsreel pools maintained some fourteen civilian crews accompanying various American fighting forces, civilian and military cameramen alike were routinely ordered to stop filming and occasionally forcefully restrained from doing so. In one case, newsreel cameramen had their equipment locked below decks to prevent them from filming a beachhead landing—in Ireland. During the Battle of the Bismarck Sea in the South Pacific, pool cameramen were grounded by the Army Air Force and forbidden to board Flying Fortresses and record the American victory. In late 1942, when the Marines began their bloody assault of the Solomon Islands, newsreel photographers had to be content with training footage of leathernecks storming the beaches at North Carolina.

Later in the war the military authorities more wisely applied restrictions *after* filming so they could confiscate likely footage for their own training films, informational archives, and commercial releases. In February 1944 Pathé News cameraman David Oliver reported that there were no restrictions on what he could film, but there was a catch. "Once, when we were shooting, an officer would tell us this or that was restricted. Now they tell us, 'go ahead and shoot what you like.' And so I make up my stories, knowing only occasionally that what I shoot will not reach the theater screen." Universal cameraman Irving Smith had the same experience covering General MacArthur's return to the Philippines. "There were no restrictions on our work. We went everywhere and photographed anything we wanted to," he told the trade press. "[Then] all the negative goes into the pool and the War and Navy department releases what it likes." A reporter for *Box Office* resentfully described the process by which military authorities exerted preemptive control:

> [In Washington] incoming negative is shown to representatives of all the services involved. As it is unreeled, somebody says: "That's out!" The "that's outs" become so numerous in a short time there is little left for public showing. Then various departments start assembling shorts and feature length films for training purposes and decide they have something which should be put into theatres.

As one newsreel editor groused, "There are about 500 would-be Cecil B. DeMilles in the government services."

Supplementing and often supplanting the pool coverage by newsreel cameramen were military photographers from the Army Signal Corps and the Navy Photographic Unit. Being locked into a lowly position in the chain of command, the cameramen in uniform were as hamstrung in their own way as their civilian colleagues. In early 1943 word filtered back to Hollywood that "despite the grandiose plan for wider use of motion picture photographers at the front, Signal Corps lensers actually in the fighting lines" were deterred by "fogey officers." *Variety* reported: "Most of the shutter boys are private or non-commissioned officers and any minor lieutenant can prevent them from even removing a lens cap. As a result, they beef, they've missed thousands of opportunities for spectacular and historic footage."

Louis de Rochemont received a letter from a former *March of Time* staffer and current Navy photographer, who reported that pictures

A weapon of war: German photographers at the Eastern front
(*above*) and in North Africa documenting Nazi victories. (Spaarnestad Foto-Archief, the Netherlands)

of the Pearl Harbor attack taken by air station photographers and the fleet camera party were nearly destroyed "on the order of an unimaginative old line officer, who apparently had no conception of their worth as documents or morale builders." In responding publicly to the charges, the Navy revealed why so many of its captains were so curiously recalcitrant about combat photography. "If de Rochemont has those letters, they probably represent a holdover from general order No. 96, in force for many years," explained Lt. Comdr. A. Donald Fraser, assistant director of photography for the Bureau of Aeronautics. "This order discouraged photography in the Navy, and [the] several courts martial resulting from the shooting of confidential material tended to make many officers shy away from allowing their cameramen freedom to shoot important actions, or any material of a confident nature." In August 1942 the order was superseded by a more elastic policy and, Fraser promised, the situation was "rapidly clearing itself [up]."

For a deadline-driven business, *what* was shown was sometimes less important than *when* it was released. In the early days of the war, when America was floundering both on the battlefield and in media exploitation, the newsreel record of combat was tardy and timorous. Terry Ramsaye, *Motion Picture Herald* editor for the duration, spoke out often and passionately on the essential role the newsreels should play in the war effort. "It is the considered opinion of the makers of newsreels that the entire war is held an entirely confidential matter by the Army and Navy," he protested in June 1942. Noting the greater latitude accorded the press and radio, Ramsaye listed a long train of abuses and lost opportunities:

> Pictures of that Pearl Harbor attack and its sequels reached the newsreel screen, in a fashion, two months after the event. The Marshall Island engagement was released in the same reluctant manner. Nothing has been had from the bombing of Tokyo, despite the fact that Colonel Doolittle, hero of the occasion, has been brought home for war cause promotions. Nothing has been had from the Coral Sea, and of course nothing is even in sight on last week's Battle of the mid-Pacific.

The progress of the Battle of Midway from sea (June 4–6, 1942) to screen (September 14, 1942) makes Ramsaye's case. Filmed in 16mm Kodachrome, the footage is among the most priceless and storied in the war record, not least because part of it was personally shot by Lt. Comdr. John Ford. Capitalizing on the coup, the Navy hoarded the choicest footage from the newsreels, opting instead for a two-reel special distributed by WAC and underwritten by the Navy, which paid for the cost of bumping up the 16mm Kodachrome to 35mm Technicolor prints. Some five hundred prints of *The Battle of Midway* were finally released the second week in September to boost a bond drive in the nation's theaters. The film's dramatic attack sequences and bombardments attracted an extraordinary amount of public attention; the newsreels had shown nothing like it.

Outmaneuvered and outranked, the newsreels leaned heavily on military photographic units for their most dynamic and timely footage. Maddeningly, despite an "understanding" that the newsreels would receive "official films prior to any other official release," the Army and Navy persisted in holding back the really exceptional combat footage for their own documentaries—whose title credits then boasted of material never shown before. In November and December 1942, Col. Darryl F. Zanuck supervised some forty-two Army, Navy, and Office of Strategic Services cameramen recording the North African campaign. As with *The Battle of Midway,* the commercial newsreels received meager excerpts from the most gripping footage, the Army saving the prime cuts for a four-reel color special released under OWI and WAC auspices and distributed by Warner Bros. WAC footed the bill for 677 Technicolor prints costing $150,000. Despite torpid pacing, *At the Front in North Africa* (released March 18, 1943) offered some of the most exciting combat footage to date and, in a dramatic break with initial War Department policy, for the first time showed glimpses of American dead and wounded on stretchers.

The cavalier treatment of the newsreels was a cause for wounded pride, but aggravating the insult was the knowledge that the military was not making effective use of the medium at its disposal. Again, when it came to the movies, the Fascists made better cineastes. The overseas branch of the OWI and the Office of Inter-American Affairs regularly expressed chagrin that the Germans consistently distributed more dynamic combat footage to wavering neutrals in South America. Terry Ramsaye complained that American military policy was "the decided reverse of that all too successful procedure of the Nazis who consider the camera an instrument of war and push it to the front where the story is." The status of the newsreels reached a wartime low in Alfred Hitchcock's *Saboteur* (1942) when a sound truck labeled "American Newsreel" is used in an Axis plot to blow up a ship at the Brooklyn Naval Yard.

Bedeviled by delays and deletions, the newsreels were also constrained by an internal, editorial uncertainty about exactly how to present the war to the homefront. Lacking compelling combat and casualty footage, editors initially rendered the war more as a glorious campaign than a nasty but necessary business. Like the dialogue of the early Hollywood feature films, commentary confused jingoistic bluster with the mature work of morale building. In 1942 *Variety* surveyed a newsreel sampling at New York's Embassy Theatre and found a "buoyant roseate picture of the war" with an "anaemic and Pollyanna slant." The trade paper caustically condemned the "tepid, serene recital of the entire world at war," intruded upon only by "a couple untoward reminders of what we ourselves are up against and of the sort of bad licks we are taking." The newsreels laid the bulk of the blame on the military; the civilians in government were inclined to agree. "Newsreel coverage is one of the log jams that block realistic war coverage," declared the OWI's Palmer Hoyt. "I'm not arguing for stories that will chill the blood of a mother or sweetheart, but we do want to know what our sons are doing."

Newsreel audiences certainly seemed ready for a less sanitized and more straightforward vision. Public dissatisfaction with aseptic war information was widespread enough to be given voice in the *March of Time*'s issue on homefront contribution, "Mr. and Mrs. America" (November 1942). Using Muncie, Indiana, as the symbolic sociological locus of Middletown America, the commentary noted that "the people have resented an official attitude which implies that they are not wise enough or strong enough to take bad news as well as good, not worthy to be admitted into full partnership in their own war." It called for "brutal candor" and boldly asserted that in its first year "the war has gone badly indeed."

Not until late 1943 were the dual problems that had bedeviled the newsreels since Pearl Harbor—delay and deletion—solved. In March 1943 representatives from the five newsreels and the film section of the Army's public relations branch came to an arrangement whereby exposed negatives of combat footage, whether taken by the newsreels or the Army, were flown by "fast plane" directly to Washington (bypassing London) for processing and censorship. The material was then to be "speedily released for film house showing." On-screen evidence of the streamlined system materialized quickly. Newsreel footage of the Sicilian campaign, more timely and exciting than anything previously available, reached theaters in a record ten days after the actual landing. The other logjam was broken up by the personal intervention of the president. In September 1943, at the urging of OWI chief Elmer Davis, FDR directed the military to cease its policy of withholding all but "cream-puff" pictures and permit the newsreels to record the realistic "albeit harrowing" side of war, including images of American dead in battle.

The reasons for the turnabout were threefold: (1) complaints from motion picture producers and Americans hungry for unadorned visuals; (2) the growing sense on the part of homefront strategists that no news was bad news, incubating rumors and anxiety; and (3) by 1943 the course of the war had favorably shifted and no armed service is ever reluctant to showcase its victories.

For exhibitors, up-to-date and dramatic newsreels suddenly acquired a box-office power of their own, regardless of the accompanying feature. "No one can honestly state to what extent [the newsreel] acts as a direct stimulus to grosses, but try cutting it out of the program and the patrons will immediately start beefing," warned *Motion Picture Herald*. "A man reads his paper or hears a broadcast about the great victory at Sicily, then he wants to see how it was done—so he goes to see it in the newsreel." Especially in the early days of the war, audiences clamored for news and documentary footage. By 1944 Francis S. Harmon of WAC estimated, with an unlikely degree of precision, that 83.6 percent of newsreel footage was being devoted to the war. Pathé's advertising claimed "today news-on-the-screen rivals the feature as a marquee attraction," which during some weeks was probably true. Leo Handel, director of the Motion Picture Research Bureau, reported that 85 percent of the public wanted to see the war in newsreels. Marquees gave prominent display to newsreel topics, announcing "first invasion pictures" or urging "see liberated Paris." "The managers of my houses have been reporting that business has been failing off badly as a result of patrons being fed up with liberty shots they've seen a hundred times," said an executive for Telenews Theatres, a circuit of eleven newsreel houses. "The Sicilian campaign [footage of August 1943] was a gift out of the blue." The sponsoring studios also took in their share of the winnings. In 1944 *Variety* estimated that "newsreel rentals for some of the majors run as high as $2,000,000 to $2,500,000 [per year] apart from their exploitation value in theaters for the parent companies represented."

The newsreels earned for themselves another kind of payoff: respect. Prior to the war, studio executives and theater managers treated the newsreels little better than cartoons. Exhibitors edited issues offhandedly and eliminated clips from tight schedules. One popular gauge of the prewar standing of the newsreel is *Too Hot to Handle* (1938), a madcap action-adventure in which Clark Gable plays a roguish cameraman who cheerfully fabricates combat footage and stages news events under the nose of his not overly scrupulous editor. After 1941, when combat news and war information pushed aside bathing beauties and sports roundups, the newsreels became, in the words of *Box Office* editor Ben Shlyen, "a vital motion picture entity." "The newsreel was never so important as it is today," he wrote in 1942. "The public was never more interested. Many people say that the newsreel is their favorite film subject." In theatrical appeal and journalistic credibility, moving-image news attained new stature. "The newsreel won for itself a wider, more attentive audience [during the war]," recalled documentary writer and narrator Newton E. Meltzer in 1947. "No longer is its appearance on the screen considered an opportune time to visit the lavatory or discuss the merits of the feature picture."

Eager to spot a son, husband, or father, women attended avidly to the newsreel screen. Paramount News provided relatives of fighting men with still-frame enlargements of their sons, fathers, and husbands while smalltown theater managers usually obliged locals with private screenings of the reels after hours. Exhibitors experienced some awkward moments when several girls-back-home requested clips of the same boy-over-there. After a woman spotted her MIA son in a Universal News clip, captured German footage of American POWs received microscopic analysis. As the images became more explicit, theater managers came to dread more sorrowful flashes of recognition: a stricken mother shrieking "That's my boy!" At Boston's Metropolitan, a woman noticed her son among the wounded in newsreel clips from Salerno and "lost control." Patrons comforted her as best they could, but neither her composure nor a moviegoing spirit was regained.

By late 1943 an accommodating military, cooperative pool coverage, and proven channels of development and distribution achieved for the newsreels something like speed and topicality. Footage of the

Marine landings on Tarawa and the United Nations conferences in Cairo and Teheran reached American screens within two weeks. Coverage of the invasion of the Marshall Islands was even better, being not only timely (delivered to newsreels within fifteen days of the event) but comprehensive in narrative and spectacular in imagery. Newsreel scenes showed the approaching task force, the bombardment of Kwajalein by sea and air, Amtracs coming ashore, and soldiers digging in and "blasting the Japs off the island."

Sicily, Teheran, the early campaigns in the Pacific—all were dress rehearsals for the newsreel coverage of the Normandy invasion, the largest amphibian assault in history, on June 6, 1944. Top secrecy notwithstanding, the anticipated invasion received an extraordinary amount of public debate and frank speculation on the radio and in the newsreels and screen magazines. The "what" known, Americans everywhere debated—some wagered on—the where and when. Observing that "nothing can inhibit the citizen's right to reasonable surmise and logical conjecture," the *March of Time* devoted its June 1943 issue ("Invasion!") to the subject and released an updated version in April 1944. A panel of experts discussed possible invasion sites and alternative strategies, illustrated by maps and arrows (one of which thrust into Normandy) and featuring vignettes of public speculation.

Not incidentally, one target audience of the "Invasion!" issue was the Axis leadership itself. The intimidating inventory of American resources—depots bulging with armored vehicles, warehouses stocked to the ceiling with equipment, factories humming at capacity—made for potent psychological warfare. Over a mosaic of newspaper headlines, the commentator makes a logical conjecture about the Axis warlords within "Festung Europa," contemplating the prospect of an Allied invasion backed by the arsenal of democracy: "The Fascist and Nazi underlings and quislings already know that the hour of retribution can no longer be indefinitely delayed. For since many months, the war of nerves which they invented and exploited has been turned against them." The nervy proclamation from the *March of Time* of its own part in the setup underlines the Allied psychological advantage even as it expresses the newly won propaganda slickness.

With a fast-breaking story, however, radio was still the best medium to tune in to. In April 1944 radio station WNEW, a 10,000-watt independent station in New York City, listed its media advantages ("around the clock," "as fast as it's released") and demonstrated just how open sensitive military operations might be in a democratic culture at war:

> *Around the clock,* when the great attack comes, you'll get all the official news—by tuning in WNEW, 1130 on your dial. . . . *Invasion is coming!* Exact day and minute are known to only a chosen few. But for every WNEW listener the word "Attack" will throw into operation a remarkable plan of invasion news coverage. Through WNEW you, the listener, will move in with the first invasion wave . . . set foot on enemy soil . . . hear *every bit of news as fast as it's released.*

Under such stimulus, as the spring of 1944 wore on the country and the media contracted a bad case of "invasion jitters" and experienced a nasty eruption on Saturday, June 3, when AP wires flashed a false report the invasion had begun. The first authenticated reports from network correspondents arrived via shortwave between 2:00 and 4:00 A.M. Tuesday morning, and most of the country woke up to the news. Ever media-wise, FDR had provided diversion and given no hint of the action in his radio address that Monday evening at 8:30— when the invasion had already been set in motion.

Motion picture exhibitors announced "invasion" updates from the stage and typed news flashes on mattes for projection on the screen. Loews Theaters unreeled a specially prepared briefie consisting of a prayer and choral music. Nonetheless the superior speed and immediacy of the rival medium was never denied. Throughout the afternoon and evening of June 6, 1944, theaters halted their programs and broke into main features for radio news bulletins, piped in through sound systems. That evening projectors were stopped for President Roosevelt's 10:00 P.M. address to the nation.

Meanwhile, military photographic units covered the invasion like a blanket, assigning a total of four hundred men and designating twenty-one for motion picture photography and 190 for still shots. In addition, two cameramen from the newsreel pool went in with the troops. Photographers mounted some fifty 35mm cameras on landing barges and tanks, set them on universal focus, and started them going at an opportune time. (Forty-seven cameras were smashed.) The Army Air Force mounted cameras in gunsights to capture the first shots of strafing and bombing launched in support of the beachhead landing. Exposed negative was immediately flown stateside by fast plane, and within sixty hours of embarkation, invasion pictures were being screened in Washington.

Even under the best of circumstances, editing and mixing raw footage and printing and transporting the reels required forty-eight hours for venues in proximity to New York, several days for the "nabes" in the hinterlands. As the news had broken on radio on Tuesday the 6th, the absolute earliest the newsreels could expect to get footage into theaters was over the weekend (by issuing a special) or, more realistically, in the regular issue on the following Tuesday, the 13th. In fact, the issue for the first postinvasion date—Thursday, June 8— was already "in the can" and devoted to Gen. Mark Clark's push on Rome. The government, however, had other plans. Frank Capra had prepared a two-reel orientation film entitled *Eve of Battle,* a nontopical review that had been ready for weeks. In a controversial move, the War Department and the OWI deposited the official government report on the commercial newsreels, with the request that it play in place of the regular issue distributed on Thursday, June 8. At so grave a crossroads, under the compulsion of wartime unity, the newsreels could only comply with what was more than a request but less than an order. The OWI vigorously denied undue pressure—"There was no badgering, no beating anybody over the head at all," asserted OWI film assistant Taylor Mills—but defender of the newsreel realm Terry Ramsaye was furious at the annexation. "The nonchalance which assumed that because somebody wanted it the whole system of newsreel production was to be upset at a nod is not to be forgiven," he wrote in a blistering editorial. A Universal Newsreel intertitle made the best of necessity: "In co-operation with the War Department Universal Newsreel is privileged to present these official pictures of the prelude to invasion." Opting in the end for thoroughness over dispatch, the newsreels withheld embarkation and aerial footage from the Tuesday the 13th issue and waited on the arrival of ground-level, beachhead material. Thus, although preliminary invasion footage arrived stateside in sixty hours, a complete newsreel account of the invasion wasn't released until Thursday, June 15.

That weekend theaters around the country ballyhooed "First Invasion Pictures!" Vivid, gripping, and comprehensive, the invasion record warranted special exploitation. The issue deployed the full catalog of newsreel devices—gunsight mounted camera shots of aerial attacks, point-of-view shots from incoming landing crafts, and footage from captured Nazi films. The tone was resolute and tempered.

In one sequence, an American soldier is shot, brought down, rises, then collapses lifeless in the water. From the 10,000 feet of raw footage available, each of the newsreels culled 1,000 feet (about ten minutes and slightly longer than a regular wartime issue). Despite the stateside glitch over *Eve of Battle,* the military censors, the newsreel pools, the Army photographers, and WAC had finally greased the system. Col. Curtis Mitchell, chief of the Pictorial Section of the War Department's Bureau of Public Relations, called it "the greatest pictorial team play in history."

The last year of the war witnessed accelerating speed, comprehensiveness, and explicitness. By way of influence and competition, the newsreels were forced to become less of a journalistic hodgepodge. Unable to compete with radio for sheer immediacy, they abandoned the tabloid headline style and adopted the newsweekly as a model. In particular, RKO-Pathé turned to a magazine-style format that emphasized interpretation, employed library footage for background orientation, and relied extensively on maps and diagrams. By devoting whole issues to the extensive coverage of landmark events, the newsreel came to resemble a minidocumentary that might build in drama. Incorporating newsreel footage made under the nose of the Nazis by French Resistance cameramen and MGM News of the Day stringer Gaston Madru, two back-to-back RKO-Pathé issues on the liberation of Paris, "Paris Is Free!" (September 7, 1944) and "Victory in Paris" (September 12, 1944) were instant watersheds. The company's intertitle was on the money: "Pathé News presents . . . from inside Paris. . . . what its editors believe to be one of the most stunning newsreel subjects ever made." Including the famous shot of Madru atop a truck above a sign reading "Please don't kill the French Cameraman," the issues recorded street-to-street fighting and death on the pavement. "Watch this action closely," instructs narrator Dwight Weist. "Bullets spatter around the fallen Nazi"—and a female Resistance fighter strips him of his weapon. Sadly, the gallant Madru was one of the many casualties of war from the cameramen's ranks, killed April 19, 1945, by a German sniper's bullet in Leipzig.

For its October 4, 1944, issue, "Allies Enter Germany," RKO-Pathé News again devoted its entire program to the single story, in what was described as "one-story magazine style." "It is a method which has suggested itself out of the unity of the material, all part of one big story," explained RKO editor Walton C. Ament. "We would be doing it again with material of equal importance and equal homogeneity." The company continued its service with a one-reel special issue on the Battle of the Bulge in February 1945. Featuring "special maps outlining each theater of action and informative narration," it "marked the first attempt [by a newsreel issue] to give the public an overall pictorial record of recent events in the European war theatre." For the recapture of Manila and the battle of Iwo Jima, each of the five newsreels devoted all their footage to the single stories (released March 1 and March 8, 1945, respectively). A trade observer noted that "whether the documentaries have learned from the newsreels, or whether the newsreels are at times influenced by the documentaries, there is a trend toward a more consistent narration in newsreel treatments." Ultimately, as the war reached anticipated climaxes, the newsreels prepared reels to meet the expected occasion. V-E Day, celebrated wildly in Times Square on Monday, May 7, 1945, and officially announced on Tuesday, May 8, was chronicled in newsreel special issues on Wednesday, May 9.

After the invasion coverage established the standard to beat, the newsreels reached for new records in speed of delivery. With film shipments assured priority treatment on Army Transport Service planes, the certainty of regular delivery as much as topicality enhanced newsreel planning. The final battles of the Pacific war came to the homefront screen with an unprecedented and (for the time) dizzying pace. The spectacular and brutal Iwo Jima footage that reached newsreel screens on March 8, 1945, had left the island on February 21, 1945, in the personal custody of Lt. Comdr. John W. McLain. Film taken of the battle of Okinawa on March 22, 1945, arrived in Washington on March 29 (Thursday) and hit newsreel screens the next week, Tuesday, April 3. The footage was then shipped *back* to Okinawa for viewing by Admiral Nimitz and his aides by April 13. "Pictorial coverage of the war is just now reaching a new height—something never before attempted in the way of speed and dramatic power," reported *Box Office*. "Nothing like this has ever been done before in either peace or war."

The newsreel also refined its combat soundtrack. For most of the war, the additional burden in equipment and the concomitant danger of exposure made forfeiture of on-the-spot sound recording the better part of valor. Though a meticulous and time-consuming intermediary step, the process of dubbing in sound effects, mixing in appropriate commentative music, and recording the voice-over narration was more wisely done in the newsreels' New York offices. For aural "sweetening" the companies relied on prerecorded files of "war noises." Canned sounds (the accelerating roar of a divebombing plane, the distinctive explosions from different caliber ordnance, and the trademark "squish" of the flamethrower) became conventional aural cues and soothing leitmotifs for newsreel combat. Moments of sound-on-sound authenticity were exceptional. Commenting on one of the rare on-site recordings, Liane Richter, newsreel analyst at the Library of Congress, was as impressed by what she heard from Iwo Jima as what she saw:

> The recording was faulty and blurred, but it had the impact of the real thing; it included scraps of barely audible conversation which, compared to the glib tones of the narrator, were like actuality shots of servicemen's faces compared to polished Hollywood perform-ances. Another reel showed a soldier giving a fuller-than-usual ac-count of his experiences in a tank. The soldier's talk was obviously unrehearsed and unedited; it included hesitation, a slip of the tongue; his account by its very spontaneity led to an intimate knowledge of the episode he described.

As the newsreels extended coverage and picked up speed, they also became more explicit and cold-blooded. In tandem with the stark combat documentaries the military was releasing through WAC, the newsreels screened images once untolerated by the Code and con-sidered anathema to audience sensibilities. Though the full horror of combat and its grisly impact on the human frame never reached the homefront screen, the depiction of death and destruction was hardly sanitized or "Disneyfied." Naturally, enemy dead—contorted in death, rotted in foxholes, burned by flamethrowers—were more emotionally acceptable and widely showcased than American dead. Naturally too, given the peculiar ferocity and racist cast of the war in the Pacific, Japanese dead were a special occasion for unblinking satisfaction. A Universal Newsreel report on the campaign for Peleliu is offhandedly cruel about a point-blank killing. "Watch this Jap care-fully," instructs the commentator as a singed soldier darts out of a pillbox. "He won't get far." He doesn't.

Less explosive though no less explicit civilian depredations, per-formed away from the chaos of battle, were also screened for the first time. As the Allied armies liberated occupied territory, vengeful citizens exacted swift retribution on their former oppressors. Out-breaks of mob justice and harsh executions were captured by the photojournalism in *Life* and the Eyemo cameras of the Army Signal Corps. Newsreel commentary reported the scenes with a grim appreciation. Italy contributed the two most gruesome examples. On September 20, 1944, a mob of vengeful Romans broke into the Palazzo Corsini courthouse. After token resistance from the guards, they fell upon Fascist flunky and prosecution witness Donato Carretta, gouged out his eyes, tossed him into the Tiber River, and watched him drown. Three days later cameras recorded the execution of former Rome chief of police Pietro Caruso, who was tied to a chair, facing backwards. Riflemen aimed for the nape of his neck, the method the Gestapo had used to murder 336 Italians fingered by Caruso for a Nazi reprisal. The aftermath of the Carretta slaying (a naked corpse hung upside down on a wall) and the Caruso execution (bullets hitting the back of his head) escaped the usual Code censorship of gratuitous violence and close-up bloodletting. The same treatment was accorded the mutilation and display of the bodies of Mussolini and his mistress, which were shown hanging from the rafters of a gas station in the issues of May 18, 1945. Paramount News, which before the war had balked at showing a dead body, signposted its report with a flippant intertitle: "Duce's Last Mob Scene."

The final indelible images of the Second World War were not of combat, not of the atomic bombings that finally ended the conflict, not like anything anyone had ever seen before. The first glimpses came at New York's Embassy Theatre on April 26, 1945, with the release of Artkino's one-reel *Nazi Atrocities.* From the silence of a projection room screening, *Variety*'s Abel Green heard a stunned whisper: "This doesn't seem possible." On May 1, 1945, the five newsreels issued the most horrifying images ever screened in American theaters, the official Army Signal Corps footage of the concentration camps at Buchenwald, Ohrdruf, Hadamar, and Nordhausen. Fox Movietone News provided a cautionary preface: "These scenes of horror are an awesome indictment of Nazi bestiality. To the civilized mind such inhuman cruelty is incredible. We show these films as documentary evidence and warn you not to look at the screen if you are susceptible to gruesome sights." Exposing the furnaces and half-cremated corpses at Buchenwald, Universal Newsreel took a different tack. "Don't turn away," orders commentator Ed Herlihy. "Look."

In an age in which the horrific image has become a living-room commonplace, when children rent a videotape series called *Faces of Death,* it is difficult to appreciate the unprecedented impact of the

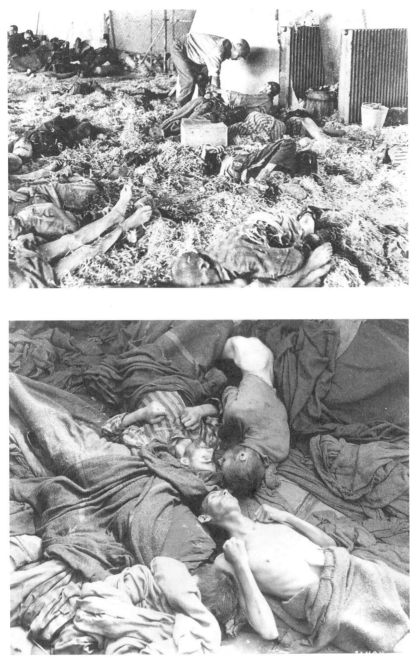

Not like anything anyone had ever seen before: Army Signal Corps photographs of the Nazi concentration camps at Nordhausen (*above*) and Dachau, April 1945. (Courtesy of the National Center for Jewish Film, Brandeis University)

Army Signal Corps footage of the crematoria at Nordhausen: the photographic image demands eyewitness verifications—from a former camp inmate and an Allied onlooker. (Courtesy of the *Stars and Stripes*)

concentration camp footage, the reaction it elicited, and the incredulity it inspired. Shown surveying stacks of corpses and rows of crematoria, Eisenhower, Bradley, and Patton, none of whom were armchair generals, are ashen-faced and visibly repelled. The anti-Hun histrionics of the Great War had left many Americans skeptical of reports of genocide. The newsreels verified that the Nazis had surpassed the imagination of the most fevered propagandist at the OWI.

But if the documentary evidence from the liberated camps validated the eyewitness accounts, the images themselves were so unbelievable they in turn required eyewitness corroboration. The footage could scarcely be credited as real. The Army conducted excursions through the camps—forcing German soldiers and local burghers to behold the national handiwork—and arranged for government, press, and Hollywood officials to visit the actual locations. At Eisenhower's request, the camp footage was shown nationwide, and audiences seem to have responded with an appalled solemnity. Some gasped, a few hissed obscenities at the Germans, but most sat in shocked silence. In London, reportedly, patrons tried to flee the theaters—only to be constrained by servicemen who compelled the civilians to confront on the newsreel screen some of what the soldiers had experienced in action.

"100% MCCOY BATTLE FOOTAGE"

Working in cultural concert with the commercial newsreels was the combat report, a warrior's eye view of frontline action. Newsreel accounts of any major military action were followed up by a documentary recapitulation from the featured branch of the service. The reportorial practice matched the wishes of the OWI's Stanton Griffis, who argued that the "first newsreel flashes from the battle front should be followed as quickly as feasible by a full documentary report." After a couple of months, a two- to four-reel government issue reviewed the campaign and traced again its movements, reassuringly containing and cinematically framing the completed action.

The dual newsreel/documentary containment of the military push up the boot of Italy to Rome illustrates the process. The campaign began with the landing of the Army at Anzio (May 11, 1944) and climaxed with the entry into Rome (June 4). Newsreels reached stateside, following in sequence and functioning as guidance, about ten days later. The narrative coherence and dramatic unity was then reasserted with a twenty-minute War Department film *The Liberation of Rome* (released July 13, 1944). That pattern—up-to-date and explicit combat footage in the newsreels followed by a comprehensive documentary recapitulation—was held for every major campaign of the later war. Like episodes of a serial, gaining momentum in the march to victory and the certainty of closure, the combat reports unspooled in sequence.

As an addition for the duration to Hollywood's staple program, the combat reports adhered to theatrical convention and standard cinematic style. The expectations of civilian spectatorship and the requirements of military education produced combat photographers fluent in the rhythms of classical Hollywood grammar. Virtually all the wartime instructors in the Army Signal Corps and Navy Photographic Unit came from the motion picture industry. Predictably, they stressed the codes of their craft and inculcated a spectator-sensitive notion of combat photography. Under the aegis of the Motion Picture Research Council, Hollywood's ace cameramen trained military classes not only in lighting, focus, and the technical side of photography but in continuity, framing, and the elements of Hollywood technique. Lecturing to a Signal Corps class at MGM studios, cinematographer Alvin Wykoff taught the basics: "Your shots, no matter how well executed, will have no meaning unless they hold together in a clear continuity pattern."

Capt. Merle H. Chamberlain, the commanding officer of the 187th Signal Photo Corps and the former head of projection at MGM, likewise stressed studio practice. Herb Lightman, a combat photographer in the 187th, recalled the operating procedure: "According to our plan, everything was to be worked out on paper before a foot of film was run through the camera, and this diagrammed script would be followed as closely as the changing situation would permit." In the field, behind the camera, Lightman and his fellow cameramen followed directions:

> We learned to select angles and image size as to put emphasis into our stories, to give them "approach," to provide connecting links between scenes. This paid off at the front. There we could not control the action to our cameras, but the principles of continuity had become so deeply ingrained that we instinctively shot pictures that "made sense" on the screen.

Having either learned their trade in the industry or been trained by people who had, combat photographers knew how to get the shot even while being shot at. They gave homefront audiences point-of-view vantages through the slits of tanks, from the decks of landing crafts, behind flamethrowers, and over bombsights. The bluster of a British officer who had supervised the photography for the Ministry of Information's combat report *Desert Victory* expressed a prevalent ethos: "The cameramen were armed with revolvers and were instructed to use them as range finders. When they were close enough to use their revolvers—that was the time to start using their cameras." The half-joking caution in the Signal Corps ranks was "Don't pan—or you'll be back in the infantry."

Unconducive to precision creative control over lighting, focal lengths, and retakes, combat conditions fostered technical advances and on-the-spot innovations. Homefront inventors and field photographers stripped, adapted, and improved weighty and time-consuming Hollywood workhorses typified by the 35mm Mitchell. Anything that required a tripod was dangerous and impractical; anything that took precious seconds of preparation (such as threading individual rolls into the camera) was dangerous and frustrating. The Bell and Howell 35mm Eyemo, a turret and hand-holdable unit developed in the 1930s for newsreel shooting, was widely used, but even the durable Eyemo was sometimes too cumbersome a burden and inviting a target. Though a few broad-shouldered old-timers clung to the larger models, the magazine-loaded Kodak Cine-Special and the Bell and Howell 16mm Filmo model came to be the preferred weapons for under-fire action. Hand held, they were steadied by pistol grips—and the nerves of the cameraman.

Though communicating in the fluent filmic grammar and performing the same genre work as the Hollywood feature, the combat reports emphasized their unique attraction as fragments of reality obtained at hard cost. They had a sophisticated arrangement with the homefront spectator, an implied contract that said: though a documentary, we will use the familiar conventions of the Hollywood feature film to accentuate the experience, but as a documentary we want you to remember that what you behold is really real. Thus, though the combat reports used the identifiable voices of Hollywood actors for narration and dramatic readings, heavenly choirs and musical soundtracks to modulate emotion, and transparently staged scenes for expository or polemical purposes, they also insisted on their special status as authentic records of wartime action and hence cinema that warranted a special credence and respect. Wartime audiences and War Department filmmakers engaged in a mutual agreement to switch between Hollywood convenience and documentary rigor.

The first and most storied of the combat reports, John Ford's *The Battle of Midway* (September 1942), set the terms of the contract. Eager to get into battle, Ford enlisted in the Navy and finagled his way first to the Office of Strategic Services and then to the battle site at Midway Island. Wounded in the first onslaught, he continued filming and captured the first battle ever recorded in color. Ford later told Peter Bogdanovich, "I did it all—we only had one camera" (an apparent attempt to print the legend not the fact: he was actually aided by Photographer Second Class Jack McKenzie, Jr., a former RKO cameraman. In one of those sad ironies war delivers straightfaced, McKenzie was killed August 10, 1945, the day after the bombing of Nagasaki, in a jeep accident near Hollywood).

Given a choice between dumb luck and visionary talent, combat photographers elect to possess the former. Ford was twice blessed. For sheer serendipity nothing in the filmed record of the Second World War surpasses the convergence in space and time of Hollywood's poet laureate of the military with the most critical naval battle of the Pacific war. As an addition to Ford's canon, *The Battle of Midway* is as elegiac and artful as the Ann Rutledge motif in *Young Mr. Lincoln*. As naval history, it requires an addendum: Ford's beachfront perspective from the island of Midway (not at sea with the task force) actually makes the battle look like a Japanese triumph, not a great American victory. Yet to capture and come back with such images, to contain the full fury of the enemy on film, compensated for any damage inflicted on the ground. By presenting sequences of exhilarating aerial bombardment and antiaircraft defense punctuated by tacit reminders that the cameraman himself is in the thick of the action, *The Battle of Midway* outlined the true order and outcome of battle. Within six months of release, timed to coincide with a war bond campaign, it had become one of the most popular and widely seen of all the combat reports, garnering over 13,000 playdates.

In *The Battle of Midway* and subsequent combat reports, documentary style meshed smoothly with Hollywood convention. Soundtrack cues and visible notices signaled the mood (and mode) shifts in cinematic expression. The main guidepost for perceptual changeover, the visual beacon telling the spectator to switch from entertainment to authenticity, was the retention of the rough edges of photography shot under duress. Ford's gorgeous Technicolor shots of vigilant sailors standing sentinel before a Pacific sunset merge into the riveting attack sequence of Japanese planes buzzing in and dive-bombing on Midway Island—where Ford, as the luck of the Irish would have it, was waiting with camera in hand. On screen, when the image falls out of frame in the backwash from an exploding shell, the violation of normative cinematic grammar (the stationary horizontal plane, sharp focus, unobstructed vision) translated into heightened impact and added credence.

For the classical Hollywood audience, that kind of departure from studio-system quality control designated documentary reality. Prior to this revelation "most newsreel men insisted it was impossible to get a picture suited for projection on the screen without using an electrically driven standard [35mm] tripod camera," commented *Box Office*. "The war—especially the invasion reels—have shown that if the pictorial content is sufficiently dramatic, audiences will not notice any technical deficiencies of photography." Actually, that was only part of the perceptual impact. The very "technical deficiencies" anathema to the studio system accentuated the allure of combat photography. "Small cameras set on the wings make the record," says the commentator of the Army Air Force's *The Fight for the Sky* (June 1945). "Too often, [this results in] poor pictures due to gun vibration. But they let you see what happens at the instant of action as the pilot sees it" (in this case a thrilling montage of smoking, exploding, and careening enemy planes). In like manner, the authenticity of Mark L. Moody's documentary *Ravaged Earth* (1942), observed *American Cinematographer,* "is emphasized by the very lack of cinematic technique. Mr. Moody and his Bell and Howell motion picture equipment were constantly subjected to the impact of explosion and the inevitably rugged existence in a bombed and shell-shocked land where slaughter permeated the atmosphere."

So dominant was the Hollywood tradition of quality that the potential impact of the out-of-frame footage from *The Battle of Midway* (caused by the concussion knocking the film out of frame in the camera aperture) was at first not realized. When the negative was developed, the sequence was initially adjudged unusable. Ford recognized the heightened drama it lent the sequence and retained it as it was. Even so, the prejudice for professionalism was tenacious from any angle. According to a cameraman in Ford's unit, "several Hollywood technicians ... thought we had done this optically just to produce the effect." It was the most widely commented on moment in the film and, as the first combat report released to homefront theaters, set a pattern of verisimilitude-via-deficiency for its successors. *Fury in the Pacific,* for example, includes an out-of-focus shot showing the dramatic rescue of a fallen soldier.

The second combat report was a world and an enemy away, *At the Front in North Africa.* The Army Signal Corps film was supervised and partly photographed by Darryl F. Zanuck in the manner of a Great War epic (GIs are still "doughboys," "Over There" is the soundtrack anthem, and the silent vintage production style is burdened by leisurely intertitles and stiff commentary). Shot in 16mm Kodachrome and bumped up to 35mm Technicolor, it is an uneven record, starting off slowly with shots of cargo ships unloading and providing little cartographic or strategic orientation. Following the latest convention, the action sequences of midair dogfights and fiery gasoline explosions deploy a jiggly camera plane and include out-of-focus shots of Nazi bombardments. In its most stunning section, a panoramic long shot of the Tébourba battlefield takes in the high-caliber dueling of tank warfare. ("Germans are on the left, Americans on the right," says the commentator. One half expects Zanuck to yell "Action!" from off camera.) The sequence forefronts the role of the cameraman both as an assurance of realism ("These street scenes were photographed by a concealed camera and reveal the true and varied reactions of the public during the raid") and a reminder of imminent danger ("These scenes were photographed from a hill overlooking the battlefield. The cameraman is actually nearer the German lines."). That the intrepid cameraman was often Zanuck himself, who appears camera in hand, cigar in mouth, was not lost on industry-wise spectators who labeled the film *At the Front with Darryl F. Zanuck.*

For his role in *The Battle of Midway* John Ford was awarded a Purple Heart and added luster to an already formidable legend; for *At the Front in North Africa,* Zanuck got nothing but grief. Having weathered the Nazi bombs in North Africa, he returned from the front to catch flak from the United States Senate, which had launched its investigation into Hollywood contracts with the War Department. Almost as bad was the critical rejection and superior competition. Although *At the Front in North Africa* received wide distribution (some 12,848 playdates according to WAC), its glow was dimmed by a combat report from the British Ministry of Information, *Desert Victory* (April 13, 1943). Opening so soon after Zanuck's record of the North African campaign, *Desert Victory* highlighted by comparison the weakness of American combat footage and the shortsightedness of Army restrictions on battlefield photography. It was everything the American film was not: dramatic, spectacular, and new—the British too had withheld some of the best footage from the newsreels. For Hollywood and Washington alike, to be bested by the Brits on screen was intolerable. Henceforth, American combat reports were to be more violent, topical, and enticing. They would combine exciting, rough-edged combat footage with expert postproduction refurbishment.

The aesthetic of the combat report did not, however, encourage a conflation of the raw and the cooked up. A manifest visible cue is usually clearly posted, the signal for the spectator to switch over from combat reality to cinematic adornment. In John Ford's *December 7th* (1943), sections of the image are actually blacked out, overwritten with the white word "censored" and incorporated into the

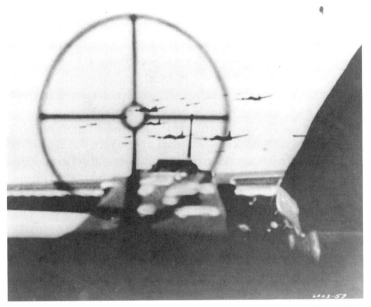

The best seat in the house: behind the crosshairs of a 50-caliber machine gun in *The Memphis Belle* (1944).

mise-en-scène. The visible evidence of military review validates the authenticity of the image: who is going to censor a dramatic recreation? *Attack! The Battle for New Britain* (June 1944) introduces itself with the assurance "the picture you are about to see is authentic in every detail. No scenes have been reenacted or staged." It then proceeds to move fluently from Hollywood vernacular—a slow dissolve on a still life of Christmas packets and letters—to a real-life view of men celebrating mass in the jungle.

The sophistication of the audience usually matched the sophistication of the moviemaking, but sometimes the combat report captured a scene so cinematic in its reality that an editorial aside was necessary to keep the metaphysics straight. At the height of the early morning air attack in *The Battle of Midway,* amidst bombs literally bursting in air, a color guard raises the American flag. "This really happened," says narrator Irving Rapper, as if to convince himself as much as the audience. An equally Fordian scene is in *Brought to Action* (January 1945), the Navy record of the Battle of Leyte Gulf. A plane lands safely on a carrier's deck, but the rear gunner has died in harness. The crew buries him at sea, at his post, with the plane as his coffin. A master shot records the solemn tableau: the crew on deck attending as the wrecked plane, with a sheet draped over the gunner's seat, slides overboard into the ocean. As the aircraft is swallowed in the ship's wake, the camera tilts upward to capture, perfectly coordinated, a fly-by tribute swooping in from the top of the frame. Heavenly intervention added powerful natural symbolism to the funeral sequence in *Report from the Aleutians* (July 1943). A somber graveside elegy, a bleak landscape of tundra, and a blanket of overcast sky suddenly brightens when clouds clear and expose a shimmering symbol of rebirth. "The chaplain commenced the service with 'In My Father's House There are Many Mansions' and with those words the fog lifted," director John Huston later recalled with some awe. "In the background, I could see a smoking volcano, widely scattered thunderstorms, and finally a half dozen rainbows." Such quiet, unbidden artistry could not but induce a conflicted response in the sensitive viewer. James Agee, always the most astute, lyrical, and guilt-ridden of film critics, meditated on the art in war: "In *Attack!* there are morning shots, getting men and material ashore in the not quite misty, sober light, which overwhelmed me with their doubleness of beauty, almost sublimity, and their almost fragrant immediacy"—visions, wrote Agee, whose occasion "made me doubt my right to be aware of the beauty at all."

Though pledged to record unvarnished reality and empowered by it, the combat reports did on occasion dissemble. Despite official injunctions forbidding the presentation of fabricated combat footage as authentic and public reiterations of authenticity from the War Department, sequences staged for expository or dramatic reasons crept into a few nominally all-real documentaries. *Tunisian Victory* (1944), a joint effort between Capra's unit and the British Ministry of Information, is the baldest case of duplicity. During the film's editing, Col. Hugh Stewart of the British Army vouched for its under-fire authenticity, dashingly remarking "you can't tell a Nazi tank to back up for a retake." Retakes, however, were possible in the California desert at night, where U.S. troops reenacted North African exploits. "We had troops moving down hills under fake artillery concentrations in the worst kind of fabrication," averred John Huston. "The material was so transparently false that I hated to have anything to do with it." Transparent it was. The counterfeit action was noted at the time by the trade press and among enough viewers to prompt the military to deny publicly charges of faking combat footage.

Such moments were exceptional, mainly because integrity was a safer policy. In reviews of *Desert Victory,* which also used staged footage to recreate the Tunisian campaign, both the *Hollywood Reporter* and *Variety* spotted the deception, and the latter articulated the danger: "The captious certainly will find room for criticism of a film sold as 100% McCoy battle footage for some of it to anyone familiar with picture making, is obviously not that." In 1944 while working at the Museum of Modern Art on the Library of Congress Film Project, OWI analyst Barbara Deming also spotted the telltale footage and offered a strained defense. "It is worth noting that *Desert Victory* makes use not only of some 'library shots' but of some specially enacted shots," she wrote. "But here instead of decreasing the reliability of the film as a document, they can be said to increase it, for they contribute to its intelligibility." Despite Deming's jesuitical distinction between "reliability" and "intelligibility," the consequences of exposure before a sharp-eyed audience were not worth the risk. The utter honesty of American footage was a cornerstone refutation to the manifest deceptions and manipulations in Axis propaganda.

The verity of *December 7th* is a more nettlesome case. Made at the direction of the president and the secretary of war, who ordered a "complete motion picture factual presentation" (note the phrasing) of the date of infamy, the film interweaves backlot recreations shot at 20th Century-Fox with the newsreel record of the attack. Though the expository scenes are avowedly dramatic reenactments (the film opens with an Uncle Sam figure lying asleep and stages conversations between an irate American reporter and a duplicitous Japanese diplomat), the extended bombardment sequence is a deft, duplicitous blend of newsreel footage, staged reenactments, and special-effects work. The full catalog of Hollywood's celluloid magic (rear-screen projection, miniatures, rapid crosscutting) conflate the real Pearl Harbor attack with the rendering of same. Especially during the rapid edits of the action sequences, the real and staged shots are indistinguishable.

Perhaps the best defense for the subterfuge in *December 7th* is that it was motivated more to spur morale and punch up emotion than to rewrite history. In rendering the destruction of the USS *Arizona*, cinematic falsification nonetheless tells the literal truth. The sequence begins with an establishing shot of a battleship, superimposed over which is a label reading "USS *Arizona*." The ship is a miniature model in a water tank. Via rear-screen projection, a squadron of attacking "Japanese" planes zooms in backframe and seemingly unloads its bombs over the toy battleship. The next shot crosscuts to sailors below deck scrabbling out of their bunks to man their battle stations. The exterior shot / interior shot pattern juxtaposes the bombing of the (miniature) battleship with the (reenacted) desperation in the ship's holds. The editing then inserts the famous newsreel footage of the *Arizona*'s explosion, a billowing fireball caught at the precise moment of detonation. The fast-paced crosscutting and quickstep synthesis can deceive the unwary, but the below-deck cutaways featuring the *Arizona*'s proxy personnel are meant to lend sympathy and identification to the men killed in the blast, to show the faces and forms behind the statistic of 1,200 dead.

Moreover, given the familiarity of the homefront audience with the extant Pearl Harbor footage, *December 7th* would not have been received with total credulity. At the height of the attack sequence, a black sailor, patently meant to stand in for Dorris Miller, is featured in medium shot on deck firing a machine gun before falling in battle. Adding visual credence to the scene is the hand-held camerawork, a calculated and innovative mimicry of newsreel-style combat photography. Yet no alert spectator would have failed to identify the figure as a surrogate for Miller or to realize that the brief forefronting of his action could only be a staged reenactment—especially since the figure, supposedly filmed in the heat of battle, is shot from two different angles.

Combat reality soon rendered forgeries unnecessary. In constructing documentary records of the uncovered or undercovered battles of the early war years, compromising the integrity of "100% McCoy battle footage" with fictional dilutions was understandable if not defensible. Irreplaceable film of the Tunisian campaign, for example, was sunk in transport at sea. By late 1943, however, the sheer scale and quantity of coverage accorded any major campaign gave filmmakers enough cover shots to be able to order battle, give approach, and create narrative interest. Also military strategists came to realize that grim, unvarnished combat footage was the best rebuff to homefront complacency, particularly in the later months of the war. *The Enemy Strikes* (March 1945), the combat report on the Battle of the Bulge, featured battle-hardened Nazis smoking Camels and Chesterfields lifted from American dead and close-up shots of GI victims of the massacre at Malmédy. "The cost of living on the Cologne plain was considerably higher than in the United States," snaps the commentator. Likewise, John Huston's *The Battle of San Pietro* (May 1945) was designed to be "stronger, more direct than any [combat report] made before by the Army Pictorial Service" said a spokesman.

The war of attrition in the Pacific theater, the inexorable movement from the West to the Far East, traced a line of frontier conquest especially suited to American vision. Maps and diagrams thrust forcefully westward to the ultimate manifest destination, Tokyo. Throughout 1944–45 the release pattern of the combat reports on the Pacific War acquired increasing momentum and the serial certainty of ultimate closure:

> *With the Marines at Tarawa* (March 2, 1944)
> *Attack! The Battle for New Britain* (June 20, 1944)
> *The Battle for the Marianas* (September 21, 1944)
> *Brought to Action* (January 11, 1945)
> *Fury in the Pacific* (March 22, 1945)
> *Target Tokyo* (May 24, 1945)
> *To the Shores of Iwo Jima* (June 7, 1945)
> *The Fleet That Came to Stay* (July 26, 1945)

For eyes not properly alert to the linear inevitability of American frontier progress, a scheme was hatched to drop copies of the *March of Time*'s documentary *The Fighting Lady* (1945) over Tokyo "so the Japanese can see the march of United States military strength across the Pacific."

The stateside distribution of Pacific theater combat reports demonstrated a high level of marketing smarts. Benefiting from the experience of the Army Signal Corps in the European theater and spurred on by interservice rivalry, the Navy's Photographic Unit and the Marine Combat Photographers expertly exploited the Pacific War as an occasion for the cinematic celebration of bluecoats and leatherjackets. For *The Battle for the Marianas,* the media-savvy marines left the editing to the professionals at Warner Bros., who culled two reels containing "not a single foot of non-combat action" from 200 reels. The Navy had also learned something about exhibition. Unlike the entries in the Army's overlong *Why We Fight* releases and *Report from the Aleutians,* the Navy documentaries sought to come in at twenty minutes on the nose, the perfect length for a featurette. "Run it as soon as you can," advised one exhibitor of *To the Shores of Iwo*

Jima, promising "a ringside seat at scenes that will make you wonder how the boys are doing this job of fighting." Often shot in 16mm or 35mm Kodachrome and printed in 35mm Technicolor, the filmed record of the Pacific battles on land and sea are vivid, thrilling, and awful.

Gratifying the backstage curiosities of a progressively cinema-savvy generation was a popular sidebar story told in tandem with the combat reports. Print journalism, newsreel segments, and issues of the *Army-Navy Screen Magazine* lavished attention on what might be called the "documentation of the documentation of combat." Just as the combat reports recorded epic battles and oriented spectators to world geography and military strategy, subsidiary reports explained the technical details of camerawork and revealed the hurdles overcome in acquiring footage under fire. Issue no. 21 of the *Army-Navy Screen Magazine* (February 1944) provided a fascinating behind-the-scenes look at the art of combat photography. The segment opens in what is described as the "cutting room" of the *Army-Navy Screen Magazine,* a workshop where Marine combat photographer Sgt. Norman Hack shares with colleagues from other branches of the service his recent experience filming the landing on Tarawa. "Armed with a pistol and a hand camera," Hack obtained 2,000 feet of action footage that "looks as though it had been taken through a frontline gunsight." Confirming the worse fears of newsreel editors in New York, Sergeant Hack leads his fellow photographers, and his all-GI audience, to a moviola viewscreen for an exclusive advance peek at a freshly edited reel. Narrated by Hack himself, the military sneak preview from the combat report that became *With the Marines at Tarawa* includes a ghastly shot of a Japanese corpse torn to shreds by machine gun fire, an image deleted from most civilian prints but retained in a military version entitled *Bloody Tarawa.* "The camera tells the truth but it doesn't give any idea of how it smells," Hack says in unruffled tones. "And the smell on that island was *bad.*" Surveying the carnage, he can only comment: "I took these pictures the day before Thanksgiving."

The most extraordinary combat footage and the most astonishing testimony to the cinematic ordering of the chaos of combat was the filming of the battle of Iwo Jima. A total of 50,000 feet of footage was shot by some sixty combat cameramen from the Navy, Marine Corps, and Coast Guard under the supervision of Lt. Comdr. John W. McLain, a former Hollywood screenwriter. Several weeks prior to the operation, McLain was given access to the Iwo Jima invasion plan, the better to storyboard his own beachhead tactics. Even under fire, his cameramen were expected to abide by proper film grammar. McLain reported that "photographers were instructed to shoot American action right to left, and enemy action left to right, thus enabling the public to get a good perspective of the action from the screen and also to help the film cutters do a better job."

The fidelity to cinematography exacted a price. Combat cameramen took incredible casualties. Six combat cameramen died filming *The Battle for the Marianas;* two of the fourteen cameramen filming *The Battle of San Pietro* were killed, and all but two were wounded. "Nine of my cameramen buddies were killed or wounded filming this picture," an illustrated marine said in the ad sheets for *Fury in the Pacific.* Images purchased at such cost were even more credible, more sacred.

The quality of postproduction work supported the fieldwork. Military action was sweetened, clarified, and reinforced on the editing table and in the sound booth. The most often used device was the artillery barrage montage, wherein a series of quick jump cuts between booming gun barrels counterpoints the tempo and assault of relentless bombardment. As the raw material for parallel editing, captured German footage lent an expanded perspective and impact to battle confrontations. The battle sequence in *The Fight for the Sky* opens with American P-51 Mustang fighters flying escort for an Allied bombing mission. A jump cut to a screaming siren and a perceptual change in film grain alerts the spectator to the Axis side of the action as Luftwaffe pilots race to their planes and take off to meet the oncoming Allies. The Luftwaffe eye view is not slighted. "The Jerries make a sneak attack on our bombers from behind," says the commentator. "Gun camera film, captured from the enemy, reveals how they hammer our bombers with their twenty-two millimeters." *Fury in the Pacific,* the most bitter and gruesome of all the combat reports, underscores the brutality of the battle on Angora and Peleliu with a coda that cinematically obliterates the enemy: a montage of diagonal "wipes"sweeps down across the screen over a series of contorted Japanese corpses that bleed into one another, the enemy doubly wiped out. The final shot is a very still life, a freeze frame close-up of the bespectacled face of a dead Japanese soldier with "The End" emblazoned across the screen and his visage.

The enemy doubly wiped out: the freeze-frame ending of *Fury in the Pacific* (March 1945).

Sound, often an unobtrusive film element, was cunningly orchestrated. Since live recording captured mainly a chaos of curses and terrified shrieks, sound in the combat report was almost always a postproduction process. Soundtrack mixes softened deafening bombardments and vocal cocophonies. Less consciously perceived than the image, the soundtrack set a mood, lent orientation, and promised safe passage through beachhead invasions and bombing missions. Sudden explosions and gunshots bushwacked spectators, but usually the sounds for ordnance were conventional and canned—the sharp report from an M-I, the thunderous roar of a big gun, the whoosh of a flamethrower. Most observer/listeners deemed the synchronous (or pseudosynchronous) sound of gunfire and artillery as more tolerable than manipulative and intrusive commentative music. Martial scores and service anthems dominated the early documentaries, but as the war of attrition dragged on the music became more symphonic, elegiac, and soft. During an edgy patrol through the jungle, *Fury in the Pacific* makes innovative use of a nerve-racking combat sound: silence.

Whether as sound or image, the discernible cinematic adornment of combat had to be applied sparingly else undercut documentary impact. In the days before color stock was the motion picture standard, the reliance on color film for the combat report kindled a critical debate on documentary aesthetics. The military was drawn to color photography for reconnaissance and intelligence because "color films show up camouflage which blends into black and white film." In 1944 an officer in the Army Air Force's First Motion Picture Unit argued that "the shadow deception on which camouflage is based is ferreted out by the motion picture camera when color film is used." A Navy officer overseeing the production of medical training films offered another practical justification. "Color provides diagnostic information," he pointed out. "Flesh wounds are far more vivid and realistic, and different parts of the anatomy and their condition readily distinguished."

Nonetheless, old-fashioned spectators questioned the appropriateness of splashy 35mm Technicolor for total war. Associated mainly with cartoons and musicals, color seemed too pleasingly attractive, too easy on the eye to render the true grit of combat. "The novelty of pyrotechnic display in exaggerated color makes war too pretty a picture," commented a troubled reviewer for *Motion Picture Herald*. The primary spectrum was unarguably apropos for two vivid wartime hues. The nightlit gasoline explosions in *At the Front in North Africa* and the splotches cascading from flamethrowers in *To the Shores of Iwo Jima* are yellow for fire. The crumpled banner of the Red Cross lying in the ruins of a bombed-out hospital in *The Battle of Midway* and the emergency transfusion in *The Memphis Belle* are crimson for blood.

To assess the legacies of the Second World War by focusing purely on the motion picture consequences risks replicating the cramped perspective of the Hollywood trade press, a self-absorbed coterie that manages to view any historical milestone, no matter how cataclysmic or solemn, through a 35mm lens. In 1945 who but a *Variety* reviewer could respond to *We Accuse,* a documentary compilation of concentration camp footage, with the cool suggestion that "nearly twenty minutes could have been trimmed from the production to snap up its entertainment value"? Conceding the parochialism of a movie-minded summation of the postwar era, a restricted focus on Hollywood and American culture since 1945 reveals an enduring, dynamic presence for the cinema of, and about, the Second World War. In domestic politics and foreign policy, in the memory of the past and outlook on the present, four years of wartime experience became a dominant frame of reference and persistent standard of measurement for an America that utterly shed the "postwar" preface only with the collapse of Soviet Communism. As the foremost purveyor and chief custodian of the images and mythos of 1941–45, the motion picture industry maintained a unique bond with its adored and idealized "public." Yet like the combat veteran, mustered out and back on native shores, returning warily to an unfamiliar spouse, Hollywood could never really take up the relationship where it left off.

"As soon as the war is over, the American motion picture industry is going to run into something it never had to face before," Jack Warner told the Screen Writers Guild in 1944. "It is going to have to compete in a world which, during the war, has become highly film conscious." The impact of motion pictures, little noted or understood before 1941, was a permanent heritage of Hollywood's war record. In a widely quoted preatomic remark, Gen. George Marshall said that the war had seen the development of two new weapons, the airplane and the motion picture. "One of the first casualties of the conflict was the 'pure entertainment myth,' " agreed the *Hollywood Quarterly* in its first editorial statement in 1946. Recalling that the war with its complex demands for training, orientation, and persuasion had emphasized "the social function of film and radio," the journal pledged itself to exploring the future role "the motion picture and the radio [will] play in the consolidation of the victory, in the creation of new patterns of world culture and understanding." No matter how remote the French village or Filipino hamlet, GIs from Chicago and Texas found themselves confronted with children mimicking James Cagney's tommygun stance and John Wayne's quick draws. For the motion picture industry, the government, and the public at large, the cultural power of American movies was a lesson learned.

Official confirmation of Washington's matriculation arrived punctually. In May 1947 a subcommittee of the House Committee on Un-American Activities (HUAC) descended on Hollywood for preliminary hearings into alleged communist infiltration of the motion picture industry. That October HUAC launched nine days of well-publicized hearings in Washington, a heady marriage of show business and politics that blended the hoopla of a gala premiere (floodlights, microphones, celebrity appearances, and starstruck spectators) with the drama of courtroom ritual (convoluted testimony, surprise revelations, and rights in conflict). At the height of the commotion, the *New Yorker*'s Lillian Ross quoted an anonymous witticism on Marxists and the movies. "They can't put their ideas in Hollywood pictures. Nobody can." It was a stale joke. In the wake of the war, in the midst of the Cold War, such smugness from the urbane literati reeked of antiquated affectation. Everyone knew that movies transmitted ideas, that the influence of the image, though difficult to gauge, was profound. The 1947 HUAC investigations and a second round of hearings held intermittently throughout 1951–52 heralded a distinctive feature of public discourse in postwar and post–Cold War America. The mass media were now the arena of choice in which to contest ideological squabbles and score political points. In this, if in little else, the House Committee on Un-American Activities was very much on the mark.

Culturally if not constitutionally, the new ground rules made sense. The motion picture industry, having proven itself pedagogically indispensable and politically responsible during the war, would henceforth be judged by different standards and held to stricter account. Not that the aptitude of the postwar tribunals measured up to the cases in the docket. As during the short-lived Senate hearings into war propaganda in 1941, the quality of congressional film criticism in 1947 was unpolished and unfocused. Neither Committee chairman J. Parnell Thomas (R–N.J.) nor chief investigator Robert E. Stripling possessed cinematic insight deeper than a recognition of certain marquee-value names. HUAC's concentration was on personnel whose communist past and present gave ipso facto confirmation of subversive intent. But though some of the Hollywood Ten, the defiant communists who held Congress in contempt and had the favor returned, were card-carrying true believers, the causal link between party membership and party-line doctrine in Hollywood scenarios was not so easily subpoenaed.

The clearest telltale trail of "ideological termites" was the "political preachment," the from-the-screen avowal of Internationale tonalities mouthed by a usefully duped star. Finding evidence of seditious burrowings demanded minimal exegetical talent. In the cold light of the Cold War, the OWI-inspired perorations to racial equality and Allied solidarity veered too faithfully to the mission of Moscow. In fact, members of the Hollywood Ten had authored many of the effusive wartime soliloquies. Albert Maltz scripted the upbeat commentary to *Moscow Strikes Back* (1942). John Howard Lawson composed the heated call for racial justice in *Sahara* (1943). Dalton Trumbo's screenplay for the suspiciously titled *Tender Comrade* (1943) had Ginger Rogers incorrectly defining democracy as "share and share alike" to her communal all-female household. The underappreciated irony was that the red-tinged dialogue was written with the advice and consent of official Washington. However, with New Deal Democrats uprooted by old-school Republicans in the congressional elections of 1946, with the Soviet Union drawing down an iron curtain on Eastern Europe, the government had changed its own party line.

The motion picture industry executives called to testify and explain themselves before a hostile committee were understandably befuddled by the turnabout in studio-government relations, the abrupt change in ground rules, and the retroactive application of same. "How did you, I, or anyone else know in 1942 what the conditions were going to be in 1947?" demanded an exasperated Jack Warner under grilling by counsel Stripling. "If making *Mission to Moscow* in 1942 was a subversive activity, then the American Liberty ships which carried food and guns to Russian allies and the American naval vessels which convoyed them were likewise engaged in subversive activities." Given his own high level of film consciousness, Warner offered a lame and patently false excuse: "The picture was made only to help out a desperate war effort and not for posterity." Louis B. Mayer admitted that MGM's *Song of Russia* (1943) was an OWI-approved "pat on Russia's back" but characterized the steppe-set melodrama as "the story of a boy and girl that except for the music of Tchaikovsky, might just as well have taken place in Switzerland or England or any other country on the earth." Better to forget the whitewash of the Reds once the gallant Russian Allies and "Uncle Joe" Stalin had reverted back into godless hordes and genocidal maniacs.

In 1941, when the Senate had charged Hollywood with premature anti-Fascism, the Motion Picture Producers and Distributors of America fought their accusers and walked away victors. In 1947, when HUAC charged Hollywood with ex post facto pro-Communism, the same organization folded like a Monogram storefront. In a contrite statement issued at New York's Waldorf Hotel, the Motion Picture Association of America (thus, the MPAA—the name changed in 1946) promised never to "knowingly employ a communist" and "to take positive action" on "disloyal elements." The positive action was a negative sanction, the blacklisting of employees deemed insufficiently vigilant in the twilight struggle.

Ironically, though, at the very moment the blacklist was wiping controversial credits off the screen, the screen itself was being more controversial than ever. In transforming Hollywood's sense of itself and the public's sense of the movies, the war had ignited a revolution in film content and filmmaker consciousness. The postwar emergence of the polemically driven production, a Hollywood feature dealing seriously and directly with a social "problem," was a direct consequence of the war-born realization of what commercial Hollywood cinema might presume. Even under the watchful eyes of Capitol Hill, the American Legion, and an alert citizenry, the late 1940s and 1950s were hardly an era of blithely uncritical and cringingly sycophantic cinema. Despite the "present atmosphere" of federally monitored orthodoxy, Hollywood's penchant for ideologically driven motion picture content intensified. Overt attacks on American capitalism or foreign policy were stifled during HUAC's 1948–54 heyday, but dozens of prestigious and contentious motion pictures, more socially conscious and boldly reformist in impulse, tackled the controversial issues of the day, sometimes through veiled allegory, often directly. Anti-Semitism, racism, juvenile delinquency, rampant materialism, middle-class complacency, business avarice, drug addiction, and sexual repression came to the screen with a forthright explicitness that, by the time of Alfred Hitchcock's *Psycho* (1960), which distilled most of the above, cumulatively shattered the Code tablets.

The literal Hollywood veterans themselves wasted no time assimilating their wartime experience into adventurous art. The first and best of the postwar social problem films was directed by the Hollywood classicist turned Army Air Force documentarian, William Wyler. *The Best Years of Our Lives* (1946), an exquisitely modulated melodrama of veteran readjustment written by Robert E. Sherwood, follows three ex-servicemen back into a homefront that is not so much callous as oblivious. The dynamic center of the film is Harold Russell, a real-life casualty of war, who plays, or inhabits, Homer, a young sailor with artificial limbs. Wyler had spotted Russell in an Army orientation film *Diary of a Sergeant* (1945) and in the first up-close look at a disabled American in mainstream Hollywood cinema, cast the amateur in one of the film's three pivotal roles. Up against seasoned actors Dana Andrews (as a former pilot landing back at his prewar job as a soda jerk) and Fredric March (as a former sergeant not making a smooth readjustment to an executive position in banking), Russell more than holds his own, which is the whole point. Blending and collapsing distinctions among high art, popular entertainment, and social realism, *The Best Years of Our Lives* seemed in one stroke to fulfill the promise of Hollywood's wartime training. When applied to the late performance of the motion picture industry, the title had not a whit of irony.

John Ford's Navy service added texture and depth to a body of work unparalleled in American film and barely matched in American letters. From *They Were Expendable* (1945) onward, the force of tradition, the burden of command, and the rules of martial behavior came to dominate his field of vision. On the Ford frontier—*Fort Apache* (1948), *She Wore a Yellow Ribbon* (1949), *Rio Grande* (1950), *The Long Gray Line* (1955), *The Wings of Eagles* (1957), *Sergeant Rutledge* (1960), *Two Rode Together* (1961), and *Cheyenne Autumn* (1964)—the code in costume and values is full-dress military. Another veteran director, John Huston, hardly needed the war to color a vision that saw glory and futility in equal measure from *The Maltese Falcon* (1941) to *The Man Who Would Be King* (1975). Of the other principal Hollywood directors who returned to the studios from uniformed service only Frank Capra failed to regain his stride. Though later revitalized by seasonal broadcasts on television, *It's a Wonderful Life* (1946) was a commercial disappointment in its time. The director who revolutionized documentary education for the War Department found some solace in his widest postwar success, a series of educational films for Bell Telephone. No less than *Why We Fight* for wartime GIs, *Our Mr. Sun* (1956), *Hemo the Magnificent* (1957), *The Strange Case of the Cosmic Ray* (1957), and *The Unchained Goddess* (1958) are embedded in the minds of a decade's worth of high school students.

A changing of the guard enacted much of the change in film content. Competing with and ultimately supplanting the classical "job of work" boys disdainful and embarrassed by the designation of "Artist"—Ford, Hawks, Wyler, McCarey, and Capra—was an insurgent breed of writers and directors only too glad to adopt the mantle of unacknowledged legislator of the world. Like their audience, the directors and producers who seized command in the postwar years had been trained by the studio system and brought up under the Code. But the practical education of four years of war was unforgettable. On the production side, the issue-oriented stance of Walter Wanger, Stanley Kramer, and Dore Schary superseded the tradition of quality upheld by Selznick, Goldwyn, and Mayer. Dark in texture, wary in outlook, the films of John Huston, Otto Preminger, Richard Brooks, Elia Kazan, and Samuel Fuller exuded the skepticism of a generation that had strayed outside the gates of Joseph Breen's cathedral. Their flagship product was the social problem film; their chosen messenger, a veteran armed with martial skills and OWI sensibilities. Reconstituted combat squads exposed anti-Semitism in *Crossfire* (1947), expedited rehabilitation in *The Men* (1950), and extinguished racism in *Bright Victory* (1951). The recurrent Judas goat was actor Robert Ryan, a real-life Marine veteran and Stevenson Democrat, who incarnated murderous prejudice against Jews in *Crossfire*, Japanese-Americans in *Bad Day at Black Rock* (1955), and black Americans in *Odds Against Tomorrow* (1959). The social problem films attracted a disproportionate measure of earnest attention because so many of them were trailblazing big-screen "firsts"—first delirious alcoholism (*The Lost Weekend*, 1945), first casual anti-Semitism (*Gentleman's Agreement*, 1947), first race riot won by blacks (*No Way Out*, 1950), and so on.

Against the shock of the new social problem film, the most significant continuity between wartime cinema and postwar cinema might be too obvious to notice: the fact that Hollywood never stopped making movies about the Second World War. Neither HUAC nor the Senate Investigation Subcommittee objected to uplifting replays of the action-adventures of 1941–45 that tactfully omitted Soviet contributions. For classicists and modernists alike, the four-year epic became a beloved backstory, a precious source of dramatic material and atmospheric settings. More than any other war—more than any other twentieth-century American experience—it was motion picture friendly. The magnetic pull of the war years wasn't merely the attraction of adventure, romance, or high melodrama but the consolation of closure and the serenity of moral certainty. For Hollywood and American culture the Second World War would always be a safe berth.

In 1944, when Clark Gable told reporters there was no comparison between soundstage war and the real thing, the *New York Times* predicted: "If Mr. Gable is right and there is no resemblance between war movies and real war then it is certain the boys back from battle will love the war pictures and eat them up; such being the nature of man and his attitude toward reality and art." Actually, most of the boys back from battle retired to lawnmowers and television. It was the boys of the boys back from battle who became the most enthusiastic and dedicated audience for motion pictures of World War II.

Unrestrained by the need to inculcate harsh war-specific lessons, assured of the final outcome, the retrospective films of the Second

World War were more flippant about the Nazis and the Japanese and less austere about "why we fight" and the cost of victory. With Fascism defeated, the motion picture "genre work" practiced and perfected between 1941–45 was no longer urgent or even absolutely necessary. Sacrifice, obedience, choral contribution, moral clarity in battle, due respect for the enemy, and the other wartime tropes endured in postwar Hollywood cinema—but as remembered and embroidered myth, not as clear and present necessity. Though postwar combat films were seldom all "guts and glory," the balance between the price and the payoffs became increasingly lopsided. In time, the American movie memory of the Second World War would conflate and confuse the contemporaneous projections of 1941–45 with the retrospective reenactments produced after 1946. The cocksure confidence of Hollywood's postwar war effaced the stern admonitions of the wartime war.

The pivotal year for the postwar combat film is 1949, distant enough to forget the bad, close enough to recall the buzz. That year saw the release and success of MGM's *Battleground, Command Decision,* and *Home of the Brave;* Warner Bros.'s *Task Force* and *Fighter Squadron;* Columbia's *Tokyo Joe;* 20th Century-Fox's *Twelve O'Clock High;* and Republic's *Sands of Iwo Jima.* Recall that prior to 1949, conventional wisdom in the motion picture industry had always held that "the public doesn't like war films," a tenet confirmed by wartime experience. However, "war proved no box office poison in 1949," proclaimed a front-page story in *Variety.* "As a matter of fact, quite to the contrary, year-end analysis shows it to have been a highly profitable subject for those filmmakers who kicked over the traditional idea that war pictures don't make money and put heavy investments in films backgrounded against the 1941–45 conflict." Listing nine films with war-related themes (including the dubious entry *I Was a Male War Bride*) that grossed a cumulative $25 million for an average domestic gross of $2.5 million each (for the time, "a whopping figure"), the showbusiness bible concluded the obvious: "more production along this line can be expected during the coming year."

And years. For the next two decades, World War II combat scenarios invigorated Hollywood production schedules. *Sands of Iwo Jima,* which became a byword for sanitized guts and glory, can stand for the lot. Dramatizing the bloodiest assault in Marine history, the moving picture works its way irrefragably to the re-creation of the most famous still picture of the Second World War, the raising of the

American flag on Mount Surabachi. *Sands of Iwo Jima* has all the generic elements of the retrospective World War II combat film—
namely, all the generic elements of the World War II combat film *plus*
historical hindsight, *minus* the necessity to instill harsh or narratively
inconvenient lessons of war. Again, few of the first wave of postwar
combat films succumbed totally to historical amnesia. The war experience was too fresh in memory, the mass audience still too mature
to pretend that war was adolescent fun. Playing Marine Sgt. John
Stryker, John Wayne is by no means a character to be naively admired. Alcoholic, divorced, insubordinate, Sergeant Stryker is among
the walking wounded; he charges an enemy machinegun nest because he has so little to lose. No dewy-eyed paean to combat glory,
Sands of Iwo Jima portrays war as unforgiving and cruel. A thought-
less coffee break causes the death of one's comrades, and the Duke
himself gets shot in a radically disruptive climax.

By most accounts, however, the textual caution signs in the post-

Postwar guts and glory: John Wayne, John Agar, and Forrest Tucker charge
a publicity photographer for *Sands of Iwo Jima* (1949). (Museum of Modern
Art/Film Stills Archive)

war combat film seldom penetrated the perceptions of an audience ever more youthful and male-dominated—especially when the publicity wraparound urged full speed ahead. Nourishing sweet Homeric dreams and luxuriating in the manly compensations of combat, trailers and one-sheet advertisements took dead aim at the teenage male temperament. The marketing campaign for *Sands of Iwo Jima,* rereleased in 1954 and circulating throughout the 1950s, is all upbeat glorification. Verifying the war-forged symbiosis between Hollywood and the military, the film's press kit portrays the leathernecks as a compliant publicity arm for Republic Pictures:

> Throughout the nation, the United States Marines Corps is on the alert—ready to give you [the exhibitor] every possible cooperation to help put *Sands of Iwo Jima* across! Every Marine Corps Unit in the country is ready to work with you on crowd-building promotion.

Relishing the prospect of the Marines storming quickstep into the exhibition end of the business, the publicity prose urged:

> Check the exploitation angles in this pressbook! Then go after that Marine cooperation for all these box office assists they can help you line up—parades, bands, displays, newspaper and radio coverage, A-Board posting—solid showmanship angles that will really sell your town on seeing *Sands of Iwo Jima.* Your local United States Marine Corps Recruiting Officer is the man to see!

If postwar films about the Second World War sometimes slighted the sacrificial and mortal consequences of combat, they were at least more candid about embarrassing fissures in American culture. Upon reflection, Nazism is no longer the sole source of racism. Typical of the films hearkening back to the war years as the crucible for ongoing social change is Mark Robson's *Bright Victory,* a moving dramatization of a dual battle against blindness and prejudice. An afflicted white Southerner (Arthur Kennedy) struggles with sightlessness together with a blinded black friend (James Edwards), whose pigmentation the son of the Confederacy knows not. The interracial conviviality is brought to an abrupt halt when the white man reveals he is not color-blind. The visual medium well illustrates the problem in perception. The two men, black and white, walk together down the hall of a veteran's hospital, laughing and joshing after a night on the town. Hearing a group of new men are due to be admitted for rehabilitation, the

The postwar social problem film: *Bright Victory* (1951) hearkens back to wartime as the crucible for progressive change. (Museum of Modern Art/Film Stills Archive)

Southerner matter-of-factly complains, "I never knew they let niggers in this ward. Did you, Joe?" The black man stops, stricken. "Yeah," he says slowly. "I've been here nearly seven months now." Later, sharing a drink with his father back in Dixie, the white soldier repents his racism. "The whole world's changing," says his patrician father approvingly. "You more than we because you helped to change it."

The Korean War did little to interrupt the wholesale excavation of the Second World War. For Hollywood cinema, the war of 1950–53 was not so much a challenge to the late mythos as an opportunity to embroider it. An early testimony to the resilience of the Second World War's mythos is the fact that three years of a "police action" more abstract in meaning, less conclusive in mission and outcome, did little to dent it.

During the Korean War, Hollywood adopted a familiar posture. "For the third time in a generation," the *Film Daily* editorialized in a year-end survey, "the awesome shadow of Mars shot full across the American industry in 1950, and, as twice before, in 1917 and again in

1941, the industry fell into line and asked for its marching orders from the government." Francis S. Harmon, the former director of the War Activities Committee, was called up and named liaison with government defense agencies, and the motion picture industry promised to do to international communism what it had done to the Axis powers.

Transported to new territory, the war film managed to retain most of the old contours. An unseemly haste infused the initial efforts, as if bringing the Korean War to the screen was a mere matter of regurgitating tropes and recostuming troops. Within days of the outbreak of hostilities on June 25, 1950, quick-witted producers recorded high-concept titles at the Title Registration Bureau of the MPAA and promptly released combat films set on the peninsula — *The Steel Helmet* (1951), *A Yank in Korea* (1951), *Fixed Bayonets* (1951), *Retreat, Hell!* (1952), *Mission Over Korea* (1953), and *The Glory Brigade* (1953). A lesser number of homefront melodramas (*I Want You*, 1952; *My Son John*, 1952) and service comedies (*Back at the Front*, 1952; and *The WAC from Walla Walla*, 1952) found Korea generically congenial. Likewise, newsreels and combat reports, notably John Ford's Navy documentary *This Is Korea!* (August 1951), reverted to well-remembered rules of reportage, orientation, and exhortation. Measured against the all-out orchestration of resources during 1941–45, Hollywood's Korean war campaign was modest, but in this its contribution reflected the scaled-down engagement of national energies.

Korea's rugged terrain did, however, provide a landscape to clear up unresolved business and settle old grievances. Welcoming in blacks, American Indians, and Japanese-Americans, the Warner Bros. platoon expanded its membership roster. Sam Fuller's *The Steel Helmet* smoothly edges a Japanese-American into the all-American combat squad in the figure of Sergeant "Buddhahead" Tanaka, played by the lately nefarious Richard Loo (still working against ethnic type). Blacks too in the now integrated Armed Forces join in with greater prominence and stature. In Fuller's ideologically sensitive combat team, neither Buddhahead nor the black Corporal Thompson (James Edwards) succumbs to a wily North Korean officer who attempts to subvert their patriotism with a recitation of an undeniable American history of unconstitutional detention and abiding bigotry.

The sorriest exception to American moral purity during World War II, the internment of Japanese-Americans, was confessed and excul-

The postwar Warner Bros. platoon: a Japanese-American (Richard Loo, *right*) and a black American (James Edwards) are recruited for Sam Fuller's Korean War combat film *The Steel Helmet* (1951).

pated with deliberate speed. In *Go For Broke!* (1951), a tribute to the 442nd Regimental Combat Team, Texas-bred Lt. Mike Grayson (Van Johnson) is forced to command Nisei soldiers. Downcast, listening to the litany of Japanese surnames in his new company, he perks up briefly at a Celtic appellation but "O-hara" turns out not to be an Irishman. In *Bad Day at Black Rock* the patriotic drunks who have secretly killed an innocent Japanese-American tenant farmer are dragged out from under their rock by one-armed Spencer Tracy. The murderer, in a fitting, fiery flashback to the vivid barbecues in the Pacific theater combat reports, is burned alive by a flaming yellow petrol bomb. *Hell to Eternity* (1960), the true story of Guy Gabaldon (Jeffrey Hunter), an American orphan raised by a Japanese-American family, is a neglected gem of the combat genre. The day after Pearl Harbor, Gabaldon accompanies his foster brothers to the recruitment center. The military rejects his Japanese-American siblings and in solidarity Gabaldon refuses to enlist. Only after his Isei foster mother, imprisoned in an internment camp, grants him leave to go to war against the Japanese, does he lend his linguistic and fighting talents to the Marines.

Off the battlefield, the peculiar ruthlessness of the war in the Pacific was a backdrop unamenable to facile appropriation by non-combat genres. A black comedy-drama like Billy Wilder's *Stalag 17* (1953) would have been unstageable in a Japanese prison camp. When the memory of the Second World War is invoked in the musical *It's Always Fair Weather* (1955) or the melodrama *The Man in the Gray Flannel Suit* (1956), the flashbacked theater of operations is European. The Caucasian cast of the continent, and the likelihood of romantic linkage with compliant French or Italian girls, made the European theater of operations the more opportunistic location for war and remembrance throughout the 1950s. As for the former "sons of heaven," the simian Japanese enemy evolved into a fetching and deferential helpmate. In the doomed interracial love affair in *Sayonara* (1957) and the yellow-faced whimsy of *The Teahouse of the August Moon* (1956), Japan became a land of rising melodrama and low comedy.

In both theaters of World War II, the combat film sustained its post-1949 momentum. *To Hell and Back* (1955), the combat bio-pic of Audie Murphy, the most decorated American soldier of the Second World War, epitomizes the second stage. When Alvin York came back from the Great War, he was besieged with movie offers. Feeling it was unethical to trade on killing, he refused. When Audie Murphy went from war to screen, the move seemed less a career change than a battlefield promotion. Though featured to good and symbolic advantage in John Huston's *The Red Badge of Courage* (1951), the baby-faced Texan mainly played laconic westerners in just-above-B-level "oaters" before being typecast for his greatest screen success. In a mind-boggling fusion of art and experience, the authentic combat hero in his own Hollywood combat film stands astride a flaming tank and acts out the action that won him the Congressional Medal of Honor. Neither Murphy nor his former employers were overawed by the convolutions. Like *Sands of Iwo Jima, To Hell and Back* went out under dual sponsorship. "The Army has officially authorized Army commanders to extend cooperation to theaters in promoting engagements of *To Hell and Back*," Universal's publicity agents informed exhibitors. "Consistent with, and dependent on, local limitations you may be able to obtain troop parades, equipment displays,

The post–World War II combat film: CinemaScope space and assured victory enhance the spectacular allure of war in Audie Murphy's bio-pic, *To Hell and Back* (1955). (Museum of Modern Art/Film Stills Archive)

weapons displays, war trophies, etc." If Murphy's private war was hell, the widescreen version held all the attractions of a holiday spot.

A few gainsayers did dwell on the close-up costs rather than the big-picture gains. Directed by Mark Robson from James Michener's bestseller, *The Bridges at Toko-Ri* (1954) finds William Holden reluctantly flying bombing missions over Korea and winding up dead in a ditch. Holden repeated the reluctant warrior turn in David Lean's *The Bridge on the River Kwai* (1957), a tale of delusion and glory-mongering in a Japanese prison camp. Here too, though, the tone is more elegiac than antagonistic, more wistful and fatalistic about the necessity of war than outraged at its existence. Stanley Kubrick's *Paths of Glory* (1957) is also passionately antiwar, but it had to be about the Great War not the Good War, the French military not the American.

Postwar antiwar cinema stopped short of pacifism because of the more persuasive anti-antiwar cinema of the Second World War. Casting longer shadows than even Hollywood's images were the documentary revelations of 1945. The concentration camp footage was decisive and irrefutable evidence of Nazi perfidy and American virtue, Exhibit A in any debate on the morality of the late war. In Orson Welles's *The Stranger* (1946) and Sam Fuller's *Verboten!* (1958), camp footage is shown to disbelievers—who flinch at the celluloid horrors. In both films too, the guide repeats the stern imperative from the original newsreel commentaries: "Look!" To clinch the case in *Judg-*

ment at Nuremberg (1961), an Army prosecutor calls on the motion picture record as his star witness, projecting images of the Holocaust to a tribunal that really sits before the bigger screen.

The aftershocks from another holocaust, so unsettling in retrospect, took years to kindle a commensurate reaction. In August 1945 most Americans greeted the news of the atomic bombing on Hiroshima and Nagasaki with unqualified relief. Where stateside audiences had been outraged and appalled by the camp footage, they sat through newsreels of nuclear obliteration with apparent equanimity. Partly, the temperate response was due to the heavy censorship of A-bomb footage, which eliminated gruesome images of charred civilians. In the clinical War Department report *The Atomic Strikes* (1946), awe-inspiring sequences juxtaposing "before" and "after" aerial shots of two former metropoli are never sullied with the mortal remains at ground zero.

But whereas the atomic annihilation in Japan had elicited little sympathy from Americans in 1945, the possibility of potential fallout at home was a different matter. During Hollywood's first postnuclear decade, the grim prospect of a Third World War negated impulses to fantasize combat-ready genre work forward in time. With mutually assured destruction holding out scant hope of victory through air power, the recollection of a securely victorious past naturally shunted aside the ghastly specter of future conflagration. When Hollywood did look ahead, the war of the future was more liable to be extraterrestrial than intercontinental. Nevertheless, the allegory was thin. Even teenagers knew that invaders from Mars stood in for missiles from Moscow.

The atomic reactions of Hollywood cinema in the 1950s did settle one old wartime score. The scientific specialist, the sole war-born authority who emerged from 1945 with more suspicion than honor, became the favorite fifth-column villain during crusades against terrors from outer space or creatures from black lagoons. Having wrought a weapon of war more earth-shattering than either the airplane or the motion picture, the once-benevolent "expert" acquired a darkly sinister coloring. In the face of alien invasion or atomic mutations, the science fiction "weirdies" of the 1950s turned for salvation to the warrior in uniform, not the white-coated scientist. A Hawksian bomber crew defeats the vegetable monster in *The Thing (from Another World)* (1951); a combat squad deploys flamethrowers against giant ants in the sewers of Los Angeles in *Them!* (1954); and the Strategic Air Command remains the best line of defense against new variants of aerial terror in *Earth vs. the Flying Saucers* (1956) and *The Deadly Mantis* (1957).

A smaller screen metastasized Hollywood's wartime images. Exploiting public-domain government films, readily retrievable newsreels, and newly unearthed and lately uncensored footage from all sides, documentaries of the Second World War were a high-profile and low-cost filler of network airtime. In prime-time tribute, television broadcast dozens of reedited combat reports on the order of NBC's *Victory at Sea* (1952), CBS's *The Twentieth Century* (1957–70), and the immensely popular U.S. Army-via-ABC series *The Big Picture* (1953–59). Journalists who had accompanied the soldiers into battle added color commentary and a you-are-there veracity to newsreels that were grainy in image but crystal clear in message.

Throughout the 1950s and on through the 1960s, Hollywood mined the pivotal campaigns and famed divisions for celebratory subject matter. Few storied regiments or brand-name battles were left unchronicled, the name alone conjuring the majesty of a beachhead assault, a military objective taken by stealth, or a unit covered in glory: *Okinawa, D-Day the Sixth of June, Tarawa Beachhead, Anzio, The Guns of Navarone, The Bridge at Remagen, Red Ball Express, The Tanks Are Coming, Thunderbirds, Merrill's Marauders, Battle Cry,* and so on and on. Whether in black and white and ladled with authentic newsreel footage or in Technicolor and widescreen CinemaScope, the American military glistened on screen.

As late as 1964, two dark visions of nuclear armageddon, lauded in their day as daring critiques and sober warnings, could not but share an unquestioned faith in the putative object of ridicule and suspicion. In both Stanley Kubrick's *Dr. Strangelove or: How I Learned to Stop Worrying and Love the Bomb* and Sidney Lumet's *Fail Safe,* resourceful bomber crews resist the best efforts of Russian *and* American defenses to penetrate Soviet air space and deliver a hydrogen payload. The gaffe that initiates the nuclear countdown is in one case instigated by a military madman and in the other a mechanical failure more supernatural than systemic. The only certainty is that the American boys on board will complete their mission and demonstrate the right stuff—whether the thirty seconds are over Tokyo or Moscow.

VIETNAM: I HATE THIS MOVIE

World War II films painted a portrait of victory and competence, of American true grit overpowering stormtrooper discipline and samurai fanaticism. Vietnam erased that image. The disrepute of the interminable war transformed military action into a code phrase for legalized atrocities and made the soldier the butt of comedy, condescension, and contempt. By the mid-1970s, according to Hollywood cinema, no crime or calumny was beyond the imagination of the White House, the CIA, and especially the Pentagon. The application of American power overseas—once just means in a just cause—had become the occasion for moral outrage. Uniforms, medals, flags, and the other talismans of honored service and intrepid skill were transmuted into signs of the villain.

As high-concept motion picture material (let alone as foreign policy), Vietnam was a hard sell. For nearly a decade, Hollywood virtually ignored it. In contrast to the police action in Korea, which immediately spawned motion pictures and engaged industry-wide participation from June 1950 onward, Vietnam inspired no flurry of production, no combat or homefront cycle during the peak years of American involvement. It was a lousy narrative with a vague beginning, an ungainly middle, and no end in sight.

Well before the cultural divisiveness of the Vietnam War generated widespread resistance and mass protests, Hollywood warily drew back from Vietnam-tainted material. In July 1965 producer Herbert Brodkin and writer Sterling Silliphant pitched a motion picture to be called *Groundswell* (based on an original Silliphant novel). The project was aberrant enough to warrant front-page coverage in *Variety,* whose straight-faced prose described what is probably the first Hollywood response to the American experience in Vietnam:

> [*Groundswell's*] plot deals with the kidnapping of the head of the Joint Chiefs of Staff by a special Viet Cong mission sent to this country for that purpose. While there is a nationwide search for the VC, they put the military man on trial for "war crimes," this taking place on Fire Island, unknown to the searchers, of course. VC okays coverage of the trial by an American war correspondent in South Vietnam.

According to Silliphant, the treatment presented both the American and Viet Cong sides of the case, but most consistently put forth "my point of view, that of the man in between, the average man who doesn't know what's happening. The picture tries to find the difference between the labels Communism and democracy. I deal with the confusion in the minds of the average American because of labels and I say it's sheer power politics, not a question of 'isms,' that what is involved is the division of power between US, Russia, and China."

Even in embryo, Silliphant's script speaks volumes. The screenwriter inverts the invasion but the plot was prophetic: it is the American who is on trial, the VC who seize the initiative and recognize the value of the media in pleading their cause. Most significant is the liberal equivocation over an American military action. In previous wars the disinterested presentation of two sides to a case with an American plaintiff was to hear one side too many. This "admittedly controversial original screenplay" was controversial not for the verdict it rendered but for bringing the case to the court in the first place. In short order, *Groundswell* was turned down by almost every major studio. As *Variety* put it in 1965, "the war in Vietnam is too hot for Hollywood."

The hands-off attitude was registered in a sensitive barometer of cultural support. The USO Camp Show circuit, an unshirkable obligation for the players of the Second World War, cast about haplessly for a fresh generation of soldiers in greasepaint. During rock 'n' roll's greatest era, no pantheon performers or prestigious popular artists on the Top Forty lists of the generation doing the grunt work went on the road to Vietnam. With precious few exceptions (namely, Ann-Margret), big-name film and musical talent avoided a Vietnam tour of duty. The USO circuit was filled out by a grizzled and very old guard epitomized by comedians Bob Hope and George Jessel and actors Robert Mitchum and John Wayne. Martha Raye, one of the original *Four Jills in a Jeep,* gallantly performed in jungle clearings and combat zones, for servicemen who might have been her children. "There is no name talent in Vietnam now," Raye said ruefully in 1965, a remark applicable not only to the entertainment industry.

The fear of being professionally burned by the land war in Asia extended to allegorical address. In 1964 Columbia bought the rights to Joseph Heller's *Catch 22* for $150,000 to "the accompaniment of much fanfare." By 1966 the company was willing to sell the property for "costs to date" to Filmways. According to Columbia executive vice president Leo Jaffe, the reason for the sale was that "we simply had a change of mind about the subject matter and felt we shouldn't make the picture at this time." Not until Robert Altman's *M*A*S*H* (1970), a surgical strike on military hierarchy in a mobile army hospital during the Korean War, did a critique of Vietnam put in a successful appearance, albeit as metaphor.

Throughout the 1960s, however, neither side of the generation gap seemed willing to indict World War II in the antiwar activity. In 1966 a trade survey listing some thirty war films planned or in production noted that with one significant exception "clearly war means World War II." The production anomaly was *The Green Berets* (1968), the sole big-budget contemporaneous film about the Vietnam War. John Wayne's critically reviled and commercially quite successful hawk's-eye view has been called a World War II combat film set in Vietnam ("a reworking of *Back to Bataan*"), but World War II combat films spoke less to "why we fight" than how best to fight. In the painful need to explain and justify the American action in Vietnam, to locate the present war within the mythos of the past war, *The Green Berets* represents the Vietnamization of a genre. Besides picket lines outside metropolitan theaters, the film begat what become a signature movie memory. In his Vietnam novel *The Short Timers*, Marine veteran Gustav Hasford describes the on-screen scene from the soldiers' perspective. Watching *The Green Berets* in Da Nang, Hasford's Vietnam grunts are spiritually linked to Ernie Pyle's screen-smart GIs but are a world away in the bitterness and betrayal brought to a Hollywood moment:

> The audience of Marines roars with laughter. This is the funniest movie we have seen in a long time. Later, at the end of the movie, John Wayne walks off into the sunset with a spunky little orphan. The grunts laugh and whistle and threaten to pee all over themselves. The sun is setting in the South China Sea—in the East—which makes the end of the movie as accurate as the rest of it.

In 1968, at around the same time *The Green Berets* was convulsing in-country spectators with Wayne's solar confusion, Richard D. Zanuck, executive vice president in charge of production at 20th Century-Fox, announced plans for the production of *Patton*, a more up-to-date version of the good war. "We wanted *Patton* because it will make a good action drama about World War II," said the son of the man who had so ardently gone off to that war in life and on screen. "There's little emotion involved today because the war was fought over twenty years ago; it's not like the many propaganda films made by all the

studios throughout the early 1940s, which played on the emotions."
Released in 1970, *Patton* was the last of the commercially successful
and critically esteemed epics of the Second World War, not least
because it managed to play equally well to Woodstock Nation and
the Nixon White House. When asked why Fox had chosen to forgo
films about the Vietnam War, Zanuck *fils* dodged. "People read about
the Vietnam war in newspapers, hear about it on the radio, and see
film clips on television. I think they've been saturated with news
about the war. Maybe in five or ten years we'll do a picture on the
subject."

Zanuck had it about right. After a decade of aversion and avoidance, Hollywood ultimately succeeded where Washington had consistently failed: in selling the Vietnam War to the American public.
Though the Oscar-winning antiwar documentary *Hearts and Minds*
(1974) was out the gate early, 1978–79 was the season that Hollywood's Vietnam first flourished. The release of four major combat
films, *The Boys in Company C* (1978), *Go Tell the Spartans* (1978), *The
Deer Hunter* (1978), and *Apocalypse Now* (1979), and one widely popular homefront rehabilitation film, *Coming Home* (1978), broke a dec-
ade-long embargo.

For a time, the subject once too hot to handle became simply hot.
Two of the films about Vietnam, Michael Cimino's *The Deer Hunter*
and Francis Ford Coppola's *Apocalypse Now,* were media-coronated
landmarks, "high seriousness" works of art literary in cast, one taking a page from James Fenimore Cooper, the other whole chapters
from Joseph Conrad. Neither was much about Vietnam as an exca-
vatable historical experience, both held stronger affinities for au-
teurism than revisionism. As self-conscious explorations of what was
being called "the dark underside of the American soul," the grandil-
oquent visions of Cimino and Coppola strained patience. Yet between
indulgent longueurs and inspired surrealism each caught the cultural
dislocation in the loss of a faith forged in 1941–45. The popular imagination locked on to two symbolic sequences. At the beginning of
Apocalypse Now a slow-motion ballet of swooping helicopters and
napalm explosions wafts through 70mm spaciousness in rhythm to
the woozy drug-rock of the Doors's "The End." At the heart of *The
Deer Hunter* a total fabrication was vivid synecdoche for the American experience in Vietnam: a soldier puts a gun to his head and pulls
the trigger.

After 1978 the absorption of the Vietnam War into the imagistic inventory of American culture was fast and furious. In undergraduate course offerings, PBS documentaries, talking-head news shows, TV movies of the week, and prime-time network action, the bad war was good copy. Vietnam backstories gave combat credentials to hipster television detectives (*Magnum, P.I.; Miami Vice*), and Vietnam-set scenarios harmonized with the episodic rhythms of serial melodrama in *Tour of Duty* and *China Beach*. At mid-decade, Oliver Stone's *Platoon* (1986) launched a second wave of Vietnam films that crested with Brian De Palma's *Casualties of War* (1989). Eventually, prolonged exposure deadened apocalyptic resonance. By the time of *Off Limits* (1988), a sordid murder mystery set in Saigon, or *Air America* (1990), a zany comedy bouncing above the Cambodian border, Vietnam might just as well have been the Philippines or Mexico, where the location shooting was usually done anyway.

No point of interest on the map of Vietnam engaged filmmakers more intensely than the position of Hollywood itself. Assuming the motion picture past as shared background and prime mover, the Vietnam film set about defacing the classical Hollywood picture. It found no larger purpose in war, ripped apart the union of the combat squad, and turned within to confront the true enemy. The Warner Bros. platoon killed the Nazis; Oliver Stone's *Platoon* killed each other.

The first rule of engagement for Hollywood's Vietnam is acknowledgment of its own patrimony. The Vietnam film presents Vietnam as a linear—no, *cinematic*—descendent of World War II films, the ignoble offspring of a hundred matinees and drive-in Saturdays. The blood ties here cut deeper than the usual anxiety of generic influence. Always, there is the whisper of complicity, the suspicion that Hollywood lent its imagination to the disaster. The notion is presumptuous, self-involved, and worth pondering: that the projections of 1941–45 mediated American entry into Vietnam by predisposing a movie-going generation to expectations of bloodless flesh wounds and Production Code endings. Before the all-too-real horrors of the in-country spectacle, Vietnam vernacular spat out a telling phrase: I hate this movie.

As if in penance for the excesses and duplicities of the past, the Vietnam combat film embraced a stony cynicism and brutal realism—or at least it appeared to. In the fanciful action-adventures of Chuck Norris (*Missing in Action*, 1984; *Missing in Action 2—The Beginning*, 1985; and *Braddock: Missing in Action III*, 1988) and Sylvester

The Vietnam combat unit: the Warner Bros. platoon implodes in Oliver Stone's *Platoon* (1986). (Museum of Modern Art/Film Stills Archive)

Stallone (*Rambo: First Blood Part 2,* 1985), the rollicking matinee spirit lives, but reflection and seriousness dominate the genre, and not just the works of the big-gun auteurs. The Hollywood film depicting combat in Vietnam presents itself as no blood-and-guts Hollywood fantasy, but the genuine item, one step removed from actually being in the bush. *Time*'s cover story on *Platoon* headlined the reigning aesthetic: "Vietnam As It Really Was."

No longer constrained by a squeamish Production Code, Hollywood rendered "Vietnam as it really was" with state-of-the-art technology and showcased the results for maximum impact. FX advances in battlefield verisimilitude (gasoline explosions, timed charges, mock-ups, mattes, and miniatures) and stunt choreography (the trademark helicopter assaults and dust-offs, often piloted by veterans-turned-stuntmen) made the Vietnam combat film an exhilarating, special-effects rollercoaster. The vivid depiction of the gruesome effect of high-tech weaponry on human flesh was not neglected: witness the shredded ligaments in *Full Metal Jacket* (1987), the chest wounds in *Hamburger Hill* (1987), and the severed limbs and smashed brains in *Platoon*. Like the pleasing Technicolor of the combat reports, the clinical attention to ultraviolence bridges realism and spectacle in ways that subvert the horrors of war: the more impressive the depiction of violence, the higher the disinterested appreciation of motion picture artistry.

Surpassing the special effects in ruthlessness was the depiction of the Vietnam veteran. As the incarnation of military defeat and moral lapse, the active duty warrior or the honorably discharged soldier became a loathsome remembrance and a cultural pariah. His demonization reached a peak in the later 1970s, waned during the 1980s, and was fully repented by the 1990s, but for the better part of a decade an intensity of hatred once'directed at an alien enemy turned inward with a vengeance. Cowardice, stupidity, and malice reigned throughout the military ranks, but was surely endemic among NCO lifers and career officers. In *The Boys in Company C,* when a soccer game is interrupted by a VC attack, a Green Beret major grabs a Vietnamese child to his chest and holds him up as a shield. In *Full Metal Jacket* an entire squad of Marines is pinned down and torn up by a lone Viet Cong sniper—and a woman at that. In *Casualties of War* a squad of average grunts rapes and murders a Vietnamese woman.

Back on the cinematic and televisual homefront, the unholy warriors had it worse than the detritus of the Great War "heroes for sale." Flashbacking furiously, Vietnam vets went on crying jags, homicidal rampages, and revenge missions. "I am a Vietnam veteran and if I acted according to what I have seen on television in the last six months or so," wrote a former Marine in 1977, "I should probably be harboring extreme psychopathic tendencies that prompt me to shoot up heroin with one hand while fashioning plastique with the other as my drug-crazed mind flashes back to the rice paddy where I fragged my lieutenant (or if I were a POW back in a Hanoi prison camp where I have just made a propaganda speech because I could not stand the torture)." Actor Bruce Dern, moving smoothly from a screen persona of motorpsycho madman into Vietnam vet malevolence, played two memorable versions of the whacked-out warrior: the gung-ho Marine officer driven mad by war and adultery in *Coming Home* and the deranged helicopter pilot who seeks to skewer a stadium full of Superbowl watchers in *Black Sunday* (1977). At best, as in *Rolling Thunder* (1977) and *Year of the Dragon* (1985), the veteran turned vigilante or cop and put his combat training to advantage by annihilating the sleazoids of the urban jungle.

The line between psycho and vigilante was thin, a reflex suspicion of the Vietnam veteran on the edge, a time bomb waiting to go off in the homefront's face. In *Taxi Driver* (1976), suited up in tattered fatigues and sporting a Mohawk, the veteran-cum-rainmaker Travis Bickle (Robert De Niro, whose off-center energy propelled a trio of Vietnam vet performances) came to wash all the scum off the street. In July 1984 a maniac "hunting humans" walked into a McDonalds restaurant in California, fired automatic weapons into the customers, and racked up a body count of twenty-one dead, nineteen wounded. A Vietnam vet, of course—but only in the popular imagination, not in reality.

The psycho and the vigilante at least possessed raw energy and combat skill. A companion type was merely pathetic, the so-called crybaby veteran. This Vietnam vet was a pitiable shell of a man, a blubbering head case doomed to psychotic episodes, alcoholism, drug addiction, homelessness, and all of the above. If he were lucky, after confronting his demons and expunging his guilt, he might be redeemed by the love of a good woman, group therapy, or political correctness—as in *Coming Home, Jacknife* (1989), and *Born on the Fourth of July* (1989). Like the nation, he suffered from a severe case of posttraumatic stress syndrome, a disease that soon entered the

Neither Sergeant York nor Audie Murphy: Hollywood-bred Vietnam veteran Ron Kovic (Tom Cruise) becomes a media-wise, antiwar warrior in *Born on the Fourth of July* (1989).

elastic lexicon of the American Psychiatric Association and the appellate tactics of trial lawyers.

Throughout the revisions and reviling, Hollywood's contempt for the military was laced with a blithe ignorance. Where the classical Hollywood directors had served in the armed forces and knew the nuances of military etiquette and the behavior of men in groups, the movie brats who rose to eminence in the 1970s simply hadn't a clue as to how men in uniform behaved. Francis Ford Coppola and Martin Scorsese knew mobsters, Steven Spielberg and Joe Dante knew the whitebread suburbs, but almost no one in the new Hollywood knew what the interior of the barracks or the base Officers Club was like. Insignia and ribbons were misplaced or worn upside down, hair length and uniforms regularly nonregulation, and gestures and personal interactions ludicrously misinformed. In *Coming Home* a cuckolded Marine officer enacts a level of unlikely derangement when in a drunken stupor he tumbles into his home dragging his drinking buddies in tow—enlisted men. In *The Package* (1989) a female lieutenant takes leave of her female commanding officer by affectionately tugging her sleeve and saying, "Gotta go now." With military service itself no longer a mainstream rite of passage, the popular audience saw no reason to laugh.

The one authentic voice and unimpeachable witness was writer-director Oliver Stone. The appearance of Stone, Vietnam combat veteran and Hollywood auteur, was greeted with a rapture bordering on desperation. *Platoon* garnered the top rewards of American popular culture: box-office and critical success, newsmagazine covers, and the Academy Awards for Best Picture and Best Director of 1986. In a gesture as symbolic as the narrative, the film's exploitation campaign was interwoven with the director's public persona and deep background screen presence. "In 1967," read the ad copy, "a young man named Oliver Stone spent 15 months in Vietnam as an infantryman in the United States Army. He was wounded twice and received a bronze star for gallantry. Ten years later Stone was a screenwriter in Hollywood, author of *Midnight Express*. It made him the only man in Hollywood with both a Purple Heart and an Oscar." Actor Lee Marvin knew better but the publicity exposed a raw cultural yearning. Wellman, Zanuck, Ford, Huston, and Wyler, the classical Hollywood artists who had earlier weathered the crucible of combat, embodied a direct connection between war film and war reality. *Platoon* became a cultural landmark not because it presented "Vietnam as it really was" but because it repaired a broken link between cinematic art and combat experience.

For civilians back in the world, television was the prime testifier and medium of transmission. Where Hollywood had shaped memories of 1941–45, televisual images determined the outlines of Vietnam territory. The media label that stuck—the living-room war—expressed the new imagistic hierarchy. It also caught the sense of distance and disorientation in homefront spectatorship, the passive noninvolvement in a war that, for most Americans at most times, was a flow of electronic dots. Against the coherence and forward order of the newsreels and combat reports, Vietnam video was a blizzard of white noise and snow, pointless statistics and random action.

Motion pictures acknowledged television's dominion over the transmission of Vietnam, but refused to concede proprietorship over the imagistic purveyance of the past. Though subordinate in power and presence to the network's channels of communication, Hollywood beat back media marginality by staking claim to cultural superiority. Around the two peaks of the Vietnam production curve (marked by *The Deer Hunter* / *Apocalypse Now* in 1978–79 and *Platoon* / *Full Metal Jacket* in 1986–87) clustered a torrent of nationwide publicity and public discussion. Visually violent and verbally obscene, expertly crafted and smoothly marketed, the major motion pictures of the Vietnam War attracted a level of self-aware self-examination designed to put video in its place.

In form and content, the major motion pictures treated television like a poor cousin, boorish and ill-equipped to tackle the difficult truths and harsh realities of a war it transmitted but failed to understand. Big-screen Vietnam appropriated and subordinated the images from small-screen Vietnam (the living-room's eye-view of war proving an eye-catching screen-within-a-screen composition). In Francis Ford Coppola's *Gardens of Stone* (1987), a mea culpa for *Apocalypse Now* set in 1968 at Arlington National Cemetery, the only on-screen combat occurs on television. For flashbacks and nostalgic period pieces, televisual atmospherics set tone and time. In *Four Friends* (1981), *1969* (1988), and other 1960s-set excursions, network news firefights fill back-frame images and broadcast body-counts mix into ambient sound. Incessantly TV-wise, Vietnam movies bow to or beat up on their rival. The Vietnam section of *More American Graffiti* (1979) duplicates a television-standard aspect ratio on the big screen. A tracking sequence in *Full Metal Jacket* features a squad of grunts in-

dividually snapping off synchronized smart-ass remarks to a TV camera crew. In another postmodern gesture of media criticism, Chuck
Norris's first act of violence in *Missing in Action* is to shoot out a
television screen.

The televisual denial of spectatorial linkage and intellectual coherence abetted the withdrawal of emotional sustenance by what
was never a true "homefront" anyway. In *Hamburger Hill* a grunt
reads a Vietnam version of a "Dear John" letter from his girl back
home. She writes not to inform him of her impending marriage to a
swell fellow she met while working in a defense plant, but to tell him
she won't be corresponding anymore because he is war criminal.
Absent the nurturing support of mothers and girlfriends back home
and nurses and WACs at the front, the Vietnam film wallows in the
cruelty and crudity of men without women. Gazed through the prism
of World War II cinema, nothing is weirder about Vietnam on screen
than its near-total exclusion of female participation. In *Apocalypse
Now* women are alien creatures dropped by helicopters into a remote
fire base. Frugging in hot pants, they incite a Dionysian frenzy in a
male world of bestial carnality. In writing of the Vietnam combat film
feminist critics search valiantly for the feminine principle—in *Platoon* it is the delicate warrior Elias, in *Full Metal Jacket* the baby-faced
Private Pyle. In World War II cinema the feminine principle is easier
to spot—she's Donna Reed, Claudette Colbert, or Margaret Sullavan.

Ultimately, the medium most committed to the divestiture of the
good war record tempered its tone. By the mid-1980s, Vietnam warriors were more likely to be heroes than war criminals. The trick was
to castigate a discredited war while crediting the morality and courage of the warrior. *Rambo: First Blood Part 2,* the most popular of all
the Vietnam films, deftly distinguishes between loyal service to
"country" (good) and "government" (bad). In a violent run through
the jungle, the muscular Indian fighter John Rambo stumbles upon
the fact that the real enemy is not the North Vietnamese Army but
the backstabbing civilian bureaucracy. His tagline threat, a rasping
"I'm coming to get *you,"* is aimed at the American in the blue suit,
not the VC in cotton trousers. For all its violence and butchery,
Rambo confirmed the vital cultural function of Hollywood genre: to
ease division and reconcile conflict through myth. Like the Vietnam
War Memorial on the Washington Mall, the Vietnam combat film
came to project a soothing ritual of atonement and celebration, a
screen reflecting back the two faces of American regret and pride.

REWIND/ERASE

With an almost sentient sense of closure, history conspired to resurrect the dormant World War II myth felled by Vietnam. "By God,
we've kicked the Vietnam syndrome once and for all," exulted President George Bush in the wake of American—rather, Allied—victory
over Iraq in 1991. If the stated geopolitical purpose of the Gulf War
was to frustrate a little Hitler and free a captive nation, the cultural
impulse was to erase the last war and replay the good war. For forty-
three days the backfire from the thousand-day war was zapped off
screen.

From August 2, 1990, the day Iraqi dictator Saddam Hussein invaded Kuwait, the crisis in the Gulf was viewed in the light of the two
wars that had worked most powerfully on the American imagination
in the twentieth century. The World War II precedent competed for
resonance with the Vietnam analogy: did going to war in the Gulf
mean to confront evil early on for a just cause or to get bogged down
in another remote killing field? Kuwait was either Arabic for Vietnam
or to 1990 what Czechoslovakia was to 1938. When the showdown
vote authorizing the president's use of military force was called in
Congress on January 12, 1991, the partisan split reflected not just
divergent generational experience or foreign policy opinion but allegiance to contrasting myths of America at war. One side envisioned
the Gulf of Tonkin Resolution and the weekly body counts from network news. The other side, with politicians old enough to remember
the Second World War (Republican House minority leader Bob
Michel, Republican Senate minority leader Robert Dole, and the former World War II fighter pilot watching from the White House), conjured the newsreel image of Neville Chamberlain deplaning from Munich waving a piece of white paper. In the end the evocation of World
War II proved more convincing, not least because the stand-in for der
Führer seemed so intent on playing his role to the hilt.

The restoration of a World War II past blurred by Vietnam com-
plemented a mission embarked on earlier at the level of national politics. The ascendancy of Ronald Reagan, Errol Flynn's sidekick in *Desperate Journey* (1942) and the voice behind so many War Department
training films, was too perfect a conjunction of Hollywood and Washington to escape interpretation as a match of culture and politics
tailor made for movie-made America. The show was not an unqualified smash ("Are we now being ruled by the fantasies of a 1940s

countersubversive B movie?" wailed a partisan opposition unable to muster attractions of equivalent marquee appeal), but by 1980 a yearning for the secure past was hardly a sign of national pathology. Vietnam backfire, Watergate disenchantment, and the Iran hostage crisis had left America's faith in its own native abilities in ruins, scattered like the helicopter wreckage in Desert One, done in by ill training, ill planning, ill winds. The representative American overseas was no longer a conquering hero, no longer even ugly, but a hostage— paraded blindfolded by mobs of howling fanatics, left to rot in bamboo tiger cages, or terrorized by swarthy hijackers with incomprehensible gripes. "America Held Hostage" headlined the network news—to uncertainly, incompetence, impotence.

Hollywood's main consolation was the rescue or extrication film, which by the late 1970s and early 1980s had become the preferred form for the military action-adventure. "Do we get to win this time?" asks a payback-minded John Rambo of his once and future Green Beret commander. Bet on it. The extrication film rendered in celluloid what the American military was agonizingly unable to deliver on the evening news screen: a deft coup de main, an uplifting display of know-how and intrepid skill. The battle plan went like this: an American, someone's spouse, buddy, or dad, is captured by Third Worldly, Uzi-toting terrorists. The State Department is timorous, the Pentagon is hapless. The protagonist, either alone or with a motley band of friends, undertakes a daring rescue mission. Utilizing their several skills, the interracial, coed, and outcast crew blasts the malefactors and extricates the hostage(s). This is the plot outline of *Rambo* and *Rambo 3, Missing in Action 1–3, The Delta Force, Iron Eagle 1* and *2, The Rescue, Uncommon Valor, Let's Get Harry, Navy SEALS,* and countless TV movies. Generically linked to the old heist or caper film, the extrication film is not about superior firepower but exquisite calculation and surgical skill, not wholesale destruction but the safe removal of captives from foreign malevolence. It lent unassailable moral clarity to combat action overseas.

Working in concert with the extrication film and sometimes collapsing into it was the military rite-of-passage film. A nation with an all-volunteer and culturally isolated Armed Forces found boot camps and elite military academies an exotic realm in formats both melodramatic (*Taps,* 1981; *An Officer and a Gentleman,* 1982; and *The Lords of Discipline,* 1983) and comedic (*Private Benjamin,* 1980; *Stripes,* 1981). Likewise, with no apologies to Warner Bros. or the War De-

Retrieving what was left behind: Sylvester Stallone is ready for action-adventure extrication in *Rambo: First Blood Part 2* (1985).

partment, the blockbuster *Top Gun* (1986) added visual flash and subtracted thematic substance to assemble a high-tech video game out of the venerable tropes of the air crew film. For adolescents of the 1980s, disciplined drill, uniform dress codes, and cropped hair seemed to present an appealingly punkish alternative to their blow-dried and Reebok-shod elders.

The cultural and budgetary comeback of the post-Vietnam military in the Reagan era was a dramatic reversal of fortune that also reflected favorably on the pre-Vietnam military. Never totally besmirched by Vietnam, the World War II mythos emerged from postwar history with its honor intact. Even in the depths of Vietnam funk and posttraumatic cynicism, the verities of the *Why We Fight* series resisted sustained revisionist assault. In literature, the shadings of irony, ambiguity, and surrealism might be grafted onto the Second World War. On screen the visual confrontation with Nazism concentrated the mind powerfully. Neither *Catch 22* (1970) nor *Slaughterhouse Five* (1972), the motion picture versions of the two best-regarded literary satires of the Second World War, attracted a popular audience. While reconciliation and common cause is allowed between Axis and Allies after defeat, even the mushiest drama of warrior reconciliation never posits moral equivalence and fraternity *during the war*. However much the ante is upped in criminality, brutality, and irreverence, the rogues and rascals of *The Dirty Dozen* (1967), *The Devil's Brigade* (1968), and *Kelly's Heroes* (1970) are blood brothers to the misfits of *Gung Ho!* (1943). Only if detached from military surroundings and historical context is the World War II enemy granted a fraternal kinship with his opponent—in *Hell in the Pacific* (1973) a Japanese and American soldier must literally be stranded on a deserted island, two men without institutions and nation, in order to approach moral equivalence. When *The Memphis Belle* (1990), a fictionalized remake of William Wyler's combat report, closed with a magnanimous dedication to "all the brave young men, of whatever nationality, who lost their lives in the air war," film critic Stanley Kauffmann dryly responded, "I'm willing to wait another century or two for the objectivity to salute the Luftwaffe." There has been no successful big-budget "deconstruction" of the Second World War mythos on screen, and as long as historical memory can conjure the Army Signal Corps footage of the Holocaust there won't be.

Nonetheless, as the past slips further and further back in time, the liberties with the historical record, the willingness to suspend disbelief, and the desire to subordinate the complexities of reality to the pleasures of entertainment proceed apace. Once sacred territory, a moral landscape can become an ill-kept and overgrown cemetery, another well-trodden ground for genre convention and narrative twists. In the science fiction fantasy *Starship Troopers* (1997) director Paul Verhoeven fused the cinematic styles of Frank Capra's *Why We Fight* series and Leni Riefenstahl's *Triumph of the Will* to create a militarist dystopia where Übermensch armies clash with hordes of giant insects. An irreverent pastiche, the film wedded the visions of the two directors whose style and substance represented the opposite poles of wartime values: totalitarianism versus democracy, racism versus equality, massed automatons versus the autonomous individual.

As a fuel propelling action-adventure pyrotechnics and melodramatic machinations, the Second World War will always provide a colorful background even as the foreground is drained of its emotional valence and moral stakes. Two films, produced more than a

DUNAGIN'S PEOPLE

"THIS MUST BE AN OLD WORLD WAR II MOVIE...
WE SEEM TO BE THE GOOD GUYS."

(Reprinted by permission of North
American Syndicate)

half century after the fact, exemplify a common type of post-postwar
wartime engagement. One was a ludicrous box office failure, the
other a critical and commercial success, but despite setting and appearances neither was really about World War II. To allow the war
as history to intrude forcefully upon the war as dramatic device is
to detract from such entertainment as each offers.

Swing Kids (1993) is a musical melodrama set in Hamburg, Germany, in 1939. A countercultural cadre of German adolescents rejects
the goose-stepping regimentation of their Hitler Youth peers for the
jungle rhythms of American jazz music. Smuggled 78-rpm records
blare subversive sounds from Harlem hot spots as blond and blue-
eyed teenagers jitterbug on ornate ballroom floors. All of this is dan-
gerously seditious because the African-American roots of the Big
Band sound defy the Wagnerian edicts of Master Race musicology.
The word never uttered is *entartete* (degenerate), the term used by
Nazi propagandists for the corrosive and corrupting influence of
modern art forms, a venereal infestation purveyed by Africans and
Jews.

"No one who likes swing can become a Nazi," avow the swing kid
insurgents, but when they are forced to join the Hitler Youth, Nazi
behavior modification turns them from hepcats to brownshirts. In
jump-cut juxtaposition, two roads diverge: scenes of uniformed recruits watching the Jew-as-vermin montage from *The Eternal Jew*

(1940) segue into the jaunty strains of Benny Goodman's "Flat Foot Fuggy," cuing an exuberant dance number. In the climax, as the last swing kid is hauled off to a forced labor camp by the Gestapo, he raises his arm in a defiant salute: "Swing Heil!"

A different kind of swinging is practiced by the war-crossed lovers of *The English Patient* (1996), a lavish widescreen romance set in the desert of North Africa in the days before the outbreak of war in Europe. Winner of nine Academy Awards, the steamy spectacle is an excursion through memory that demands historical amnesia. As in the simple-minded melodramas released during the Second World War itself, a Nazi blitzkrieg at the second act curtain disrupts the course of true love.

The English Patient is the anti-*Casablanca,* a film where private passions override patriotic duty, where the personal devotion of a man to a woman justifies collaboration with the enemy, where the problems of three little people really *are* worth more than a hill of beans. Unlike *Casablanca,* where the present at Rick's Cafe is alive with witty intrigue and smoky passion, and where the past, in Rick's gin-soaked flashback to Paris, is bucolic and banal, the flashbacks to the past in *The English Patient* are more vivid and vital than the present-day convalescence during wartime. *Casablanca* wants to engage the war; *The English Patient* wants to escape it. Literally burned by history, eased into the next world by a morphine injection from a sympathetic nurse, the English Patient dies knowing he and his beloved will always have Cairo.

If the wartime legacy is durable enough to survive the impulse to belittle or efface, the credit is due in part to the consistent presence of what might be called "caretaker films." Documentaries and dramas alike, the caretaker films seek to flesh out the picture of World War II while staying true to the history and keeping faith with the meaning. Lineal descendants of the dutiful wartime work of John Ford, Howard Hawks, John Huston, and Frank Capra, they enter World War II territory with more humility and higher purpose.

By definition backward-looking and committed to actuality, documentary films function as the sternest custodian of the Second World War's legacy on screen. Sustaining whole cable channels and weighing down the shelves of video stores with gift box sets comprised of Frank Capra's *Why We Fight* series, CBS's *Victory at Sea,* and the BBC's *The World at War,* World War II footage reissued or reedited remains the most popular, perhaps definitive, version of the archival documentary, the film genre that teaches history by way of motion pictures.

Though cable television subsidizes the proliferation of archival retreads of conventional style and predictable content (newsreel/ talking head/newsreel/talking head, etc.), the creation of new war-time documentaries from heretofore unseen footage energizes a film format prone to inertness. Constant rewinding of familiar iconography diminishes the impact of even the most chilling tableaux: of the Berlin book burnings of 1933, of Hitler looming over the Eiffel Tower in 1940, of the skeletal concentration camp inmates liberated in 1945. "Films beget films," historian Jay Leyda famously remarked, and such is the hunger for films of the Second World War that the discovery of any new cache of footage is apt to beget a new archival documentary. Sometimes the resurrection of a fresh moving image can cast an aura that is almost supernatural. The last moments of *Anne Frank Remembered* (1995) unveil a startling strip of motion picture footage. Caught by accident leaning out a window, a girl known only through a jacket photograph on her diary springs magically to life in a few feet of film.

No wonder documentaries of the Second World War devote themselves so assiduously to unearthing lost canisters of motion picture footage. Even on the battlefield, a surprising number of uniformed amateurs working without official sanction and often in violation of direct orders took private home movies. Set in relief against the official 35mm version of the big picture, the unofficial 8mm version can look truer to life, closer to the bone.

The most striking of the new caches of film tend to be in color stock, a jarring deviation from a celluloid past apprehended in the newsreel shades of black and white. Drawing on amateur color footage of Hitler's visit to Munich for an arts festival in July 1939, the BBC documentary *Good Morning Mr. Hitler!* (1993) showcases pristine color photography that might have been developed yesterday at Photomat. Proudly awash in the florid pageantry of Nazism, a shimmering, sunlit Munich beckons as a travelogue vision. Tanned, their complexions flushed in the sun, Hitler and his henchmen saunter by in a sea of color, vitally and impossibly alive. Thus reanimated, the spectacle of Nazi Germany looks downright eerie.

Likewise *Mein Krieg* (1991), a documentary enlivened by amateur color footage shot during the invasion of Russia in June 1941, seems the work of a Hollywood crew on location, not the surreptitious home movies taken by Wehrmacht troops. Cradling his trusty 8mm Siemens camera, still working after fifty years and the subzero temperatures of a Moscow winter, a former soldier of the Reich and lifelong camera buff recalls his prewar farsightedness in hoarding film stock. "Kodachrome even. I had my last Kodachrome developed in 1942." Looking at the dazzling blood red swastikas and the greens and browns of the countryside spied from atop a tank barreling eastward on a beautiful summer day, he sees only the splendor of the photography and not the squalor of the military mission: "[The color pictures] have kept very well. They turned out great." No denying it: the "fascinating fascism" of the Third Reich is all the more fascinating in all the colors of the rainbow.

Discovered in the 1980s and 1990s, edited seamlessly into future documentaries, the newly emerging color footage from the 1939–1945 period may one day render a wartime vista quite different from the one viewed on screen during the war and throughout most of the postwar era. For the past half century, the aesthetics of motion picture history have lent war on screen a color-coded valence. Just as the nightly blizzard of white noise on the television screen seems to echo the chaos and dissonance of the Vietnam War, the black-and-white prism of the newsreels suits the stark polarities and moral clarity of World War II. Color may be truer to the reality of 1939–1945, but not to the cultural memory of it, and perhaps not to its meaning—which may be why, when looking at pictures of World War II, the right colors always seem to be black and white.

TAPS AT THE MILLENNIUM: *SAVING PRIVATE RYAN* (1998) AND *THE THIN RED LINE* (1998)

By the early 1990s, conventional Hollywood wisdom considered the 1939–1945 background "box office poison" because multiplex mall crawlers and the crucial 18-to-24-year-old demographic found Frank Capra's Great Struggle as remote and irrelevant as the Peloponnesian War. A series of bellwether commercial failures underlined the folly of genre resuscitation: *The Memphis Belle; Fat Man and Little Boy* (1989), a melodrama about the creation of the atomic bomb; *For the Boys* (1991), a backstage musical that spanned Big Band and rock 'n' roll; *Shining Through* (1992), a wildly anachronistic espionage thriller; and *A Midnight Clear* (1992), a somber and quite intelligent combat film. "World War II is ancient history to the majority of the TV and movie audience—there's nothing real about it," declared a vice president for programming in 1989.

But almost as if in a final reckoning at the end of the century, before the last human links to 1939–1945 slipped away forever, American cinema turned again to its most dramatic and defining moments. Like the archival documentary, the resurgent cycle of war films often drew on lesser-known episodes of combat and captivity to inject fresh energy into tired tropes. HBO's *The Tuskegee Airmen* (1995) filled an ellipsis in the combat film genre with a tribute to African-American pilots fighting for a double victory. *Paradise Road* (1997), a melodrama about a women's choir in a Japanese prison camp, reminded audiences of the brutality of an Imperial enemy that has, over the years, managed to escape the enduring infamy of the Nazis. HBO's well-crafted *When Trumpets Fade* (1998) chronicled a forgotten chapter of the Allied thrust into Germany, the Hurtgen forest battle of November 1944, pushed off the front pages of history by the Battle of the Bulge the next month. Residual aftershocks erupted in a variety of related venues: in public debates over the shape and placement of a World War II memorial on the Washington Mall, on the comparative virtues (and lack of same) of the aging, dutiful World War II generation and their shiftless baby boomer inheritors, and in the ghosts from the past who periodically emerged from suburban America—former Nazi war criminals, now frail octogenarians, pathetic figures emanating none of the vigorous menace of young manhood but still emblems of pure evil. All testified to the tenacious grip of the great war whose shadow over American culture recedes but never quite fades.

In the cluster of caretaker films that arrived punctually on the eve of the millennium, Steven Spielberg's *Saving Private Ryan* (1998) attained instant preeminence. A popular and critical success of epic proportions, it was not just a motion picture event but a cultural milestone, an occasion for another solemn encounter with the meaning of World War II and perhaps the last chance for a face-to-face salute to the surviving warriors. *Saving Private Ryan* is best understood as a kind of sacramental rite, the baby boomer sons kneeling before their World War II fathers in a final act of generational genuflection. Perfectly timed and pitched (in both senses), it flickered less as a motion picture than as a ceremonial flame before which Americans might look back at the linchpin event of a vanishing century and contemplate the cost paid by the men who had won the Good War.

To prepare for the ritual, *Saving Private Ryan* came wrapped in an aesthetic of realism that served as a red badge of pure motives and high purpose. Prepublicity advertising massaged audience reception and dictated the terms for victory: the imprimatur from historians and the testimonials of veterans being more avidly solicited than thumbs-up signs from influential film critics. "Without exception, the veterans I've talked to on the phone or corresponded with say this film has captured the real war (as opposed to the reel war of all previous Hollywood war movies)," declared historian Stephen Ambrose, the most conscientious guardian of the wartime legacy. Of course, the blurbs and ballyhoo for combat films from *The Big Parade*

Generational genuflection: Steven Spielberg directs Tom Hanks in the blistering D-Day sequence from *Saving Private Ryan* (1998). (Courtesy of Dreamworks Pictures)

(1925) to *Platoon* (1986) all played variations of the same theme: heretofore Hollywood sanitized combat, but in this film, finally, the hell of war is shown in all its fury and horror, stripped of romance, nobility, and happy endings. *Saving Private Ryan* sold itself as *sui generis,* proclaiming something about war that no film had dared say before: that it is violent and terrifying, that good guys die, that moral verities wilt under fire.

Up on screen, the earnest verisimilitude seemed to justify the endorsements from scholars and veterans: not just in the unflinching depiction of violence (always the true measure of "realism" in American cinema), but in the set design, costuming, and supply lines. *Saving Private Ryan* reclaimed the attention to martial detail that had invested the best of the classic World War II epics, the period authenticity in arms, vehicles, uniforms, and unit insignia, every stripe and hash mark in place, down to the distinctive diamond-shaped design of a Hitler Youth dagger. In tune with the texture of the battle gear, Robert Rodat's sparse script kept an ear out for wartime vernacular and military lingo, with no subtitles for listeners who couldn't keep up (though most figured out the GI acronym FUBAR [fucked up beyond all recognition], a less known variant of SNAFU, long before it dawned on the butt of the joke).

As for Steven Spielberg, the planet's most popular director had been in training for his own World War II landing since his first 8mm one-reelers, shot on location in the deserts of the American Southwest. In *Jaws* (1975), the wartime backstory surfaced when the flinty shark hunter Quint conjured his night sea terror after the sinking of the USS *Indianapolis,* a riveting soliloquy that remains the most memorable verbal passage in any Spielberg film. At the same time, the backdrop of 1939–1945 had been the scene of his most conspicuous blunders. In three ambitious and fiscally bootless efforts, *1941* (1979), *Empire of the Sun* (1987), and *Always* (1989), Spielberg's war-themed inspirations fizzled with American moviegoers. *1941* is a tiresome and costly noncomedy mocking California's invasion fears in the wake of Pearl Harbor. *Empire of the Sun,* drawn from J. G. Ballard's prizewinning memoir of a British boy's life in a Japanese internment camp in China, has a fairy-tale quality of a kind darker than Spielberg's usual childhood fantasies. *Always* is an outright remake of *A Guy Named Joe* (1943), which for the blazing glory of fighting Nazis over Britain substitutes the glory of fighting blazes in Yellowstone National Forest. (Spielberg had originally planned to retain the wartime setting for *Always,* but shifted to a modern stage after *Empire of the Sun* foundered at the box office.)

Perhaps World War II had been the common source of Spielberg's box office and artistic failures because, though the wartime period has haunted his filmography no less than aliens and anthropologists, he had never taken Nazism seriously—certainly not in the Indiana Jones series, where the SS were clumsy fools befuddled by a bullwhip and Adolf Hitler was just another celebrity signing autographs. Not, of course, until *Schindler's List* (1993). In his close encounter with the Holocaust, Spielberg finally demanded of himself, and his audience, something more than a spellbound gaze at the screen.

Still, *Schindler's List* is a melodrama about Nazis exterminating Jews, not a combat film about Americans fighting Nazis. Spielberg's revival of the World War II combat genre thus seems the logical culmination of an auteurist obsession that began in boyhood, the most awesome action-adventure ever recorded by the moving image finally attracting the full attention of the most cinematically inspired of American artists.

Given that pedigree, the prism of World War II (the movie) not World War II (the war) filters *Saving Private Ryan.* Classic Hollywood combat war films from *Battleground* (1949) to *The Big Red One* (1980) leave visible tracks (a Sergeant Zack lookalike from *The Steel Helmet* appears briefly in the last battle sequence), but the deeper dreamwork conjures up the most popular television show of its time for a suburban youth of a certain age growing up in Phoenix, Arizona, namely *Combat* (1962–1967), the gritty black-and-white ABC series, directed from a lean, ground-level perspective. Set in the European Theater of Operations after D-Day, *Combat* was a weekly reiteration of the tropes of the classical WWII combat film and the shooting script for a thousand adolescent war games.

Since the key to genre is the tension between familiarity and variation, the conventional and the original, *Saving Private Ryan* unfolds as an uncharted minefield of sudden terrors interspersed with secure perimeters and safe bivouacs. The mission: to save the last surviving sibling of a family hit three times by death, to pluck one man from the fog of war and return him safely to home and hearth. The tale is bracketed by the present-day time frame of a graveside visit at the Normandy Memorial Cemetery (quiet, serene, respectful), and by a pair of furious combat sequences (loud, chaotic, blasphemous). For every radical disruption (American soldiers shoot surrendering Germans point blank and then crack bad jokes), a soothing nostrum restores equilibrium. Where else but in a World War II combat film does a GI warn "I don't have a good feeling about this one," a Nazi prisoner spared from summary execution return for bad result in the last reel, or the green kid turn into the unlikely hero—or does he?

The baptism of fire begins with a 27-minute battle overture depicting the Allied landing at Omaha Beach, a sequence that unnerved even teenage audiences jaded by the ultra-violence of post-Production Code Hollywood cinema. A sustained fusillade, it manages to induce not just suspense, shock, and disorientation but a kind of combat fatigue. Protected for a moment in the eggshell of a landing craft, racing through the surf to land on the most hostile of shores, GIs vomit from seasickness and fear. The doors to the craft swing open and whole squads are cut to ribbons—shot, shelled, drowned, and torn apart. Robert Capa mise-en-scène and Army Signal Corps eyelines clash in a barrage of jarring kaleidoscopic flashes: the blurry D-Day images of the famous still photographer spliced into the jostled, handheld perspective of military cameramen in the thick of it, scampering for cover, peering out from behind parapets, and peeking through the slits of pillboxes. Newsreel memories are evoked by angle of sight, jump cut-action, and subtle shifts in film grain, but the newsreels unspooled nothing like this. The jagged suturing of the editing serves as a sickening complement to the surgical violations of the human frame: a man's intestines spill out of his gut, a face blows apart, a dazed GI with a bloody stump grips his detached forearm, and a wounded man suddenly disintegrates into a shredded torso.

The rending of human flesh leaves an oceanfront awash in blood and body parts—and the spectator reeling from the emotional percussion. As the first major World War II combat film to be fashioned in the modern age of computer graphic imaging (CGI), digital sound, and forensic makeup, *Saving Private Ryan* took advantage of the shock of the new, of being able to revision, in full color carnage, a war largely censored and sanitized on the Hollywood screen. Though well-established tricks of the trade in action-adventure, horror teenpics, and the Vietnam War film, the high-tech tools of cinematic verisimilitude had never before been orchestrated for sustained visceral impact in World War II territory.

Lending a full measure of ear-witness depth involvement, the combat symphony howling on the digitally enhanced sound track underscores the visual assault: the mosquito buzz of bullets whizzing through the air, the whistles of the incoming 88s, and the three-dimensional presence of zooming aircraft and crunching tank treads—each weapon, shell, and vehicle given its own aural marker. Wisely too, the musical score by John Williams is quietly martial, not bombastic. All gentle trumpets and mild percussion, it slides in only when the combat recedes, layered almost beneath conscious registration. Throughout all of this, the guilty secret is that far from being horrifying and repulsive, the stunning spectacle of sight and sound is a joy to behold and harken to from a theater seat, pure cinema at its most hypnotic and intense.

Up and off the beach, the carnage and confusion subsides, replaced by the rational purpose of a military target, to take out a German machine-gun emplacement. Spielberg's celebration of spontaneous GI action, above and beyond the call of duty, conforms to the story of D-Day according to Stephen Ambrose, the consultant and spiritual auteur of *Saving Private Ryan:* that discrete acts of heroism and initiative by citizen soldiers assured victory on the beach that day. Mustering the remnants of tattered platoons for a forward assault, Captain Miller (Tom Hanks) bellows a line straight from the manual of Sgt. John Ryker of *Sands of Iwo Jima* or Sgt. Chip Saunders of *Combat:* "Let's get in this war!"

Scanning the CGI-generated landscape after battle, a crane shot swoops in on the backpack of a dead GI with the stenciled name, "Ryan, S." From the blood-drenched vista of Omaha Beach, the action shifts to the sepia tones of homefront America and the tap-tap-tapping of War Department secretaries typing out bad news borne by telegram, with the expressions of official regret recited in a chorus of voice-overs. The sight of an Iowa farmhouse with four blue stars in the window and a long shot of an Army staff car driving up a dirt road, spied from the vantage of a mother standing at the kitchen sink, is another kind of telegraphed message: she knows, we know she knows, but we know she knows not the worst of it.

Noteworthy in the brief homefront sequence is the saintly portrait of Army Chief of Staff Gen. George C. Marshall. The architect of victory, the indispensable man in the fight against fascism, Marshall has been almost erased from the popular memory of World War II, never granted the big-screen recognition of Generals Patton or Eisenhower. Breaking ranks with the usual Hollywood formula for portrayals of the officer corps in the post-Vietnam era (the higher up in the command, the lower the IQ and moral fiber), Spielberg treats General Marshall as reverently as Jack Warner treated FDR, a decision designed to endear the film to WWII buffs, who think Marshall's picture should be on U.S. currency. "The boy's alive and we're going to find him and we're going to get him the hell out of there," orders the general, after quoting, from memory, Abraham Lincoln's letter of condolence to Mrs. Bixby, a mother who lost five sons in the Civil War. Suitably awed, his men answer, "Yes, sir."

After the battle-scarring introduction and stateside orientation, a roulette game of ensemble attrition commences. A multiethnic sampling, the combat squad sent to extricate Private Ryan fits the Warner Bros. mold: the idealized everyman leader Captain Miller (Tom Hanks), the grizzled Sergeant Horvath (Tom Sizemore), the cynical tough guy Private Reiben (Edward Burns), the emotional "Eye-tal-ian" Caparzo (Vin Diesel), the edgy Jewish guy Melish (Adam Goldberg), the compassionate medic (Giovanni Ribisi), the Johnny Reb marksman (Barry Pepper), and the milquetoast clerk pressed into infantryman's boots, Corporal Upham (Jeremy Davies). Bearing the symbolic weight of the moral and statistical stakes, the elusive Ryan (Matt Damon) is an Iowa farm boy straight from the pages of *Guadalcanal Diary*. One half expects William Bendix to pop up with a wisecrack about the Brooklyn Dodgers.

If the cannon fodder on Omaha Beach presents a blur of bodies and nameless faces, the combat squad personalizes the cost of war: Caparzo, whose heart overrules his head and whose fate punctuates the cold logic of combat ("And *that's* why we can't take children!" barks Captain Miller); the up-close death of the medic, a physician who cannot heal himself, who knows the diagnosis is terminal when his liver has been hit; and the excruciating duel to the death between a Nazi Übermensch and Melish, wherein the Jewish GI is penetrated by a blade in a deadly pas de deux that plays like an act of coitus. In vintage combat film fashion, ethnic and religious colors shade in the character details. Catholics clutch rosaries and cross themselves, priests administer last rites to gasping soldiers, and the fundamentalist sniper recites scripture. The Second World War being the crucible of assimilation for Italian-Americans, a vowel in the last name vents a complimentary slur. "All the guineas are buying it," cracks Reiben as the men rummage through a pile of dog tags looking for the Irish surname. Oddly, or maybe not so oddly, Spielberg seems off-balance in limning the Jewish guy Melish, an overdetermined Nazi-

Reviving the World War II combat genre: Captain Miller (Tom Hanks) and Sergeant Horvath (Tom Sizemore) in Steven Spielberg's *Saving Private Ryan* (1998). (Courtesy of Dreamworks Pictures)

hater, who breaks down in tears when clutching a Hitler Youth dagger ("Now it will be a *Shabbat hallah* cutter") and taunts German POWs by waving a Star of David and hissing "Juden, Ja, Juden!"

In the tension between the aesthetic of realism and the satisfactions of genre, Tom Hanks is the man on the tightrope. Just as the hierarchy of the studio star system worked against the grain of the values of the classic World War II combat film (ensemble players as combat unit doing an unglamorous job of work), the certainty that Hanks will die not in the first but in the last reel works against the chaos theory of war. (*Of course* he will be killed in action: the way to tell a serious war film from a juvenile war film is that in a serious war film the most likable character dies.) Captain Miller embodies the Frank Capra version of the American soldier, the antithesis of the Wehrmacht automaton, a schoolteacher who becomes a warrior of necessity not bloodlust, who wants only to finish the job and get back home to his wife in smalltown Pennsylvania. He is also a natural leader who might have sprung from a Walter Mitty daydream. He is made mortal by a mild case of the nerves, a shaky right hand, a physical tic and visual symbol that will have a wrenching emotional payoff in his last seconds of animation.

Filling the quiet spaces between the combat action are discussions of the bond of brotherhood by that rear echelon essayist Ralph Waldo Emerson, one soldier's off-the-cuff translation of an Edith Piaf tune wafting on a scratchy phonograph in the prebattle calm, droll GI grumbling ("The Statue of Liberty is kaput?" Miller asks dryly, harkening to the news from a Nazi loudspeaker. "That's disconcerting."), and meditations on the connect-the-dots theme ("This time the mission *is* a man"). The patches of verbal eloquence share space with glimpses of austere beauty: a strangely serene landscape after battle, a quiet night in a demolished cathedral, and a combat squad silouhetted against flashes of artillery light at dawn, the Wehrmacht sharing the affinity of Hollywood cinematographers for the dappled chiaroscuro of the "magic hour." "That's quite a view," says Miller, waxing Spielbergian as he gazes out over Omaha Beach, now secure, cluttered with men, equipment, ships, blimps, and bodies.

Spielberg's watchmaker's skill with every unit of cinematic grammar is always breathtaking: seeing the gears turning and the bells chiming on cue never diminishes astonishment in the precision of the instrumentation. The shot–reverse shot duel to the death between two snipers, one who spies the other through his scope and sees the flash of gunfire a split second too late for his own shot; a forward assault rendered through the passive point of view of Corporal Upham; or Miller, near death and beyond caring, futilely firing his pistol at an oncoming tank, impossibly igniting it, as the camera tilts upward to reveal the true source of the explosion, a plane climbing in an arc out of its attack dive. The squadron of P-51s, the alert spectator may recall, would not be in the sky had not Miller ordered his reluctant men to take out a German radar installation earlier, a decision that caused the death of the beloved medic.

When Captain Miller and his squad finally find the man who is the mission, he refuses to abandon his fraternity and remains "with the only brothers I have left." "The world has taken a turn for the surreal," comments Captain Miller, anachronistically, incorrectly. Actually, this is as classical and traditional as it gets.

After the last battle, with the armored cavalry riding up and the

P-51s zooming above, the combat zone is secure enough for the exit line. "Earn it," whispers the dying Miller to Private Ryan, as the camera looks down to his once-trembling hand, now stilled. Neither a benediction nor a curse, it is a reminder aimed not at Private Ryan— he has already earned it—but at his posterity, the callow inheritors of the sacrifice of the wartime generation, middle-age boomers and twentysomething Gen-Xers alike. General Marshall's godlike voice-over delivers the eulogy for Captain Miller, Sergeant Horvitz, Private Caparzo, T/4 Medic Wade, et al., quoting again from Lincoln's letter to Mrs. Bixby, offering the solace that America's sons have died on "the altar of freedom."

The words are not ironic and neither is the last image, echoing the first, of the American flag flying in the harsh breezes of the memorial cemetery at Normandy. This is not the flag that unfurls in *Born on the Fourth of July* or *Rambo,* a stained prop of fake glory and scoundrel patriotism, but the real item, the star-spangled banner yet waving, the symbol of Spielberg's American anthem and an emblem of his own eagle eye for hitting Americans right where they live.

Released six months after *Saving Private Ryan* and inevitably landing in its shadow, Terrence Malick's version of James Jones's *The Thin Red Line* (1998) underscored the comeback of World War II on screen. It also marked something of a comeback for writer-director Malick, the auteur of two of the most sumptuously lensed films of the 1970s, *Badlands* (1973) and *Days of Heaven* (1978).

Despite his self-imposed twenty-year hiatus from cinema, however, Malick's natural affinities were still with nature. Oceans away from Jones's source novel and the previous motion picture version filmed in 1964, *The Thin Red Line* overlays the ravishing cinematography of *Days of Heaven* onto the narrative contours of *Guadalcanal Diary,* but in the struggle for generic dominance, the straightforward plotline of the combat film fades before the visual delights of Malick's luxurious pastoralism. Where *Saving Private Ryan* is fast, furious, grim, and graphic, *The Thin Red Line* is languid, meditative, serene, and artful. And where Spielberg strives for verisimilitude with the rough edges of combat-like photography, Malick splashes his canvas with the colors and sights of a biosphere that is never less than gorgeous.

Set in the Pacific theater of operations, *The Thin Red Line* is defined by a sense of place, not history or politics. Where a military tactician scans the battleground for enemy encampments and defensible positions, Malick looks over no man's land like a natural scientist bent on discovering new species of plant life. In one sense at least, his outlook reflects the original wartime perspective. To American eyes, the combat landscape of the Pacific appeared as alien territory, primeval and Darwinian, the humid jungles and volcanic ash of obscure atolls possessing none of the reassuring familiarity of the postcard monuments of the tourist capitals of Europe. The inhabitants—Melanesian natives and Japanese invaders alike—were no less strange and otherworldly. Moreover, in the Pacific archipelago, against the Japanese, the ground fighting tended to be more vicious, the enemy less liable to be kept at arm's length: symbolically and significantly, the favored war trophy for veterans of the Pacific war was the samurai sword; for veterans of the European theater of operations, a German lugar.

Of course, the other big difference between the two theaters of war was the race of the enemy—and a medium amenable to sinister caricatures and overripe character acting did more than its bit to imprint the racist dimensions of the war against Japan. By the late 1960s, however, as the issue of race pressed ever more into the forefront of American reconfigurations of its own history, the Japanese role as a pillar of the Axis triad tended to fade from popular depictions of WWII on screen. A symbolic touchstone was the *Rashomon*-like epic *Tora! Tora! Tora!* (1970), a balanced appraisal of the attack on Pearl Harbor from the Japanese and American point of view, itself basically a bilateral coproduction with Japanese and American directors. In defeat, Japan presented a wholly new face to the world, a picture of earnest technophiles and well-mannered businessmen, not fierce warriors schooled in brutality and prone to atrocities. American shame over the internment of Japanese-Americans and the exterminationist temper of wartime propaganda encouraged a cultural amnesia that (though Japan had far more to forget) served both sides. Tellingly, the longest-running portrait of the Japanese enemy in American popular culture came by way of the coded figures of the Klingons, the extraterrestrial race of imperialist samurais in television's original *Star Trek* (1966–1969), an alien species that by the time of the sequel *Star Trek: The Next Generation* (1987) had been peacefully assimilated for service on the deck of the resonantly named *Starship Enterprise*.

Not least, the relative paucity of recent combat films set in the Pacific reflects a powerful profit motive. Hollywood spectacles about

Japanese villainy during World War II make dubious exports into an increasingly lucrative Japanese market, where box office rentals sweeten the dividends from North America theaters. Throughout *The Thin Red Line*, whether as a result of revisionist intentions or commercial calculations, Japanese soldiers appear mainly as shadows in the grass or defeated victims of American war crimes (reversing the national identities in a well-known rumor of the Pacific war, a ghoulish GI collects gold fillings from the bodies of dead Japanese).

The stray line of dialogue aside, then, Malick's Guadalcanal diary is more a meditation on nature than an evocation of war: the main characters are neither the American GIs of Charlie Company nor the barely glimpsed Japanese enemy, but the flora and fauna of the jungle location. Shot in the Solomon Islands and the Daintree Rain Forest in Queensland, Australia, and projected in spectacular widescreen Panavision, *The Thin Red Line* shimmers like a big-budget travelogue. The first image reveals the snout of a crocodile, whose elongated reptilian form slithers into the widescreen frame. "What is this war in the heart of nature?" asks the AWOL Private Witt (Jim Caviezel). "Why does nature vie with itself?" Presumably, the snake is already in the garden, but the beauty of the lush foliage and the innocence of the noble Melanesian savages belie any intimation of a heart of darkness in the heart of nature. Witt swims in the crystal-clear ocean, frolics with the native children, and bakes himself bronze in the sun. It is not crocodiles but Caucasians who violate the purity of the prelapsarian paradise. When a U.S. Navy warship cruises into sight on the blue horizon, "et in arcadia ego" might be painted on the bow.

As voice-overs recite the interior monologues of unusually eloquent and philosophical GIs ("War doesn't ennoble men—it turns them into dogs, poisons the soul") and gauzy flashbacks call up the memory of homefront America, a meandering story emerges, slowly. The men—boys, really—of Charlie Company must seize the high ground from a well-dug-in emplacement of Japanese machine guns. So orders the demonic Colonel Tall (Nick Nolte), a martinet in the Captain Queeg mold, driven batty not by war but by the tedium of the peacetime military and the humiliation of being "passed over" for the eagle of the bird colonel. Like the cinematic war lovers played by George C. Scott in *Patton* and Robert Duvall in *Apocalypse Now*, he is invincible and charmed, not even flinching when a mortar explodes nearby. Gravel-voiced and gung-ho, the larger-than-life Colonel Tall is also by far the most animated character in the company.

"What's this war at the heart of nature?": Private Bell (Ben Chaplin), Captain Gaff (John Cusack), and Private Witt (Jim Caviezel), in Terrence Malick's pastoral version of James Jones's *The Thin Red Line* (1998). (Courtesy of Twentieth Century Fox)

"Go straight up that goddamn hill!" he orders, not oblivious to the human toll but heedless of the cost.

Less motivated is Captain Staros (Elias Koteas), who balks at the suicide mission, and Sergeant Welsh (Sean Penn), a loner whose still waters run deep. Cleverly, Malick delays the onset of violence, foreshadowing the horror to come with the grisly discovery of two bodies of tortured Marines, creating tension simply by having nothing happen. When the combat erupts, it hits suddenly and matter of factly, but even amid the hard rain of the technology of war the director never goes too long without getting back to nature. The elemental fluid bottled up in the supply lines is not gasoline but water. "Nature is cruel, Staros," Colonel Tall says when he relieves the soft-hearted captain from command, picking up on the recurrent theme.

Weighed against its fated frame of comparison, *The Thin Red Line* offers few of the dramatic or cultural satisfactions of *Saving Private Ryan*. Malick lacks Spielberg's sure sense of narrative drive, of carrying an audience into the fabula, even of creating a convincing historical past or compelling genre film. Certainly, amid the pantheistic sightseeing, the sporadic wartime cliché unfolds: GIs gripe in the accents of the Bronx and Dixie, the devoted husband pining for his wife receives a predictable letter at mail call ("It just got too lonely, Jack"), and Private Witt enjoys a prolonged death scene and sentimental graveside homage. Also, as in latter-day combat epics such as *The Longest Day* (1962) and *A Bridge Too Far* (1977), name-brand American stars march by for a few seconds of screen time: John Travolta as an unctuous brigadier general, Woody Harrelson as a luckless sergeant clumsy with a hand grenade, and George Clooney as a smug officer. Like the Melanesian islanders, however, the thin red line of men in Charlie Company walk through a mythic state of nature beyond history, not Guadalcanal Island or any other real geographical site or battlefield milestone. In case anyone misses the point, Tall reminds his subordinates that at West Point he read Homer, in the original Greek: the original wartime myth.

Not that Malick lacks an agenda. In ideology no less than topography, *The Thin Red Line* evokes the Vietnam combat genre, where the worst enemy of the American soldier is his commanding officer. The taciturn sergeant Welsh expresses the generic allegiance when he utters a line that is commonsensical in the Vietnam jungle but heretical in World War II territory: "If you die, it's gonna be for nothing."

Finally, though, the true bloodlines of *The Thin Red Line* are not cinematic but botanical and zoological. Malick revels in the sights of a fecund environment oozing with natural energy, churning out life and death in equal measure, indiscriminately. Beams of sunlight break through the jungle canopy for a "rosy fingered dawn." Owls watch alertly, vampire bats hang ominously, and carrion birds circle eerily. Weirdly festive in blue and red, parrots stand out against the browns and greens of the jungle and the khaki of the GI fatigues. Under withering machine-gun fire, a soldier is threatened by a coiling snake, attacked at once by man and nature. A mountainside of tall grass trembles in a gentle breeze, the wafer-thin reeds giving the illusion of cover from shot and shell. Bathed in the reflection of yellow flames, the faces of young GIs glow in the chiaroscuro of Renaissance portraiture. Even the landscape after battle, where vegetative nature and flesh-and-blood men are burnt to a crisp and dogs feast on cadavers, seems healthy and biodegradable, a wondrous part of the great chain of being. Before such radiant cinematography and environmental splendor, one may feel, like the wartime spectators who beheld the Technicolor beauty of *To the Shores of Iwo Jima* (1945) with more guilt than pleasure, that Terrence Malick has made of World War II too pretty a picture.

Whatever the commercial destiny of World War II on the theatrical screen in the wake of *Saving Private Ryan* and *The Thin Red Line,* the age of cable narrowcasting guarantees the visual persistence of the motion picture record. Seldom missing a wartime anniversary without a commemorative archival documentary, the History Channel thrives on the grainy black-and-white footage from the newsreels and military photographic units. The Arts and Entertainment network rebroadcasts the *Why We Fight* series and the BBC's monumental *World at War* documentaries so incessantly that teenagers refer to A&E as "the World War II channel." Calling on seemingly bottomless inventories from the MGM, Warner Bros., and RKO libraries, American Movie Classics and Turner Classic Movies are treasure troves of wartime feature films and short subjects. Via 800 numbers, mail-order catalogs, and the Internet, the dissemination on video of newsreel compilations, *March of Time* reissues, and combat reports proceeds with a speed and sweep beyond the ken of the War Activities Committee. That the choicest footage and best documentaries—even many of the commercial features—have passed into the public domain assures longevity and ubiquity.

Of course, transmission alone is no guarantee of clear reception. If the images from the wartime past are to sharpen the vision of American culture, if the motion picture record is to be more than "a set of dusty spectacles," an alert understanding must inform the eyes of the beholder. Actuarial tables and SAT verbal scores alike attest to a pressing need for another kind of transmission, the communication through time, across the generations, of historical experience—of what happened, and why, and what might have happened otherwise. To a postwar world that has fallen somewhat short of OWI aspirations and Production Code standards, Hollywood's projections of war can yet illuminate the real legacies of the years from 1939 to 1945.

Hollywood's Most Popular Films, 1941–1945

Gauging the popularity of Hollywood films is not simply a matter of dollars and cents—perhaps fortunately because box-office figures for the war years are elusive and imprecise. *Variety*, the trade journal of box-office record, did not begin issuing complete year-end figures for box-office gross until 1946. Moreover, the phrase "box-office gross" itself has shifted in meaning. In wartime trade parlance a film's reported "gross" generally referred to income received by the distributor, *not* box-office revenues. In the parlance of today's industry, "gross" (the money taken in at the box-office window) and "rental" (the money the exhibitor pays back to the distributor) are quite separate tabulations.

A revolution in economic structure adds to the trouble with terminology. Until the Supreme's Court's Paramount Decree in 1948, the major studios could legally own and operate all three rungs of the motion picture business—production, distribution, and exhibition. In 1945, Paramount, 20th Century-Fox, Warner Bros., RKO, and Loews, Inc., MGM's parent company, controlled among them nearly

20 percent of all domestic theaters. For member exhibitors who were component parts of their parent studio's vertically integrated business, the tripartite division was more organizational than entrepreneurial. For nonaffiliated theaters, however, the financial arrangement between exhibitor and distributor, the percentage of box-office income the one contracted to pay back to the other, varied depending on a film's perceived prospects. During the Second World War, the standard cut among the three principles of the motion picture industry was: exhibitor: 65 percent; distributor: 10 percent; and producer: 25 percent. Then as now, however, distributors with must-see, big-budget motion pictures negotiated special deals more to their advantage, usually on a sliding scale downward that swung more to the exhibitor's advantage the longer a film played at the theater. Thus the terms of the deal really determine the box-office success of any film: huge profits for the distributor might be only a break-even proposition for the exhibitor.

Since profit does not necessarily mean popularity, the gauge offered below is from the year-end surveys of *Showmen's Trade Review*, which based its hierarchy on responses from the nation's exhibitors as to their most popular films. Believing there was "no more accurate estimate of the public's taste in entertainment than the record revealed by the majority report of the showmen who are in daily contact with the people who pay to see the pictures," the exhibitors' list of motion picture favorites tended to be films that played in one theater for many weeks and thus accrued more money to the exhibitor. Note too that the year of a film's greatest popularity may well be the year *after* its official release date. Of course, no financial gauge can measure the tenacity of memorable lines or indelible moments at the time or as time goes by—else *It Ain't Hay* would loom as large in historical memory as *Casablanca*.

The "Leading Productions" of *Showmen's Trade Review:*

1941
Men of Boys Town (MGM)
Buck Privates (Universal)
Caught in the Draft (Paramount)
The Shepherd of the Hills (Paramount)
North West Mounted Police (Paramount)
Sergeant York (Warner Bros.)

In the Navy (Universal)
Virginia (Paramount)
Honky Tonk (MGM)
The Philadelphia Story (MGM)
Hold That Ghost (Universal)
A Yank in the RAF (Fox)
Blossoms in the Dust (MGM)
Moon Over Miami (Fox)
Sun Valley Serenade (Fox)
Andy Hardy's Private Secretary (MGM)
Billy the Kid (MGM)
The Strawberry Blonde (Warner Bros.)
Kitty Foyle (RKO)
The Great Dictator (UA)
Life Begins for Andy Hardy (MGM)
Dive Bomber (Warner Bros.)
I Wanted Wings (Paramount)
Penny Serenade (Columbia)
Tin Pan Alley (Fox)

1942
Mrs. Miniver (MGM)
How Green Was My Valley (Fox)
To the Shores of Tripoli (Fox)
Look Who's Laughing (RKO)
Reap the Wild Wind (Paramount)
The Fleet's In (Paramount)
Pardon My Sarong (Universal)
Keep 'Em Flying (Universal)
Holiday Inn (Paramount)
One Foot in Heaven (Warner Bros.)
Ride 'Em Cowboy (Universal)
Kings Row (Warner Bros.)
Captain of the Clouds (Warner Bros.)
Babes on Broadway (MGM)
Rio Tita (MGM)
Wake Island (Paramount)
Eagle Squadron (Universal)
My Sister Eileen (Columbia)
The Bashful Bachelor (RKO)

Remember Pearl Harbor (Republic)
Somewhere I'll Find You (MGM)
Beyond the Blue Horizon (Paramount)
Song of the Islands (Fox)
Louisiana Purchase (Paramount)
My Gal Sal (Fox)

1943
Special Award:
   This Is the Army (Warner Bros.)
Random Harvest (MGM)
Yankee Doodle Dandy (Warner Bros.)
Hitler's Children (RKO)
My Friend Flicka (Fox)
Stage Door Canteen (UA)
Hello, Frisco, Hello (Fox)
Star Spangled Rhythm (Paramount)
Coney Island (Fox)
So Proudly We Hail! (Paramount)
For Me and My Gal (MGM)
Springtime in the Rockies (Fox)
Pride of the Yankees (RKO)
The Road to Morocco (Paramount)
Hit the Ice (Universal)
The Human Comedy (MGM)
The More the Merrier (Columbia)
Crash Dive (Fox)
Dixie (Paramount)
Bataan (MGM)
Air Force (Warner Bros.)
It Ain't Hay (Universal)
Casablanca (Warner Bros.)
Who Done It? (Universal)
Salute to the Marines (MGM)
The Major and the Minor (Paramount)

1944
Special Awards:
   For Whom the Bell Tolls (Paramount)
   Wilson (Fox)
   Song of Bernadette (Fox)

Going My Way (Paramount)
Since You Went Away (UA)
A Guy Named Joe (MGM)
The Story of Dr. Wassell (Paramount)
White Cliffs of Dover (MGM)
See Here, Private Hargrove (MGM)
The Miracle of Morgan's Creek (Paramount)
Cover Girl (Columbia)
Home in Indiana (Fox)
Destination Tokyo (Warner Bros.)
Madame Curie (MGM)
Thousands Cheer (MGM)
Lady in the Dark (Paramount)
Two Girls and a Sailor (MGM)
Up in Arms (RKO)
Arsenic and Old Lace (RKO)
Pin Up Girl (Fox)
Bathing Beauty (MGM)
Shine On Harvest Moon (Warner Bros.)
Guadalcanal Diary (Fox)
Old Acquaintance (Warner Bros.)
Dragon Seed (MGM)
In Society (Universal)
The Fighting Seabees (Republic)
Casanova Brown (RKO)

1945
Thirty Seconds Over Tokyo (MGM)
National Velvet (MGM)
Meet Me in St. Louis (MGM)
State Fair (Fox)
Thrill of a Romance (MGM)
God Is My Co-Pilot (Warner Bros.)
A Song to Remember (Columbia)
Anchors Away (MGM)
Hollywood Canteen (Warner Bros.)
Incendiary Blonde (Paramount)
Son of Lassie (MGM)
Thunderhead (Fox)
A Tree Grows in Brooklyn (Fox)
Christmas in Connecticut (Warner Bros.)

Song of Bernadette (Fox)
For Whom the Bell Tolls (Paramount)
Valley of Decision (MGM)
The Story of G.I. Joe (UA)
Up in Arms (RKO)
Music for the Millions (MGM)
Wilson (Fox)
Billy Rose's Diamond Horseshoe (Fox)
I'll Be Seeing You (UA)
Along Came Jones (RKO)
Our Vines Have Tender Grapes (MGM)

Victory Films Released through the War Activities Committee of the Motion Picture Industry, 1941–1945

1941
Power for Defense (Tennessee Valley Authority) (February 8, 1941)
12 Army Recruiting Trailers (February 18, 1941)
Calling All Workers (War Jobs) (April 9, 1941)
American Preferred (War Bonds) (May 20, 1941)
Where Do We Go (USO) (May 28, 1941)
Bits and Pieces (OEM—Office of Emergency Management) (June 5, 1941)
Army in Overalls (Civilian Conservation Corps) (June 5, 1941)
America Builds Ships (June 5, 1941)
Bomber (OEM) (October 3, 1941)
Pots to Planes (Scrap Aluminum) (November 22, 1941)
Ford for Freedom (December 9, 1941)
Women in Defense (December 24, 1941)
Red Cross Campaign Trailer (December 24, 1941)

1942
Safeguarding Military Information (January 16, 1942)
Tanks (Building) (January 23, 1942)

The New Spirit (February 2, 1942)
Any Bonds Today (April 2, 1942)
Lake Carrier (Iron Ore) (April 2, 1942)
Fighting Fire Bombs (April 2, 1942)
Ring of Steel (Morale) (April 2, 1942)
United China Relief (April 14, 1942)
War Bond Appeal (Treasury Secretary Henry Morgenthau) (April 21, 1942)
Keep 'Em Rolling (War Production Board) (May 25, 1942)
Winning Your Wings (Recruiting) (May 28, 1942)
Mr. Gardenia Jones (USO) (May 29, 1942)
Vigilance (Forest Saboteurs) (June 9, 1942)
U.S. Coast Guard (Recruiting) (June 18, 1942)
Your Air Raid Warden (July 25, 1942)
Frying Pan to Firing Line (Save Fats) (September 8, 1942)
The Battle of Midway (Navy) (September 14, 1942)
The World at War (OWI Feature) (September 18, 1942)
Salvage (War Production Board Chairman Donald Nelson) (October 8, 1942)
Your American Tragedy (October 8, 1942)
Scrap Drive (Newspapers) (October 8, 1942)
Manpower Missing (October 29, 1942)
Fuel Conservation (November 12, 1942)
Japanese Relocation (November 12, 1942)
Henry Brown, Farmer (November 15, 1942)
Dover (British Morale) (November 26, 1942)
Night Shift (Factory Women) (December 10, 1942)
Colleges at War (December 24, 1942)

1943
Community Transportation (January 7, 1943)
You, John Jones (United Nations relief) (January 14, 1943)
Paratroops (January 21, 1943)
Negro Colleges in War Time (January 25, 1943)
Farm Battle Lines (January 29, 1943)
The Spirit of '43 (War Taxes) (February 4, 1943)
Troop Train (Army Transportation) (February 11, 1943)
Since Pearl Harbor (Red Cross Service) (February 18, 1943)
Point Rationing of Food (February 25, 1943)
Farmer at War (March 11, 1943)
At the Front in North Africa (March 18, 1943)

Food for Fighters (Army Rations) (April 1, 1943)
Right of Way (Travel) (April 15, 1943)
Mission Accomplished (Bombing Nazis) (April 29, 1943)
Doctors at War (May 13, 1943)
Wings Up (Army Air Force Training) (May 27, 1943)
Prelude to War (Army Feature) (May 27, 1943)
Message from Malta (June 10, 1943)
War Town (Community Problems) (June 24, 1943)
Lift Your Heads (British Morale) (July 8, 1943)
Report from the Aleutians (July 30, 1943)
Black Marketing (August 19, 1943)
One Day Sooner (War Bonds) (September 2, 1943)
Glamour Girls of '43 (Women in Industry) (September 2, 1943)
Winston Churchill Buys War Bond (September 9, 1943)
Last Will of Tom Smith (National War Fund) (September 9, 1943)
Oil Is Blood (Saga of Oil) (September 23, 1943)
Angels of Mercy (U.S. Cadet Nurses) (September 30, 1943)
American Saboteur (October 1, 1943)
Day of Battle (Aircraft Carrier) (October 7, 1943)
Suggestion Box (War Industry) (October 21, 1943)
Let's Share and Play Square (Rationing) (October 28, 1943)
Family Feud (Home Conservation) (November 4, 1943)
Tin Can Salvage (November 11, 1943)
Battle of Russia (November 11, 1943)
Food and Magic (Conserve Food) (November 18, 1943)
Is Your Trip Necessary? (November 25, 1943)
Chief Neely Reports to the Nation (Waves) (December 2, 1943)
Save Waste Paper (December 9, 1943)
Brothers in Blood (Blood Donors) (December 16, 1943)
Destination Island X (Seabees) (December 23, 1943)
No Exceptions (Homefront Support) (December 30, 1943)

1944
What If They Quit? (Treasury) (January 6, 1944)
The Price of Rendova (What capture of island cost in men and materials) (January 6, 1944)
Help Save Fighting Fuel (January 20, 1944)
At His Side (Red Cross) (January 27, 1944)
File Your Income Tax Return Early (Treasury) (February 3, 1944)
Help Your Grocer (WPB—War Production Board) (February 18, 1944)

Help Save Tires Now (WPB) (March 2, 1944)
With the Marines at Tarawa (Combat Report) (March 2, 1944)
Why of Wartime Taxes (March 9, 1944)
Prices Unlimited (Rationing) (March 16, 1944)
Fight Waste (WPB) (March 23, 1944)
America's Hidden Weapon (Food) (March 30, 1944)
A Personal Message to the Black Market (OPA—Office of Price Admin-
    istration) (April 6, 1944)
The Negro Soldier (April 13, 1944)
The Memphis Belle (April 13, 1944)
Women and Victory (WMC—War Manpower Commission) (April 20,
    1944)
It's Your War Too (Women in Uniform) (April 20, 1944)
No Alternative (Gasoline Rationing) (April 27, 1944)
Conserve Paper (May 4, 1944)
Skirmish on the Home Front (Economic Stabilization) (May 11, 1944)
Victory Gardens (WPB) (May 18, 1944)
Road to Victory (5th War Loan) (May 18, 1944)
Reward Unlimited (Cadet Nurses) (May 18, 1944)
Treasury Bulletin (War Loan) (June 1, 1944)
Movies at War (Film-troops overseas) (June 8, 1944)
Victory Vacation (WPB) (June 20, 1944)
Attack! The Battle for New Britain (Combat Report) (June 20, 1944)
Young America Backs "Fighting Fifth" (War Loan) (June 22, 1944)
The Liberation of Rome (Army Combat Report) (July 13, 1944)
The Last Furlough (WPB) (July 13, 1944)
Prepare for Winter (WPB) (July 20, 1944)
Battle Stations (Spars) (July 27, 1944)
Manning the Victory Fleet (Recruiting Seamen) (August 3, 1944)
Memo for Joe (National War Fund) (August 10, 1944)
Are You a High School Graduate? (Back to School) (August 17, 1944)
Report to Judy (Waves Recruiting) (August 24, 1944)
The War Speeds Up (September 7, 1944)
Car Sharing (September 14, 1944)
Battle for the Marianas (September 21, 1944)
Red Cross Home Nursing (September 21, 1944)
It's Murder (Loose Talk) (October 12, 1944)
Target Japan (Navy) (October 26, 1944)
American Enemy (Department of Agriculture) (November 1, 1944)
169th Anniversary of the Marine Corps (Bonds) (November 2, 1944)
A Message from Lt. Tyrone Power (Bonds) (November 9, 1944)

V-1 the Robot Bomb (November 16, 1944)
Admiral Nimitz Reports on the Pacific (November 23, 1944)
Weapon of War (December 14, 1944)

1945
Brought to Action (Naval Philippines Battle) (January 11, 1945)
What's Your Name (How Workers Aid Fighters) (January 18, 1945)
Seeing Them Through (Red Cross) (February 1, 1945)
Story with Two Endings (Fight Against Inflation) (March 1, 1945)
The Enemy Strikes (Army—Battle of the Bulge) (March 15, 1945)
Fury in the Pacific (Navy, Army, Marine Corps Combat Report) (March 22, 1945)
Watchtower Over Tomorrow (United Nations) (March 29, 1945)
The Two Way Street (Lend Lease explained) (April 12, 1945)
All Star Bond Rally (Treasury) (April 26, 1945)
The Battle of San Pietro (May 3, 1945)
Two Down and One to Go (General Marshall and Points) (May 10, 1945)
Target Tokyo (B-29 Campaign Reports) (May 24, 1945)
On to Tokyo (General Marshall on Japanese Task) (May 31, 1945)
To the Shores of Iwo Jima (Marine Combat Report) (June 7, 1945)
War Comes to America (Capra's *Why We Fight*) (June 14, 1945)
Fight for the Sky (Allied Combat Pilots) (June 21, 18945)
Something You Didn't Eat (Disney on Balanced Diet) (June 28, 1945)
The Fleet That Came to Stay (Navy at Okinawa) (July 26, 1945)
Here Come the Yanks (National War Fund) (August 30, 1945)
What Every Veteran Should Know (September 13, 1945)
The True Glory (Eisenhower's Final Film Report) (October 4, 1945)
That Justice Be Done (Justice Jackson Indicts Nazis) (October 18, 1945)
Hollywood Victory Caravan (Victory Loan) (November 1, 1945)
To Win the Peace (Victory Loan) (November 11, 1945)
Welcome Home (Army Veteran's Bureau) (November 22, 1945)
We've Got Another Bond to Buy (Victory Loan) (November 25, 1945)
Appointment in Tokyo (MacArthur's Final Film Report) (December 8, 1945)
UNRAA Reports to the U.S. (December 20, 1945)
Freedom and Famine (December 27, 1945)
    Source: War Activities Committee

This section lists research sources and a few observations, cued by page number and identifying phrase. Although not strictly necessary bibliographically, the trade press headlines were too tantalizing to omit.

Chapter 1: Hollywood's War

Page 1. **Veronica Lake shears:** "Ado about Hair-Do," *Motion Picture Herald*, February 20, 1943, p. 9.

Page 2. **From the nickelodeon:** Among the notable studies of Hollywood and the Second World War are Bernard F. Dick, *The Star-Spangled Screen: The American World War II Film* (Lexington: University Press of Kentucky, 1985), a thorough overview of Hollywood's war work; Clayton R. Koppes and Gregory D. Black, *Hollywood Goes to War: How Politics, Profits, and Propaganda Shaped World War II Movies* (New York: Free Press, 1987), which makes extensive use of Office of War Information (OWI) archives; Colin Schindler, *Hollywood Goes to War: Films and American Society 1939–*

1952 (London: Routledge and Kegan Paul, 1979), a lively and industry-wise discussion; and Lawrence H. Suid, *Guts and Glory: Great American War Movies* (Reading, Mass.: Addison-Wesley, 1978), a study that combines a military and motion picture expertise. The essential contemporary works are *Movie Lot to Beach Head: The Motion Picture Goes to War and Prepares for the Future* (Garden City, N.Y.: Doubleday, Doran, 1945), and *Movies At War*, the War Activities Committee (WAC) official record. Otto Friedrich paints a vivid portrait of the motion picture community in the 1940s in *City of Nets: A Portrait of Hollywood in the 1940s* (New York: Harper and Row, 1986).

Page 2.   **David Denby vented:** David Denby, "Fighting the Good Fight on Film," *Premiere* (August 1989), p. 23.

Page 2.   **Walt Whitman remarked:** From the "Specimen Days" section of Whitman's *Specimen Days and Collect* (1882–83), reprinted in *The Norton Anthology of American Literature* (New York: Norton, 1989), pp. 2104–2105. Whitman's comment on the refusal of the artist to render the true horror of the Civil War is taken up by literary historian and World War II combat veteran Paul Fussell in *Wartime: Understanding and Behavior in the Second World War* (New York: Oxford University Press, 1989). Yet in his bitter assault on the lies and duplicities of public rhetoric during 1941–45, Fussell hardly deigns to consider the "Disneyfied" motion picture record as worthy of contempt.

Page 3.   **Disposable as art:** David Bordwell, *Making Meaning: Inference and Rhetoric in the Interpretation of Cinema* (Cambridge: Harvard University Press, 1989), sizes up the shifting templates of academic film criticism.

Page 3.   **Thus Guy Debord:** Guy Debord, *Society of the Spectacle* (Detroit: Black and Red, 1983), sec. 8.

Page 3.   **I can't help thinking:** Michael Herr, *Dispatches* (New York: Avon Books, 1978), p. 223; also 199–202.

Page 7.   **Playing against expectations:** Rudy Elie, Jr., "American Servicemen in the Pacific Put Ceiling on Sex—for USO Shows," *Variety*, May 30, 1945, pp. 1, 55.

Page 7.   **They showed a movie:** Ernie Pyle, *Last Chapter* (New York: Henry Holt, 1946), p. 87.

Page 7.   **He must weigh:** "Ernie Pyle Sets Rules for Own Role in Pic," *Variety*, March 29, 1944, p. 3.

Page 7.   **Producer Lester Cowan:** Meredith himself recalls that the fix was in from the start and that presidential aide Harry Hopkins personally phoned him with the offer. Leonard Maltin, "FFM Interviews Burgess Meredith," in Maltin, ed., *Hollywood: The Movie Factory* (New York: Popular Library, 1976), p. 218.

Page 7.   **On June 9, 1945:** "Ernie Pyle's 'GI Joe' Pic Preem June 9 in Okinawa," *Variety*, May 30, 1945, p. 7.

Page 8. **When I see Japs:** *Yank*, June 16, 1944, p. 14.

Page 8. **Occasionally remarked a mordant:** *Yank*, December 10, 1943, p. 18.

Page 9. **A GI in Sicily:** "Real War Lacks Reel Touch," *Motion Picture Herald*, April 12, 1943, p. 51.

Page 9. **In 1944 the Department:** "U.S. Survey Shows Films Get 80% to 85% of Amusement Coin," *Variety*, July 19, 1944, pp. 1, 38.

Page 10. **Classical Hollywood cinema:** Margaret Farrand Thorpe gives a good reading of the industry's sense of itself on the eve of war in "Eighty-Five Million a Week," the opening chapter of *America at the Movies* (New Haven: Yale University Press, 1939).

Page 13. **Actually if you stop:** Abel Green, " 'WB's Patriotic Cycle, in Its Service to U.S., Worth Any Price'—J. L. Warner," *Variety*, July 28, 1943, pp. 2, 46.

Page 13. **The main thing:** "Spyros Skouras Brushes Off Industry Beefs—'War Effort the Main Thing,' " *Variety*, May 20, 1942, p. 5.

Page 13. **At present boasted:** Mori Krushen, "Films Big Gains in Decade," *Variety*, December 8, 1943, pp. 1, 47.

Page 14. **Jack Warner dated:** Jack Warner, *My First Hundred Years in Hollywood* (New York: Random House, 1964), p. 249. Regarding Jack Warner's premature anti-Nazism: Warner was certainly one of Hollywood's earliest and most passionate anti-Nazis, but there is a curious ellipsis in the explanation he gives for his motivation. In his autobiography Warner claims that the murder of one Joe Kauffman, whom he identifies as Warner Bros.'s chief salesman in Germany, animated his antipathy toward the Third Reich. According to Warner, Kauffman was beaten to death in 1937 in a Berlin back alley by Nazi thugs. The incident is noted in Schindler, *Hollywood Goes to War*, p. 9; Lester D. Freidman, *Hollywood's Image of the Jew* (New York: Frederick Ungar, 1982), p. 82; and Neil Gabler, *An Empire of Their Own: How the Jews Created Hollywood* (New York: Crown, 1988), p. 342. All three authors cite Warner as their sole source. However, after a painstaking and somewhat obsessive search of the likely archives and numerous bothersome inquiries to patient film scholars, this author has been unable to find any independent verification of Warner's story or indeed the very existence of a Joe Kauffman.

Page 14. **At 20th Century-Fox:** "Skouras Nephew Executed by Nazis," *Hollywood Reporter*, February 24, 1943, p. 1.

Page 14. **George J. Schaefer:** "George J. Schaefer's Son, Lt. James Gerard, 27, a D-Day Casualty," *Variety*, June 28, 1944, p. 21.

Page 14. **Joseph I. Breen:** "Two Breen Boys Wounded," *Variety*, August 15, 1944, p. 15.

Page 15. **I am thrilled:** Darryl F. Zanuck, *Tunis Expedition* (New York: Random House, 1943), pp. 25, 27.

Chapter 2: Leni Riefenstahl's Contribution to the American War Effort

Page 16. **In a less escapist:** Alfred Kazin, *Starting Out in the Thirties* (Boston: Little, Brown, 1962), p. 166.

Page 17. **In the waning days:** "Melancholy Baby," *Motion Picture Herald*, May 26, 1945, p. 9.

Page 18. **Like the Nuremberg rallies:** Among the many studies of Nazi propaganda are Jay W. Baird, *The Mythical World of Nazi War Propaganda, 1939–1945* (Minneapolis: University of Minnesota Press, 1974) and David Welch, ed., *Nazi Propaganda: The Power and the Limitations* (London: Croom Helm, 1983). For a provocative analysis of the aesthetics of Nazism, see Peter Cohen's film *The Architecture of Doom* (1989).

Page 20. **We have seen:** "Coe Sees Films Helping to Win World Peace," *Motion Picture Herald*, August 7, 1943, p. 18.

Page 20. **Although never commercially released:** On the international release and distribution of *Olympia* see Cooper C. Graham, *Leni Riefenstahl and Olympia* (Metuchen, N.J.: Scarecrow Press, 1986), pp. 154–249, esp. pp. 210–26 on the American market. Graham notes that *Triumph of the Will* was screened in German enclaves in the big cities and that *Olympia* was shown, probably in a pirated print, in New York in 1940.

Page 20. **Visiting Germany in 1938:** The Josef von Sternberg quote is in Leni Riefenstahl, *Memoiren* (München: Albert Knaus, 1987), p. 300. Although von Sternberg's autobiography omits any plaudits for *Triumph of the Will*, he regally numbers Riefenstahl among "students of my work" and recalls that along with the rest of Weimar Germany, she hung around the set of *The Blue Angel*. Interestingly, he misremembers the film title as *The Will to Triumph*. Von Sternberg, *Fun in a Chinese Laundry* (New York: Macmillan, 1965), p. 144.

Page 20. **Siegfried Kracauer:** Siegfried Kracauer, "Propaganda and the Nazi War Film" (1942), reprinted in *From Caligari to Hitler: A Psychological Study of the German Film* (Princeton: Princeton University Press, 1947; London: Dennis Dobson, 1947), pp. 303, 278. Less cinematically minded observers were not as attentive to Riefenstahl's contribution. In a 1938 survey of the Nuremberg rallies for *Public Opinion Quarterly*, Thorton Sinclair makes no mention of either *Triumph of the Will* or Riefenstahl. Sinclair, "The Nazi Party Rally at Nuremberg," *Public Opinion Quarterly* (October 1938): 570–83.

Page 20. **Photos show her:** The captions are from the Associated Press photos of Riefenstahl's New York arrival, on file at the Stichting Nederlands Foto-& Grafisch Centrum, Haarlem, the Netherlands.

Page 21. **The fashionable coverage:** For the trade angle on *Olympia*, see

"Riefenstahl Coming to Peddle Picture," *Hollywood Reporter*, November 3, 1938, p. 11. Riefenstahl's version of her American tour is in *Memoiren*, pp. 322–32. Like most ex-Nazi memoirs, the need to exculpate and excuse vies with a selective memory. Susan Sontag's "Fascinating Fascism," reprinted in Bill Nichols, ed., *Movies and Methods*, 2 vols. (Berkeley: University of California Press, 1976), 1:31–44, remains the essential essay on the Leni Riefenstahl mystique.

Page 21. **Nowhere did Riefenstahl:** "Leni Riefenstahl Still Getting Film Business' Brushoff," *Variety*, December 7, 1938, pp. 1, 55. See also "Rambling Reporter," *Hollywood Reporter*, November 30, 1938, p. 2. According to Riefenstahl, director King Vidor admired her work, but Vidor makes no mention of Riefenstahl in his autobiography, *A Tree Is Still a Tree* (New York: Harcourt, Brace, 1952). The anti-Riefenstahl ad is in the *Hollywood Reporter*, November 29, 1938, p. 5. A fine account of Riefenstahl's American trip and Hollywood's reaction is in Glenn B. Infield, *Leni Riefenstahl: The Fallen Film Goddess* (New York: Thomas Y. Cromwell, 1976), pp. 175–85.

Page 21. **It scared the hell:** Capra made the remark in his discussion of *Triumph of the Will* with Bill Moyers in "World War II: Propaganda Battles" from the PBS series *A Walk through the Twentieth Century* (1982).

Page 22. **Thirty years later:** Frank Capra, *The Name Above the Title* (New York: Macmillan, 1971), pp. 362–63.

Page 22. **Triumph of the Will:** Philip Dunne, "The Documentary in Hollywood," in Richard Meran Barsam, ed., *Nonfiction Film Theory and Criticism*, (New York: E. P. Dutton, 1976), p. 159.

Page 23. **At MOMA Iris Barry:** Letter from Iris Barry to Nelson Rockefeller, Coordinator of Inter-American Affairs, November 24, 1942, on file at the Washington National Records Center (hereafter WNRC), Suitland, Md. (RG 229, Box 211, Entry 1, "German Films" file).

Page 23. **Throughout the war she:** Reports of Riefenstahl's "liquidation" are mentioned in Sgt. Alfred W. Rhodes, Jr., "German Propaganda Movies in Two Wars," *American Cinematographer* (January 1943), pp. 10–11, 28.

Page 24. **While public screenings:** Richard Thompson, *Film Propaganda: Soviet Russia and Nazi Germany* (London: Croom Helm, 1979), p. 177.

Page 24. **When Army Chief of Staff:** Capra, *The Name Above the Title*, pp. 361–62.

Page 24. **By common agreement:** "Film Biz Pressing Our Government for Better Coverage of the War," *Variety*, July 22, 1942, pp. 4, 18.

Page 25. **In an address:** Francis S. Harmon, "Movies as Propaganda," in *The Command Is Forward: Selections from Addresses on the Motion Picture Industry in War and Peace* (New York: Richard R. Smith, 1944), pp. 8–9. In his 1945 account of the Hays Office, Raymond Moley offered a caveat that underlined the popular usage, "I have used the word 'propaganda' with no sinister implications." Moley, *The Hays Office* (Indianapolis and New York: Bobbs-Merrill, 1945), p. 112. A notable departure from Hollywood's traditional aversion to overt intrusion into politics occurred during Upton Sinclair's 1934 campaign for governor of California. With a sophistication and unscrupulousness worthy of the Reichsfilmkammer, MGM filmed bogus man-on-the-street interviews and presented the well-rehearsed anti-Sinclair smears as "newsreels" in theaters throughout the state. The spots were widely thought to have torpedoed Sinclair's chances. See Upton Sinclair, "The Movies as Political Propaganda," in William J. Perlman, ed., *The Movies on Trial* (New York: MacMillan, 1936), pp. 192–94.

Page 25. **Ford looked at me:** Robert Parrish, "Fact Meets Fiction in a World War II Celluloid Face-off," *Smithsonian* (March 1986), p. 164. See also Parrish, "The Battle of Midway," in *Growing Up in Hollywood* (Boston: Little, Brown, 1976), pp. 144–51.

Page 26. **In 1943 American Cinematographer:** Rhodes, Jr., "German Propaganda Movies in Two Wars," p. 11.

Page 26. **In 1942 Variety shamefully:** "D.C. Brasshats' Short Sightedness on Propaganda Pix Nearing a Crisis," *Variety*, August 19, 1942, p. 47.

Page 26. **These films were shown:** "Nazis Are Using Films for Conquest and Pacification," *Hollywood Reporter*, September 21, 1942, p. 7.

Page 27. **According to discomforting reports:** "Film Biz Pressing Our Government for Better Coverage of the War," *Variety*, July 22, 1942, pp. 4, 18.

Page 27. **Lacy W. Kastner:** "OWI Film Aim Is to Beat Nazis Among Neutrals," *Motion Picture Herald*, August 1, 1942, p. 16.

Page 27. **Ruefully observing how:** Kracauer, *From Caligari to Hitler*, p. 278.

Page 27. **When the Motion Picture Society:** "Propaganda Lesson," *Motion Picture Herald*, January 30, 1943, p. 9. During the segment from *Triumph of the Will*, the *Hollywood Reporter* heard chuckling from the crowd at "der Führer's strutting" and disapproved sternly of such "a prideful and frivolous reaction" to so "cunningly planned and darkly prophetic [an] example of threatening propaganda."

Page 27. **Films are a field:** "Elmer Davis Says Mellett's Govt. Film Bureau Will Continue Its Function; Embarrassed by Praise," *Variety*, June 17, 1942, p. 4.

Page 28. **Lowell Mellett head of:** "Mellett's Trial Balloon Bursts; Prods. Stand Pat," *Hollywood Reporter*, December 21, 1942, p. 7.

Page 28. **Col. Kirke B. Lawton:** Hearings Before the Special Senate Committee Investigating the National Defense Program, 78th Cong., 1st sess., February 16, 1943, p. 6903.

Page 29. **Announcing the screening:** "American Soldiers See German Film of War," *Stars and Stripes*, January 29, 1943, p. 4.

Page 29. **In the combat report:** "Propaganda in Reverse," *Motion Picture Herald*, March 3, 1945, p. 5.

Page 29. **Circulated stateside:** "Hitler, Plus Lambeth Walk Equals a Panic," *Box Office*, January 17, 1942, p. 11.

Page 29. **Every night soldiers:** Sgt. Arthur Barschdorf, "Japs Broadcast to U.S. Troops Presents Popeye and Poppycock," *Yank*, July 9, 1943, p. 6.

Page 30. **In 1944 with the:** " 'Tokyo Rose,' Other Propagandists for Japs Get U.S. Radio 'Sponsor,' " *Variety*, August 9, 1944, p. 1.

Page 34. **We have not sought:** "Academy Hears Mellett Make 'Faith' Award," *Motion Picture Herald*, March 6, 1943, p. 19.

Page 35. **As the Hollywood Reporter:** "Axis Influence in No. Africa Being Overcome by U.S. Pix," *Hollywood Reporter*, January 18, 1943, p. 5.

Chapter 3: Production Codes

Page 36: **The familiar and unquestioned:** Joseph Breen's version of his epoch-making role in the Production Code enforcement system is told in Jack Vizzard, *See No Evil: Life Inside a Hollywood Censor* (New York: Simon and Schuster, 1970), pp. 44–56. For a guided excursion through the PCA archives see Leonard J. Leff and Jerold L. Simmons, *The Dame in the Kimono: Hollywood Censorship and the Production Code from the 1920s to the 1960s* (New York: Grove Weidenfeld, 1990).

Page 37. **Breen a man notoriously:** "Code Stands in War Too Says Breen," *Motion Picture Herald*, June 27, 1942, p. 40.

Page 38. **In 1942 Breen issued:** "Brief in Regard to *In Which We Serve*," *In Which We Serve* Production Code Administration file (hereafter, PCA file), Academy of Motion Picture Arts and Sciences, Margaret Herrick Library, Beverly Hills, California (emphasis added). All PCA communications went out under Breen's name.

Page 38. **The power of Casablanca's:** Robert B. Ray, *A Certain Tendency of the Hollywood Cinema, 1930–1980* (Princeton: Princeton University Press, 1985), pp. 110, and 89–112.

Page 38. **It is bad taste:** "Purity-Sealer Breen Sees Little Change in What's Bad for Pictures," *Variety*, June 10, 1942, p. 7 (emphasis added). See also "Industry Awaits Orders on Its Future in War," *Motion Picture Herald*, December 13, 1941, p. 13.

Page 39. **On June 5, 1940:** "In Announcing Griffiths' OWI Post, Hoyt Plugs Film Biz's Co-op with U.S.," *Variety*, August 29, 1943, p. 22.

Page 39. **With the progressive decline:** Bernard F. Dick, *The Star-Spangled Screen: The American World War II Film* (Lexington: University Press of Kentucky, 1985), pp. 67–68.

Page 39. **Singling out the trailblazing:** " 'Nazi Spy' Spears Hitler Regime," *Hollywood Reporter*, December 6, 1938, pp. 1, 6. See also "Hollywood to Ask Exhib Co-op on War on Nazis," *Film Daily*, December 12, 1938, pp. 1, 10.

Page 40.   **In September 1941:** Hearings Before a Subcommittee on Interstate Commerce into "Moving Picture Screen and Radio Propaganda," 77th Cong., 2d sess., September 9–26, 1941.

Page 42.   **After Pearl Harbor:** For examples of industry gloating on the first anniversary of Pearl Harbor, see "Leading Productions," *Showmen's Trade Review*, December 26, 1942, p. 19, and "With an Eye to the Future," *Box Office*, December 16, 1942, pp. 6–7.

Page 42.   **On December 18, 1941:** Again, the most extensive discussion of Hollywood and the OWI is Clayton R. Koppes and Gregory D. Black, *Hollywood Goes to War: How Politics, Profits, and Propaganda Shaped World War II Movies* (New York: Free Press, 1987). See also Cedric Larson, "The Domestic Motion Picture Work of the Office of War Information," *Hollywood Quarterly* 3 (1947–48): 434–44.

Pages 42–43.   **In June 1942:** "Information, Please," *Motion Picture Herald*, June 20, 1942, p. 9.

Page 43.   **The agency that some:** Statement by Sen. Harry F. Byrd (D–Va.), press release May 2, 1942, on file in the Quigley Archives, Special Collections, Georgetown University Library.

Page 43.   **It is not possible:** William Weaver, "Three Government Units Deal Direct with Studios," *Motion Picture Herald*, July 11, 1942, p. 13.

Page 43.   **In January 1943:** William Weaver, "OWI Outlines 'Voluntary' Propaganda Requirement," *Motion Picture Herald*, January 9, 1943, p. 15.

Page 44.   **Speaking to the press:** "Censored," *Motion Picture Herald*, January 15, 1944, p. 9. A marvelous firsthand account of the journalistic rites of wartime Washington is "Press Lords and Reporters," in David Brinkley, *Washington Goes to War* (New York: Ballantine, 1988), pp. 165–92.

Page 45.   **On board of their:** "Films for Friendly Nations Must Avoid Provocation, Please OWI," *Variety*, October 21, 1942, p. 1.

Page 45.   **I want no censorship:** "President Calls Screen to War, Defines Nature of Restrictions," *Motion Picture Herald*, December 27, 1941, p. 13. FDR's reassurance is quoted in "Trade's Alarm over Mellett-OWI Censorship Ideas Begins to Abate," *Variety*, December 12, 1942, p. 6.

Page 45.   **The most widely circulated:** "Manual of Themes," *Motion Picture Herald*, July 4, 1942, p. 9.

Page 46.   **The emphasis in:** "The OWI Critiques," *Motion Picture Herald*, September 19, 1942, p. 9.

Page 46.   **Typical was the presumption:** "Hollywood Spanked for 'Sloughing' Cause of Democracy in War Films," *Variety*, June 17, 1942, p. 1.

Page 47.   **The OWI has entrusted:** Walter Wanger, "OWI and Motion Pictures," *Public Opinion Quarterly* (Spring 1943): 103.

Page 47.   **Martin Quigley:** Martin Quigley, "The OWI-Policy and Performance," *Motion Picture Herald*, March 6, 1943, p. 2.

Page 47.   **Annoyingly keen on:** Weaver, "Three Government Units Deal Direct with Studios," pp. 13–14. For representative resentful remarks on

Poynter see "Mellett's Trial Balloon; Prods. Stand Pat," *Hollywood Reporter*, December 21, 1942, p. 7 ("Poynter's proffered interference proceeded out of bounds in his criticism of pictures that had nothing to do with the war"), and Will Hays, *The Memoirs of Will Hays* (New York: Doubleday, 1955), p. 532 ("Nelson Poynter, sent as a government representative to the Coast, created some added complications and was later relieved of his duties there. . . . Experienced movie producers could hardly be expected to take kindly to 'advice' much less supervision from an inexperienced layman—government or no").

Page 47. **Nicholas M. Schenck:** "Nick Schenck–Mellett Statement," *Variety*, December 30, 1942, p. 6.

Page 47. **In his official communications:** Weaver, "Three Government Units Deal Direct with Studios," p. 13.

Page 47. **In 1942 Sam Goldwyn:** "Too Hot," *Motion Picture Herald*, August 29, 1942, p. 9.

Page 47. **Smelling a power grab:** "Mellett Trial Balloon Bursts," *Hollywood Reporter*, December 21, 1942, p. 1.

Page 48. **Responding with an exculpatory:** Earl A. Dyer, "Another Government Film Experiment Ends," *Box Office*, July 17, 1943, pp. 22, 25–26. Written on the occasion of Mellett's resignation, Dyer's article is a tempered, comprehensive, and exceptionally useful review of OWI–film industry relations.

Page 48. **More maladroitly Elmer Davis:** "OWI Chief Says U.S. Has No Idea of Censoring Pix," *Hollywood Reporter*, December 24, 1942, p. 4.

Page 48. **On March 15, 1943:** Dyer, "Another Government Film Experiment Ends," p. 25.

Page 49. **The filming of General:** "Indie Buys Life of General Mitchell over Army Frown," *Hollywood Reporter*, June 10, 1942, p. 1.

Page 49. **According to chief censor:** "Set Up U.S. Boards to Check Incoming and Outgoing Films for Propaganda," *Variety*, June 10, 1942, p. 6. The Office of Censorship Code, issued December 11, 1942, is reprinted in the *Hollywood Reporter*, December 14, 1942, p. 4. Hollywood paid more attention to the Office of Censorship than the other way around. In the agency's official history, issued when it closed shop in November 1945, the motion picture industry is barely mentioned. Cable, postal, press, and radio censorship took precedent. The Office of Censorship places Hollywood production in fairly insulting company: "Censorship Boards of Review were set up to censor motion picture films leaving and entering the country. One was established in New York City to censor motion picture newsreels, one in Hollywood to censor feature motion pictures, and a third in Rochester, N. Y. to handle amateur and still motion pictures." *A Report on the Office of Censorship* (Washington, D.C.: GPO, 1945), p. 12. See also "Films Lauded for Fine Job During War Export Period; End Censorship," *Variety*, May 30, 1945, p. 7.

Page 49. **It took an intense:** Red Kann, "On the March," *Motion Picture Herald*, June 26, 1943, p. 14.

Page 49. **Among the films banned:** "Censors Ban Three Films," *Hollywood Reporter*, August 12, 1942, p. 13.

Page 50. **Another unsavory disturbance:** "OWI Kayoes 'Tomorrow the World'; Seen As 'Too Sympathetic' to the Nazis," *Variety*, January 24, 1945, p. 1.

Page 50. **As far as the:** "Only U.S. and Axis Citizens Can Be Villains Now," *Hollywood Reporter*, January 19, 1943, p. 7.

Page 50. **In 1942 Republic Pictures:** "Fu Manchu Shelved," *Hollywood Reporter*, July 9, 1942, p. 1, and "Fu Manchu Whitewash," *Hollywood Reporter*, July 27, 1942, p. 7.

Page 50. **What really distinguished:** William Weaver, "OWI Keeps Watchful Eye on Films Despite Cut," *Motion Picture Herald*, August 14, 1943, p. 30.

Page 51. **Foreign markets for:** "OWI Kayoes 'Tomorrow the World; Seen as Too Sympathetic to Nazis," *Variety*, January 24, 1945, p. 1.

Page 51. **The overseas branch:** Weaver, *Motion Picture Herald*, August 14, 1943, p. 30.

Page 51. **At the overseas branch:** "Riskin Bans His Own Picture from Overseas," *Hollywood Reporter*, March 4, 1943, p. 1.

Page 51. **In 1943 Cowboy Commandos:** Kann, "On the March," p. 16.

Page 52. **For your information:** Teletype to George A. Barnes, Washington, D.C., from Ulric Bell, San Francisco, November 12, 1943, and teletype to Alan Murray, Washington, D.C., from Ulric Bell, Hollywood, December 11, 1943, WNRC (RG 208, Box 3509, Entry 566).

Page 52. **Likewise, after V-E Day:** "While Censorship Off OWI Can Still Hold Up U.S. Film Shipments," *Variety*, June 6, 1945, p. 25.

Page 52. **The war years were:** Leff and Simmons, *The Dame in the Kimono*, p. 122.

Page 53. **We remind you again:** Breen to Maurice Pivar, Universal Pictures, July 9, 1943, and July 19, 1943 (*Gung Ho!*, PCA file).

Page 53. **Cautioning that:** Breen to William Gordon, RKO Pictures, October 13, 1942 (*Hitler's Children*, PCA file).

Page 54. **Similarly for the depiction:** Breen to William Gordon, April 21, 1943 (*Behind the Rising Sun*, PCA file).

Page 54. **A mid-1943 conference:** "Bad War News As Well As Good Will Be Given Public," *Hollywood Reporter*, September 7, 1943, pp. 1, 2.

Page 54. **Like Breen, Will Hays:** "Hays Tells How Screen Serves War Cause," *Motion Picture Herald*, April 17, 1943, p. 18.

Page 54. **Applying the prewar standards:** "He Man, Fighting Words in Coward's 'Serve' (UA) and *March of Time*'s Pic, 'Marines,' May Revise Prod. Formulas," *Variety*, December 12, 1942, p. 46.

Page 54. **The March of Time appealed:** "MOT Wins Point But No Changes in Code," *Film Daily*, January 22, 1943, pp. 1, 5.

Page 54.   **We went through hell:** Bill Formby, "Hell of a Fuss," *Box Office*, January 1, 1943, p. 18.

Page 56.   **In the most ridiculed:** Raymond Moley, Moley, *The Hays Office* (Indianapolis and New York: Bobbs-Merrill, 1945), p. 94. See also "UA Loses to Hays in Battle of Bastard," *Hollywood Reporter*, December 7, 1942, p. 1.

Page 56.   **Playwright Lillian Hellman:** "Hollywood in Wartime," *Yank*, September 24, 1943, p. 21.

Page 56.   **The cinematically astute censor:** Breen to Col. Jason Joy, 20th Century-Fox, June 14, 1943 (*Happy Land*, PCA file).

Page 56.   **The most lascivious:** A full discussion of *The Outlaw* controversy is in Leff and Simmons, *The Dame in the Kimono*, pp. 112–40, and Murray Schumach, *The Face on the Cutting Room Floor: The Story of Movies and Television Censorship* (New York: DaCapo Press, 1975), pp. 51–62.

Page 57.   **Prior to the war:** Mike Wear, "Newsreel Execs Pass Buck Back to Gov't for Any 'Pollyanna' Hue," *Variety*, March 18, 1942, p. 6.

Page 57.   **Paramount profited:** "Par Won't Salve Legion on 'Stalingrad' Despite 'B,' " *Variety*, September 20, 1944, p. 8.

Page 57.   **Pennsylvania's Board:** "Pa. Censors Clip 'Battle of Russia' Scenes As 'Indecent,' 'Too Gruesome,' " *Variety*, November 24, 1943, p. 9.

Page 58.   **Seeing too much blood:** "Ohio Censors Slap Soviet War Film," *Hollywood Reporter*, July 6, 1943, p. 9.

Page 58.   **The Army of course:** "The True Glory Goes to Columbia for October Release," *Motion Picture Herald*, August 4, 1945, p. 22.

Page 58.   **Thus the Army subscribes:** "On the March," *Motion Picture Herald*, August 11, 1945, p. 18.

Page 58.   **Nonetheless, part of:** "U.S. Rushes Teheran Films," *Motion Picture Herald*, December 11, 1943, p. 15.

Page 58.   **The Hays Office censored:** "Nazi Atrocity Films Go to Indies After Hays Nixes 'em for MPPDA" and "Hays Action No Ban," *Variety*, May 9, 1945, p. 18.

Pages 58–59.   **The material from Buchenwald:** "Music Hall Atrocity Film Ban Protested," *Hollywood Reporter*, May 7, 1945, p. 1.

Page 59.   **In 1947 when asked:** Hearings Before the Committee on Un-American Activities, 80th Cong., 2d sess., October 20, 1947, p. 75.

Chapter 4: Government Work

Page 60.   **According to the final:** *Movies at War: Reports of the War Activities Committee of the Motion Picture Industry*, vol. 4 (War Activities Committee, 1945), p. 28.

Page 61.   **In a serviceable separation:** "Will Hays Outlines Role of the Screen in War," *Motion Picture Herald*, April 4, 1942, p. 27.

Page 61. **Saving what Walt Disney:** "Inside Stuff," *Variety*, June 24, 1942, p. 25.

Page 61. **Safeguarding Military Secrets:** " 'Military' Film Is Released to Public," *Hollywood Reporter*, July 14, 1942, p. 5.

Page 61. **Jack Warner boasted:** Abel Green, " 'WB's Patriotic Cycle, in Its Service to U.S., Worth Any Price'— J. L. Warner," *Variety*, July 28, 1943, p. 46.

Page 62. **An advertisement for Kodak:** *Motion Picture Herald*, June 30, 1945 (inside back cover).

Page 62. **Overseen by the Navy's:** "On the Navy's Smokestack Circuit," *Business Screen* (December 1944): 221.

Page 62. **The philosophy behind:** Rear Adm. C. H. Woodward, "The Motion Picture Program of the Incentive Division, U.S. Navy," *Journal of the Society of Motion Picture Engineers* (February 1944): 114.

Page 63. **And a measure of perspective:** "Films in the War Effort," *Motion Picture Herald*, August 1, 1942, p. 43.

Page 63. **The production of training:** A concise and comprehensive treatment of the military's motion picture work is in Richard Dyer MacCann, *The People's Films: A Political History of U.S. Government Motion Pictures* (New York: Hastings House, 1973), pp. 118–72.

Page 63. **The full range:** Capt. Edmund North, "The Secondary or Psychological Phase of Training Films," *Journal of the Society of Motion Picture Engineers* (February 1944): 119.

Page 63. **Branches of the armed forces:** The official three-volume history of the Army Signal Corps in World War II is the essential military-minded guide to the various services, branches, and units involved in motion picture production and liaison with what the Office of Military History called "the west coast film industry." George Raynor Thompson et al., *The Signal Corps: The Emergency, the Test, the Outcome* (Washington, D.C.: GPO, 1957), esp. pp. 387–426 of vol. 2.

Page 63. **In February 1943:** All quotes from Hearings Before the Special Committee Investigating the National Defense Program, 78th Cong., 1st sess., February 16, 1943. The wording is slightly different in Andrew H. Older, "Army Lauds Pix Execs. to Senate Committee," *Film Daily*, February 17, 1943, pp. 1, 8.

Page 65. **That April:** All quotes from Hearings Before the Special Committee Investigating the National Defense Program, 78th Cong., April 3, 1943. Again, the wording is slightly different in "Text of Patterson Statement," *Hollywood Reporter*, April 5, 1943, pp. 7, 8. Leonard Mosley, *Zanuck: The Rise and Fall of Hollywood's Last Tycoon* (Boston: Little, Brown, 1984), pp. 197–209, discusses Zanuck's wartime activities. A collection of relevant documents is reprinted in David Culbert, ed., *Film and Propaganda: A Documentary History*, vol. 2 (New York: Greenwood Press, 1990). On the question of motion picture industry malfeasance, Culbert avers: "One turns in vain to these conclusions in a quest for scandal" (p. xvii).

Page 65.   **At a paper delivered:** Lt. William Exton, Jr., USN, "Training Films in the U.S. Navy," *American Cinematographer* (June 1942): 253, 281. Exton later amended his objection to "the *arbitrary* introduction into the training film of the paraphernalia of the entertainment motion picture." Exton, "The Navy's Utilization of Film for Training Purposes," *Journal of the Society of Motion Picture Engineers* (December 1942): 335.

Page 66.   **In September 1942:** North, "The Secondary or Psychological Phase of Training Films," pp. 120–21.

Page 66.   **Capt. Edmund North:** North, "The Secondary or Psychological Phase of Training Films," p. 122.

Page 67.   **Truly, Hollywood:** Col. Kirke B. Lawton, "Role of Film in Carrying GI Recreational Load," *Variety*, January 5, 1944, p. 23.

Page 67.   **I think it made:** Peter Bogdanovich, *John Ford* (Berkeley: University of California Press, 1978), p. 80. See also William K. Everson, "John Ford Goes to War—Against V.D.," in Leonard Maltin, ed., *Hollywood: The Movie Factory* (New York: Popular Library, 1976), pp. 224–29.

Page 67.   **Three Cadets:** Newton E. Meltzer, "The War and the Training Film," *American Cinematographer* (July 1945): 230.

Page 67.   **In Enemy Bacteria:** Hilda Black, "Lucite and Lantz Come Through for the Navy," *American Cinematographer* (November 1945): 372–73, 392.

Page 67.   **Army Air Force trainees were taught:** Lt. William R. McGee, "Cinematography Goes to War," *Journal of the Society of Motion Picture Engineers* (February 1944): 111. See also the brief survey by Maj. Ellis Smith, "Animation in Training Films," *Journal of the Society of Motion Picture Engineers* (September 1943): 225.

Page 68.   **They worked on:** Red Kann, "On the Line," *Motion Picture Herald*, November 6, 1943, p. 16.

Page 68.   **Creative personnel:** Carl Nater, "Walt Disney Studio—A War Plant," *American Cinematographer* (May 1944): 156, 175.

Page 68.   **In 1943, 94 percent:** "Disney Net for Year $431,536," *Motion Picture Herald*, January 15, 1944, p. 55.

Page 68.   **Sandbags and antiaircraft:** "Disney Necessary," *Motion Picture Herald*, March 13, 1943, p. 8. For a book-length study, see Richard Shale, *Donald Duck Joins Up: The Walt Disney Studio During World War II* (Ann Arbor, Mich.: UMI Research Press, 1982).

Page 69.   **In a remark:** Lawton, "Role of Film in Carrying GI Recreational Load," p. 23.

Page 69.   **From the hundreds:** Joseph H. Hazen, "How Films Serve the Army," *Variety*, January 6, 1943, pp. 2, 65.

Page 70.   **The war gave:** Charles F. Hoban, Jr., *Movies That Teach* (New York: Dryden Press, 1946), p. ix. Also relevant is the special issue devoted to "A

Report on the Training Film Program of the United States Navy," *Business Screen* (June 1945).

Page 70. **Recalling his own:** Forrest C. Pogue, *George C. Marshall: Organizer of Victory 1943–1945* (New York: Viking, 1973), pp. 91–92. In an interview with Pogue, Marshall states, "I required that every soldier see [*Prelude to War*] before he left the United States." Probably unaware of the commercial failure of the first entry, he adds, "I always thought it was very tragic that our people [civilians] didn't get the chance to see the pictures."

Page 70. **I want our generals:** "Senator Holman Would Like to Forget About It," *Film Daily*, February 18, 1943, p. 9.

Page 70. **In his factually suspect:** Frank Capra, *The Name Above the Title* (New York: Macmillan, 1971), pp. 361–62. A less Capraesque version of the director's life is in Joseph McBride, *Frank Capra: The Catastrophe of Success* (New York: Simon and Schuster, 1992). On Capra's films, see Richard Glatzer and John Raeburn, *Frank Capra: The Man and His Films* (Ann Arbor, Mich.: University of Michigan Press, 1975), and especially Robert Sklar's "The Imagination of Stability: The Depression Films of Frank Capra" and Richard Meran Barsam's "Why We Fight," in Barsam, ed., *Nonfiction Film Theory and Criticism*, (New York: E. P. Dutton, 1976), pp. 121–38, 149–54. The official military designation for Capra's unit was the 834th Signal Service Photographic Detachment.

Page 74. **One of Hitler's:** "Films Important Aid to Training," *Motion Picture Herald*, March 28, 1942, p. 45.

Page 74. **In the wake of:** "Footage Dearth Stymies Newsreels' Nazi Expose," *Film Daily*, November 21, 1938, p. 10.

Page 75. **By mid-1943:** "New Projectors in ETO Movies," *Stars and Stripes*, August 11, 1943, p. 4.

Page 75. **An approximation of:** Sgt. Bill Davidson, "They Fight with Film," *Yank*, March 5, 1943, pp. 20–21.

Page 75. **Hollywood producers:** "Fan Mags Put Favorable Spotlight on Hollywood's All-Out War Work," *Variety*, January 20, 1943, p. 20.

Page 75. **By 1945 the Army:** "Pix Used as GI Battle Therapy," *Variety*, January 24, 1945, p. 3.

Page 75. **At one time the:** "Facts," *Motion Picture Herald*, March 4, 1944, p. 8.

Page 75. **In language that:** "Special Services Set for Second Front," *Stars and Stripes*, June 2, 1944, p. 2.

Page 75. **In a trade agreement:** "Hot Films Sent U.S. Prisoners," *Stars and Stripes*, February 8, 1944, p. 4.

Page 77. **The unit historian:** Narrative History of the 4th Photo Recon Group (Pacific), July 23, 1942–December 31, 1943, on file at the USAF Historical Research Center at Maxwell Air Force Base, Montgomery, Alabama (hereafter USAF-HRC).

Page 77. **Up on Bouganville:** *Movies at War*, vol. 3 (War Activities Committee, 1944), p. 4.

Page 77. **Another soldier wrote:** "GIs No Like Over S-A USO Femme Troupers or Anti-Negro Pictures," *Variety*, April 25, 1945, p. 11.

Page 77. **More remarkable stories:** Admittedly, this sounds dubious. However, the official record of the War Activities Committee, anticipating skepticism, reproduces a handwritten letter from a GI relating the story. The same letter recounts a less felicitous tale (the GI won't vouch for its accuracy) in which fourteen Japanese in Okinawa were killed in a theater area during a showing of *Hotel Berlin* (*Movies at War* 3:11).

Page 79. **Those who liked:** "What This Picture Did for Me," *Motion Picture Herald*, December 19, 1942, p. 52.

Page 79. **It supplied 150 prints:** "To Show Capra Army Films in War Plants," *Motion Picture Herald*, March 3, 1943, p. 42.

Page 79. **Though Prelude to War:** For the exhibition record of *Prelude to War* see "Capra Pic Goes to Exhibs Free," *Hollywood Reporter*, April 27, 1943, pp. 1, 8; "Better Real War Pix Demanded," *Hollywood Reporter*, May 12, 1943, pp. 1, 4; "Army Cold on Public Showings," *Hollywood Reporter*, June 14, 1943, pp. 1, 6.

Page 79. **I guess I've lost:** "10 Cameramen in Italy Killed in Action—Capra," *Film Daily*, April 12, 1944, p. 10.

Page 80. **Something You Didn't Eat:** "Inside Stuff—Movies," *Variety*, May 30, 1945, p. 25.

Page 81. **An exceptionally stolid:** "Review of *Right of Way*," *Motion Picture Herald*, April 3, 1943, p. 1239.

Page 81. **In 1943 WAC:** Francis S. Harmon, *The Command Is Forward* (New York: Richard R. Smith, 1944), p. 23 (emphasis added).

Page 81. **For more urgent:** "War Shorts Program Okayed; Hoyt Silent on OWI Film Head," *Hollywood Reporter*, July 27, 1943, pp. 1, 9.

Page 82. **Fearing government intervention:** "Industry Police System Proposed to Ensure 100% Showing Gov't Shorts," *Variety*, March 25, 1942, p. 4.

Page 82. **The next month:** "94% Using 'Em," *Variety*, April 15, 1942, p. 5.

Page 82. **Early on:** "Movies Stay: FDR," *Motion Picture Herald*, March 14, 1942, p. 8.

Page 82. **Responding to a call:** "Rubber Matinees," *Motion Picture Herald*, July 7, 1942, p. 60.

Page 83. **The New York premiere:** "Bond Opening Nets $5,750,00 for War Effort," *Motion Picture Herald*, June 6, 1942, p. 69.

Page 83. **Up to now:** Oscar A. Doob, "War Work," *Motion Picture Herald*, April 25, 1942, p. 53.

Pages 83–84. **The worthiest and most:** "First 'Plasma Premiere' a Big Success in Cincinnati," *Box Office*, February 12, 1944, p. 20.

Chapter 5: Genre Work

Page 85. **The fact that no:** Chester Bahn, "For Victory," *The 1942 Film Daily Year Book of Motion Pictures*, p. 36.

Page 86. **Marching as a unit:** Will H. Hays, "Films' Postwar Mission," *Variety*, January 5, 1944, p. 2.

Page 86. **Industry officials loved:** Francis S. Harmon, *The Command Is Forward* (New York: Richard R. Smith, 1944), p. 21.

Page 86. **After film critic Robin:** Robin Wood, "Ideology, Genre, Auteur," *Film Comment* (January–February 1977), p. 47.

Page 86. **The work of genre:** The phrase is from Jack Shadoian, *Dreams and Dead Ends: The American Gangster/Crime Film* (Cambridge: MIT Press, 1979). Thomas Schatz defines and discusses genre in *Hollywood Genres: Formulas, Filmmaking, and the Studio System* (New York: Random House, 1981).

Page 87. **In 1917 disgusted:** Randolph S. Bourne, "The War and the Intellectuals," *Seven Arts* 2 (June 1917), reprinted in *War and the Intellectuals: Collected Essays, 1915–1919* (New York: Harper and Row, 1964), p. 4.

Page 88. **A special government agency:** All subsequent quotes from Creel are from George Creel, *How We Advertised America: The First Telling of the Amazing Story of the Committee on Public Information That Carried the Gospel of Americanism to Every Corner of the Globe* (New York: Harper, 1920), p. 117, and passim; and Creel, *Complete Report of the Chairman of the Committee on Public Information 1917–18–19* (Washington, D.C.: GPO, 1920), pp. 53, 89–90, 93–94. A collection of relevant documents is reprinted in Richard Wood, ed., *Film and Propaganda in America: A Documentary History*, vol. 1, *World War I* (New York: Greenwood Press, 1990). David M. Kennedy, *Over Here: The First World War and American Society* (New York: Oxford University Press, 1980) provides an overview of the Great War homefront.

Page 89. **A. P. Waxman:** A. P. Waxman, "Film Men Made Military History in World War I," *Variety*, January 7, 1942, p. 36.

Page 90. **The declamations:** The title of the standard history of the Creel Committee reveals the media hierarchy and lingering verbal outlook: James R. Mock and Cedric Larson, *Words That Won the War: The Story of the Committee on Public Information 1917–1919* (Princeton: Princeton University Press, 1939).

Page 90. **By 1941 no American:** Plans to reintroduce the practice were never fulfilled. See "4 Min. Men to Spiel from Screen," *Variety*, April 15, 1942, p. 1.

Page 90. **According to film historian:** Terry Ramsaye, "National Film Library," *Motion Picture Herald*, November 18, 1944, p. 7.

Page 90. **Shortly after the Armistice:** Terry Ramsaye, "Report on War," *Motion Picture Herald*, January 1, 1944, p. 7.

Page 91. **By 1944 John G. Bradley:** "For the Records," *Motion Picture Herald*, July 7, 1944, p. 8. Craig W. Campbell surveys the newsreel record of the Great War in *Reel America and World War I: A Comprehensive Filmography and History of Motion Pictures in the United States, 1914–1920* (Jefferson, N.C.: McFarland, 1985), pp. 224–54.

Page 91. **World War I adjudged:** Terry Ramsaye, "On Film Front," *Motion Picture Herald*, August 7, 1943, p. 7.

Page 91. **Limiting itself:** "Screen History Is Repeated," *Motion Picture Herald*, January 16, 1943, p. 13.

Page 92. **Like the poetry:** Although devoted largely to the British scene, Paul Fussell, *The Great War in Modern Memory* (New York: Oxford University Press, 1976) traces the literary legacy of the Great War.

Page 92. **A reporter from Variety:** "Memories of 1918," *Variety*, November 11, 1925, p. 37.

Page 94. **You should take all:** The trope refuses to die. In Frankie Goes to Hollywood's pre-glasnost music video, "Two Tribes" (1983), Andropov and Reagan lookalikes duke it out in a sand pit.

Page 95. **They gave me Wings:** Kevin Brownlow, *The Parade's Gone By . . .* (Berkeley: University of California Press, 1968), p. 174.

Page 95. **The pilots on both:** The knightly gesture is replayed without apparent irony in Blake Edwards's Great War romantic adventure, *Darling Lili* (1970).

Page 97. **In Wings the wild:** The silent cinema compensated as best it could at the more elaborately orchestrated big-city screenings. In the metropolitan engagements of *Wings*, backstage sound effects simulated "the whine and drone of motors in two tones to denote the American and enemy planes." "Review of *Wings*," *Variety*, August 17, 1927, p. 21.

Page 98. **In eruptions of Warner Bros.:** Andrew Bergman interprets this Warner Bros. "social consciousness" in *We're in the Money: Depression America and Its Films* (New York: Harper Colophon Books, 1972), pp. 92–109.

Page 100. **Exhibitors not cognizant:** "Reissue of 'Pacifist' Films at This Time Clashes with Our War Effort," *Variety*, February 25, 1942, pp. 1, 18.

Page 101. **Setting up to aim:** The gesture is mimicked in the movies as well, in *Guadalcanal Diary* (1943) and *The Thing* (1951).

Page 102. **The combat, depicted:** On the Great War reverberations of the Lindbergh cult, see Modris Eksteins, *Rites of Spring: The Great War and the Modern Age* (Boston: Houghton Mifflin, 1989), pp. 241–74.

Page 102. **Released and ballyhooed in:** "Inside Stuff—Pictures," *Variety*, September 29, 1943, p. 24.

Page 102. **According to several Selective:** "Sgt York Film's Influence on War Objectors," *Variety*, December 31, 1941, p. 1.

Page 103. **Warner Bros.'s Air Force:** A word on military nomenclature: In June 1941, a long overdue reorganization within the War Department created the Army Air Force, the ancestor of today's Air Force, which became a separate branch of the Armed Forces in 1947. Under the command of Gen. H. H. Arnold, the Army Air Force comprised the Air Corps (service) and the Air Force Combat Command (combat). Since contemporary references in screen dialogue and studio documents, sometimes even military screen credits and War Department pronouncements, tend to conflate the various different air commands, and since the distinctions can be confusing even when used correctly, the designation "Army Air Force" has been used throughout. For a complete organizational map, consult Wesley Frank Craven and James Lea Corte, eds., *The Army Air Forces in World War II*, vol. 1 (Chicago: University of Chicago Press, 1949), pp. 114–15.

Page 104. **As film historian Jeanine:** Jeanine Basinger, *The World War II Combat Film: Anatomy of a Genre* (New York: Columbia University Press, 1986). Basinger presents a comprehensive catalog and convincing taxonomy for the WWII combat film as a distinct genre.

Page 104. **The practice of aerial bombardment:** H. Bruce Franklin offers a contrary view of the bombing ethos in *War Stars: The Superweapon and the American Imagination* (New York: Oxford University Press, 1988), pp. 91–111.

Page 108. **A famous Hollywood anecdote:** Col. Barney Oldfield, "Dayton's Air Force Museum Owes Much to Hollywood's Morale Films," *Variety*, December 9, 1964, p. 70.

Page 109. **By late 1944:** "Liberator Bombers Want a L'il Plug Too," *Variety*, November 4, 1944, p. 1.

Page 111. **Air Force recruits:** Robert B. Ray discusses "Classic Hollywood's Holding Pattern: The Combat Films of World War II," in Ray, *A Certain Tendency of the Hollywood Cinema, 1930–1980* (Princeton: Princeton University Press, 1985), pp. 113–25.

Page 115. **The OWI wanted:** "Palmer Hoyt Facing Showdown On Shorter Army Pix for Public Showing," *Variety*, July 28, 1943, p. 22.

Page 115. **Released in long form:** "Film Bulletins Get 16,844 Playdates," *Box Office*, January 8, 1944, p. 51.

Page 117. **The interphone dialogue:** The production sheet for *The Memphis Belle* on file at USAF-HRC confirms the postproduction soundtrack work. In PBS's *American Masters* tribute to William Wyler, the director movingly recalls the fear that his hearing would render him unemployable in postwar Hollywood. He is on the verge of tears but calls himself up short. "A lot of guys had it a lot worse," he says.

Page 117. **The Memphis Belle was:** " 'Memphis Belle' Story," in the *Box Office Showmandiser*, June 3, 1944, p. 2.

Page 119. **OWI film analyst:** The OWI report by Barbara Deming—later the author of the idiosyncratic moviegoing memoir *Running Away from Myself: A Dream Portrait of America Drawn from the Films of the Forties* (New York: Grossman, 1969)—is on file at the Motion Picture Division of the Library of Congress.

Page 119. **A box-office report:** *Box Office Showmandiser*, January 22, 1944, p. 12.

Chapter 6: Properly Directed Hatred

Page 122. **In Communiqué:** William R. Weaver, "Films Fostering Hate for Axis Approved," *Motion Picture Herald*, October 3, 1942, p. 34 (emphasis added).

Page 123. **After complaints:** " 'Kill' Song Too Grim," *Variety*, July 14, 1943, p. 1. See also Laurence Bergreen, *As Thousands Cheer: The Life of Irving Berlin* (New York: Viking, 1990), pp. 420–21.

Page 123. **In a thoughtful paper:** John G. Bradley, "Motion Pictures and the War Effort," *Journal of the Society of Motion Picture Engineers* (May 1943): 284.

Page 123. **Americans, the theory:** "Hollywood Cued on Hitler and Hirohito, But Doesn't Even Bother with Musso," *Variety*, May 20, 1942, p. 1.

Page 123. **An OWI film analyst:** The OWI analysis of *This Is the Army* is on file at the Motion Picture Division of the Library of Congress.

Page 124. **The Society for the Prevention:** "Authors See More Than 'Hitler Gang' to Blame for War," *Variety*, June 28, 1944, p. 1.

Page 124. **Noting the difficulties:** "Films Wary of Treatment of Nazis," *Variety*, February 3, 1943, p. 45.

Page 124. **The anti-Hun hysteria:** Pertinent is the study by Otto Klineberg, "Race Prejudice and the War," *Annals of the Academy of Political and Social Sciences* (September 1942): 190–98. Klineberg comments: "Most observers agree that so far in this war Americans have shown remarkably little of that hysterical prejudice against everything of enemy origin which characterized 1917–18."

Page 125. **In cartoons:** On wartime animation, see Michael S. Shull and David E. Welt, *Doing Their Bit: Wartime American Animated Short Films, 1939–1945* (Jefferson, N.C.: McFarland, 1987), and Shale's *Donald Duck Joins Up: The Walt Disney Studio During World War II* (Ann Arbor, Mich.: UMI Research Press, 1982).

Page 126. **The Great Dictator:** Charles J. Maland discusses *The Great Dictator* in *Chaplin and American Culture: The Evolution of a Star Image* (Princeton: Princeton University Press, 1989), pp. 159–94.

Page 126. **To Be Or Not To Be:** William Paul discusses *To Be or Not To Be* in *Ernst Lubitsch's American Comedy* (New York: Columbia University Press, 1983), pp. 223–56.

Page 127.   **A fiery New York Times:** Melchior Lengyel, " 'You Cannot Outwit Wit' Sez Lengyel, Defending H'wood's Satire of Fascism," *Variety*, April 1, 1942, pp. 4, 5.

Page 129.   **There are some very:** From the OWI analysis of *Once Upon a Honeymoon* on file at the Motion Picture Division of the Library of Congress.

Page 130.   **An exhibitor's report:** *Motion Picture Herald*, February 12, 1944, p. 52.

Page 130.   **In an influential front-page:** Robert Gessner, " 'Need Bitter War Films,' " *Variety*, March 11, 1942, pp. 1, 16.

Page 131.   **John Grierson:** "Canada's John Grierson Gives Ideas on Propaganda Function of Gov't Pix," *Variety*, August 26, 1942, p. 27.

Page 131.   **Lowell Mellett:** Abel Green, "U.S. Will 'Cue' Hollywood," *Variety*, May 6, 1942, p. 5.

Page 132.   **Over a report:** "Hollywood Cued on Hitler and Hirohito, But Doesn't Even Bother with Musso," *Variety*, May 20, 1942, p. 1.

Page 132.   **An enemy portrayal:** "RKO Injecting Comedy in All War Background Pix," *Hollywood Reporter*, November 5, 1942, p. 8.

Page 132.   **It was a fine line:** For an overview of the industry consensus on the kinds of war pictures deemed "objectionable to the public, either in whole or in part," consult Bill Formby, "Men and Events," *Box Office*, April 8, 1944, p. 10.

Page 134.   **John Dower's landmark:** John W. Dower, *War without Mercy: Race and Power in the Pacific War, 1941–1945* (New York: Pantheon, 1986), esp. pp. 94–117. Also relevant is Harold Isaacs, *Scratches on Our Minds: American Images of China and India* (New York: J. Day, 1958).

Page 135.   **Derogatory reference:** "Hollywood Cued on Hitler and Hirohito, But Doesn't Even Mention Musso," *Variety*, May 20, 1942, p. 54.

Page 135.   **In a memo:** Memo from Ulric Bell, December 20, 1942, WNRC (RG 208, Box 3509, Entry 566).

Page 136.   **The OWI was apprehensive:** "Studios Await Gov't Edict on Jap Atrocity Pix; Fears Nip Reprisals," *Variety*, October 17, 1943, p. 3.

Page 136.   **The first and only:** "U.S. Meticulously Laying Off Needless Censorship of Films," *Variety*, December 8, 1943, p. 4.

Page 136.   **There will be no trouble:** "War Dept. to OK Scripts on Jap Atrocity Films," *Variety*, March 1, 1944, p. 9.

Page 136.   **Although the Emperor:** Teletype from Robert E. Sherwood to Ulric Bell, January 31, 1944, WNRC (RG 208, Box 3509, Entry 566). See also "Jap Atrocity Revelations Cue U.S. 'Go' Sign on H'wood Propaganda Pix," *Variety*, February 2, 1944, pp. 1, 16.

Page 136.   **The hate revival:** "Jap Atrocities Hypo 3 at B.O.," *Variety*, February 9, 1944, p. 5.

Page 137.   **A lobby display:** *Box Office Showmandiser*, March 3, 1944, p. 12.

Page 137. **This stand may:** "Review of *Behind the Rising Sun,*" *Hollywood Reporter*, July 14, 1943, p. 4.

Page 141. **Shortly after Pearl Harbor:** "How to Tell Japs from the Chinese," *Life*, December 22, 1941, p. 81.

Page 142. **A satisfied Nelson Poynter:** Memo from Nelson Poynter to Lowell Mellett, May 11, 1943, WNRC (RG 208, Box 3509, Entry 566).

Page 143. **The few Japanese-Americans:** "Me No Moto," *Variety*, December 31, 1941, p. 1.

Page 143. **A trade reviewer:** "Review of *Secret Agent of Japan,*" *Variety*, March 11, 1942, p. 8.

Page 143. **Another trouble with cross-racial:** Edward Dmytryk, *It's a Hell of a Life, But Not a Bad Living* (New York: New York Times Books, 1978), p. 56.

Page 143. **Eschewing laugh lines:** "Inside Stuff—Pictures," *Variety*, October 24, 1944, p. 22.

Page 144. **With Communist fellow-traveling:** Because of the postwar investigations by the House Committee on Un-American Activities, Hollywood's modest foray into pro-Soviet melodrama has received more than its fair share of critical and historical attention. One of the most incisive essays is David Culbert's "Our Awkward Ally: *Mission to Moscow* (1943)," in John E. O'Connor and Martin A. Jackson, eds., *American History/American Film: Interpreting the Hollywood Image* (New York: Frederick Ungar, 1979), pp. 121–45.

Page 146. **In 1943 the Stars and Stripes:** "U.S. Jap Combat Team," *Stars and Stripes*, March 15, 1943, p. 6, and "Loyal Americans," *Stars and Stripes*, May 8, 1943, p. 2.

Page 146. **Yank, whose Pacific correspondents:** For example, *Yank*, August 10, 1945, p. 18.

Page 148. **In 1943 Lt. Col. R. P. Presnel:** Lt. Col. R. P. Presnel, "Training Film Production Problems," *Journal of the Society of Motion Picture Engineers* (September 1943): 220.

Chapter 7: Women Without Men

Page 150. **In 1930, writing:** Ruth Morris, " 'Western Front' Is Greatest War Sermon," *Variety*, May 14, 1930, p. 61.

Page 150. **Unfortunately, All Quiet:** "Inside Stuff: The Movies," *Variety*, May 14, 1930, p. 28.

Page 150. **But after 1941, American women:** The recent explosion of feminist scholarship on women, gender, and the Second World War includes Karen Anderson, *Wartime Women: Sex Roles, Family Relations, and the Status of Women During World War II* (Westport, Conn.: Greenwood Press, 1981); Maureen Honey, *Creating Rosie the Riveter: Class, Gender, and Propaganda During World War II* (Amherst: University of Massachusetts Press,

1984); Leila Rupp, *Mobilizing Women for War: German and American Propaganda, 1939–1945* (Princeton: Princeton University Press, 1978); and Susan M. Hartmann, *The Homefront and Beyond: American Women in the 1940s* (Boston and New York: Twayne Publishers, 1982).

Page 150. **In 1942 pollster:** " 'Men Top Pic Fans'—Gallup," *Variety*, August 5, 1942, pp. 3, 18.

Page 151. **In a wry response:** "Pollock Challenges Gallup Findings, Sez Women Sway Men's Pic Choices," *Variety*, August 12, 1942, p. 12 (emphasis added).

Page 153. **Pollock's notion:** "Sex Up the Beautiful Hunk of Men in Film Ads to Lure Unescorted Females," *Variety*, March 11, 1942, pp. 1, 53.

Page 153. **If a face:** Jonah Ruddy and Jonathan Hill, *The Bogey Man: Portrait of a Legend* (London: Souvenir Press, 1965), pp. 71–72.

Page 154. **According to exhibitors:** "Femmes Shying Away from War Pictures," *Variety*, November 18, 1942, pp. 1, 54.

Page 154. **We get walk outs:** "Exhibitors Protest at Flood of War Film, Ask Entertainment," *Motion Picture Herald*, May 8, 1943, p. 13.

Page 154. **As today's feminist documentaries:** Exemplary is Connie Field's documentary *The Life and Times of Rosie the Riveter* (1980) and Aretha Franklin and Annie Lennox's music video "Sisters Are Doin' It for Themselves" (1986).

Page 157. **Might mislead ambitious girls:** From the OWI analysis of *She's in the Army*, on file at the Motion Picture Division of the Library of Congress.

Page 157. **When Congressman John Martin Costello:** "Inside Stuff—Pictures," *Variety*, May 31, 1944, p. 27. The WASPs were formed in August 1943 from the WAFS and the Women's Flying Training Detachment (WFTI). The "acronym sounded catchy for women flyers," remarks Marianne Verges in *On Silver Wings: The Women's Airforce Service Pilots of World War II* (New York: Ballantine, 1991).

Page 158. **Zoot suits:** "Zoot Suits Banned in Films by Hays," *Hollywood Reporter*, April 26, 1943, p. 6.

Page 159. **Paulette Goddard's attire:** "Covering Paulette," *Motion Picture Herald*, December 18, 1943, p. 8.

Page 159. **Luxury clothes:** "Picture Heroines Now Must Be Glamourous in Work Clothes," *Hollywood Reporter*, October 13, 1942, p. 7.

Page 159. **The golden bathtub:** "But Glamourous," *Hollywood Reporter*, December 3, 1942, p. 11.

Page 165. **Even in a war:** John Morton Blum, *V Was for Victory: Politics and American Culture During World War II* (New York: Harcourt Brace Jovanovich, 1976), p. 45.

Page 165. **In adjudging and ranking:** "Glamour in Overalls," *Variety*, January 14, 1942, pp. 5, 16.

Page 166. **Air raids and lights-out drills:** "Washington Disagrees with Hollywood on Comedy Theme," *Hollywood Reporter*, December 2, 1942, p. 8.

Page 177. **Tears and audible bouts:** A Brooklyn exhibitor reported his audience "laughed at the early life of the Sullivans and cried like babies at the end." *Box Office Showmandiser*, July 8, 1944, p. 1.

Page 177. **To an Ohio theater owner:** *Motion Picture Herald*, February 5, 1944, p. 62.

Page 177. **Invite all gold star mothers:** *Box Office*, February 12, 1944, p. 508.

Chapter 8: Keep 'Em Laughing

Page 180. **In my humble opinion:** "Service By Entertainment," *Motion Picture Herald*, May 30, 1942, p. 7.

Page 180. **Valuable as a temporary:** "Films Will Keep National Spirit Soaring," *Motion Picture Herald*, January 17, 1942, p. 22.

Page 181. **Hays's notion:** "Gottlieb Will Entertain Not Instruct in Universal Pix," *Hollywood Reporter*, March 23, 1943, p. 6.

Page 181. **The medicinal metaphor:** "Film Therapy," *Motion Picture Herald*, July 31, 1943, p. 8.

Page 181. **Overwhelmingly preponderant:** "Exhibitors Protest at Flood of War Film, Ask Entertainment," *Motion Picture Herald*, May 8, 1943, pp. 12–14.

Page 182. **For Harry Warner:** "Not Overfed with War Pictures, Says Warner," *Motion Picture Herald*, May 22, 1943, p. 25.

Page 182. **Send more escapist films:** "Boys in So. Pacific Say They Know All About the War, So Send Escapist Pics," *Variety*, December 15, 1943, pp. 4, 55.

Page 182. **Sitting among an unruly:** "Go-Git-'Ems War Pix Fliv with Service Men; Correspondent Details Why," *Variety*, August 11, 1943, p. 3.

Page 182. **At the top of:** "Marines Prefer," *Motion Picture Herald*, July 21, 1945, p. 8 (emphasis added).

Page 183. **In 1943 Paramount's executive:** " 'Paramount Will Cut Down on War Pix,' Says de Sylva," *Hollywood Reporter*, February 23, 1943, p. 3.

Page 183. **Originally slated to end:** Red Kann, "Signals in the Breeze," *Motion Picture Herald*, June 12, 1943, p. 16. Significantly, in its 1951 rerelease *The Sullivans* was rechristened *The Fighting Sullivans*, the title frame in most television prints of the film.

Page 185. **To a 1942 trade:** "Service by Entertainment," *Motion Picture Herald*, May 30, 1942, p. 7.

Page 188. **It was actually:** Sandy Sturges, ed., *Preston Sturges by Preston Sturges: His Life in His Works* (New York: Simon and Schuster, 1990), p. 294.

Page 188. **The age differential:** "Pix Go Hunting for Gals," *Variety*, June 6, 1942, p. 3.

Page 189. **In the later war:** On the wartime musical, see Allen L. Woll, *The Hollywood Musical Goes to War* (Chicago: Nelson Hall, 1983).

Page 189. **At the box office:** "Shift to Comedy," *Motion Picture Herald*, June 5, 1943, p. 8.

Page 190. **Expressing a rankled vox:** "Hollywood Canteen," *Yank*, June 29, 1945, p. 19.

Page 191. **In 1942 Melvyn Douglas:** "Political Friend of Hollywood Scours D.C. Bias as Exemplified by Hullabaloo over Douglas, et al.," *Variety*, February 18, 1942, pp. 5, 55. Incidentally, as a direct result of his insulting remarks about the motion picture industry, Congressman Ford was roundly defeated in the next election by Democrat Will Rogers, Jr. Ford's former district had included Los Angeles.

Page 191. **The next year the:** Hearings Before the Special Committee Investigating the National Defense Program, 78th Cong., 1st sess., April 3, 1943.

Page 191. **In 1942 Yank published:** Sgt. Bill Davidson, "Hollywood in Wartime," *Yank*, August 19, 1942, p. 18. See also "AFRA Protests Slur; Radio's Patriotism," *Variety*, February 18, 1942, p. 4, for a trade reaction to legislative "snide digs" at the entertainment industry during discussion of that year's Appropriations Bill for the Office of Civilian Defense.

Page 191. **Lowell Mellett summed up:** "Washington Paradox," *Variety*, February 11, 1942, p. 5.

Page 192. **In February 1942 General Hersey:** "Rush to Enlist Could Put Serious Crimp into Hollywood; Pros and Cons on Hersey's Ruling," *Variety*, February 11, 1942, p. 4.

Page 193. **Responding to Hersey's initial:** "SAG Wants No Special Preference; Also Votes Support to Douglas," *Variety*, February 11, 1942, p. 21.

Page 193. **MPPDA Vice President Y. Frank Freeman:** "Washington Paradox," *Variety*, February 11, 1942, p. 5.

Page 193. **We agree that the:** "OWI Makes First Move to Get Talent Deferred; Supports Kyser Appeal," *Variety*, March 10, 1943, p. 21.

Page 193. **Variety claimed the big:** "Rush to Enlist Could Have Put Serious Crimp into Hollywood; Pros and Cons on Hersey's Ruling," *Variety*, February 1, 1942, p. 21.

Page 193. **The stumbling block is:** "Actors Status Up to Public," *Hollywood Reporter*, April 2, 1943, pp. 1, 9.

Page 193. **The Selective Service head:** "Non-Essential Status for Show People Guided by Public Opinion, Sez Hersey," *Variety*, April 7, 1943, p. 3.

Page 194. **The apparently fit crooner:** William Manchester, *The Glory and the Dream: A Narrative History of America 1932–1972* (Boston: Little, Brown, 1973), p. 309. See also "What and Why Is Frank Sinatra?" *Yank*, January 12, 1945, p. 14 ("He is of draft age but not draft material because of a punctured eardrum"). Sinatra's symbolic wartime status is discussed in Dana Polan, *Power and Paranoia: History, Narrative, and the American Cinema, 1940–1950* (New York: Columbia University Press, 1986), pp. 124–27.

Page 195. **Dreading the stigma:** Mori Krushen, "Talent and Manpower Problems," *Variety*, January 6, 1943, p. 64.

Page 195. **Clark Gable heartbroken:** "FDR Tells Gable He's More Valuable Making Pictures for Civilian Morale," *Variety*, April 4, 1942, p. 1.

Page 195. **I have no interest:** "Gable Into Army as Private," *Hollywood Reporter*, August 11, 1942, pp. 1, 10.

Page 195. **At Pueblo Air Base:** Leon Pearson, "Davis, Mellett Duck Pix Issue," *Hollywood Reporter*, March 3, 1943, p. 8.

Page 195. **Gable's voluntary demotion:** "Gable Becomes Aerial Gunner; He Wins His Wings the Hard Way," *Yank*, January 27, 1943, p. 8, and Andrew A. Rooney, "Clark Gable Is Just a Two-Bar Joe Doing a Job," *Stars and Stripes*, June 7, 1943, p. 3. Gable was put on the inactive list in June 1944.

Page 196. **At the Pentagon, Gable:** "Real War Differs from War Movies, Says Gable," *Motion Picture Herald*, November 6, 1943, p. 64.

Page 197. **Jimmy Stewart:** The Editors of *Look*, *Movie Lot to Beachhead* (New York: Doubleday, Doran, 1945), pp. 81, and 70–81. Stewart is the only Hollywood actor to whom the *Look* editors devote an entire chapter.

Page 198. **Besides the standard intimations:** Mori Krushen, "Talent and Manpower Problems," p. 64.

Page 198. **Not until early 1943:** Ralph Wilk, "MGM Rooney Appeal Not Trade Test Case," *Film Daily*, March 3, 1943, pp. 1, 8, and "Greetings Again," *Motion Picture Herald*, March 11, 1944, p. 8.

Page 198. **Writer-director Garson Kanin:** "Kanin Vox Pops Ye Ed," *Variety*, August 26, 1942, pp. 4, 25.

Page 199. **In 1939 average weekly:** Figures are from *The 1940 Film Daily Year Book of Motion Pictures* and *The 1946 Film Daily Year Book of Motion Pictures*, respectively.

Page 199. **Following movie-marked money:** "Box Office Is Unbelievable," *Hollywood Reporter*, October 17, 1942, pp. 1, 4. In this case, box-office gross indicates the money taken in at the theater window and should not be confused with rentals (the payment the exhibitor returns to the producer/ distributor).

Page 199. **For the commerce-minded:** "Review of *Hangmen Also Die*," *Variety*, March 24, 1943, p. 20.

Page 199. **Implying a special relationship:** Harry Warner, "Entertainment and Education Comprise Today's Screen Mission," *Variety*, January 6, 1943, p. 64.

Page 200. **Banking on the south:** "Inside Stuff—the Movies," *Variety*, July 7, 1943, p. 25.

Page 200. **In June 1944 producer:** "Wagner Agenda?" *Motion Picture Herald*, June 24, 1944, p. 9.

Page 200. **The more somber and therapeutic:** William Weaver, "Studios Turn to Psychiatry as New Picture Theme," *Motion Picture Herald*, June 3, 1944, p. 28.

Page 201. **Prior to the war:** Arthur L. Mayer, "Fact into Film," *Public Opinion Quarterly* (Summer 1944): 207.

Page 202. **Distributors reported that:** "Documentaries a Part of War News-reels," *Motion Picture Herald*, March 7, 1943, p. 68.

Page 202. **By 1942 the number:** "Russe Pic Sends 42nd St. House to $75c Top; Vodka Films' OK Biz," *Variety*, April 15, 1942, p. 20.

Page 202. **In the next two years:** "War Themes Drop to 12% of Product for 1944–45," *Motion Picture Herald*," July 29, 1944, p. 13.

Page 204. **In 1943, without a trace:** "Limit On War," *Motion Picture Herald*, May 29, 1943, p. 8.

Page 204. **Another scheme from RKO:** "Hedge on Hitler," *Motion Picture Herald*, August 21, 1943, p. 8.

Page 204. **Placing the bottom line:** Samuel D. Berns, "Story Material for Hollywood," in Alicoate, ed., *The 1946 Film Daily Year Book of Motion Pictures*, p. 83.

Chapter 9: The Negro Soldier

Page 205. **A survey on American:** Surveys Division, Office of War Information, Memorandum no. 59, "The Negroes' Role in the War: A Study of White and Colored Opinions," July 8, 1943. Reprinted in Morris J. MacGregor and Bernard C. Nalty, eds., *Blacks in the United States Armed Forces: Basic Documents*, vol. 5, *Black Soldiers in World War II* (Wilmington, Del.: Scholarly Resources, 1977), pp. 216–17, 236.

Page 205. **In line with the:** Gen. Benjamin O. Davis, "History of the Special Section of the Inspector General," April 17, 1946, in MacGregor and Nalty, *Blacks in the United States Armed Forces* 5:459.

Page 205. **For reasons the Surgeon:** Memorandum of the Surgeon General for Assistant Secretary McCloy, September 3, 1941, in MacGregor and Nalty, ibid., 5:139.

Page 207. **In 1944, New York:** C. D. Reddick, "Educational Programs for the Improvement of Race Relations: Motion Pictures, Radio, Press, and Libraries," *Journal of Negro Education* (Summer 1944): 369. See also Leonard C. Archer, *Black Images in the American Theatre: NAACP Protest Campaigns—Stage, Screen, Radio, and Television* (New York: Pageant and Poseidon, 1973), pp. 183–224.

Page 207. **On the margins of:** *The 1944 Film Daily Yearbook of Motion Pictures* lists 421 "Negro Houses" in the United States. Douglas Gomery discusses "Movie Theaters for Black Americans" in *Shared Pleasures: A History of Movie Presentation in the United States* (Madison: University of Wisconsin Press, 1992), pp. 155–70.

Page 207. **In July 1942 Walter:** Walter White, *A Man Called White: The Autobiography of Walter White* (New York: Viking, 1948), pp. 200–203.

Page 208. **Demanding a better break:** "Film Executives Pledge Better Roles for Negroes in Movies," *New York Age*, August 8, 1942, p. 10, and "Movie

Moguls Show Change of Heart," *Philadelphia Tribune*, August 7, 1942, p. 10.

Page 208. **The ultimate goal:** "Score for the Movies," *The Crisis* (October 1944): 312.

Page 208. **One unrepentant screenwriter:** "Censoritis Smothers Genius of H'wood Writers, Scripter Complains," *Variety*, October 13, 1943, p. 2.

Page 208. **In 1943 Hollywood began:** "H'wood's Negro Flacking," *Variety*, September 8, 1943, p. 1. See also "Hollywood Holding Up Pix Releases in Which Whites, Negroes Mix," *Variety*, June 30, 1943, p. 27.

Page 211. **On behalf of the:** "NAACP Lauds 'Bataan,' " *Hollywood Reporter*, June 2, 1943, p. 7.

Page 212. **Variety correctly noted:** "Salute Dignified Treatment of U.S. Negroes in Films," *Variety*, June 30, 1943, pp. 1, 27.

Page 212. **Until 1943 the Army Air:** Yielding to pressure, the Army did establish and train a black bomber unit, the 477th Bombardment Group (M) (Colored). The group was never deployed in combat for reasons put succinctly by military historian Alan L. Gropman. "The unit lost all its effectiveness, and did not become combat ready before the war's end, because its combat training was subordinated to the question of who could enter the base officer's club." Gropman, *The Air Force Integrates, 1945–1964* (Washington, D.C.: Office of Air Force History, 1978), pp. 17 and 1–31.

Page 213. **In the same spirit:** "Minutes of Meeting of Advisory Committee on Negro Troop Policies," February 29, 1944, in MacGregor and Nalty, *Blacks in the United States Armed Forces* 5:329 (emphasis added).

Page 213. **The most notable official:** Thomas Cripps and David Culbert discuss *The Negro Soldier* in "*The Negro Soldier* (1944): Film Propaganda in Black and White," *American Quarterly* (Winter 1979): 616–40.

Page 214. **It had in fact:** "Negroes' Part in War," *Variety*, January 26, 1944, p. 4.

Page 215. **Sitting down to:** Michael Carter, "Preview of Film: The Negro Soldier," *New Jersey Afro-American*, March 4, 1944, pp. 1, 14.

Page 216. **General Davis, whom FDR:** Gen. Benjamin O. Davis, "History of the Special Section of the Inspector General," April 17, 1946, in MacGregor and Nalty, *Blacks in the United States Armed Forces* 5:460–63.

Page 216. **WAC made up forty:** E. B. Rea, "Memphis Censor Board Freezes Soldier," *New Jersey Afro-American*, July 22, 1944, p. 10.

Page 216. **Our concept of proper:** Herman Hill, "Reviewer Praises Film on Colored Soldier," *Pittsburgh Courier*, February 26, 1944, p. 15. See also George C. Moore, "Aberdeen GIs Say Whites Should See 'Soldier' Film," *New Jersey Afro-American*, July 15, 1943, p. 10.

Page 216. **Goldberg lost the case:** "War Dept's Negro Pic Can Now Be Released," *Variety*, May 10, 1944, p. 9.

Page 216. **MGM floated the idea:** " 'Uncle Tom' Will Be Color Special At

MGM," *Variety*, February 2, 1944, p. 9, and "MGM Not to Film 'Uncle Tom'; Leader Denies Offer of Casting," *Pittsburgh Courier*, February 19, 1944, p. 20.

Page 216. **Another borderline miscalculation:** "Tennessee Johnson" file, WNRC (RG 208, Box 3509, Entry 566). See also " 'Tennessee Johnson' Gets Mellett's Okay," *Film Daily*, January 5, 1943, p. 1.

Page 216. **MGM ended up spending:** "Salute Dignified Treatment of U.S. Negroes in Films," *Variety*, June 30, 1943, pp. 1, 27.

Page 217. **No Hollywood films had more:** When *Gone With the Wind* played in his hometown, the youngster who became Malcolm X recalled: "I was the only Negro in the theater, and when Butterfly McQueen when into her act, I felt like crawling under the rug." Malcolm X with Alex Haley, *The Autobiography of Malcolm X* (New York: Ballantine, 1965), p. 32.

Page 217. **In 1942 a contemplated:** "Censors Sharpen Axes," *Variety*, December 23, 1942, p. 18, and "Censors Bar Nation Film," *New Jersey Afro-American*, January 1, 1944, p. 8.

Page 217. **In 1944 David O. Selznick:** "Selznick Plan to Musicalize 'Wind' for Pictures Distresses Many Negroes," *Variety*, February 7, 1945, pp. 1, 25.

Page 217. **Protests and adverse commentary:** "Salute Dignified Treatment of U.S. Negroes in Films," *Variety*, June 30, 1943, pp. 1, 27. In headlining another cancellation, the *New Jersey Afro-American* beat *Variety* at its own game: "Uncle Tom's Cabin Film Now Gone with the Wind," February 2, 1944, p. 11.

Page 217. **A thunderstruck reviewer:** E. Washington Rhodes, "Movie Shows Negro in New Kind of Role," *Philadelphia Tribune*, August 1, 1942, p. 3.

Page 218. **In a widely quoted:** "Blackface Hollywood a la Mode," *New Jersey Afro-American*, February 5, 1944, p. 10. See also Peter Furst, "Hollywood and Minorities," *American Cinematographer* (September 1943): 326–27.

Page 218. **In May 1944 the Entertainment:** "Show Biz Endorses Negro 'Principles,' " *Variety*, May 24, 1944, pp. 1, 32.

Page 218. **The American Red Cross:** "Red Cross to Delete Colored Shot from Film," *New Jersey Afro-American*, April 15, 1944, p. 8.

Page 219. **So venerable and reliable:** Joseph Boskin traces the Sambo figure in American culture in *Sambo: The Rise and Demise of an American Jester* (New York: Oxford University Press, 1986).

Page 219. **A smalltown exhibitor:** *Box Office Showmandiser*, January 22, 1944, p. 1.

Page 219. **In 1945 a soldier:** "GIs No Like Over S-A, USO Femme Troupers or Anti Negro Pictures," *Variety*, April 25, 1945, p. 11, and "Inside Stuff—Motion Pictures," *Variety*, May 16, 1945, p. 20.

Page 220. **Against that record:** Reddick, "Educational Programs for the Improvement of Race Relations," p. 377.

Page 220. **After four years:** "Negro Ass'n Raps WB's Tolerance Film Short," *Variety*, June 13, 1945, p. 2.

Page 220.   **The Writers War Board:** "Negroes' War Efforts Get H'wood Brush Off; Writers Complaining," *Variety*, March 15, 1944, pp. 1, 32.

Page 220.   **The board's survey:** "Stage 'Most Liberal' of Show World in Treatment of Minority Groups," *Variety*, March 21, 1945, p. 11.

Page 220.   **The calculated cuts:** "Omissions from Newsreels," *The Crisis* (February 1944): 39, and "Soldiers Cheated Out of Credit," *The Crisis* (November 1944): 344.

Page 220.   **As the New Jersey Afro:** "Movies Cut Troops: 5 Companies Delete Our Soldiers from Overseas Newsreels," *New Jersey Afro-American*, January 8, 1944, p. 1.

Page 220.   **In February 1944 the Pittsburgh:** "Film to Show Negro Troops," *Pittsburgh Courier*, February 26, 1944, p. 1.

Page 221.   **The newsreels have been:** "Soldiers Cheated of Credit," *The Crisis*, (November 1944): 344.

Page 221.   **A weekly issue founded:** "Negro Newsreel Seen by 4,000,000," *American Cinematographer* (November 1943): 408.

Page 221.   **An obvious red flag:** Paul Demis, "The Negro in Show Business," *Negro Digest* (February 1943): 36–37.

Page 221.   **After the Detroit race:** "Hollywood Holding Up Pix Releases in Which Whites, Negroes Mix," *Variety*, June 30, 1943, p. 27.

Page 222.   **Knoxville censored a scene:** "More Negro Scenes Cut Out in Dixie Set Problem for Pix Producers," *Variety*, July 12, 1944, pp. 1, 32.

Page 222.   **The notoriously scissor-happy:** "Memphis Again Cuts Negro Phase from Pic," *Variety*, June 13, 1945, p. 10.

Page 222.   **Branding the inimitable Eddie:** "Banned," *Motion Picture Herald*, April 4, 1945, p. 9. See also "Rochester 'Inimical'?" *Variety*, April 6, 1945, pp. 1, 46.

Page 223.   **A letter from:** "GI's Burn at Memphis Mayor's 'Jimcrowism' vs Rochester in Film," *Variety*, June 27, 1945, pp. 1, 27.

Page 224.   **Shut out totally from:** "Inside Stuff—Pictures," *Variety*, September 13, 1944, p. 18.

Chapter 10: The Real War

Page 228.   **If "reality" as Vladimir:** Vladimir Nabokov, *Lolita* (New York: Berkeley Books, 1977), p. 283.

Page 228.   **The moving-image news:** The standard account of the commercial Hollywood newsreel is Raymond Fielding, *The American Newsreel 1911–1967* (Norman: University of Oklahoma Press, 1972), and the essential bibliographical companion is K. R. M. Short, *World War II through the American Newsreels 1942–1945: An Introduction and Guide to the Microfiches* (New York: Oxford Microfilm Publications, 1985). A useful overview is David H. Mould, "Historical Trends in the Criticism of the Newsreel and Television News," *Journal of Popular Film and Television* (Fall 1984): 118–26.

Page 229. **Two-thirds of the nation's:** "Film Bulletins Get 16,844 Playdates," *Box Office*, January 8, 1944, p. 51.

Page 229. **Two screen magazines offering:** Respective sources include Raymond Fielding, *The March of Time, 1935–1951* (New York: Oxford University Press, 1978), and Richard Meran Barsam, " 'This Is America': Documentaries for Theaters, 1942–1951," in Barsam, ed., *Nonfiction Film Theory and Criticism* (New York: E. P. Dutton, 1976), pp. 115–35.

Page 229. **The quantity of the:** On newsreel theaters, see Douglas Gomery, *Shared Pleasures: A History of Movie Presentation in the United States* (Madison: University of Wisconsin Press, 1992), pp. 141–54.

Page 230. **In 1943 when the:** "Industry Will Fill War Gap Left By OWI," *Motion Picture Herald*, July 31, 1943, p. 15.

Page 231. **In a seemingly scripted:** "Filming Pearl Harbor(s)," *Motion Picture Herald*, February 2, 1942, p. 9.

Page 231. **The eagerly anticipated:** "More Criticism on 'Pollyanna' War Newsreels," *Variety*, March 11, 1942, pp. 4, 27.

Page 232. **Not until December 10:** "Pearl Harbor Scenes Only Movietone's; Jap Attack Shown," *Hollywood Reporter*, December 11, 1942, p. 1. The rule of thumb is 90 feet of film per minute of screen time.

Page 233. **Assenting to the principle:** Frederick Ullman, Jr., "Newsreel War Coverage Will Be a Matter of Luck," *Variety*, January 7, 1942, p. 11.

Page 233. **During the Battle of:** "Yank Air Victory Pix Had to Come from Anzaccs; More Brass-Hatism," *Variety*, April 21, 1943, p. 7.

Page 233. **In late 1942 when:** John C. Loeser, "Newsreel Crews, Shooting for U.S. Marine's Anni This Week, Grabbed Tough Training Pix at N.C. Base," *Variety*, November 11, 1942, p. 6.

Page 234. **In February 1944 Pathé:** "Army Uses Censored Newsreel Footage," *Motion Picture Herald*, February 26, 1944, p. 28.

Page 234. **Universal cameraman Irving Smith:** "Cameramen Here After Three Years at the Front," *Box Office*, March 17, 1945, p. 41.

Page 234. **A reporter for Box:** James M. Jerauld, "Newsreel Editors Chafing as Delays Hurt Timing," *Box Office*, August 7, 1943, p. 10.

Page 234. **In early 1943 word:** "Army's Battle Films Train Soldiers," *Variety*, March 3, 1943, p. 47.

Page 236. **If de Rochemont has:** "Navy Photographic Units Turning in Excellent Pix," *Film Daily*, March 12, 1943, pp. 1, 4.

Page 236. **It is the considered:** Terry Ramsaye, "War and the News," *Motion Picture Herald*, June 13, 1942, p. 7. Ramsaye also sounded off in "Rationed News," *Motion Picture Herald*, August 22, 1942, p. 7, and "Newsreels," *Motion Picture Herald*, November 14, 1942, p. 7.

Page 237. **Some five hundred prints of:** "Pictures Ahoy," *Motion Picture Herald*, September 5, 1942, p. 8.

Page 237. **Maddeningly, despite an understanding:** "African Invasion Films to U.S. Newsreels," *Hollywood Reporter*, November 16, 1942, p. 2. See also "War Dept. Says 99% of Newsreel Combat Films Reach Theater Screens," *Variety*, March 22, 1944, p. 6.

Page 237.   **As with the Battle:** "Zanuck Special," *Motion Picture Herald*, February 20, 1943, p. 9, and "North African Battle Seen in 'At the Front,' " *Motion Picture Herald*, February 27, 1943, p. 22.

Page 237.   **Despite torpid pacing:** "African Invasion Films to U.S. Newsreels," *Hollywood Reporter*, November 16, 1942, p. 2.

Page 237.   **Terry Ramsaye complained:** Terry Ramsaye, "Reporters' Rights," *Motion Picture Herald*, October 24, 1942, p. 7.

Page 238.   **Lacking compelling combat:** "Newsreels Sugarcoat War," *Variety*, March 4, 1942, pp. 1, 22, and "More Criticism on 'Pollyanna' Newsreels," *Variety*, March 11, 1942, pp. 4, 27.

Page 238.   **In 1942 Variety surveyed:** "Review of Embassy Newsreel Theatre, New York," *Variety*, March 11, 1942, p. 49.

Page 238.   **Newsreel coverage is one:** "Hoyt Asks More Realism in War News Coverage," *Motion Picture Herald*, October 2, 1943, p. 14.

Page 238.   **In March 1943 representatives:** "New Speed-Up for War Front Reels," *Variety*, March 10, 1943, p. 6.

Page 239.   **In September 1943 at:** "More and Better War," *Motion Picture Herald*, September 11, 1943, p. 8, and "Harmon Is Army's No. 1 'Poison Guy' In Scrap Releasing Censored Reels," *Variety*, September 8, 1943, p. 4.

Page 239.   **No one can honestly:** Chester Friedman, "The Newsreel *Is* Important," *Motion Picture Herald*, July 17, 1943, p. 73.

Page 239.   **By 1944 Francis S. Harmon:** "Harmon Points Out Film's War Value," *Motion Picture Herald*, December 16, 1944, p. 14.

Page 239.   **Leo Handel, director:** "Show Us the War," *Motion Picture Herald*, August 15, 1942, p. 9.

Page 239.   **The managers of my:** "Theatres Push Newsreels as War Shots Improve," *Motion Picture Herald*, August 7, 1943, p. 25.

Page 239.   **In 1944 Variety estimated:** "WB's Own Newsreel (When and If) May Be of the Magazine Format," *Variety*, December 13, 1944, p. 5.

Page 240.   **After 1941, when combat:** Ben Shlyen, "The Newsreel Makes News," *Box Office*, January 2, 1943, p. 3.

Page 240.   **The newsreel won:** Newton E. Meltzer, "Are the Newsreels News?" *Hollywood Quarterly* 2 (April 1947): 271.

Page 240.   **Eager to spot:** "Looking for Loved Ones in Detroit War Newsreels Ups Femme Pix Interest," *Variety*, March 31, 1943, p. 23.

Page 240.   **Paramount News provided relatives:** George W. Harvey, "Relatives of Fighting Men (When On Screen) Given Photos by Par," *Variety*, October 20, 1943, p. 9; "Families May Get Pictures of Soldiers in Newsreels," *Hollywood Reporter*, January 25, 1943, p. 4; and "Kin War Reels Cue Pvt. Family Shows," *Variety*, June 28, 1944, p. 21.

Page 240.   **After a woman spotted:** "Newsreel 'Finds' Son Missing in Action," *Variety*, January 24, 1945, p. 2.

Page 240.   **As the images became:** "War Newsreels Showing Home-Town Boys Now a New Headache for Mgrs," *Variety*, October 13, 1943, p. 7.

Page 240.   **By late 1943:** "U.S. Rushes Teheran Films," *Motion Picture Herald*, December 11, 1943, p. 15.

Page 241.   **Newsreel scenes showed:** "Expect Quicker Screening of War Pictures," *Motion Picture Herald*, February 26, 1944, p. 28.

Page 241.   **In April 1944 radio:** Advertisement in *Variety*, April 26, 1944, p. 24.

Page 242.   **Under such stimulus:** "D-Day Biggest Radio Story," *Variety*, June 3, 1944, p. 42. See also "News Tieups Being Made for Big Invasion Flash," *Box Office Showmandiser*, June 3, 1944, p. 2.

Page 242.   **The first authenticated reports:** "Cinema Moves with Invasion Fronts," *Motion Picture Herald*, June 10, 1944, p. 13.

Page 242.   **Throughout the afternoon:** "D-Day Marked in Theaters," *Film Daily*, June 7, 1944, pp. 1, 12.

Page 242.   **Meanwhile, military photographic units:** "Organization of D-Day Newsreeling a Saga of Adventure in Itself," *Variety*, July 5, 1944, pp. 3, 12.

Page 242.   **Exposed negative was immediately:** Memo from the Motion Picture Services Officer to the Assistant Chief of Air Staff Operations, June 9, 1944, on file at USAF-HRC.

Page 243.   **Frank Capra had prepared:** Many sources, including the Office of the Chief of Military History, list the title of the War Department's D–Day film as *Eve of Battle*. However, the print on file at the National Archives reads *Eve of Invasion*.

Page 243.   **In a controversial move:** "OWI Denies Pressure for 'Eve of Invasion,'" *Film Daily*, June 14, 1944, p. 2.

Page 243.   **The nonchalance which assumed:** Terry Ramsaye, "War and the Newsreel," *Motion Picture Herald*, June 24, 1944, p. 7.

Page 243.   **Opting in the end:** "Newsreels of Invasion Hit U.S. in Four Days," *Box Office*, June 17, 1944, p. 9. Throughout and below, newsreel screening dates were culled by cross-referencing listings in *Motion Picture Herald* and *Box Office* with the newsreel call sheets on file at the National Archives. Although official release days for the two weekly newsreel issues were Tuesday and Thursday, an urgent story such as the Normandy invasion would disrupt normal scheduling. Also, the closer a venue was to New York editorial offices, the earlier it obtained and thus might screen an issue. An overview of the D-Day coverage in *Variety*, July 5, 1944, p. 12, reported: "First camera crews hit beach at H-hour plus 30. By noon of D-Day, Army officials [in London] were looking at first shots, those made over the battlefield by the U.S. Eighth Air Force and two days later London theaters were showing the embarkation stuff. First air films arrived in the

U.S. in 60 hours, but were held up to give American audiences a rounded picture of D-Day."

Page 244. **From the 10,000 feet:** John Sturges, "First Newsreels of the Invasion Take Audience to the Beachheads," *Motion Picture Herald*, June 17, 1944, p. 9.

Page 244. **Col. Curtis Mitchell:** *Variety*, July 5, 1944, p. 3.

Page 244. **Sadly, the gallant Madru:** "Nazi Sniper Kills Madru, News of the Day Ace," *Film Daily*, April 24, 1945, p. 2.

Page 244. **For its October 4:** "Newsreel Pattern," *Motion Picture Herald*, October 7, 1944, p. 8. See also "Newsreels' Trend to 'Magazine' Coverage," *Variety*, September 20, 1944, p. 8.

Page 245. **The company continued:** "Pathé Releases Subject on Western Front Action," *Motion Picture Herald*, February 17, 1945, p. 20.

Page 245. **V-E Day, celebrated wildly:** "V-E Newsreels Ready for Exhibition Today," *Variety*, May 9, 1945, p. 2.

Page 245. **With film shipments assured:** "Newsreels Set for Record Invasion Coverage," *Box Office*, March 20, 1944, p. 15.

Page 245. **The spectacular and brutal:** J. M. Jerauld, "Iwo Jima Camera Work Real Record for Speed," *Box Office*, March 10, 1945, p. 45.

Page 245. **Film taken of the battle:** J. M. Jerauld, "Okinawa Newsreel Films Arrive in Seven Days," *Box Office*, April 7, 1945, p. 29.

Page 245. **Though a meticulous:** Bill Formby, "Around the Clock Is Newsreel Pace," *Box Office*, June 3, 1944, p. 43.

Pages 245–246. **For aural sweetening:** "Movietone News Pioneer in Sound-on-Film Field," *Box Office*, March 24, 1945, p. 33.

Page 246. **Commenting on one of:** Liane Richter, "Notes on Newsreels," April 25, 1945, reprinted in K. R. M. Short, *World War II through the American Newsreels*.

Page 247. **From the silence of:** Abel Green, "Newsreels Tell Shocking Story of Nazis' Murder Mills," *Variety*, May 2, 1945, p. 2.

Page 247. **Fox Movietone News provided:** "Horror Pictures," *Motion Picture Herald*, May 5, 1945, p. 5.

Page 249. **Some gasped, a few:** For audience reaction to the footage see "Report from Germany," *Motion Picture Herald*, April 28, 1945, p. 9; "Atrocity Pix Breaking Newsreel House Records," *Film Daily*, May 3, 1945, pp. 1, 6; "Horror Pictures Shock Patrons, But None Protest," *Motion Picture Herald*, May 5, 1945, p. 14; "Nazi Atrocity Film Real Shockers, But U.S. Audiences Take It; Some Cuts," *Variety*, May 9, 1945, pp. 6, 18. *Variety* estimated that 90 percent of the nation's theaters complied with Eisenhower's request and screened the atrocity newsreels unedited. See "Inside Stuff—Pictures," *Variety*, May 16, 1945, p. 20.

Page 250. **The reportorial practice matched:** "Toward Timeliness," *Motion Picture Herald*, January 29, 1944, p. 8.

Page 250. **Newsreels reached stateside:** "WAC Film Shows Rome Campaign," *Motion Picture Herald*, July 8, 1944, p. 39.

Page 251. **Herb Lightman, a combat:** Sgt. Herb A. Lightman, "Shooting Production Under Fire," *American Cinematographer* (September 1945): 296–97, 306; and Sgt. Herb A. Lightman, "The Men Behind the Combat Cameraman," *American Cinematographer* (October 1945): 332.

Page 251. **The bluster of a British:** "Brit Officer Who Shot 'Victory' Here," *Hollywood Reporter*, April 8, 1943, p. 4.

Page 252. **Ford later told Peter:** Peter Bogdanovich, *John Ford* (Berkeley: University of California Press, 1978), p. 82.

Page 252. **He was actually aided:** "Inside Stuff—Pictures," *Variety*, October 14, 1942, p. 6, and McKenzie's obituary in *Variety*, August 22, 1945.

Page 253. **Within six months:** "WAC Sets 660,000 Bookings for Shorts," *Variety*, March 10, 1943, p. 4.

Page 253. **Prior to this revelation:** "Viewpoints Are Varied on Newsreels' Trend," *Box Office*, June 24, 1944, p. 54.

Page 254. **In like manner:** "Ravaged Earth Brings Fame to M. L. Moody," *American Cinematographer* (August 1944): 283.

Page 254. **According to a cameraman:** Lt. Arthur E. Arling, USNR, "Cameramen in Uniform," *American Cinematographer* (October 1943): 385.

Page 255. **Although At the Front:** "Film Bulletins Get 16,844 Playdates," *Box Office*, January 8, 1944, p. 51.

Page 257. **The chaplain commenced:** In his autobiography, John Huston retells the rainbow scene as an act of divine intervention (God's, not his). Huston, *An Open Book* (New York: Alfred Knopf, 1980), p. 94.

Page 257. **James Agee, always:** James Agee, *The Nation*, June 24, 1944; reprinted in Agee, *Agee on Film*, vol. 1 (New York: Grosset and Dunlap, 1969), p. 271.

Page 257. **Despite official injunctions:** "War Shots Faking Officially Denied," *Hollywood Reporter*, April 1, 1943, p. 8, and "Army Forbids Faking of Any Battle Shots," *Hollywood Reporter*, April 21, 1943, p. 2.

Page 257. **During the film's editing:** "Complete Editing of Army's Tunisia Film," *Variety*, February 9, 1944, p. 5.

Page 257. **We had troops moving:** Huston, *An Open Book*, pp. 102–103.

Page 257. **In reviews of Desert Victory:** "Review of *Desert Victory*," *Variety*, March 31, 1943, p. 8. "Desert Victory: Hailed as Finest Picture of the War" (*Hollywood Reporter*, March 19, 1943, p. 4) skirted the issue, but the next month "Army Forbids Faking of Any Battle Shots" (*Hollywood Reporter*, April 21, 1943, p. 2) noted "a few shots in British *Desert Victory* were staged."

Page 257. **In 1944 while working:** Barbara Deming, "The Library of Congress Film Project," *Library of Congress Quarterly* (July–August–September 1944): 8.

Page 258. **The verity of December 7th:** These comments are based on the 34-minute version released in 1943. Long buried deep in the National Archives, the Navy's original 84-minute version of *December 7th* was recently disinterred for a fiftieth-anniversary commemorative videotape from Kit Parker Films. Allegedly censored by military brasshats for undue criticism of Navy preparedness, the longer version is actually more pallid and xenophobic than the shorter version. It eliminates the Arizona newsreel footage, and a long opening section impugns the loyalty of Hawaii's Japanese-American population. Jeanine Basinger's discussion of the 34-minute *December 7th* deems it "hardly a documentary at all." Basinger, *The World War II Combat Film: Anatomy of a Genre* (New York: Columbia University Press, 1986), pp. 127–30.

Page 260. **Likewise John Huston's:** "Army Gives Film Report on Horror and Cost of War," *Motion Picture Herald*, March 17, 1945, p. 27.

Page 260. **For eyes not properly:** "Premiere over Tokyo," *Motion Picture Herald*, February 17, 1945, p. 8.

Page 260. **Run it as soon:** "The Exhibitor Speaks His Mind," *Motion Picture Herald*, July 14, 1945, p. 36.

Page 261. **A total of 50,000:** "Newsreels Bring Bloody Iwo Home," *Motion Picture Herald*, March 10, 1945, p. 36.

Page 264. **In 1944 an officer:** Lt. William E. McGee, "Cinematography Goes to War," *Journal of the Society of Motion Picture Engineers* (February 1944): 108.

Page 264. **A Navy officer overseeing:** Lt. Gordon L. Hough, "Medical Films at War," *Business Screen* (June 1945): 104. See also Lt. Walter Evans, "The Contribution of Color to Navy Training Films," *Business Screen* (June 1945): 60–61.

Page 264. **The novelty of pyrotechnic:** "Stark Realism of War Recorded in Iwo Jima Film," *Motion Picture Herald*, June 2, 1945, p. 26.

Chapter 11: Legacies

Page 265. **In 1945 who but:** "Review of *We Accuse*," *Variety*, May 30, 1945, p. 16.

Page 266. **As soon as the war:** "Films Must Have Part in Peace Talks— Warner," *Motion Picture Herald*, September 23, 1944, p. 30.

Page 266. **In a widely quoted:** Arthur C. Mayer, "Fact into Film," *Public Opinion Quarterly* (Summer 1944): 206.

Page 266. **One of the first:** "Editorial Statement," *Hollywood Quarterly* (Berkeley: University of California Press, 1945–46).

Page 266. **That October HUAC launched:** The scholarship on HUAC and Hollywood is voluminous. A sampling: Larry Ceplair and Steven Englund, *The Inquisition in Hollywood: Politics in the Film Community* (New York:

Anchor Books, 1980); John Cogley, *Report on Blacklisting*, vol. 1, *The Movies* (New York: Fund for the Republic, 1956); and Stephen J. Whitfield, *The Culture of the Cold War* (Baltimore: John Hopkins University Press, 1991), esp. pp. 127–52.

Page 266. **At the height of:** Lillian Ross, "Onward and Upward with the Arts," *The New Yorker*, February 21, 1948, p. 32.

Page 268. **How did you, I, or anyone:** All quotes from Hearings Regarding the Communist Infiltration of the Motion Picture Industry, 88th Cong., 2d sess., October 20, 1947, pp. 39 and 7, 74, 77. For a content probe see Dorothy B. Jones, "Communism in the Movies: A Study in Film Content," in Cogley, *Report on Blacklisting* 1:196–233.

Page 270. **Though later revitalized by:** Jeanine Basinger, *The "It's a Wonderful Life" Book* (New York: Alfred A. Knopf, 1986), pp. 52–60.

Page 271. **In 1944, when Clark Gable:** "Real War Differs from War Movies, Says Gable," *Motion Picture Herald*, November 6, 1943, p. 64.

Page 272. **That year saw:** "World War II Pix Kayo B.O. Pacifism with $25,000,000 Gross in 1949," *Variety*, December 28, 1949, pp. 1, 45.

Page 275. **For the third time:** Chester B. Bahn, "1950: A Review," in *The 1951 Film Daily Yearbook of Motion Pictures*, p. 53.

Page 280. **In August 1945 most:** A typical reaction from the wartime generation is the title essay in Paul Fussell, *Thank God for the Atom Bomb and Other Essays* (New York: Summit, 1988), pp. 13–44. Paul Boyer, *By the Bomb's Early Light: American Thought and Culture at the Dawn of the Atomic Age* (New York: Pantheon, 1985) finds more moral equivocation in the American response. My own survey of the contemporary film record detected absolutely no intimations of regret for the events of August 1945 or doubt about their necessity.

Page 280. **The atomic reactions:** The military, the scientist, and sundry "pods and blobs" are discussed in Peter Biskind, *Seeing Is Believing: How Hollywood Taught Us to Stop Worrying and Love the Fifties* (New York: Pantheon, 1983), pp. 101–59.

Page 282. **The project was aberrant:** "New Film's Plot: Viet Kidnaps U.S. Military Brass," *Variety*, July 21, 1965, pp. 1, 21. Technically, Sam Fuller's *China Gate* (1957) and Joseph L. Mankiewicz's version of Graham Greene's novel *The Quiet American* (1958)—the latter starring a subdued Audie Murphy—predate Silliphant's scenario, as does the curio obscurity *A Yank in Vietnam* (1964). But none of these pre-1965 films engage the Vietnam War during the peak—and hence most controversial—years of American involvement.

Page 283. **As Variety put it:** "Viet Tale Too Hot for Hollywood," *Variety*, September 18, 1965, p. 4.

Page 283. **There is no name:** A. D. Murphy, "Martha Raye Graphically Details Need for U.S.O. Troops in Vietnam," *Variety*, June 16, 1965, pp. 1, 63.

Page 283. **In 1964 Columbia bought:** "Catch as 'Catch 22' Can: Columbia Ducks Satire and Ransohoff Takes Over," *Variety*, February 23, 1966.

Page 284. **In 1966 a trade survey:** Robert B. Frederick, "New War Pic Cycle Gathers Momentum Or Maybe Military Always in Fashion," *Variety*, August 10, 1966, p. 4.

Page 284. **John Wayne's critically reviled:** Julian Smith, *Looking Away: Hollywood and Vietnam* (New York: Scribners, 1975), p. 129.

Page 284. **In his Vietnam novel:** Gustav Hasford, *The Short Timers* (New York: Bantam, 1979), p. 38.

Page 284. **We wanted Patton:** Tom Gray, "Fox Tackles Controversial Themes," *Motion Picture Herald*, February 7, 1968, p. 1.

Page 285. **After a decade:** The Vietnam genre is interpreted in Albert Auster and Leonard Quart, *How the War Was Remembered: Hollywood and Vietnam* (New York: Praeger, 1988); Gilbert Adair, *Hollywood's Vietnam: From The Green Berets to Full Metal Jacket* (London: William Heinemann, 1989); and Michael Anderegg, ed., *Inventing Vietnam: The War in Film and Television* (Philadelphia: Temple University Press, 1991).

Page 287. **Time's cover story:** *Time*, January 26, 1987.

Page 288. **Flashbacking furiously, Vietnam vets:** On the "crybaby veteran" see Timothy J. Lomperis, *"Reading the Wind": The Literature of the Vietnam War* (Durham, N.C.: Duke University Press, 1987), pp. 36–54.

Page 288. **I am a Vietnam veteran:** Robert Brewin, "TV's Newest Villain: The Vietnam Veteran," *TV Guide*, July 19, 1975, p. 4.

Page 291. **The media label:** Michael J. Arlen's *Living-Room War* (New York: Viking, 1969) helped make the phrase common parlance.

Page 292. **In writing of:** For example, Susan White, "Male Bonding, Hollywood Orientalism, and the Repression of the Feminine in Kubrick's *Full Metal Jacket*," in Anderegg, *Inventing Vietnam*, pp. 204–30.

Page 293. **Are we now being:** Michael Rogin, *Ronald Reagan, The Movie and Other Episodes in Political Demonology* (Berkeley: University of California Press, 1987), p. 3.

Page 296. **I'm willing to wait:** Stanley Kauffmann, "From the Present, From the Past," *New Republic*, November 12, 1990, p. 27.

Page 301. **By the early 1990s:** John Demsey, "WWII: From Boom to Bust in Ratings," *Variety*, December 20, 1989, pp. 37–38.

Page 301. **Saving Private Ryan is best understood:** In an article surveying reactions to *Saving Private Ryan,* critic Vincent Canby expressed a consensus view: "Once again, Spielberg has made a connection to the American public of almost messianic proportions." Vincent Canby, "Saving a Nation's Pride of Being," *New York Times,* August 10, 1998: B1, B3.

Page 302. **Without exception:** Stephen Ambrose, " 'Private Ryan' Tells Our War Story," *New York Daily News,* August 12, 1998.

Page 315. **If the images:** The phrase is from Fredric Jameson, *Postmodernism, or the Cultural Logic of Late Capitalism* (Durham, N.C.: Duke University Press, 1991), p. 18.

FILM INDEX

INDEX